august 1995

How Close Are We?

Dave Hunt

HARVEST HOUSE PUBLISHERS
Eugene, Oregon 97402

Scripture quotations in this book are taken from the King James Version of the Bible.

The author's free monthly newsletter may be received by request. Write to:

> Dave Hunt
> P.O. Box 7019
> Bend, OR 97708

HOW CLOSE ARE WE?

Copyright © 1993 by Harvest House Publishers
Eugene, Oregon 97402

Library of Congress Cataloging-in-Publication Data

Hunt, Dave.
    How close are we? / Dave Hunt.
        p.   cm.
    ISBN 1-89081-904-1
      1. Rapture (Christian eschatology)   2. Second Advent.
    I. Title.
    BT887.H86   1992   91-47624
    236'.9—dc20   CIP

Printed in the United States of America.

Dedicated to all those citizens of heaven for whom this world has lost its appeal. And who, loving Christ with their whole heart, long to be at home with Him in His Father's house.

To Helen,

"Let Not your heart be troubled; believe in God, believe also in Me. In my father's house are many dwelling places; if it were not so, I would have to you; for I go to prepare A place for you. And if I go And prepare A place for you, I will come AgAin, And receive you to Myself." John 14:2,3

Happy birthday Helen
God Bless And Keep you.
Your brother in Christ,
Tony Smith

Contents

HOW CLOSE ARE WE?

"I Will Come Again"

$\diamond$

> Let not your heart be troubled: ye believe in God, believe also in me. In my Father's house are many mansions: if it were not so, I would have told you. I go to prepare a place for you. And if I go and prepare a place for you, I will come again, and receive you unto myself; that where I am, there ye may be also (John 14:1-3).

"I will come again." What a promise from our Lord! Yet there has been a consistent blindness from the very beginning to the true meaning of these words—a blindness even going back all the way to those who first heard this comforting pledge from His own lips. The indisputable fact is that when Christ made this startling declaration on the eve of His betrayal, not one of His astonished disciples understood what He meant. Even John the Baptist, though chosen by God to introduce the Messiah to Israel, was as ignorant as were Christ's sworn enemies, the rabbis, of the momentous truth that two Messianic comings had been prophesied.

That blindness to the Old Testament prophecies created great confusion concerning Christ's identity and the purpose of His first advent. If we are to gain accurate insights into the Second Coming, we must go back to discover the reasons for the misunderstandings when Christ first came. And we must make certain that we do not fall prey to a similar confusion.

The problem was not skepticism concerning the prophesied coming of the Messiah. Almost everyone in Israel in Christ's day was looking for that promised One—and so are the Jews today. But that He should come *twice* was and still is unthinkable heresy to a Jew. Surprisingly, a similar prejudice against the thought of two comings of Christ being yet future is growing even in the evangelical Church.

The Mystery of Two Comings Remains

Christians have no problem with two comings of Christ, if one is in the past and one in the future. He came once, and will come again as He promised. That there are yet two comings still in the future, however—the Rapture and the Second Coming—separated by seven years, is not generally accepted in the Church. Yet we will see that the Bible clearly indicates that Christ's promise, "I will come again," refers not to one event but two, seven years apart. The rejection of this fact in our day is creating a serious misunderstanding among many Christians, a misunderstanding similar to that which caused such confusion at Christ's first advent.

For the Jews in Jesus' day, the thought of two comings had serious implications. It could only mean that the Messiah would be rejected the first time, perhaps even killed. Otherwise, why would He have to come again? At the very least it would mean that His mission would be aborted and the Kingdom not established. Yet the Kingdom was the very reason for the Messiah's coming. It had to be established! That He would come *twice* was therefore unthinkable!

The same view prevails among Jews today. Visit Israel and ask any Israeli if he or she is expecting the Messiah. Almost without exception the answer will be in the affirmative, some even declaring with conviction that He is somewhere on the earth already, waiting to be recognized. And what about *two comings*? No, it couldn't be possible that He has already come once—certainly not that Jesus was the rejected, crucified Messiah! Never!

The ultimate purpose of the Messiah's coming is clearly stated in Scripture: to establish a Kingdom of everlasting peace. Jesus didn't do that. It is therefore reasoned that He couldn't have been the Messiah. Whoever establishes peace in the Middle East and throughout the world—and it will be established temporarily—will be hailed as the long-awaited Messiah, both by Israel and the world. That man, for whom the entire world waits, will, in fact, be the Antichrist. "Him ye will receive," said Christ (John 5:43), and all for a lack of understanding what the prophets have said!

Truth by Implication

There is absolutely no excuse for such ignorance today. Nor was there any excuse when Jesus came the first time. The Hebrew prophets, whose utterances concerning Messiah's advent comprise a major part of Scripture, had clearly indicated that He would come *twice*. After coming to Israel through a lowly virgin birth, He would leave this earth and then, after a period of great persecution for Jews worldwide and their return to their homeland, He would come again in glory and power to rescue His chosen people at Armageddon and rule the world from Jerusalem. It was all there in the writings of the prophets for anyone who had eyes to see. Oddly, however, the meaning was hidden even from rabbis who read the Hebrew prophets religiously each day.

Of course, the specific words, "two comings of the Messiah" or "Messiah will come twice," were not to be found in the pronouncements of the prophets. The truth was there by implication only. All that the prophets had revealed concerning the Messiah obviously could not occur in one time frame and one event. There were seeming contradictions, which could be reconciled in no other way than by two comings. For example, He would be "cut off out of the land of the living" (Isaiah 53:8) yet He would "prolong His days [forever]" (53:10); He would be rejected and killed (53:3,9) yet would reign forever (Isaiah 9:7). The deduction was inescapable. The Messiah *had* to come twice. It was as simple as that.

Despite the most diligent study of the Scriptures, there was not one rabbi in Israel at the time of Christ's first advent who comprehended the two comings of the Messiah. Rabbi Nicodemus, in contrast to the other religious leaders, believed that Jesus was the Messiah sent by God. Yet even he did not understand that the Messiah had to be rejected and slain. Surely had he understood, he would have attempted to point out the relevant prophecies to his colleagues, but he did not.

How was such blindness possible? Even more important, could it happen again? Astonishingly, a prophetic ignorance of equal magnitude characterizes our own day. This is true among both Jews and Christians, making a book such as this not only necessary but urgent.

A Prevailing Prophetic Illiteracy

A lack of interest in the Rapture and the Second Coming (the distinction between the two will be examined later), and the ignorance that inevitably accompanies indifference, have settled like an obscuring fog over the Church. Few, indeed, are the Christians today who could point out and explain the meaning of the key Old Testament prophecies of which Christ's contemporaries were so tragically ignorant. This is true even among those who pride themselves on their general knowledge of God's Word.

"I will come again!" After nearly two millennia, that wonderful but as yet unfulfilled promise remains shrouded in misunderstanding. What should be one's attitude today concerning this solemn promise made by Christ to His disciples and to each of us? If the promise is to be taken literally, then why such a long delay?

Yes, a very long time has passed since Christ gave His pledge to return. No matter how many centuries have come and gone, however, the One who conquered death must be taken seriously—both as to His promise and the warnings He uttered—lest His return take us by surprise and find us uninterested and unprepared.

Unfortunately, the same prophetic illiteracy which contributed largely to the rejection of Christ the first time He came is still with us and could have equally serious consequences upon

His return. Our purpose is to clarify the misunderstandings and to bring Christ's promise into clear focus once again. It is, of course, axiomatic that without a proper understanding of Christ's first coming one could hardly expect to have any real insight as to His Second Coming.

Jewish Lineage of the Messiah

Genesis 3:15 gives us the first promise of the Messiah's coming and explains the purpose: to destroy Satan and to rescue mankind from God's judgment. Nine chapters later we learn that the virgin-born "seed of the woman" will be a descendant of Abraham (12:3). How else could a blessing come to "all the families of the earth" except through the Messiah? Next we learn that through Isaac's lineage all the world will be blessed (Genesis 26:4); then we are told it will be through the seed of Jacob (28:14). The Messiah's ancestral line is further narrowed down to the tribe of Judah (Genesis 49:10), then the family of Jesse (Isaiah 11:1) and finally to the house of David (2 Samuel 7:12-16; Psalm 89:3,4,28-36; Jeremiah 23:5).

No wonder the New Testament begins with the genealogy of Jesus. It is traced through Joseph in Matthew 1:1-16 (though not His father, he was head of the house), and through Mary, his mother, in Luke 3:23-38, beginning there with Joseph's father-in-law, Heli. That Jesus was descended from David was absolutely essential, for the Messiah had to fulfill every relevant prophecy and His lineage was foundational. As Christ emphasized to His disciples:

> All things must be fulfilled, which were written in the
> law of Moses, and in the prophets, and in the psalms
> concerning me (Luke 24:44b).

Numerous and very specific are the Old Testament references to the coming Messiah: That He would be born in Bethlehem (the city of David), that He would be called out of Egypt, that He would live in Nazareth, that His own people would hate and turn Him over to the Gentiles, who would crucify Him. Many more details were prophesied, as we shall see. Why? A major reason, of course, would be so that the Messiah, when He came, could be identified beyond any shadow of doubt.

That the life, death and resurrection of Jesus of Nazareth fulfilled to the letter all of the requisite prophecies cannot be denied by any honest investigator. The evidence establishes beyond question that Jesus of Nazareth was and is the Messiah. His first coming to earth is an indisputable fact of history. As Peter declared in his second sermon in Jerusalem to thousands of Jews who had been eyewitnesses and knew the facts about Jesus:

> But those things, which God before had shewed by the mouth of all his prophets, that Christ should suffer, he hath so fulfilled (Acts 3:18).

Exactly as Christ's first advent fulfilled God's promises to His people—promises which the Hebrew prophets recorded centuries earlier in the Old Testament—so His second advent will fulfill in equally precise detail numerous additional prophecies. Therein lies the only source of information we have concerning Christ's return.

With the destruction of the temple and Jerusalem in A.D. 70, the genealogical records were destroyed. Since that time, therefore, it has been too late for any would-be Messiah to prove himself to be a descendant of David. Such inability, however, will not inhibit the Antichrist, for, as we shall see, he will be received, even by Israel, without regard to the Messianic prophecies.

That the Messiah would be a Jew and that His coming would be first of all to His own people is a matter both of history and prophecy fulfilled. That He must come again specifically to His genealogically related people, the Jews, is also plainly stated in the Scriptures. Thus we must come to an understanding of the Messiah's relationship to Israel, and of the role of Israel in both advents, or we cannot gain an accurate insight into either the Rapture or the Second Coming.

CHAPTER 2

The God of Prophecy

$\Diamond$

> I am God, and there is none else; I am God and there is none like me, declaring the end from the beginning, and from ancient times the things that are not yet done, saying, My counsel shall stand, and I will do all my pleasure (Isaiah 46:9-10).

> I have even from the beginning declared it to thee; before it came to pass I shewed it thee: lest thou shouldest say, Mine idol hath done them, and my graven image ... hath commanded them (Isaiah 48:5).

What does one say to a professed atheist when he demands "proof" that God exists? One could, of course, challenge him to prove that God doesn't exist, and to justify the preposterous scenario that the universe and even the human brain just happened by chance. The life and health of all creatures depends upon the fact that DNA molecules replicate exact duplicates of themselves. Only if the DNA, through chance foul-ups in its mechanism, failed to function properly could evolutionary changes occur.

That billions of intricately designed creatures, each with its proper food, and the delicately balanced ecological relationship between them—to say nothing of the nervous system, eye, and human brain—are the result of a series of chance mistakes in the DNA is too preposterous for belief. Yet those who reject God are left with no other alternative. The consequences of that theory, which is aggressively promoted in America's public schools and media, are not only morally and spiritually destructive, but logically fallacious as well. C.S. Lewis wrote:

> If minds are wholly dependent on brains, and brains on biochemistry, and biochemistry on the meaningless flux of the atoms, I cannot understand how the thought of those minds should have any more significance than the sound of the wind. . . .

Lewis's simple logic destroys Darwinism. If man is the chance product of impersonal evolutionary forces, then so are his thoughts—including the theory of evolution. Nevertheless, all of today's psychology, whether Christian or secular, rests upon Darwinism. Such was the basis of Freud's atheistic medical model which remains the key element in the attempt to establish a "science of human behavior."

As a result, man came to be viewed as a stimulus-response conglomeration of protein molecules driven by overpowering urges programmed into his unconscious by past traumas. Sin, for which one is morally accountable to God, became a mental illness beyond one's control. No longer a moral problem for which one was personally responsible, wrong behavior could only be corrected by the newly-invented ritual of psychotherapy. It was a new ball game with new rules and goals.

Even the Church went along with psychology. For evangelicals, the Bible, though still inerrant, was no longer *sufficient*. Biblical answers to spiritual problems were now perceived as inadequate and were at first supplemented and then replaced by "scientific" diagnoses and cures unknown to prophets and apostles. The *salvation of sinful souls* through Christ alone somehow metamorphosed into the *cure of sick minds* through psychotherapy.

A "Scientific" Explanation?

Christ's mission took on new meaning. His coming to earth was seen as more akin to a heavenly psychiatrist's visit to help us feel good about ourselves than that of a holy God descending among sinners to judge sin and bring salvation. Paul warned that in the last days professing Christians would have "a form of godliness while denying the power thereof" (2 Timothy 3:5). Lip service is still given to the power of the Holy Spirit and the gospel, but as a practical matter, far more faith is placed in the ritualistic power of psychotherapy to change lives. "Getting in touch with one's feelings" and "understanding oneself" rendered obsolete Christ's supernatural solution to a problem of evil which began with Lucifer's rebellion.

By claiming to offer a "scientific explanation" for human behavior, psychology invaded the realm of soul, spirit, morals, and religion. It thus posed a greater challenge to belief in God and the gospel than had physics or chemistry, which proposed no explanation for the universe or man's existence. Many of this century's greatest scientists have issued grave warnings against trying to mix science and religion. Einstein said, ". . . scientific theory has nothing to do with religion." Nobel laureate Erwin Schroedinger added, "[Science] knows nothing of . . . good or bad, God and eternity." Pretending to know what it couldn't, psychology offered a religious science of the mind and claimed to present new evidence for God's existence: the harmony of psychology and Scripture. The truth is that the two are irreconcilable.

Einstein, Schroedinger, and their colleagues were right: Science has nothing to say about God or morals. It can no more prove that God does or doesn't exist than it can prove that one sunset is beautiful and another is not. Moreover, proofs are really beside the point. It is impossible scientifically to prove one's own existence—but who doubts it? Then why is a proof of God's existence necessary? If God really is, then He should be able to make Himself known. And if He can't do that, then whether He exists or not would be irrelevant to practical concerns.

Natural Inability to Know God

Of course, the problem may not be that God isn't making Himself known but that mankind fails to recognize Him when

He does so. Even the natural world suggests such a probability. Consider, for example, energy. It is invisible and intangible, though its effects can be seen and felt everywhere. And though those effects bombard us constantly, mankind was for thousands of years unaware of the existence of energy as we now understand it.

The invisible component out of which all things were made remained unrecognized, not because it didn't manifest its presence and power, but in spite of that fact. Its effects were commonly known, but no one was capable of recognizing the presence of energy behind the phenomena it produced and which so abundantly proved its existence. Even today, though we know much about it, no scientist knows what energy is, how it originated, or why it functions as it does. Nor do we know what gravity is, or space, or light or any other basic ingredient of the universe.

Could it not be the same way with God? If He created energy, would He not be even more elusive and incomprehensible than anything He made? To be the creator of all, God (by very definition) would have to be infinite and thus beyond human understanding. He would have to reveal Himself, or we could never know Him. Yet how could He make Himself known to finite beings? Our self-centered ignorance and blindness to truth posed a major difficulty.

How could God make Himself known in such a way that a finite man would be absolutely certain that God was revealing Himself? To ask such a question is not an attempt to avoid the issue. It raises a very practical problem which God, if He exists, would have to overcome and honest skeptics must acknowledge.

From the innermost depths of the atom (which we haven't yet been able to explore) to the furthermost reaches of the cosmos, the intricately organized universe God made adequately reveals His infinite intelligence and power. It is something else, however, for God to manifest His love and will for mankind. To do so, He must make Himself known *personally* in such a way that a finite man would realize beyond a shadow of doubt that the infinite God was revealing Himself. How could an infinite God unveil Himself personally to finite beings?

Suppose God thundered from the sky with an audible voice. How would anyone know for certain that it was God who had spoken? Suppose He made some great display of power. How would it be known that God had acted and that it was not some natural phenomenon? Suppose He made Himself visible in some earthly form? If He came as a man, who would believe that He was God? Yet how could He reveal Himself to finite creatures unless He became one of them?

Suppose, instead, that God manifested Himself in some transcendent form. How could anyone know that it was God and not some highly evolved extraterrestrial visiting earth? How, indeed! Miracles, no matter how spectacular, would not suffice, for skeptics could argue that highly advanced technology seems miraculous to those who don't know how it works. And yet, if God really existed and was the creator of mankind, surely He would want to communicate not only His existence but His will to the creatures He had made and to whom He had given the capacity to know Him.

There Is Only One True God

Here we confront the many religions in the world. Each one claims to follow the revelations of the true god or gods—yet even in their basic concepts of deity there are sharp contradictions. Obviously, contradictory views can't all be right. Hinduism, for example, embraces millions of gods and worships idols which supposedly represent them, since *everything* is god. Islam, on the other hand, denounces idol worship and pantheism/polytheism and claims that its Allah is the only true God. Buddhism, in contrast, needs no god.

Allah was, in fact, the name of the chief god in the Kaabah, the pagan temple that Muhammad "purged" by destroying the more than 300 idols contained in it. Muhammad likely kept the name of this ancient pagan moon god and the symbol of the crescent moon because it would be easier to convert idolaters to his new religion if he could offer something with which they were familiar. Muslims see no contradiction in this strategy, nor even in keeping the chief object of worship in the ancient Kaabah, the black stone that Muslims kiss and revere today, even as idolaters did before Muhammad incorporated it into Islamic religious practice.

The God of the Bible states unequivocally: "Before me there was no God formed, neither shall there be after me. I, even I, am the Lord; and beside me there is no saviour" (Isaiah 43:10-11). He does not simply ignore the gods of other religions. He denounces them all, including Allah, as imposters who actually front for Satan or his demons. The great apostle Paul wrote, "The things which the Gentiles [non-Jews] sacrifice [to their gods], they sacrifice to devils" (1 Corinthians 10:20). Nor is such a denunciation narrow-minded or dogmatic. What could be more important than properly identifying the one true God, and what blasphemy could be worse than suggesting that God is something or someone who He is not?

Some well-meaning people, forgetting that the issue is truth and not wanting to cause offense, insist that the gods of all religions are simply different names for the same Being or Force. Such an idea, however, is like a man declaring that all women in the world, no matter what their names and individual identity, are one and the same person—and that each of them is his wife. The particular woman to whom he is married would not accept that fraud, nor would the other women to whom he is not married allow him to treat them as though each were married to him.

Irreconcilable Differences

While there are some similarities, the distinctions between the gods of major world religions are far greater than those between individual men and women. The adherents of competing religions take very seriously the identifying attributes of their deities. Thus, it is not generosity but a cynical trivialization of that which is vital and sacred to suggest that the gods of all religions are the same. It is an affront to Muslims to insist that Allah is the equivalent of the many gods in Hinduism; or to tell a Christian that his God, who gave His Son to die for the sins of the world, is the same as Allah, of whom it is specifically stated that he has no son.

To say that all religions are the same denies the meaning of language and is an insult not only to the followers of these religions but to intelligence itself. The difference is particularly glaring when it comes to Christianity. It stands alone on one side of a theological chasm, with all other religions on the other side—a chasm that renders any ecumenical union impossible without destroying Christianity itself.

One cannot deny, for example, the irreconcilable conflict between the belief that Christ died for our sins and rose again (which is the very heart of Christianity) and Islam's blasphemous claim that Christ did not die on the cross, much less for sin, but that someone else died in His place. To sweep such differences under an ecumenical rug (as Roman Catholicism, and specifically Vatican II, seeks to do) is not kindness but madness.

Nor is it possible to reconcile the claim of all non-Christian religions that sin is countered by good works with the Bible's oft-repeated declaration that only Christ, because He was sinless, could pay the penalty for sin, and that to do so He had to die in our place. Of course Christ's claim, "I am the way, the truth and the life; no man comes to the Father except by me" (John 14:6), is the strongest possible rejection of all other religions as Satanic counterfeits.

The very subject of this book, the *Second Coming of Christ*, is a belief which is unique to Christianity and separates it from all of the world's religions by a chasm that cannot be bridged by any ecumenical sleight-of-hand. Muhammad never promised to return, nor did Buddha, nor did the founder of any other of the world's religions. Only Christ dared to make this promise, and only He made it credible by leaving behind an empty tomb. That undeniable fact is reason enough to take seriously His assertion that He would return to this earth in power and glory to execute judgment upon His enemies.

Prophecy, Evidence, and the Bible

That the Bible, which provides the historical account of the life, death, and resurrection of Jesus Christ, is unique for this and many other reasons becomes obvious from even a superficial comparison with all other sacred writings. The Hindu scriptures, for example, are obviously mythological. There is no historical evidence that the characters ever existed or that the fantastic tales refer to events that actually occurred. The same is true of much that is recorded in the scriptures of other religions.

Take, for example, the Book of Mormon. Not one pin or coin or the tiniest shred of evidence of any kind has ever been found to verify that the peoples, much less the events, to which the Book of Mormon refers were real. Not even a mountain or river or any piece of topography or geography described in the Book of Mormon has ever been located. And this in spite of the fact that the Mormon Church has zealously pursued an intensive search of North, Central, and South America in its attempt to find some evidence of the great nations which the Book of Mormon describes as having lived there.

In contrast, the world's museums contain vast stores of evidence of all kinds confirming the historicity of the Bible. Yes, the skeptics have attacked the biblical record; but in *every* case, when the archaeological work has been done, the skeptics have been proved wrong and the Bible right. As only one example, critics at one time denied that the Hittites mentioned in the Bible had ever lived, because no record of their existence had as yet been found. Today in Ankara, Turkey, there is an entire museum devoted to the Hittites. Their relics are contained in museums around the world; and their history as we now know it agrees exactly with what the Bible has claimed for thousands of years.

In Israel's public schools the children are taught the history of their people and land directly from the Old Testament. Archaeologists in the Middle East use the Bible as a guide that tells them where to dig for ancient cities. The historical, geographical, and scientific accuracy of the Bible has been vindicated repeatedly as have no other sacred writings.

The Bible was written by men who claim to have been inspired by God and to have recorded the message He wanted them to convey to mankind. So specific are the Bible writers that each claims to have written down, not a paraphrase or a vague recollection, but the very words of God verbatim. Those words speak with convicting power to the human conscience and bear their own testimony (Hebrews 4:12). The Bible claims that just as all men recognize the same moral standards, because God has written His law in their hearts (Romans 2:14,15), so the gospel of Jesus Christ recorded in the Bible bears witness in every conscience as well (John 1:9; 2 Corinthians 4:2).

What About Objective Evidence?

The ardent skeptic, however, insists upon something more objective and convincing. The Bible declares that the universe all around us, so intricately organized and so subjected to precise and ingenious laws that it could not possibly have happened by chance, bears eloquent testimony to God's existence (Romans 1:19,20). Unfortunately, modern man has been misled into believing that science has some explanation for the universe and human life, though this is not the case at all. Sir Arthur Eddington declared, "Ought [i.e., right and wrong] takes us outside chemistry and physics." Schroedinger reminds us: "Whence came I and whither go I? That is the great unfathomable question . . . for every one of us. Science has no answer to it."

The average person, however, has been led to believe that science does in fact have the answers, but that they are too complex for ordinary people to understand. Thus they remain blind to the testimony of creation all around them. One of the beauties of the Bible is that it provides a very simple evidence for God's existence that anyone can easily and fully comprehend. It gives an equally simple and unequivocal way to identify which one of the sacred Scriptures claimed by the world's religions was inspired of God, and Who is the only Savior of the world.

What is this simple yet profound evidence which the Bible offers? It is prophecy fulfilled, an irrefutable verification reserved to the Judeo-Christian Scriptures alone. No honest person can remain an unbeliever after even a brief study of prophecy, as we hope to demonstrate in the pages following.

As we have already noted, prophecy is the missing element in all other sacred scriptures of the world's religions. It is not to be found in the Koran, the Hindu Vedas, the Bhagavad-Gita, the Book of Mormon, the sayings of Buddha, the writings of Mary Baker Eddy. By contrast, prophecy comprises about 30 percent of the Bible.

The God of Prophecy

It is not surprising, then, that the God of the Bible identifies Himself as the One who accurately foretells the future and makes certain that it unfolds as He said it would. In fact, God points to prophecy as the irrefutable evidence of His existence and the authenticity of His Word. The verses at the beginning of this chapter offer an example. Yet the fact that God uses prophecy in this manner is scarcely recognized even by evangelicals.

Prophecy, of course, is the topic which we will pursue in the following pages. Our approach, however, will be different from what one usually encounters in books of this nature. There are many individual prophecies in the Bible with which we will not concern ourselves because they lack universal interest and may be argued by skeptics. There are, however, two major topics of prophecy which must be studied if one is to have any understanding of the Bible. They are: 1) Israel; and 2) the Messiah, who would come to Israel and, through her, to the world. These two major topics involve undeniable specific fulfillments of prophecy and they hold the key to the timing of the Second Coming.

The Bible does not waste its time, as philosophers so foolishly have for centuries, in any attempt to provide some academic proof for the existence of God. The God to whom the Bible bears testimony is capable of communicating with mankind and promises to reveal Himself to all who sincerely desire to know Him and earnestly seek Him. "You will seek for me and find me, when you seek for me with all your heart" (Jeremiah 29:13) says the Old Testament. The New Testament echoes the same promise: "He [God] is a rewarder of those who diligently seek him" (Hebrews 11:6).

In communicating Himself and His will, God balances subjective evidence with objective proof. The Bible records God's provision of many tangible signs to those who wanted to know Him and His will. To "put out a fleece" is a common expression that is understood worldwide. It comes from Gideon's use of a sheep's fleece to be certain of God's will. Placing it on the ground overnight, he asked God for two signs: dew on the fleece and not on the ground one morning, then dew on the ground but not on the fleece the next (Judges 6:36-40). God honored his request because Gideon's heart was right and such evidence was necessary for the unusual task to which God was calling him.

That is not to say that God will honor every "fleece" which any person may by whim or stubborn demand lay before Him. Those who neglect to study diligently and heed the Scriptures which God has provided and preserved through the centuries need not expect some new word of prophecy or some miraculous sign. Those who make such demands fall into the hands of Satan, who is only too glad to provide the "signs and wonders" which they seek and thereby lead them astray.

Israel: Irrefutable Proof

There is a sign which God has given to the entire world for all generations. That sign is the land and people of Israel. God speaks of "Israel my glory" (Isaiah 46:13) and refers to her as the one "in whom I will be glorified" (Isaiah 49:3). How would this glorification come about? It could only be by God's specific dealings with Israel before a watching world, after having prophesied precisely what would happen (2 Chronicles 7:20). Referring to the rescue of Israel at Armageddon, the subject of many Old Testament prophecies, Ezekiel 38:23 declares: "Thus will I [God] magnify myself, and sanctify myself; and I will be known in the eyes of many nations, and they shall know that I am the Lord."

The Bible declares that the prophecies it provides concerning Israel supply the irrefutable evidence for God's existence and for the fact that He has a purpose for mankind. History is not merely happenstance. It is going somewhere. There is a plan. Prophecy reveals that plan in advance. And at the heart of that plan biblical prophecy places Israel as God's great sign to the world.

It was to Israel that the Messiah, the Savior of the world, was sent. As predicted by her own prophets, Israel rejected Him. How ironic that in rejecting Jesus the Jews fulfilled prophecies that identified Him as the Messiah! If we are to understand anything of Christ's Second Coming, then we must gain some insight into Israel's key role as revealed by the Old Testament prophets and by Christ and His apostles.

CHAPTER 3

An Irrefutable Sign

◇

> Behold, I will make Jerusalem a cup of trembling unto all the people round about, when they shall be in the seige both against Judah and against Jerusalem. And in that day will I make Jerusalem a burdensome stone for all people: all that burden themselves with it shall be cut in pieces. . . . For I will gather all nations against Jerusalem to battle; and the city shall be taken . . . then shall the Lord go forth to fight against those nations (Zechariah 12:2,3; 14:2,3).

The fulfillment of hundreds of specific prophecies in the ancient and modern history of the Jewish people is God's great sign to mankind—a sign that no one can mistake or deny. God's unique dealings with Israel before a watching world constitute an irrefutable proof that He exists and that He is guiding history. He is not the god of the deists, but is intimately involved with earth's inhabitants, for whom He has great love and definite plans which He will carry through to their conclusion. Both Israel and her Messiah are vital to God's purpose for mankind.

That God gave Israel her land, took her out of it and scattered her throughout all the world, then brought her back to it centuries later is a saga unique in the annals of history. It is beyond the possibility of chance and without ordinary explanation. Her future in the promised land with the Messiah eventually ruling the world from Jerusalem on David's throne has been assured by God. Woe to those who try to revise His plan!

Even before He brought the descendants of Abraham, Isaac, and Jacob (whom God later named Israel) into the land of Canaan as He had promised, God warned them through Moses: "If thou wilt not hearken unto the voice of the Lord thy God, to observe to do all his commandments and his statutes... ye shall be plucked from off the land whither thou goest to possess it. And the Lord shall scatter thee among all people, from the one end of the earth even unto the other... and thou shalt become an astonishment, a proverb, and a byword among all nations..." (Deuteronomy 28:15,63,64,37).

Other prophets continued to plead and warn. Typical are the following: "I will make you to be removed into all the kingdoms of the earth... and I will make the cities of Judah a desolation without inhabitant (Jeremiah 34:17,22).... For, lo, I will command and I will sift the house of Israel among all nations" (Amos 9:9).

In spite of God's guidance, blessing, protection, and patient warnings, Israel repeatedly rebelled against Him. She worshiped the false gods of the nations around her, even as God had foretold she would. Warnings such as those just quoted were repeated many times by the Hebrew prophets as God, reluctant to punish His people, pleaded with them to repent. The day came, however, when He could withhold His judgment no longer.

God's Reluctant Judgment

The people of Israel persisted in their rebellion for nearly five centuries. At last God reluctantly fulfilled His word. Jerusalem and the temple were destroyed by Nebuchadnezzar, then restored and rebuilt, then later destroyed once again. Exactly as His prophets had foretold, God scattered His people, Israel, throughout the entire world (Leviticus 26:33; Deuteronomy 4:27, 32:26; 1 Kings 14:15; Nehemiah 1:8; Jeremiah

9:16, 49:32, etc.). Today, the "wandering Jew" is found in every corner of the earth.

Though God used the nations into which she was disbursed to discipline Israel, all the world will be held accountable for their mistreatment of His people. The Lamb of God, who came in meekness to die for our sins, will return as the Lion of the tribe of Judah to execute judgment.

That Israel was cast out of her land and scattered worldwide exactly as God said represents a fulfillment of prophecy involving so many people, so many nations and such a lengthy span of time that no one can honestly remain a skeptic, much less an atheist. Jewish history stands as a universally visible monument to God's existence, to the fact that the Bible is His infallible Word, and the Jews are His chosen people.

Approximately 2500 years have passed since the Babylonian captivity and more than 1900 years since the latest Diaspora when Jerusalem was destroyed by the Romans in 70 A.D. During the ensuing centuries the wandering Jews had no homeland. Yet they were never absorbed into the nations among which they had been scattered. These hated, despised, and persecuted people, who had every reason to intermarry and lose their identity, remained an identifiable ethnic unit. That in itself is miraculous. God fulfilled His promise through the prophets to preserve His people in order to bring them back to their land as He had sworn He would.

Those who insist that God is finished with Israel have closed their eyes to specific and numerous prophecies to the contrary. The following is only one example among many:

> Therefore fear thou not, O my servant Jacob, saith the Lord, neither be dismayed, O Israel: for, lo, I will save thee from afar, and thy seed from the land of their captivity. . . . For I am with thee, saith the Lord, to save thee: though I make a full end of all nations whither I have scattered thee, yet will I not make a full end of thee: but I will correct thee in measure, and will not leave thee altogether unpunished (Jeremiah 30:10,11).

Listen once more to what God has said about this people who are of such great significance in His plan of redemption and who are such a visible sign to the world. So important are they that if the natural order in the world is to be preserved, then Israel must be preserved also, as Jeremiah tells us:

> Thus saith the Lord, which giveth the sun for a light by day, and the ordinances of the moon and of the stars for a light by night, which divideth the sea . . . the Lord of hosts is his name: if those ordinances depart from before me, saith the Lord, then the seed of Israel also shall cease from being a nation before me for ever (Jeremiah 31:35,36).

Ten Lost Tribes?

It is often argued that Israel was not preserved but that ten tribes were lost, carried away captive into Assyria (2 Kings 15:29, 17:6,18). If that is the case, then the Bible is filled with false prophecies about the 12 tribes being brought back to their land in the last days. One must believe either this theory or Scripture—both cannot be true. The prophecies cited above refer to all of Israel and were spoken by God long after the ten tribes were supposedly lost.

In fact, the theory of "ten lost tribes" is an antisemitic myth. Space does not permit the detailed discussion which this subject perhaps deserves. However, a careful reading of the history of Israel in Scripture denies what must be considered a Satanic doctrine, for it destroys in theory (as others have sought to do in practice) the continuity of Israel. That continuity was repeatedly assured by God and is essential for the major prophecies of Scripture to be fulfilled in the last days.

There are sound scriptural reasons for rejecting the lost tribes theory. First of all, the ten tribes were not taken far from Israel. Why then would they be lost? It is unreasonable to imagine, with all the ebb and flow of kings and kingdoms in the ensuing centuries, that none of these people would return to their land, and that all of them would forget their ethnic identity. Such a presumed cultural memory loss goes against everything we know of the persistence of these people to retain their Jewish heritage. Those who were carried captive into Babylon returned, so why not those taken a lesser distance to Assyria?

Secondly, it would be unrealistic to imagine that every last person was removed. That many remained in the land of Israel in spite of the Assyrian captivity, even as many remained in Judah during the Babylonian captivity, is evident. For example, many members of the ten tribes of Israel were still living in their land during the spiritual revival in Judah under King Josiah—a revival which occurred nearly 100 years after the carrying away into Assyria.

A few years before the Assyrian captivity, Hezekiah had called upon those from the ten tribes of Israel as well as from Judah to repent. He sent messengers "throughout all Israel and Judah . . . saying, Ye children of Israel, turn again unto the Lord God of Abraham, Isaac, and Israel, and he will return to the remnant of you, that are escaped out of the hand of the kings of Assyria" (2 Chronicles 30:6). In fact, we are told that a multitude of people from Ephraim, Manasseh, Issachar, and Zebulun came to keep the Passover in Jerusalem at that time.

Likewise, the revival a century later under Josiah affected many from the ten tribes. We read that there were in existence functioning "cities of Manasseh, and Ephraim, and Simeon, even unto Naphtali" (2 Chronicles 34:6). The Levites even went through the cities of Israel, gathering funds from "Manasseh and Ephraim, and of *all the remnant of Israel*" (34:9) to finance the repairing of the temple in Jerusalem. Multitudes from six of the ten allegedly lost tribes, still in contact with Judah, came to Jerusalem, tender to the call of the prophets to repent and keep the feasts of Jehovah.

Remember Anna, who came into the temple in Jerusalem, just when Joseph and Mary had brought in the eight-day-old Jesus, and identified Him as the Redeemer? We are told that she was "of the tribe of Asher" (Luke 2:36). So here is evidence of a survivor of a seventh tribe of the "lost" ten. We need not say more. Let us accept God's Word on this subject.

A Shameful Chapter in Human History

The persistent and infamous persecution of Jews down through the centuries is undeniable. It also defies any ordinary explanation. Such continual abuse at the hands of their fellow man was a perpetual reminder that, though chosen of God and greatly beloved, they had sinned and were under His judgment. It was also a reminder of something else equally remarkable—that Satan was determined to destroy them.

God had promised that His Messiah, the Savior of Israel and of the world, would come through these people. God's battle with Satan could only be won by the Messiah. He alone could wrest mankind from Lucifer's evil grasp. Consequently, if Satan could destroy Israel there would be no Messiah and he would have won the battle for the universe. That there has been not only a supernatural aspect to Jewish (and by Jewish we mean all 12 tribes) persecution but a certain diabolical element, as well, is a matter of history. Even those who call themselves Christians have often been the instruments of Satan in this battle of the ages.

For centuries the Roman Catholic Church, claiming to have taken Israel's place in God's favor, consigned the Jews to ghettos and forced them to wear identifying insignia. Luther persisted in this persecution even after his break with Rome, giving Jews the option of converting to Christianity or having their tongues torn out. The forced "conversion" of Jews in the Roman Catholic Inquisition and at other times in history is well known. To this day the Vatican has never acknowledged Israel's right to exist.

Hitler justified his tactics against the Jews on the basis of what the officially recognized Christian church, both Catholic and Protestant, had done for centuries. That highly educated, scientifically advanced and "civilized" nations would single out a group of fellow human beings for extermination is not only incredible but betrays a Satanic element. That these people, in spite of such a programed destruction, would be preserved, retain their ethnic identity and would even multiply in numbers around the world is almost beyond belief.

Surely God has kept the Jews from genocide and from losing their identity as a national people exactly as He promised. The theory of "ten lost tribes," or of British Israelism, or that the real Jews became the white Europeans and Americans, stands in the fullest contradiction to a major theme and repeated testimony of God's Word.

Miraculous Restoration to Her Land

Even more indicative of God's hand behind the scenes is the fact that, just as the Bible declared, the descendants of Abraham, Isaac, and Jacob have been restored to their ancient land and reborn as a nation in today's modern world (Jeremiah 30:3,10,11; 31:8-10; Ezekiel 11:17; 28:25, etc.). Nearly 1900 years after the last destruction of the nation of Israel and the scattering of her people all over the earth, the nation of Israel is in place once again in the land that God gave to her nearly 4000 years ago. It is a restoration unique in human history, in fulfillment of numerous and specific prophecies, and it bears the unmistakable imprint of the hand of God. Yet there is an even more astonishing aspect of this story.

The passage quoted at the beginning of the chapter is among the most remarkable in the Bible. It was recorded by Zechariah, under the inspiration of the Holy Spirit, nearly 2500 years ago. To appreciate his prophecy fully, one must remember that at the time the words were uttered Jerusalem was in ruins and the land around it, mostly desert or swamp, was a largely uninhabited wilderness—and it remained that way for centuries. Any chance that Jerusalem could recover its ancient glory, much less that it would be of international importance in today's modern world, was nil.

Under those hopeless conditions, God, through His prophet, made three unbelievable declarations: 1) that the day would come when Jerusalem would be the focus of attention for all mankind; 2) that the entire world would at that time tremble in its concern over Jerusalem; and 3) that one day the armies of all nations would gather against Jerusalem to destroy it.

For centuries this prophecy seemed to be a grand mistake that had no rightful place in the Bible. The land of Israel remained largely a wasteland with a few nomads feeding their flocks on its sparse growth and scratching out a bare existence from its arid soil. Zechariah's prophecy could not have come from God but rather from his own madness. So it must have seemed for 2000 years. Yet today, as foretold, Jerusalem, though still of negligible size and in a location of no significance, is the center of international attention. The impossible has happened and for reasons that are still not understood by the world!

"A Cup of Trembling"

Not only is Jerusalem the center of world attention, but just as Zechariah foretold, it has become a "cup of trembling" for a modern world. Whether atheist or believer, Hindu, Buddhist, Muslim, or Jew, all mankind knows that the next world war, when it occurs, will break out over Jerusalem! Could any intellectually honest person deny that only God could have inspired such an incredible prophecy 2500 years in advance?

Smaller than Holland, Israel occupies about one-sixth of 1 percent of the land possessed by the Arabs surrounding her. The latter have the oil and the wealth and influence that goes with it. Israel has nothing: no oil or gas, no precious metals, no great rivers, no high mountains nor the vast fertile valleys they create. Then why the international concern over this postage stamp piece of arid real estate and the four million refugees who have fled there to escape persecution? It makes no sense. Yet the prophets foretold this situation precisely as it exists today.

The major nations of the world have their diplomats working day and night to effect a peace treaty between Israel and her Arab neighbors. Why? Because all mankind knows that the peace of Jerusalem is the key to the peace of the entire world exactly as God said through His prophets!

For centuries such a prophecy seemed the height of absurdity. Yet today, Jerusalem hangs like a millstone around the necks of 5.2 billion people who cannot escape the necessity of either bringing peace to this despised people or destroying them. Those who favor the latter alternative are growing in numbers and power.

Yes, to some extent, Jerusalem is the focus of attention because it is sacred to Catholics, Muslims, and Jews. But neither Catholics nor Muslims existed when these prophecies were made. Nor does Jerusalem's sacredness to these three religions explain why the whole world is concerned with establishing peace in the Middle East. That peace will be guaranteed by the Antichrist and will ultimately lead to the most destructive war in earth's history. Sadly, one day soon and precisely as prophesied, all of the nations of the world will bring their armies against Israel to destroy her people.

The Bible's prophecies concerning the Jews, Jerusalem, and Israel are specific, preposterous, and impossible—yet they are being fulfilled to the letter. How could anyone doubt that God is the author of the Bible, the Jews are His chosen people, and Israel is the land God gave them! Woe to those who seek to frustrate the promises which God has given to Israel, His chosen!

CHAPTER 4

God's Chosen People

◇

> I will give it unto you to possess it, a land that floweth
> with milk and honey: I am the Lord your God, which have
> separated you from other people. And ye shall be holy
> unto me: for I the Lord am holy, and have severed you
> from other people, that ye should be mine (Leviticus
> 20:24,26).

Whatever one may choose to believe, God's Word declares
repeatedly and unequivocally that Israel is His specially chosen people and that they will never lose that singular status.
Israel's unique destiny, ordained by God to fulfill His will for
mankind, is the dominant theme of Bible prophecy. The
prophecies concerning the Messiah are inextricably linked
with His people, Israel. It was to Israel, and through her to the
world, that the Messiah, Himself a Jew, was to come.

Therefore, a clear insight into the prophecies pertaining to
Israel's past, present, and future is foundational to any understanding both of the first advent of Christ and of His promise to
"come again." Israel, as we have already noted, is God's
prophetic timepiece, the great sign which He has given to the
world to prove His existence and to demonstrate that He is in
charge of history. Like it or not, the Jews are God's chosen
people.

A chosen people? Chosen by God? That favor seems to have
brought more than its share of troubles. In *Fiddler on the Roof*,

Topol echoes many a Jew's bewildered protest, "How about choosing somebody else!" Obviously that plea won't change the facts. There is no escaping God's purpose or the biblical record.

Refusing to face the overwhelming evidence, skeptics contemptuously dismiss the very suggestion that there could be a special "chosen people." Atheists deny the existence of any God to do the choosing. Nevertheless, that biblical claim, even though widely rejected, has focused attention upon the Jews. In many cases it has brought persecution from those who hate the Jews, as though they were the ones who conceived the idea that God had some special affection and plan for them.

Muslims, on the other hand, insist that it was not the descendants of Isaac but those of Ishmael who were chosen by God. Muhammad's Quraish tribe claimed to trace themselves back to Ishmael and through him to Abraham. Therefore, it is argued, the land of Israel (which Muslims insist was promised to Ishmael) belongs to the Arabs. This claim, however, is without any foundation. The Bible declares otherwise: that the land of Israel belongs to the descendants of Isaac. As for the Koran, it fails even to mention Jerusalem or any part of the land of Israel—an omission which is fatal to Islamic claims at this late date.

Five Distinguishing Characteristics of Israel

Let us take a closer look at this remarkable "chosen people." There is no better place to start than the book of Genesis. There we meet a man named Abram, whom God chose and later renamed Abraham. Both Arabs (through Ishmael) and Jews (through Isaac) claim him as their father. In fact, there is no evidence that the Arabs are descended from Abraham through Ishmael. As Robert Morey has pointed out in his excellent book *The Islamic Invasion*: "The prestigious *Encyclopedia of Islam* traces the Arabs to non-Abrahamic origins." The evidence that Jews are Abraham's descendants, however, is overwhelming. Here is where the story begins:

Now the Lord had said unto Abram, Get thee out of thy country . . . unto a land that I will shew thee: and I will make of thee a great nation . . . and I will bless them that bless thee, and curse him that curseth thee: and in thee shall all families of the earth be blessed (Genesis 12:1-3).

The Lord thy God hath chosen thee to be a special people unto himself, above all people that are upon the face of the earth (Deuteronomy 7:6).

There are five distinct elements in the covenant God made with Abraham, Isaac, and Jacob (Israel), which set their descendants apart from all other peoples on the earth. Here they are in the order in which they were given: 1) the promise that the Messiah would come to the world through Israel; 2) the promise of a particular land that was given to Israel as a possession forever; 3) the Mosaic law and its accompanying covenants of promise, which defined a special relationship between God and Israel; 4) the visible manifestation of God's presence among them; and 5) the promised reign of the Messiah, on the throne of David in Jerusalem, over His chosen people and over the entire world.

We will defer the first and last promises above, which pertain specifically to the Messiah, until later and deal with the others now. The verses quoted from Genesis 12 contain the first promise of a land that was to be given to Abram and his descendants after him. The next few verses in that chapter record Abram's obedient departure from Ur of the Chaldees, the land of his nativity, where his family had lived in idolatry for many years after the dispersion of the builders of the Tower of Babel. Around the ruins of that Tower the city of Babylon was built. It would become the capital of the first world empire, the place of Israel's later captivity, and of great importance concerning Christ's return to this earth, as we shall see.

We very quickly find Abram arriving in "the land of Canaan." Its inhabitants were already known as Canaanites and they possessed the land at that time. This was the land that God identified to Abram as the land which his descendants would possess about 400 years later. Thus it became known as "the promised land" and is still referred to as such. The following are a sampling of God's many confirmations of this special promise concerning the land:

> And the Lord appeared unto Abram, and said, Unto thy seed will I give this land . . . for all the land which thou seest, to thee will I give it, and to thy seed for ever.

> I am the Lord that brought thee out of Ur of the Chaldees, to give thee this land to inherit it. . . . Thy seed shall be a stranger in a land that is not their's [Egypt], and shall serve them. . . . But in the fourth generation they shall come hither again.

> In the same day the Lord made a covenant with Abram, saying, Unto thy seed have I given this land, from the river of Egypt [in the Sinai desert] unto . . . the river Euphrates [and there follows a description of the exact territory] (Genesis 12:7; 13:15; 15:7,13-16,18-21).

The same promise is repeated to Abraham's son, Isaac, on more than one occasion. For example: "For unto thee, and unto thy seed, I will give all these countries, and I will perform the oath which I sware unto Abraham thy father . . . and in thy seed shall all the nations of the earth be blessed" (Genesis 26:3-5). The twin promise of the land and the Messiah is repeated again to Jacob, whom God later named Israel: "I am the Lord God of Abraham thy father, and the God of Isaac: the land whereon thou liest, to thee will I give it, and to thy seed . . . and in thy seed [i.e., the Messiah] shall all the families of the earth be blessed" (Genesis 28:13,14).

God's Self-Identification

Linking His very name with these promises, the God of the Bible identifies Himself at least ten times as "the God of Abraham, Isaac, and Jacob" (Exodus 3:15,16; 1 Chronicles 29:18; Matthew 22:32; Acts 3:13, etc.). He revealed Himself as such to Moses at the burning bush. At the same time, He gave

Moses His name, "Yahweh," which means "I AM THAT I AM." He is the self-existent One whose existence depends upon no other, and upon whom the existence of all else depends. Jesus uses the fact that Yahweh is known as "the God of Abraham, Isaac, and Jacob" to argue for the resurrection:

> But as touching the resurrection of the dead, have ye not read that which was spoken unto you by God, saying, I am the God of Abraham, and the God of Isaac, and the God of Jacob? God is not the God of the dead, but of the living (Matthew 22:31,32).

"God" is not a name but a generic term that could apply to any god. Therefore, the God of Abraham, Isaac, and Jacob gives us His name. It is "Yahweh." Thus He is distinguished from all the gods of the world's religions. Yahweh is definitely not Allah for many reasons. Their character is exactly the opposite. Yet the highest officials of the Roman Catholic Church—in Vatican II and elsewhere—declare that the God of the Muslims and of the Christians is one and the same. Even evangelicals, trying to be broadminded and ecumenical, are suggesting that Muslims worship the same God as do Christians. Nothing could be further from the truth!

Here again we find clarification through an understanding of Israel's role. Allah is surely not "the God of Abraham, Isaac, and Jacob" but their sworn enemy who desires the extermination of their descendants! Allah is a proper name—a name that existed long before Muhammad invented the anti-Israel and anti-Christian religion of Islam. Allah was, as we have already noted, the name of the moon god, which was represented by the chief idol in Mecca's Kaabah. Hence the symbol of the crescent moon. For all of Islam's rejection of idolatry, Allah had a long pre-Islamic history as a pagan god represented by an idol—certainly not the God of the Bible at all!

The gods of the heathen, represented by idols, are consistently and repeatedly denounced in the Bible and those who worship them are condemned by Yahweh's prophets. Never is there the least hint or suggestion that any such god is or could be an unwitting representation of Yahweh. Indeed, Paul, as we've noted, declares that those who worship idols really worship the demons who identify themselves with them.

"Chosen" by an "Impartial" God?

Even among Christians there is increasing controversy over whether Israel any longer has a special place in God's plans. This controversy is accompanied by a growing rejection of the biblical teaching that the land of Israel belongs to the Jews. Some argue that for God to choose Israel would mean that He was unfairly playing favorites. After all, the Bible says that God is "no respecter of persons" (Acts 10:34).

Such impartiality on God's part was not easily revealed to Peter, for the Jews (and the early Christians were all Jews) considered all Gentiles to be without hope under the law of Moses. It took miraculous signs to convince Peter that the gospel was not only for Jews but for the Gentiles also. Even many Christians today cannot believe that God loves every person equally and desires that all should be saved, though the Bible teaches it plainly: "For God so loved *the world . . .* who will have *all men* to be saved. . . . The Father sent the Son to be the Saviour *of the world*" (John 3:16; 1 Timothy 2:4; 1 John 4:14, etc.).

How can God's impartiality be reconciled with the idea of a chosen people? God made it very clear on a number of occasions that it was not "respect of persons" that caused Him to choose Israel. He chose them *in spite of their unworthiness and unattractiveness*, not because He found them more appealing than other peoples. In fact, they were rebels who deserved nothing but judgment. It was these unworthies in whom He decided to demonstrate His love, grace, and mercy to the world. Listen as He speaks to Israel through His prophets:

> The Lord did not set his love upon you, nor choose you, because ye were more in number than any people; for ye *were* the fewest of all people: But because the Lord loved you, and because he would keep the oath which he had sworn unto your fathers [Abraham, Isaac and Jacob], hath the Lord brought you out [of Egypt] (Deuteronomy 7:7,8).

This is a rebellious people, lying children, children that will not hear the law of the Lord: which say . . . to the prophets, Prophesy not unto us right things, speak unto us smooth things, prophesy deceits (Isaiah 30:9,10).

Son of man, I send thee to the children of Israel, to a rebellious nation that hath rebelled against me: they and their fathers have transgressed against me, even unto this very day (Ezekiel 2:3).

God's Unsearchable Grace

The Bible repeatedly says that the Jews, like all mankind, are rebels who are unworthy of anything except judgment. Even so, God blesses Israel by grace without any merit on her part because of His promises to Abraham, Isaac, and Jacob. Moreover, this grace is made possible by the Messiah's redemptive death. The contradiction between the Bible and the Koran could not be clearer on this point.

Although Allah is called "the Merciful Compassionate One," he is, in fact, compassionate only with a few, merciless with most, and has no basis for mercifully forgiving the sinner. In contrast to the biblical gospel of God's grace, Islam's salvation is by works and is merited by keeping the law. The Koran has no concept of divine mercy and grace and the penalty for man's sin having been paid in full by the Redeemer.

The Koran declares that Muslims receive God's blessing, not by grace, but because they are worthy: "Ye are the best of Peoples, evolved for mankind, enjoining what is right, forbidding what is wrong, and believing in Allah" (Sura 3:110). This same verse goes on to call the Jews "perverted transgressors." Sura 4:52,53 calls the Jews the people "whom Allah hath cursed . . . [who] have no one to help [them]."

It is commonly argued today, even by evangelicals, that the return of millions of Jews to their land is merely a chance happening of history without any prophetic significance. Surely God would not have brought the Jews back to Israel, it is argued, because they aren't worthy of it. A large percentage of them are atheists or agnostics and nearly all have rejected their Messiah. Many are humanists, materialists, New Agers.

Certainly Israel has not always acted in perfect righteousness toward the Arab Palestinians or toward her neighbors. With such a litany of sins to her credit stretching back to ancient times, how could Israel enjoy God's special blessing?

Grace and Promise

Israel's imperfections are beside the point. As the above verses and hundreds like them in the Bible attest, Israel has been rebellious from the very beginning. Her present condition is nothing new. God has punished Israel for her sins. The worst punishment, however, lies ahead during the Great Tribulation, which will culminate in the battle of Armageddon. Yet the promises to Abraham, Isaac, and Jacob remain and will be fulfilled by God's grace. For if God's blessing comes only to those who are worthy of it, then all mankind is doomed. For as the Bible reminds us, "all have sinned" (Romans 3:23; 5:12).

There is no way for a sinner to pay for his own sins. Even one violation of the law puts the lawbreaker in a hopeless condition before God. Keeping the law perfectly in the future (even if that were possible) could never make up for having broken the law even once in the past. Obviously, there is no extra credit given for perfect compliance with every precept, for that is exactly what the law demands. Thus, good deeds can never obtain God's forgiveness for past sin.

The debt must be paid by One who is without sin and who is able to bear the judgment that the guilty deserve. Such is God's solution to evil—and to pay that debt was the primary mission of the Messiah. It was through His death for our sins that He judged and destroyed Satan. Hence, the good news of the gospel: "For by grace are ye saved, through faith, and that not of yourselves, it is a gift from God" (Ephesians 2:8).

Part of God's punishment upon Israel in the past was to scatter her people throughout all nations. He is now bringing them back to their land in unprecedented numbers, not because they merit it but because of His promise to Abraham, Isaac, and Jacob to do so. It has been a modern phenomenon far exceeding the original exodus of their ancestors from Egypt into the promised land.

A Promise for the "Last Days"

Of particular amazement to the world has been the recent collapse of communism and the shredding of the Iron Curtain. One major bonus has been the resultant astonishing flood of Jews pouring back into Israel by the hundreds of thousands from the former Soviet Union—a land that only recently refused to allow them to leave.

What a sight it is to watch the daily influx of grateful immigrants arriving at Tel Aviv's Lod airport from all parts of the world, but especially from the northern land of Russia! It is deeply moving to see many of them kiss the ground when they exit the plane, weeping for joy.

An observer of this uniquely emotional scene who was familiar with the Hebrew prophets could not help but recall the promise God made 2500 years ago and which He said He would fulfill in the last days:

> For thus saith the Lord: Sing with gladness for Jacob, and shout among the chief of the nations: publish ye, praise ye, and say, O Lord, save thy people, the remnant of Israel. Behold, I will bring them from the north country, and gather them from the coasts of the earth, and with them the blind and lame, the woman with child and her that travaileth with child together; a great company shall return thither. They shall come with weeping, and with supplications will I lead them: I will cause them to walk by the rivers of waters in a straight way, wherein they shall not stumble: for I am a father to Israel, and Ephraim is my firstborn. Hear the word of the Lord, O ye nations, and declare it in the isles afar off, and say, He that scattered Israel will gather him, and keep him, as a shepherd doth his flock. . . . Therefore they shall come and sing in the height of Zion, and shall flow together to the goodness of the Lord (Jeremiah 31:7-12).

Why was this promise to be fulfilled in that period of time called "the last days"? The reason is obvious and of great importance to our subject. The Second Coming could not take place without Israel having become a nation once again in her own land—for it is to Israel that Christ returns in the midst of Armageddon, to rescue her from the enemies who are intent upon exterminating her.

How close are we to that day? The fulfillment at this particular time in history of the many ancient prophecies that immigrants would flood into Israel in the last days is a major sign of the nearness of Christ's return.

Yahweh does not violate His promises. If He failed to keep His Word, whether to bring blessing or judgment, His character would be tarnished and His holy name dishonored. As He often said through His prophets concerning His intention to bring Israel back into her land in the last days: "I do not this for your sakes, O house of Israel, but for mine holy name's sake" (Ezekiel 36:22); "Thou art my servant, O Israel, in whom I will be glorified" (Isaiah 49:3).

What a great and convincing "sign" is Israel's return to her land after 2500 years! Today, in fulfillment of prophecy, the eyes of the world are upon that seemingly insignificant and tiny piece of arid real estate. She is, exactly as foretold, a "cup of trembling" for all nations—a trembling concerning what may happen there.

Can anyone honestly compare the prophecies concerning Israel with her history and remain an atheist? Or can anyone deny that Jesus Christ is the only Savior? His advent, prophesied by the same Spirit-inspired mouthpieces for God, is intimately connected to Israel and her tortured history of dispersion and return to her land. We will come back to that subject later.

The other great theme of biblical prophecy is the Messiah who was to come through and to Israel. Those specific and numerous prophecies concerning Christ's coming, and their fulfillment in the life, death, and resurrection of Jesus of Nazareth, provide conclusive identification of Jesus as the Christ. They also constitute a further irrefutable proof for the existence of the God who inspired the Hebrew prophets.

CHAPTER 5

An Unlikely Prophetic Scenario

—————————— ◇ ——————————

The assembly of the wicked have inclosed me: they
pierced my hands and my feet.... They part my garments among them, and cast lots upon my vesture [robe]
(Psalm 22:16,18).

They gave me also gall for my meat; and in my thirst
they gave me vinegar to drink (Psalm 69:21).

It was the night of April 9, A.D. 32, a Wednesday. The scene
was the "last supper" and Jesus was alone with the twelve who
comprised the inner circle of His disciples. Only three days
earlier, on Sunday, April 6—a day now celebrated as Palm
Sunday—the acclaim awarded Jesus of Nazareth had reached
a crescendo. He had ridden into Jerusalem that day, mounted
not as one would expect of a hero, but, strangely enough, on a
donkey. Nevertheless, throngs of people had spontaneously
lined the approach to the Holy City to welcome Him. Waving
palm branches and shouting for joy, the multitudes had hailed
Him as Israel's long-awaited Messiah. Few, if any, in that
joyous crowd realized that they were fulfilling a prophecy
made part of Scripture about 500 years earlier:

Rejoice greatly, O daughter of Zion; shout, O daughter
of Jerusalem: behold, thy King cometh unto thee: he is
just, and having salvation; lowly, and riding upon...a
colt the foal of an ass (Zechariah 9:9).

47

Following that astonishing event Jesus had remained day after day in the vicinity of Jerusalem as though He were presenting Himself in a new way to Israel. He had never before lingered at Jerusalem in this manner. It was extremely dangerous to do so, because the rabbis were determined to arrest and kill Him. Now, however, He seemed to have thrown away all caution. Though secreting Himself in a safe place at night, He returned each day to walk among the people and teach in the temple.

Unable to take Jesus into custody because of the crowds of admirers surrounding Him at all times, the increasingly frustrated rabbis were confounded as they watched His popularity grow by leaps and bounds. It was, of course, a time of excited, almost breathless, anticipation for Christ's disciples. The establishment of His kingdom was obviously at hand!

Alone with their Lord now, in the upper room, the twelve could scarcely contain their elation. Surely the One whom they had followed for more than three years was about to assert His right to rule on David's throne. The rabbis could never stop Him now, for the people were behind Him in overwhelming numbers.

A Frightening Turn of Events

The hour for which His inner circle of disciples had been waiting so long had come at last. So they thought, but how wrong they would soon discover themselves to be! In a seemingly impossible and frightening turn of events, their Master would in a few hours be arrested, condemned to death, mockingly crowned with thorns, and crucified like a common criminal. Dreams shattered, the disciples would flee in shame and fear for their own lives.

During His brief earthly ministry, Christ had repeatedly foretold His rejection and death at the hands of Israel's religious leaders. He had also declared publicly that He would rise from the dead after three days and had pointed His hearers to the Old Testament prophets who had already declared the same concerning the Messiah. Still, no one had understood.

Peter had even rebuked Him for holding such a negative thought: "Be it far from thee, Lord: this shall not be unto thee" (Matthew 16:22,23). Instantly had come Christ's stern rebuke: "Get thee behind me, Satan!"

The prophets had clearly declared that the Messiah, when He came, would be rejected by His own people, crucified, and raised again from the dead. Yet neither the rabbis, who studied the Scriptures daily, nor the disciples, to whom Christ had tried to explain these things, comprehended what the prophets had foretold. Had they understood their own Scriptures, many of the religious leaders might have realized that Jesus of Nazareth was indeed the Messiah. Certainly the disciples would have acted differently had they grasped the messianic prophecies.

Today a similar confusion surrounds the Scriptures that pertain to Christ's return to planet earth. Even among evangelicals there is not only disagreement on the subject but blindness to many of the pertinent prophecies. Consequently, an indifference prevails toward the most staggering event in history—an event which is much nearer than most Christians suspect.

That the prophesied Messiah, instead of ruling on David's throne as expected, would be rejected by His own people and killed was completely alien to the thinking of Christ's disciples. It was as though they hadn't even heard His words when He tried to tell them so. And now, in this last intimate moment with His faithful few before the cross, the Lord sought to explain further the purpose of His pending crucifixion. "I am going away to prepare a place for you," He told them.

Here were words whose meaning they understood but which did not fit their expectation. Going away? At the moment of triumph when all Jerusalem was hailing Him as the Messiah? It didn't make sense. Going where? Why? What about the kingdom?

Confusion Concerning the Kingdom

Visible consternation reflected from the anxious faces gathered about the table. What about the Davidic kingdom the

Messiah was supposed to reestablish? Christ had promised that they would reign with Him on 12 thrones, judging the twelve tribes of Israel. He couldn't go away now! Was He having second thoughts—perhaps even preparing them for some disappointment? Had they been deceived? Too disturbing to face, the thought was drowned in the irrepressible flood of self-centered ambition and optimism.

Again it was the disciples' lack of understanding of what the prophets had so clearly declared that created such costly confusion. Ultimately, their lack of discernment would cause them to be unfaithful to Christ at the very time when they should have been most loyal to Him. How could they have been so ignorant of what their own Hebrew prophets had foretold concerning the messianic kingdom!

A similar ignorance prevails today. As a result, confusion is growing in the 1990s, even among evangelicals, concerning the kingdom of God. This topic will be addressed more fully in later chapters because of its relevance to the return of Christ.

To the chagrin of the disciples sharing the "last supper" with their Lord, that kingdom in which they eagerly anticipated playing a leading role would have to await its appointed time. Though that time was revealed in the Scriptures and known to Christ, His followers and the rabbis were abysmally ignorant of such prophecies. That very night Jesus, the prophesied King of Israel, would be led away in apparent helpless defeat to be condemned to death at a mock trial. The disciples, disillusioned and shattered, would all forsake Him. Fervent pledges of loyalty and love forgotten, they would flee to protect their own lives.

Betrayal and Cowardliness in the Inner Circle

Knowing all that would transpire, Christ solemnly warned the 12 that they would all desert Him. He even quoted the prophecy which foretold their cowardliness: "Smite the shepherd, and the sheep shall be scattered" (Zechariah 13:7; Matthew 26:31)—a prophecy which none of them understood even when He pointed it out to them.

Peter, the most outspoken in swearing his fidelity ("I will lay down my life for thy sake"—John 13:37), was given special attention by the Lord. Jesus told him plainly: "Simon, Simon, behold, Satan hath desired to have you, that he may sift you as wheat: but I have prayed for thee, that thy faith fail not. . . . [Nevertheless] the cock shall not crow this day, before that thou shalt thrice deny that thou knowest me" (Luke 22:31-34).

Again the words were incomprehensible. That rugged fisherman, convinced that he knew his own heart, insisted that he would die before he would be unfaithful to the One he so fervently loved. So said all of the other disciples as well. In spite of their good intentions, however, they would prove the prophets right that very night. The entire spectacle would transpire exactly as it had all been written centuries earlier in surprising detail under the inspiration of the Holy Spirit.

Jesus knew all that would happen, even what the prophets had not foretold, for He had inspired them. Significantly, He told His disciples, "I tell you before[hand] . . . that, when it is come to pass, ye may believe that I am *he*" (John 13:19). The word "he" is in italics and does not appear in the original. Jesus was declaring once again that He was Yahweh, the I AM of Israel, who "declares the end from the beginning, and from ancient times the things that are not yet done" (Isaiah 46:9,10).

Nor did Christ hide from this inner circle the awful treachery within their own ranks. Once again He showed the disciples that He was the God of Israel by revealing the secret intentions of the one who would betray Him. Sorrowfully, He challenged the shallowness of their commitment and understanding with this shocking declaration:

> Verily I say unto you, One of you which eateth with me shall betray me. . . . The Son of man indeed goeth, *as it is written of him*; but woe to that man by whom the Son of man is betrayed! good were it for that man if he had never been born (Mark 14:18-21).

After that horrifying pronouncement, the disciples should have allowed no one to leave the room until the culprit had confessed and repented! Instead, this prophetic utterance by their Lord elicited only the briefest flurry of concern among the disciples. Each one with seeming innocence and sincerity asked, "Lord, is it I?" Christ answered Judas in the affirmative. Incredibly, none of the others seemed to notice.

Almost immediately the disciples' selfish ambitions came again to the fore and they returned to their argument over who would be the greatest in the kingdom. Surely it would be inaugurated very shortly! So they thought. And why not? The crowds that were daily shouting Christ's praises would insist upon it.

"As it is written of him"! That all-important reference by the Lord to what the prophets had said seemed to mean nothing to any of those present. Inexcusable blindness to the prophetic Scriptures would be costly not only to the betrayer but to all of the disciples.

A Pawn in Satan's Hands

Judas was too full of his own secret aspirations to bother with arguing about his place in the kingdom. Why waste time on a dream that was not to be? Judas had inside information that Jesus was not going to take David's throne after all. The rabbis would see to that—with no small help from him. The crucial time had come to betray his Master to the religious leaders for crucifixion.

Intoxicated with the greedy anticipation of what he would do with 30 pieces of silver, the traitor muttered an excuse and slipped out into the night. The whole idea of a messianic kingdom was a grandiose delusion. In spite of the seeming miracles Jesus had performed, it was only a matter of time until this One whom so many had followed in the mistaken belief that He was the Messiah would be hunted down and arrested by the rabbis. So why not help them, since they were willing to pay handsomely? Why let that money go unclaimed or to someone else?

Judas was a man bereft of conscience. At first he had fought the temptation to steal from the small fund that came from occasional donations and which he had volunteered to keep track of and to guard. But after yielding that first time, the second theft came much easier, then the third and the fourth. It was not long until stealing, and lying to cover up, had become a challenging and seemingly rewarding way of life.

Satan had found his instrument; Judas was now a pawn in his hands. It couldn't be so wrong to realize a tidy profit by hastening what was surely inevitable. So he told himself once again as he made his furtive way to the rendezvous that would make him rich—and seal his soul's doom.

The name Judas would ever after be synonymous with treachery and betrayal. What a pitiful figure he was, driven by greed, inspired by Satan. And all the while he was oblivious to the fact that both his infamous deed and his tragic end lay before his very eyes in Scripture. David had written, "Yea, mine own familiar friend, in whom I trusted, which did eat of my bread, hath lifted up his heel against me" (Psalm 41:9).

Judas had prided himself on the sweet deal he had negotiated. It had not been easy, but he had succeeded in driving the haggling, skinflint rabbis up to 30 pieces of silver—a fabulous retirement nest egg.

Overlooked by the betrayer were the staggering words of the prophet Zechariah: "So they weighed for my price thirty pieces of silver . . . a goodly price that I was prised at of them" (11:12,13). That Judas would in bitter remorse, but too late, throw that blood money back at the rabbis' feet; that they would use it to buy a field for burying the destitute (Zechariah 11:13); and that he would kill himself (Psalm 55:12-15) had also all been foretold.

The Kingdom—Key to the Puzzle

The other disciples were oblivious to the historic drama in which they would play such cowardly roles. Each continued unabashedly to boast of his own qualifications for highest ranking, next to Christ, in the kingdom—a kingdom about whose advent and timing they were so terribly mistaken. They, like the rabbis, were heedless of the very Scriptures they read daily. Numerous prophecies, which they should have known, indicated clearly that the Messiah would not ascend to David's throne at His first coming, as they were so eagerly expecting. How their entire outlook and conduct would have changed had they but understood the prophets!

Disillusioned with predictions offering dates for the Rapture, most of those who call themselves Christians today have little interest in prophecy. Consequently, misunderstanding similar to that of the disciples concerning the timing and establishment of the kingdom now prevails in the Church. In fact, confusion regarding the kingdom of God is prevalent even among those who retain a deep interest in the return of Christ. Yet the kingdom, as we shall see, is a key part of the puzzle. Without it there would be no Second Coming. The prophets made that abundantly clear.

The first coming of Christ nearly 2000 years ago fulfilled specific prophecies concerning the kingdom of God—prophecies which had been a matter of record in the Old Testament for centuries. So must His Second Coming, which will also fulfill additional prophecies about that kingdom provided in the New Testament. The fact that everything prophesied concerning Christ's first appearance took place exactly as foretold provides absolute confidence that all of the prophecies concerning His return will also surely come to pass.

What those prophecies are, both in the Old and New Testaments, which foretell the Second Coming and the establishment and other details of the kingdom—and why they have been neglected, overlooked or misunderstood—is a fascinating study. Nor is it just an academic inquiry, but one of great practical value, as we shall see.

Strange Proof of Being the Messiah

On that shameful night of His betrayal Jesus knew exactly what Judas had planned and what the rabbis were determined to do. In obedience and in love, and to procure our redemption, He would take that bitter cup from His Father's hand and pay the debt we owed to Infinite Justice for our sins. Ironically,

Israel's religious leaders were unaware of the fact that their evil designs against Christ would prove Him to be the Messiah. In arresting and condemning Him to be crucified, they would unwittingly be fulfilling precisely what God had decreed and what the Hebrew prophets they claimed to honor had foretold.

Completely overlooking what they should have seen in their own Scriptures, the rabbis would think that in crucifying Him they had destroyed this One whom they so passionately hated. In fact, through death He would destroy Satan and break forever his evil power. Yes, even that unbelievably brilliant strategist, who had inspired Judas to betray his Lord, had no better insight into the Old Testament prophecies. Though he could quote the Bible, as he had when tempting Jesus in the wilderness, Satan did not understand it either. "That old serpent, the Devil" (Revelation 12:9) would be caught by surprise by the stunning defeat he was about to suffer.

Hanging naked upon a cross as a condemned criminal, jeered and taunted by the rabbis and rabble, Jesus of Nazareth, ex-carpenter and itinerant preacher, would seemingly be stripped of all messianic pretense. His ignominious decease would look like hopeless defeat to His disenchanted and cowardly disciples. Instead, by fulfilling specific prophecies, His crucifixion would prove conclusively that Jesus was the Christ. Blind to this fact, the seemingly victorious powers of darkness would gloat in obscene anticipation of taking over the world and the universe. Surely God's Son had failed in His rescue mission to planet earth!

In reality, that humiliating and seemingly tragic death would be Christ's triumph. It would be the glorious fulfillment of the purpose for which the Son of God had been incarnated as a man into this world. As the old hymn says:

> By weakness and defeat,
> He won the victor's crown;
> Trod all His foes beneath His feet,
> By being trodden down.
> He Satan's power laid low.
> Made sin, He sin o'erthrew.

> Bowed to the grave, destroyed it so—
> And death, by dying, slew!

Christ had explained His mission to His disciples a number of times, but to no effect. They were so obsessed by their own self-centered anticipation of wielding great power in the messianic kingdom that His words fell without meaning upon their ears. Though His crucifixion would fulfill Scripture authenticating Him as the Messiah, to His disciples as well as to the rabbis it would seem to prove the opposite.

"We thought He was the Messiah, but of course He couldn't have been because they killed Him!" So went the pathetic lament of the two on the road to Emmaus (Luke 24:19-21). They were only expressing the embarrassing and humiliating disillusionment felt by all of the erstwhile disciples of Christ who were now in hiding. How could they have been so deceived by this messianic pretender? Perhaps the rabbis were right after all that no prophet could come out of Galilee (John 7:52).

Their champion was dead. That was proof enough. As it is today, even among many who call themselves Christians, so it was then—the cross did not fit human concepts of greatness and power.

CHAPTER 6

Victory by Defeat

◇

Except a corn of wheat fall into the ground and die, it abideth alone: but if it die, it bringeth forth much fruit. . . . Now is the judgment of this world: now shall the prince of this world [Satan] be cast out. And I, if I be lifted up from the earth [on a cross], will draw all men unto me [either to salvation or judgment] (John 12:24, 31,32).

Let us go back and take a closer look at events leading up to Christ's crucifixion. We want to see the faith-inspiring correlation between what the prophets foretold and what actually transpired. Particularly, we want to have burned into our hearts and minds how a failure to understand the Old Testament prophecies caused the religious leaders and Christ's own disciples to dishonor God and fail to recognize who the Messiah was and why He came. That lesson should provide sufficient incentive for each of us to take another careful look at prophecy with renewed interest and appreciation.

For months the scribes, Pharisees, and Sadducees had been plotting to kill Jesus. Fearful of losing their positions and authority and encouraged by satanic enticement, Israel's religious leaders were blinded to the truth by pride and self-protective jealousy. Their hearts were filled with envy and hatred toward this One who defied their traditions and who spoke truth with an authority that pierced their hardened consciences like a sword. Had they truly been willing to know and do God's will, they would have understood His Word (John 7:17). Without that willingness to submit to His truth, no one can understand the Scriptures.

It was common knowledge by now that Jesus of Nazareth had healed multitudes of every kind of disease, made the lame walk, opened the eyes of the blind, even raised the dead. Those public miracles, witnessed by so many, could not be denied. No wonder the self-centered religious leaders both hated and feared Him. His growing popularity with the masses threatened to put them out of business. They were serving themselves instead of God and His people. As John tells us:

> Then gathered the chief priests and the Pharisees a council, and said, What do we? for this man doeth many miracles. If we let him thus alone, all men will believe on him: and the Romans shall come and take away both our place and nation.
>
> . . . Caiaphas . . . said unto them, Ye know nothing at all, . . . it is expedient for us, that one man should die . . . and that the whole nation perish not (John 11:47-50).

This Crafty Imposter

How could the rabbis justify even to themselves such malice? It was quite easy, as rationalization always is. The miracles had to be an elaborate trick with the aid of unknown accomplices. This Jesus of Nazareth was such a crafty, slippery impostor! Whomever the Sanhedrin hired to engage Him in public debate in order to expose Him as a fraud was made to look abjectly foolish. How had He acquired such knowledge and brilliance? He confounded their best lawyers with an ease and wisdom which was obviously far beyond anything being taught in their rabbinical schools—or in any other centers of learning on this earth.

This audacious Nazarene had even said that His kingdom was "not of this world." What did that mean? Was He deliberately baiting them? Multitudes were treating Him as though

He were indeed a king. The situation had become so explosive that the Romans might very well step in suddenly with military force. Something had to be done!

Intoxicated by the seeming miracles—especially by His apparent ability to feed thousands of followers with a few loaves and fishes—the impetuous populace was murmuring against Caesar and hinting that this Jesus ought to be installed as King of the Jews. His followers, now numbering in the thousands, were under His hypnotic spell. Falling for His staged triumphal entrance into Jerusalem, they had openly hailed Him as the Messiah. Threats by the religious leaders to excommunicate anyone who even so much as whispered such heresy had failed to stifle the insidious rumors or to stem the growing tide of His popularity.

In opposing this Galilean and being made out to be fools for their trouble, the rabbis had lost the respect and attention of the common people. Even the children swarming around Him in the temple were crying, "Hosanna to the son of David" [i.e., Messiah]. When the chief priests and scribes reproved Him for accepting such praise, Jesus had boldly replied: "Yea, have ye never read, Out of the mouth of babes and sucklings thou hast perfected praise" (Matthew 21:16)?

Those who had once obeyed with reverence the edicts of the ruling Sanhedrin now ignored them. Instead, they hung with rapt attention on every word of this upstart Nazarene, as though He were God Himself—which, indeed, He blasphemously claimed to be. That had been the last straw! Surely now they had legal cause under the Mosaic law for a public execution. No one could complain.

He Claimed to Be God!

"Unless you believe that I AM [that was the name with which God revealed Himself to Moses!] you will die in your sins, and where I go you cannot come" (John 8:21-4). Utter blasphemy, to be sure, but what did He mean by "where I go you cannot come"? He kept throwing in these strange ideas as a diversionary tactic. So blinded were the rabbis by self-interest that their consciences were dulled to the voice of truth when He spoke in their very midst.

, The statements He made about Himself were staggering: "I AM the Bread of Life come down from heaven" (John 6:33-35); "I AM the light of the world, he who follows me shall not walk in darkness" (John 8:12); "I AM the door, by me if any man enter in he shall be saved" (John 10:9); "I AM the Son of God" (John 10:36); I AM the resurrection and the life . . . he who believes in me shall never die" (John 11:25,26). Anyone else who persisted in making such incredible claims would be dismissed as insane—but not this man. He spoke these words with an authority that couldn't be challenged. The rabbis had tried.

This cunning rabble-rouser deliberately used the words "I AM" in a way that not only outraged but dumbfounded and frightened the scribes and Pharisees. There could be no doubt that He was claiming to be God. Yet He cleverly avoided boasting about it, as one would expect some egomaniac to do. He made His dignified and seemingly sincere claim to deity with His use of "I AM" in exactly the same way Yahweh had revealed Himself to the prophets. One was afraid to stand near Him when He made these brazen declarations for fear lightning would strike or the ground would open up to swallow Him as it had Korah and his followers (Numbers 16:32)!

"Before Abraham was, I AM" (John 8:58). There it was again! On that occasion even the common people within earshot had been so scandalized that they had joined the rabbis in taking up stones to kill Him. Yet He walked unscathed through their midst and they were powerless to stop Him. And now the rabble were thoroughly convinced and on His side. The Romans were complaining about the restlessness among the people! What could be done? Multitudes were treating Him as though He really were the Messiah!

How dare any man in his right mind make such grandiose claims for himself—even that he was God! Yet this obviously pious and otherwise seemingly humble Galilean was no self-deluded simpleton. He knew the Scriptures better than anyone! Israel's cleverest lawyers had tried to trip him up with trick questions about the law of Moses and He had turned the tables on them every time. He had to be eliminated for the good of the nation.

A Frustrated Manhunt

Where had He gotten His education? Certainly not in their rabbinical schools, which He had never attended—yet the people reverently called Him "Rabbi!" It was galling and infuriating for the religious leaders to hear a title they had labored so long to earn applied admiringly to this uneducated Galilean. Without any conscience at all He accepted such adulation: "Ye call me Master and Lord: and ye say well; for so I AM" (John 13:13). He seemingly had no compunction about applying God's unspeakable name to Himself!

This carpenter-turned-itinerant-preacher was an enigma. He was no mere reckless liar—far worse than that. There was no mistaking the fact that He knew exactly what He was saying and obviously believed His grandiose claims, for He pronounced them with great conviction. "Destroy this temple, and I will raise it up in three days!" He was an incurable braggart as well as a blasphemer of the most impertinent kind.

Such flagrant defiance of the law demanded the death penalty. That just verdict had been secretly agreed upon by the authorities long ago—but how to take Him when admiring mobs surrounded Him at all times was the problem. Jesus of Nazareth had headed the list of "most wanted" criminals for so long that it had become an embarrassment. Even the temple guard who had been sent to arrest Him returned empty-handed, mumbling helplessly, "Never man spake like this man" (John 7:46).

Why was He still at large? His arrest and death had been sought diligently for months, but no one had been able to lay a hand upon Him. And now, at last, here was the chance they had so long awaited—a stroke of good fortune! He would not elude them this time!

A Break for the Sanhedrin

One of Christ's own inner circle had surprised the rabbis with an opportunity they had never expected. Judas had told them that, for some strange reason, unlike His past caution, Jesus was staying on at Jerusalem. It would be a simple matter to lead a band of soldiers to an isolated night rendezvous where they could take Him all alone without the protection of the crowd that always surrounded Him in the city.

Although the rabbis had nothing but contempt for that greedy traitor, they were only too glad to use him to their own ends. He had driven a hard bargain. Thirty pieces of silver was a large sum—but more than worth it to the Sanhedrin. Before the night was over, with Judas guiding them to Jesus's hiding place and with no admiring rabble flocking around to protect Him, they would arrest this blaspheming troublemaker and turn Him over to the Romans for execution. He would die like the common criminal He was. At long last they would be rid of Him.

What a relief it would be when this great impostor was out of the way and the people were once more under their power. Oh, yes, He had said He would rise from the dead the third day—claimed that was what He meant about raising up the temple, that He was referring to the temple of His body. So be it. They would seal the tomb and set a guard so the disciples couldn't steal the body and claim a resurrection. This lie would be His last—the final proof that would explode the myths surrounding Him and break the spell that held even His most ardent followers. That charlatan would soon be forgotten, like so many pretenders before him who had gathered a following only to die in disgrace, their disciples scattered in disillusionment.

So the Sanhedrin thought. It was not, however, the connivings of Judas and the rabbis which determined the shameful events of that dark night and the following day. The plotters were oblivious to the fact that they were the unwitting instruments of God's will. Christ's mock trial and crucifixion, which the rabbis thought proved their power over Him, would prove instead what they so furiously denied—that He was indeed the Messiah.

All According to God's Plan

Prophecies by the dozens, recorded centuries before by Israel's acknowledged prophets, were being fulfilled to the letter by those who sought His death. Every move the religious leaders made added one more proof that Jesus of Nazareth was the Christ. That astounding fact, when at last he understood it, would be Peter's dramatic revelation in his first sermon on the Day of Pentecost. The betrayal, Pilate's sham judgment, and the crucifixion had already been decreed by the "determined counsel and foreknowledge of God" (Acts 2:23) long before the world was even created (Ephesians 1:4; 1 Peter 1:20). All would occur exactly as the prophets had foretold.

How could the future be known and revealed before it happened? Surely such an outrageous idea had to be a myth! Astrologers deceitfully used ambiguous phrases that could apply to almost any occasion or event. Likewise, the words of the Hebrew prophets contained in the Scriptures were often so cryptic that they could be interpreted in many ways. So why waste valuable time on such vain speculations?

Such skepticism toward prophecy caused it to be a neglected topic in the Israel of that day. Prophecy is likewise largely in disfavor even in the evangelical Church in our time, and because of similar unbelief. Yet the words are clear for those hungry to know God's revealed will and wise enough to seek and obey it. To them He unfolds the future, as Daniel was told: "None of the wicked shall understand [prophecy]; but the wise shall understand" (Daniel 12:10). As we shall clearly see, there is no more exciting and enlightening topic to study than prophecy!

The very Scriptures which the rabbis read with such pomp and ceremony in the synagogues each Sabbath plainly declared the horrendous outrage against heaven which they were determined to carry out. The perpetrators of the most heinous crime in the history of the universe were acting out the fulfillment of prophecy and were not even aware that they were doing so. What terrifying judgment they were bringing upon themselves—judgment which could have been avoided had they but known and heeded the prophets!

The Enigma of Two Comings

Isaiah, the prophet who had written so much about the Messiah's endless reign of perfect peace, had also declared unequivocally that He would be "despised and rejected" (Isaiah 53:3) by Israel and even slain (53:8,9). How could He be killed, and yet reign over the promised kingdom? The contradiction seemed impossible to reconcile, so the prophecies of His rejection and death were simply ignored. Of course, if these prophecies referred to *two comings* of the Messiah—one in weakness as the "Lamb of God" (John 1:29) to die for our sins, the other in power and glory as the "Lion of Judah" (Revelation 5:5)—then the contradiction disappeared.

Such a likelihood, however, never occurred to the Jews in Christ's day, causing them in ignorance to fulfill the Scriptures by crucifying their Lord. In like manner most Christians today reject the possibility that *two comings* for Christ yet remain in the future. We shall see that, after examining all the relevant prophecies and comparing them carefully one with another, there is no other conclusion which one can logically reach.

David, greatest of Israel's kings, upon whose throne the Messiah would eventually reign, had foretold the same astonishing rejection of the Messiah by His own people (Psalm 22:6,7). He had even described the manner of His death—that this Holy One would be crucified (Psalm 22:16). That prophecy was inspired of God and written into Scripture many centuries before this method of execution had been adopted by the Romans as a means of putting down uprisings following their conquests. David and the other prophets had to be divinely inspired, for who but God could know the future so far ahead and with such accuracy?

There was more. The God who inspired David to prophesy the crucifixion had also promised him that the Messiah would be his descendant and would reign on the Davidic throne in

Jerusalem: "I will set up thy seed after thee . . . and I will establish . . . the throne of his kingdom for ever" (2 Samuel 7:12-17). To be despised and rejected by Israel and crucified—and yet to reign over His people in Jerusalem? Clearly both could not occur at the same time.

Surely Messiah had to come *twice* to fulfill two such divergent prophecies. And since His reign would never cease, He had to be crucified the first time, rise from the dead—and ascend to David's throne at a later coming. For the learned rabbis not to recognize that fact was inexcusable.

Victory in Apparent Defeat

The cross was Christ's triumph—a victory that would establish His kingdom through apparent defeat. Through death He destroyed "him that had the power of death, that is the devil" (Hebrews 2:14). That same victory over sin and over the forces of darkness is now available to Christ's followers. It comes for them, as for their Lord, not by bravado nor with the guarantee of immunity from suffering, but by way of meekness, submission to the Father's will and apparent defeat in the death of the cross. As Jesus said, "If anyone will come after me, let him deny himself, and take up his cross and follow me" (Matthew 16:24).

Not that Christians must all die on literal crosses, though martyrdom has been the fate of many. The flagellation of the flesh accomplishes nothing. Victory is in *His* cross, not in some other cross one might bear. Christ alone could pay the full debt for sin. Through faith in His substitutionary death upon the cross for all mankind, those who believe are eternally set free from sin's penalty. It is a gratuitous gift of God's grace.

And what of sin's power to deceive and enslave? Freedom from both sin's penalty and power come in the same way—through embracing His death as one's very own. When Christ took our place, God's justice required His death. Those who believe He died in their place acknowledge that they justly deserved the death penalty and confess that they have died in Him. Sin no longer has any power over those who are dead, nor does this world hold any enticements for them.

The greatest promise, however, is that He will take us to His Father's house in heaven, where we will be free from sin's presence forever. Through paying upon the cross the full debt demanded by Infinite Justice, Christ has delivered us from the penalty of sin, is delivering us from its power, and will one day deliver us eternally from its very presence.

This snatching away of His followers from earth is known as the Rapture. The word is found in the Latin translation of the New Testament. It simply means an ecstatic catching away. How close are we to that incredibly wonderful event? That's the major question we want to pursue in the following pages.

CHAPTER 7

A "Passover Plot"?

◇

> Paul, a servant of Jesus Christ, called to be an apostle,
> separated unto the gospel of God, (Which he had prom-
> ised afore by his prophets in the holy scriptures,) con-
> cerning his Son Jesus Christ our Lord, which was made
> of the seed of David according to the flesh; and declared
> to be the Son of God with power, according to the spirit
> of holiness, by the resurrection from the dead (Romans
> 1:1-4).

The very accusation with which Israel's religious leaders
self-righteously condemned Jesus of Nazareth—that He claimed
to be the Son of God and was therefore equal with the Father—
was the fundamental credential of the Messiah. One of Israel's
greatest prophets had put it so clearly: "Behold, a virgin shall
conceive, and bear a son, and shall call his name Immanuel"
(Isaiah 7:14). That name meant "God with us"—not in a
general way, i.e., that God was on Israel's side, but that He was
personally present. Naming this virgin-born child Immanuel
could only mean that He was God come as a man.

Of course! To be the Savior, the Messiah *had* to be God, for
God Himself had said that He was the only Savior:

> For I am the Lord thy God, the Holy One of Israel, thy
> Saviour . . . I, even I, am the Lord; and beside me there is
> no saviour (Isaiah 43:3,11) . . . there is no God else beside

me; a just God and a Saviour; there is none beside me.
Look unto me, and be ye saved, all the ends of the earth"
(Isaiah 45:21-22).

Jesus was condemned for blasphemy because He said that
God was His Father, thus making Himself equal with God
(John 5:18). Indeed, He declared, "I and my Father are one"
(John 10:30), thus claiming to be one in essence with Jehovah,
the God of Israel. According to the prophets, the Messiah
could be no less than God. Yet the Sanhedrin, in complete
contradiction of the Scriptures, dogmatically insisted that the
Messiah, though a great man, could be no more than human.

In like manner, various modern cults, such as the Mormon
Church and Jehovah's Witnesses, deny that Christ is God.
They interpret Christ's "I and my Father are one" to mean
merely "one in purpose, work, interest." Jesus, however,
clearly meant *one in essence*—for if He were anything less He
could not be the Messiah, the Savior of the world. *"Beside me
there is no savior!"*

The Messiah's Deity in the Old Testament

Isaiah had made it so clear that the long-awaited One who
would rule "upon the throne of David" and establish a kingdom of everlasting peace would be no less than "the mighty
God, the everlasting Father":

> For unto us a child is born, unto us a son is given: and
> the government shall be upon his shoulder: and his name
> shall be called Wonderful, Counsellor, The mighty God,
> the everlasting Father, the Prince of Peace. Of the
> increase of his government and peace there shall be no
> end, upon the throne of David and upon his kingdom, to
> order it, and to establish it with judgment and with
> justice from henceforth even for ever. The zeal of the
> Lord of hosts will perform this (Isaiah 9:6,7).

Though the word itself is not found, the teaching of the
Trinity is all through the Bible, including the Old Testament.

The following is only one example: "Come ye near unto me, hear ye this; I have not spoken in secret from the beginning; from the time that it was, there am I: and now the Lord God, and his Spirit, hath sent me" (Isaiah 48:16). Clearly John refers to the same event and gives a New Testament commentary upon it when he declares: "The Father sent the Son to be the Saviour of the world" (1 John 4:14).

The One who is speaking in this passage in Isaiah is obviously God. He has existed and spoken from the very beginning and is the One who reveals God to man. And yet He says, "the Lord God, and his Spirit, hath sent me." (Three distinct personalities are presented as God. One who is God was sent by God and the Spirit of God.)

This One who speaks as God and in revelation of God can only be the One whom John calls "the Word" and identifies as God and the creator of all: "In the beginning was the Word [*logos*], and the Word was with God, and the Word was God . . . all things were made by him" (John 1:1-3). Yet the speaker, though God, has been sent by God and His Spirit. We could not have Father, Son, and Holy Spirit presented any more clearly.

We see these three persons of the godhead acting together again at the baptism of Christ. On this occasion, which marked the start of our Lord's public ministry, the Father speaks audibly from heaven, and the Holy Spirit is seen as a dove resting upon the Son as He comes up out of the waters of baptism. What an appropriate confirmation of the passage in Isaiah, and what a powerful identification of Jesus as the Messiah!

Clearly, the New Testament, rather than presenting something new and discontinuous, simply elaborates upon and carries a step further that which has already been revealed in the Old Testament. The deity of Christ is absolutely necessary on the basis of Old Testament Scriptures, for He is both the Savior (who must be God) and the Word of God, the One who is the expression of God to mankind. That Christ is God, though stated more directly in the New Testament, is clearly presented in the Old.

In using the Greek term *logos*, which simply means a spoken expression, John did not begin his gospel, as some argue, by borrowing from Alexandrian Greek thought. On the contrary, he was taking a truth already stated in the Old Testament and, under the inspiration of the Holy Spirit, elaborating upon it. *Logos* was not the exclusive property of the philosophers but was used by everyone in ordinary conversation.

Prophecy Is the Foundation for the Gospel

It is vital to realize that Christianity was not a first-century invention. Far from being a new cult, it was the culmination of a long Jewish heritage. The life-transforming gospel which the early Church brought to the world was founded solidly upon the consistent message which the Hebrew prophets had declared for centuries. The apostles boldly used the Old Testament Scriptures to prove that Jesus was the Christ, the Savior of the world. Taking what the Hebrew prophets had said concerning the Messiah and showing how it had all been fulfilled in Jesus of Nazareth was standard procedure for the early Church in "turning the world upside down" (Acts 17:2-4,6).

In the passage quoted at the beginning of this chapter, note how Paul describes the message he preached: "the gospel of God, which he had promised afore by his prophets in the holy scriptures" (Romans 1:1,2). Basing his entire presentation of the gospel upon what the prophets had written was Paul's *modus operandus*:

> And Paul, as his manner was . . . reasoned with them out of the scriptures [i.e., the messianic prophecies] . . . that Christ must needs have suffered, and risen again from the dead; and that this Jesus, whom I preach unto you, is Christ (Acts 17:2,3).

Here is an approach to evangelism almost unknown among evangelicals today, yet it is the biblical method and the most powerful means of winning souls to Christ.

Jesus Himself used the same approach with the two disciples on the road to Emmaus. He rebuked them for not realizing that the prophets had clearly foretold that the Messiah would be rejected of His people and would be crucified. In fact, His language was rather harsh, showing that each of us is responsible to know what the prophets have said:

> Then said he unto them, O fools, and slow of heart to believe all that the prophets have spoken: Ought not Christ to have suffered these things, and to enter into his glory? And beginning at Moses and all the prophets, he expounded unto them in all the scriptures the things concerning himself (Luke 24:25-27).

That God came to this earth as a man, Jesus of Nazareth, through a virgin birth, nearly 2000 years ago, to be the Savior of the world is indisputable. We can make this statement with great confidence. There is no other explanation for the fact that the life, death, and resurrection of Jesus Christ fulfilled not only the few prophecies we have mentioned thus far but dozens of others involving unmistakable, specific details. Anyone, Jew or Gentile, who takes an honest look at what the prophets foretold and compares it with the historical record concerning Jesus of Nazareth can come to no other conclusion.

There is much earnest talk today about returning to the simple and powerful Christianity of the early Church. Yet there is scarcely a mention of the important role which prophecy would play in such a revival of first-century zeal and effectiveness. Thus we see how lacking today's Christians are in understanding the major part played by prophecy in first-century evangelism. This is not to say, of course, that if we used Paul's prophetic approach in preaching the gospel we would see a universal ingathering of converts. "Whosoever will" is still the key. Those who want an excuse for not believing will find or manufacture one.

Millions of both Jews and Gentiles refuse to admit the truth, even when faced with the overwhelming facts. They will accept any other explanation, no matter how fantastic, that will allow them to escape admitting the truth about Jesus Christ and the consequences of that truth for their own lives. Nevertheless, we must continue to set forth the evidence from prophecy, for this is the biblical approach to presenting the gospel.

A Farfetched Scenario

Some skeptics have gone so far as to suggest that Jesus attempted to authenticate Himself as the Messiah by deliberately acting out the Old Testament prophecies—and even persuaded a well-meaning Judas to help Him. That absurd proposal was presented in *The Passover Plot*, a popular book that was made into a movie some years ago. While such a scenario might conceivably explain a small part of what transpired, it could not possibly account for most of the fulfilled prophecy.

David had declared, for example, that the soldiers who crucified the Messiah would, in the process of dividing His clothes among them for souvenirs, gamble for His robe (Psalm 22:18) and give Him vinegar and gall to drink (Psalm 69:21). This was exactly what happened. How could Christ have arranged for that to occur while He hung helpless on the cross? Isaiah had foretold that He would be executed in the company of criminals (Isaiah 53:9). How did Christ arrange to have Himself crucified between two thieves?

The common practice was to break the legs of those crucified so they could no longer support their weight and would collapse and suffocate. Although the soldiers broke the legs of the thief on either side of Him, they did not do so to Jesus, thus fulfilling the Scripture: "He keepeth all his bones, not one of them is broken" (Psalm 34:20). Instead, one of the soldiers plunged a spear into His side—a seemingly inexplicable act which fulfilled yet another prophecy: "They shall look on me whom they pierced" (Zechariah 12:10).

Are we to assume that certain Roman soldiers were part of the plot and acted out the applicable prophecies? What would be their motive in trying to make it look as though Jesus were the Messiah? If they were bribed to do so, what was the source of the money? Certainly Jesus Himself had no funds with which to finance such an elaborate deceit. Moreover, how could He have known which soldiers would be assigned to the cross in order to pay them in advance?

Furthermore, who would be fool enough to willingly die a horrible death in the hope of convincing a few uneducated and inept followers that he had fulfilled messianic prophecies? What good would that do Him when He was dead? In spite of His many previous explanations, they hadn't yet understood what the prophets had foretold and would be even less likely to come to an understanding in His absence. It makes no sense.

Unwittingly Proving That Jesus Was the Messiah

And what about Judas? What could his motive have been? Why would he destroy himself in the hope of deceiving the Jews into following a fake Messiah? It is outrageous to suggest that Judas returned the money to the rabbis and hung himself in order to fulfill prophecy as part of some mysterious "Passover Plot"! Yet those self-destructive acts did fulfill specific prophecies!

Judas and the soldiers were hardly such fools as to act out a cheap charade that could only fall of its own weight and bring neither them nor their phony "Messiah" any benefit whatsoever in the long run! The fact is that all of the players in this incredible drama unwittingly played out the roles that God had ordained in Scripture. And in so doing they put the stamp of authenticity upon Christ in a manner that cannot be explained away.

What about the rabbis? Their actions, too, fulfilled prophecies which proved that Jesus was the Messiah—clearly the last thing they wanted to do! Take, for example, the 30 pieces of silver which Judas threw down in the temple, as the Scriptures had foretold he would (Zechariah 11:13). Dividing that tempting sum among themselves would have been the natural thing for the rabbis to do. After all, it no longer belonged in the treasury but had been paid out to the betrayer. If he chose to return it, that was his loss and their gain and no laws would have been violated.

Instead of keeping the money for themselves, however, the rabbis magnanimously used it to buy a "potter's field," as it was called, for burying strangers—exactly as the prophet said they would. Why? Surely the religious leaders, who hated Jesus with a passion, were not part of a conspiracy to authenticate His messianic claims! They weren't even aware that they were fulfilling prophecy.

There is no escaping the fact that, like Judas and the soldiers, the rabbis also, in their treatment of Jesus, fulfilled ancient messianic prophecies. Of their own free will, and with raw malice, they unwittingly followed precisely what the prophets had said Israel's religious leaders would do to the Messiah. These and the many other fulfillments of specific prophecies in the life, death, and resurrection of Christ are conclusive evidence that He was indeed the Messiah, the Savior of whom the prophets spoke.

When Was Your Jehovah Pierced?

Zechariah 12 is an astounding chapter, to which we shall return later. It is quite clear that Yahweh Himself, the God of Israel, is speaking through His prophet. What He says in verse 10 is remarkable: "They shall look on *me*, whom they have pierced." Ask Jehovah's Witnesses or Jews the question, "When was your Jehovah (Yahweh) pierced?" They have no answer, yet Zechariah 12:10 is straightforward and indisputable: God would become a man and be pierced to the death; He would come back to life and return to Jerusalem in the midst of Armageddon to rescue Israel. It's all there for those with eyes to see.

The way Jehovah speaks in this verse is instructive. He says, "They shall look on *me* whom they pierced," and "they will mourn because of *him*." The pronouns "me" and "him" refer to two individuals; yet they seem to be the same person. Why, if the "me" was pierced, would Israel mourn about what they had done to "him"? Zechariah presents exactly what Jesus declared: "I and my Father are one." In piercing Jesus, Israel pierced her God, Yahweh, the "I AM," who Jesus claimed to be—indeed, who He had to be or He couldn't be the Savior, as we've seen.

In the Hebrew, that word *pierced* meant not what nails had done to hands and feet or thorns to brow, but a piercing to the death by sword or spear. Remember, this is God speaking about Himself having been put to death. How could God be slain? The only possible answer to that question was given in the prophecies we have already considered concerning a virgin-born Son who would be "the everlasting Father" Himself.

The Hebrew prophets made it clear that the Messiah would have to be God Himself born upon earth as a man through a virgin. He would have to be crucified, pierced to the death, rise from the dead, go back to heaven, and then return to planet earth. It was all there for the rabbis and Christ's disciples to see. Yet these prophecies were hidden from them behind the veil of their own preconceived ideas. In seeking to understand the Second Coming, we must be careful to allow the prophets to speak God's Word to our hearts instead of giving what they have written our own biased interpretation.

Joseph's New Tomb

That Christ's body was placed in a new tomb "wherein never man before was laid" (Luke 23:53) was a beautiful picture of the fact that He died a death that no one had yet experienced—a death that He endured for all who would believe in Him and receive the eternal life He offered. Whence came that particular sepulcher into which Christ's body was laid? Tombs were local family burying places in use for centuries and filled with the bones of ancestors. Where could one be found that had not yet been used?

The Scripture gives us the answer to that question. The tomb belonged to Joseph of *Arimathea*—a man who had lately moved from that place to Jerusalem. Far from the family burial plot, he had to build a new one. The Garden Tomb that one can visit today just outside Jerusalem's wall seems to qualify. It was never quite completed. Surely Joseph, having given to Jesus the partially constructed tomb, would not thereafter have finished it and used it for himself and his family.

Only a man of considerable substance could afford to donate an expensive tomb hewn out of rock. Joseph of Arimathea, so the Scripture says, was wealthy. That Christ was laid in a rich man's tomb fulfilled yet another Scripture: "and with the rich in his death" (Isaiah 53:9). Chance could not possibly explain the fulfillment in the birth, life, death, and resurrection of Jesus of Nazareth of each of dozens of specific messianic prophecies. Nor could He, or anyone else, have arranged for all of these events to occur precisely as the prophets had foretold. The conclusion is inescapable.

Much more, however, was required to pull off this alleged scam. Jesus would have had to engineer a staged resurrection to fulfill that part of the prophecies. The logistics of such a "plot" clearly place it beyond the realm of reason for a handful of rather poor outsiders. Jerusalem was under the heel of Rome and religiously controlled by insecure rabbis who had their spies everywhere.

Certainly neither the secular nor religious authorities would have been a party to making it appear that Jesus was the Messiah. A new religion with a miracle-working, godlike leader who had supposedly been resurrected and claimed to be King of the Jews was the last thing either Pilate or Caiaphas wanted. Yet this was exactly how they viewed Christianity. It threatened their base of power and created a major disruption of civic order. Miracles were being done by the apostles and thousands were becoming the followers of this Jesus of Nazareth. The most powerful persuasive, however, was the claim that this man whom the authorities had crucified and whom hundreds had seen hanging on a cross just outside the city wall had risen from the dead.

Furthermore, that bold claim was being preached with a fearlessness that was entirely out of character for the disciples who had proved themselves so cowardly on the night of their

Master's betrayal. They had gone into hiding for fear of their own lives. Yet now, suddenly, they were out in public again, risking arrest and crucifixion themselves and speaking with an authority that was reminiscent of this very One whom they claimed now lived by His Spirit in each of them.

CHAPTER 8

Back from the Dead!

◇

> For David speaketh concerning him [the Messiah]
> ...thou wilt not leave my soul in hell...[nor] suffer
> thine Holy One to see corruption.... David is both dead
> and buried, and his sepulchre is with us to this day.
> Therefore being a prophet, and knowing that God...
> would raise up Christ to sit on his [David's] throne; He
> seeing this before spake of the resurrection of Christ.
> ...This Jesus hath God raised up, whereof we all are
> witnesses [from Peter's first sermon preached to thou-
> sands in Jerusalem at Pentecost] (Acts 2:25-32).

The resurrection of Jesus Christ is one of history's most impeccably substantiated events. That both the religious and secular authorities did everything in their power to stamp out the "new sect" of Christians preaching this message is a matter of history. That they never took the one obvious action which would have conclusively disproved the resurrection is sufficient evidence that they could not do so. This indisputable fact bears authentic testimony to the validity of the resurrection.

The claim of an empty tomb would have been easy to disprove if it were a fraud, for Jesus did not send His disciples off to India or Siberia to begin preaching the gospel. He instructed them to start right in Jerusalem, the scene of both His crucifixion and resurrection. Testifying to these publicly known events was the disciples' simple but powerful message. On that basis, and backed by the Old Testament prophecies He had fulfilled, Christ's transformed followers declared that He had died for the sins of the world and that His resurrection was proof that sin's debt had been paid. Forgiveness of sin and eternal life were now offered as free gifts of God's grace to all who would believe.

The good news (gospel) the disciples preached was delineated by Paul:

> How that Christ died for our sins according to the [Old Testament] scriptures; And that he was buried, and that he rose again the third day according to the [Old Testament] scriptures: And that he was seen of Cephas [Peter], then of the twelve: After that he was seen of above five hundred brethren at once, of whom the greater part remain unto this present [time]... after that, he was seen of James; then of all the apostles. And last of all he was seen of me [Paul] also (1 Corinthians 15:3-8).

Confronting the Empty Tomb

The resurrection, as Paul further explained, was the very heart of the gospel:

> And if Christ be not risen [from the dead], then is our preaching vain, and your faith is also vain. Yea, and we are found false witnesses of God; because we have testified of God that he raised up Christ. . . . And if Christ be not raised . . . ye are yet in your sins. Then they also which are fallen asleep [died] in Christ are perished. If in this life only we have hope in Christ, we are of all men most miserable [because we're suffering and dying for and preaching a lie] . . . but now is Christ risen from the dead (1 Corinthians 15:14-20).

The new message the once-frightened but now bold-as-lions disciples preached was not a religious philosophy to be argued.

Nor was it a matter of opinion or hearsay. The incredible assertion was being made that the Savior they proclaimed had conquered death and had come out of the grave alive three days after His lifeless corpse had been placed in it. And they were making that claim in the very place where it could easily have been disproved if it had not been true. A short walk to the tomb was all it would have taken to expose the delusion.

"Go take a look for yourself!" would have been the sarcastic response to the gospel. "The stone is still in place with the Roman seal intact. Empty tomb indeed!" In a very short time all Jerusalem would have been armed with the facts. And if, perchance, the disciples had persisted in stirring up the people with their lies, the authorities could have rolled aside the stone and made a public display of Christ's corpse. Yet they didn't. Obviously they couldn't.

Thousands were becoming Christ's followers and saying that He was coming back to execute judgment upon those who refused to believe in Him. Jerusalem was in an uproar. Neither the Romans nor the rabbis could afford to allow the public disruption to persist. That the authorities had every reason to display the corpse but didn't—and that the tomb was verifiably empty—is a matter of historic record.

Why didn't the Romans place another corpse inside, roll the stone across it, seal the tomb once again and station a guard outside who would swear that the grave was still occupied by the body of Jesus? By the time that ploy may have been thought of, too many curious observers had gone there to see for themselves that the body was gone.

The fact that the tomb was empty could not be disputed. The Roman seal had been contemptuously ripped apart and the stone rolled aside, exposing the entrance to the large rock-hewn sepulcher. Anyone could go inside, and many did, verifying the fact that there was no recent corpse nor any remains from previous burials, for this, remember, was a new tomb. The authorities could not deny that Christ's grave was empty. They were left with no alternative but to find an explanation to fit that fact.

A Preposterous Concoction

The best the rabbis could come up with was an unbelievable tale. It was carefully "leaked" to the public that the disciples had stolen the body and buried it secretly. That transparent lie, however, was too preposterous to convince anyone except those who wanted to believe it. Who would dare to break the Roman seal and risk the death penalty! Certainly not the disciples. That small band of confused and terrified country bumpkins had neither the brains nor the *chutzpah* to challenge Rome. Those cowards had all fled to protect their own skins when Jesus had been arrested. Surely they were the last ones to have the genius and courage to pull off such an audacious escapade.

Yet such was the pitifully contrived story whispered about, which, for obvious reasons, as anyone with common sense knew, only the rabbis could have originated. Supposedly the well-trained Roman soldiers, notorious for their robotlike obedience and flawless discipline, had *all* fallen asleep on duty. As the impossible fiction went, the disciples had sneaked up (getting the courage from who knew where), rolled the stone aside, and trotted off with the corpse without awaking anyone. How the soldiers knew who had done this astounding deed while they were sound asleep was irrational enough. But there were more questions equally embarrassing.

Why hadn't the disciples been arrested for the crime of which they were supposedly guilty? And what about the soldiers? They hadn't been disciplined at all. Yet this alleged breach of duty, a most serious one, carried the death penalty. They should have been promptly nailed to crosses where Jesus had just been crucified. It didn't add up. Something was rotten at the top.

The "disciples-stole-the-body" story had to be a fabrication which had the approval of the rabbis and the Roman military hierarchy, or heads would have rolled instantly. The tale had enough holes in it for several Roman legions to march through. It was so poorly contrived that it could only have been concocted in a moment of panic and desperation. There were witnesses, in fact, to the very panic that fit the case. They claimed to have seen an angel, shining as bright as lightning, rolling back the stone from the tomb and terrified soldiers, at first frozen in fear, then fleeing the scene.

The Three-Day Factor

That the body was gone there was no doubt. If it had indeed been stolen, that deed could only have happened after the soldiers were no longer guarding the tomb. A sensible and believable account would have been that the soldiers remained on guard until several hours after the expiration of the three days within which the impostor had said He would rise from the dead. They then left the graveside with the governor's seal still intact on the entrance stone. Any body snatching thereafter would have come too late.

Had the soldiers given sworn testimony that they had remained at the tomb until the end of their assignment and then left with the body still inside it would have exposed the disciples' "resurrection tale" for a lie. That the soldiers filed no such report is of great significance. The "body-stolen-while-the-soldiers-slept" tale was an admission that the body disappeared while the soldiers, who had been assigned to guard the tomb until the end of the third day (Matthew 27:64-66), were still there on duty. Otherwise the fabrication of such a fantastic falsehood wouldn't have been necessary. That such an absurd fiction was being circulated fit precisely the amazing scene that several women claimed to have witnessed.

Just before dawn on the morning of the third day after His crucifixion an angel of terrifying appearance had rolled the stone away and sat upon it, exposing the empty tomb to the world. The soldiers had been stricken with terror, as had the women who observed it all from close at hand. When the heavily armed guards recovered enough from their frozen fright to move their limbs, they had fled in panic to the rabbis to tell the ominous story.

The soldiers must have reported also that there had been witnesses to the fact that the grave had been empty before the three-day deadline had expired. Thus the authorities were stuck with the ludicrous scenario of the body having been stolen while the soldiers slept.

The Unbelieving Disciples

The initial reaction of Christ's followers also testified to the truth of their sworn testimony. Stunned by the news that His tomb was empty, and still fearing for their own safety, the eleven remaining disciples gathered secretly that evening to discuss this latest development. Their dream of ruling over the messianic kingdom had turned into a nightmare. Perhaps by talking over the unbelievable sequence of events they could help each other make some sense of the strange saga they had jointly shared and which now seemed to place their lives in jeopardy.

A resurrection was the last thing they expected. They were not even able to believe it after the fact. Upon the first report from the women who had seen Him alive, which no one believed, Peter and John had run to the tomb and verified that it was indeed empty (John 20:2-10). Jesus had later appeared to Peter alone, confronted him gently, and had forgiven him for his cowardly denial. Yet even Peter was still as confused as the rest of them.

Far from scheming to fabricate a "back-from-the-dead" fable, the frightened disciples were shocked by the staggering developments. They had been earnestly discussing what these appearances might mean—and how to put their shattered lives back together again—when suddenly there He was standing in their midst! Without opening door or window and without a sound their Lord had mysteriously entered the securely locked room to confront the unbelief of those who had abandoned Him in fear of their own lives. And even now, with Christ standing in their midst, they couldn't believe what their senses were telling them. They were petrified with fear. It had to be His ghost (Luke 24:36,37)!

Jesus extended His hands toward them and spoke reassuringly in the calm, authoritative voice they knew so well:

"Behold my hands and my feet, that it is I myself: handle me, and see; for a spirit hath not flesh and bones, as ye see me have." The eyewitness account continues:

> And when he had thus spoken, he shewed them his hands and feet. And while they yet believed not for joy, and wondered, he said unto them, Have ye here any meat? And they gave him a piece of a broiled fish, and of an honeycomb, And he took it, and did eat before them. And he said unto them, These are the words which I spake unto you, while I was yet with you, that all things must be fulfilled, which were written in the law of Moses and in the prophets, and in the psalms, concerning me. Then opened he their understanding, that they might understand the scriptures (Luke 24:39-45).

Forty Days of "Infallible Proof"

To remove any possible doubt whatsoever concerning His resurrection, Christ remained with His now joyful disciples for 40 days. During that time He repeatedly demonstrated "by many infallible proofs" (Acts 1:3) that He was indeed alive. We have the complete and irrefutable account of eyewitnesses who were with Him and heard and saw it all.

During that time, He spoke to them of the kingdom about which they had been so confused, though we are not told what He said. "When will you restore the kingdom to Israel?" they eagerly asked Him. "It is not for you to know the times or the seasons, which the Father hath put in his own power," was His cryptic and only reply (Acts 1:6,7).

At the "last supper"—in another world long ago and far away it now seemed—Christ had explained that He was going to return to His Father's house in heaven. That was the place from whence He had come and to which He had promised to take them. First, however, He must return to the Father alone, leaving them to tell the world of His death for sin and His resurrection.

Why must He go away? These were troubling words which, once again, they did not understand. They were still expecting the kingdom to be established momentarily.

All too soon that incredibly marvelous 40 days which Christ spent with His own to restore their faith came abruptly to an end. Suddenly and without any warning He left them. The disciples watched in astonishment as, with hands outstretched in blessing, Christ rose from this earth and disappeared far above them in a cloud. His last words moments before had been: "Ye shall receive power, after the Holy Ghost is come upon you: and ye shall be witnesses unto me both in Jerusalem, and in all Judaea, and in Samaria, and unto the uttermost part of the earth" (Acts 1:8).

"The Power of His Resurrection" (Ephesians 1:18-21)

It cannot be emphasized enough that the life Christ gives to those who believe in Him is *resurrection life*—a new life which only those who have died in Him can receive. No longer for them the bewilderment of the twelve on the dark night of Christ's betrayal, but the confident assurance of eternal life received as a free gift of God's grace.

That the physical remains of Buddha, Muhammad, or the founders of other religions still occupy their graves does not detract from those belief systems. The world's religions consist basically of rules left behind by the founders concerning how their disciples should live. It matters not that the originators of such religions are dead, for their teachings live on. Whatever rewards such religions offer, from enlightenment to nirvana, they must be earned by the efforts of those who seek them.

Christianity is altogether different. It, too, is a way of life, but not one to which the individual Christian can attain. The standard is so high that no one but Christ ever lived or could live the Christian life. Everything depends upon a *living relationship* with Christ, who, therefore, must Himself be alive. To explain that intimate union, Christ likened Himself to a grapevine in which His disciples are the branches, drawing their sustenance from and bearing their fruit through the life that He provides.

"Because I live, you shall live also," Christ promised (John 14:19). Christ "*is* our life" (Colossians 3:4) said Paul. Through the indwelling Holy Spirit, He lives His resurrection life in those who put their faith in Him. Paul's exultation is for all who believe: "I am crucified with Christ: nevertheless I live; yet not I but Christ liveth in me: and the life which I now live in the flesh I live by the faith of the Son of God, who loved me, and gave himself for me" (Galatians 2:20).

The Saul/Paul Factor

Perhaps even more astonishing than the transformation in the lives of the disciples because of Christ's resurrection was that which took place in Saul of Tarsus. A strict Pharisee and one of the instigators of the stoning of Stephen, the first martyr, Saul emerged as the chief enemy of the infant church. "Breathing out threatenings and slaughter against the disciples of the Lord" (Acts 9:1), Saul "made havock of the church, entering into every house, and haling men and women committed them to prison" (Acts 8:3).

Yet this man, in an incredible about face, suddenly became a follower of Christ. No one could believe what had happened. The Christians "were all afraid of him, and believed not that he was a disciple" (Acts 9:26). But Paul, as he now called himself, began to preach the gospel and to dispute with both the Jews and the Greeks, proving with irrefutable arguments from logic and the Scriptures that Jesus was the Christ.

Paul knew from the very moment of his conversion that he would suffer an even worse fate than the other Christians. Having become one of those whom he had persecuted with such zeal, he was now the chief target of the rabbis, who almost immediately plotted to kill him (Acts 9:23,29, etc.). Paul describes something of the life he experienced, which culminated with his martyrdom in Rome:

> Are they [church leaders who criticized Paul] ministers of Christ? (I speak as a fool) I am more; in labours more abundant, in stripes above measure, in prisons more frequent, in deaths oft. Of the Jews five times received I forty stripes [with the cat-of-nine-tails] save [less] one. Thrice was I beaten with rods, once was I

stoned [and left for dead], thrice I suffered shipwreck, a
night and a day I have been in the deep [swimming
because the ship sank]; in journeyings often, in perils of
waters, in perils of robbers, in perils by mine own coun-
trymen, in perils by the heathen, in perils in the city, in
perils in the wilderness, in perils in the sea, in perils
among false brethren; in weariness and painfulness, in
watchings often, in hunger and thirst, in fastings often,
in cold and nakedness (2 Corinthians 11:23-27).

What would cause an admired rabbi to abandon the religion
to which he had devoted his life and to adopt contrary beliefs—
indeed, beliefs of which he had been the chief opponent? To all
appearances, by so doing he had nothing to gain and everything to lose! It seemed insane to exchange a comfortable,
prestigious life for one of abuse, persecution and eventual
martyrdom. As Paul himself said, "in every city . . . bonds and
afflictions await me" (Acts 20:23). Why would he become a
Christian, one of those whom he hated most?

Paul declared that he had personally met the resurrected
Christ. If true, that would explain everything—but what proof
did he offer? That he was now willing to suffer persecution and
to die for Christ, as he eventually did, would seem to be proof
enough. Skeptics, of course, could say that he had hallucinated
Christ's appearance to him. He was sincere, but deluded. Such
an argument would not hold, however, because Paul evidenced
a knowledge which he could have received in no other way than
from Christ Himself.

For example, Paul described what had taken place at the last
supper, though he hadn't been present. He could not have heard
the details from one of the apostles who had been there for he
knew none of them. Paul insisted that he had gotten this
information from the resurrected Lord Himself (1 Corinthians
11:23). He solemnly swore that he had received none of his
ideas or beliefs from the apostles:

I certify you, brethren, that the gospel which was
preached by me is not from man. For I neither received it

of man, neither was I taught if, but by the revelation of Jesus Christ. . . . When it pleased God . . . to reveal himself in me . . . immediately I conferred not with flesh and blood: neither went I up to Jerusalem to them which were apostles before me (Galatians 1:11,12,15-17).

The original apostles had to acknowledge that Paul's teachings, which he had not learned from them, were authentic. They had spent more than three years being personally trained by Christ; yet Paul, this newcomer, knew more than they did. Paul became the chief of the apostles and wrote most of the epistles. He even corrected Peter, who had been the chief apostle before him.

There is no other explanation for the transformation of Saul, the chief persecutor of the church, into Paul, its chief leader, than that, as he testified, he had personally met Christ risen from the dead! That Paul, who had not known Christ before His death, had been taught by Him could not be denied. No greater proof for the resurrection is needed.

The Promise of a "Second Coming"

Back to the Mount of Olives again. As the disciples gazed upward in bewilderment, two angels stood by them and announced that He would return to that very place on the Mount of Olives from which He had just ascended. Moreover, He would come again in the same manner in which He had left: in a visible descent from the heavens. Other Scriptures make it clear that He will come in glory and power and "every eye shall see him" (Revelation 1:7). The exact words of the angelic messengers were: "This same Jesus, which is taken up from you into heaven, shall so come in like manner as ye have seen him go" (Acts 1:11).

"Science fiction?" some would ask. No! In fact, it is a scenario far more amazing than that. Nor should this angelic declaration have been startling or new to the disciples. The prophet Zechariah had already stated it clearly, including the fact that this One who would return to the Mount of Olives was God:

> Then shall the Lord [Yahweh] go forth, and fight
> against those nations [surrounding Jerusalem at Arma-
> geddon]. . . . And his feet shall stand in that day upon the
> Mount of Olives, which is before Jerusalem (Zechariah
> 14:3,4).

The prophet Zechariah adds this interesting commentary in
the next verse: "And the Lord my God shall come, *and all the
saints with thee.*" There can be no doubt that Zechariah 12–14
refers to the return of the Messiah at Armageddon to rescue His
people Israel from those who have them surrounded with
overwhelming force and are about to annihilate them. Clearly
this is the same event which John reveals in Revelation 19. One
whose name is "The Word of God" (v. 13)—surely the same
One to whom we've already referred, who has been the expression of God from the beginning (Isaiah 48:16)—Christ Himself, comes to Armageddon accompanied by "the armies
which were in heaven."

The Necessity of a Previous "Rapture"

The heavenly "armies" which John says will accompany
Christ must be the "saints" of whom Zechariah writes. There
can be no doubt that both passages describe the same event.
Jude tells us that this coming of the Lord in power and glory
was foretold by Enoch thousands of years earlier: "And Enoch
also, the seventh from Adam, prophesied of these, saying,
Behold, the Lord cometh *with ten thousands of his saints*, to
execute judgment upon all" (Jude 14,15).

It is clear, then, that the "saints" of all ages, which would
certainly include all Christians, accompany Christ from heaven
when He returns to the Mount of Olives at His Second Coming.
It takes no genius to conclude that for His saints to come back
to earth with Christ *from heaven* they must have been taken up
there previously. We are faced, therefore, with the inescapable conclusion that Christ, sometime prior to the Second
Coming, takes all those who have believed in Him (the resurrected dead and the transformed living) to heaven.

Many Christians will never die physically. Their resurrected Savior has promised that when He returns to raise those believers who have died, He will catch away from this earth all living Christians as well and transform their physical bodies to be like His resurrected body of glory. That occasion is called the Rapture, which, as we have already noted, simply means an ecstatic catching away. It is a promise which is absolutely unique. Neither Muhammad, Buddha, nor any other of the founders of the world's religions ever dared even to make such an offer. Dead men don't "Come again."

Again, Paul, who was not with the original disciples when the Lord spoke to them of His return, became the chief authority on the subject. He provided details about the Rapture which none of the other apostles explained. Paul described it in these words: "And the dead in Christ shall rise first: then we [Christians] which are alive and remain shall be caught up together with them in the clouds to meet the Lord in the air: and so shall we ever be with the Lord" (1 Thessalonians 4:16,17).

It is clear, from Scriptures which we will examine later, that Christ's promised return involves two distinct events. At the Rapture, Christ comes *for* His saints to catch them up from this earth. At the Second Coming, He comes *with* His saints from heaven to rescue Israel and execute judgment upon Antichrist and his followers. These two events will be separated by seven years, a period during which Antichrist will be in control of this earth. Biblical justification for this belief will become overwhelming as we proceed.

CHAPTER 9

The "Blessed Hope"

———————— ◇ ————————

> Let not your heart be troubled: ye believe in God,
> believe also in me. In my Father's house are many man-
> sions: if it were not so, I would have told you. I go to
> prepare a place for you. And if I go and prepare a place
> for you, *I will come again, and receive you unto myself,*
> that where I am, there ye may be also (John 14:1-3).

What overpowering emotions stirred within the disciples as
they watched their Lord disappear into heaven, then heard
from the angels the promise of His return to the Mount of
Olives! Their thoughts must have gone back immediately to
what Christ had told them at the last supper. That solemn
occasion was taking on more significance each day as their
understanding deepened. On the eve of His betrayal Christ had
given them similar assurance of His return with the words, *"I
will come again."* Yet there seemed to be a puzzling contradiction.

Christ had declared that He was going back to His Father's
house, from whence, after a short while, He would return to
take them up there as well to be with Him forever. His promised return would be for a specific purpose: *"I will receive you
unto myself."* They had understood Him to mean that He was
going to take them to heaven, to His Father's house, *"that
where I am, there ye may be also."* So His coming again had to

be for the purpose of catching them up to heaven to be with Him.

Yet the angels, when they said He would come back to the Mount of Olives, had made no mention of anyone being taken to heaven. If that were indeed the purpose of His coming, it surely wouldn't be necessary for Him to return all the way to this same place outside Jerusalem. He could catch His followers up to meet Him far above the earth. That He would indeed do so was the revelation which the Holy Spirit would later speak through Paul who, at this time, was the sworn enemy of Christ and His church.

Moreover, the prophet Zechariah had said that when the Messiah's feet stood upon the Mount of Olives He would bring with Him from heaven "all the saints" (Zechariah 14:5). Rather than taking anyone to heaven, He would have come back to earth to rescue Israel when she would be surrounded by the armies of the world gathered to destroy her. In fact, the Messiah would destroy those armies and immediately set up His millennial kingdom over which He would reign from David's throne in Jerusalem.

There seemed to be a glaring contradiction. Christ's return to do battle with Israel's enemies at Armageddon didn't sound at all like His promise to take His own to heaven. Something wasn't right. And if they were going to rule with Him in Jerusalem, how could they have been taken to heaven? There was apparently much which they still didn't understand.

Presumably the disciples saw the apparent contradiction and puzzled over it. Most Christians today don't even recognize the seeming contradiction, much less know how to reconcile it. Let us, however, defer that problem for the moment.

The "Blessed Hope"

Christ's promise had been unequivocal: *"I will come again, and receive you unto myself; that where I am there you may be also!"* For the first time, having watched Him caught up to heaven, the disciples found hope in those electrifying words which they had never understood before. Surely their resurrected Lord would return very soon to take them to His

Father's house. In fact, He had said, "Ye shall not have gone over the cities of Israel until the Son of Man be come" (Matthew 10:23). That couldn't take long!

To make up for past failures they would show Him how quickly their assigned task could be accomplished—perhaps in a few weeks, surely not longer than a few months. He was sending the Holy Spirit from heaven to empower them to be His witnesses. The sooner they completed that important work the sooner He would return to take them to His Father's house in heaven as He had promised.

With Christ's *I will come again!* still fresh in memories, the early Christians eagerly waited and watched for their Lord's return. He had said that they were not of this world, but that He had chosen them out of it. Paul would soon write under His Lord's inspiration: "For our conversation [citizenship] is in heaven; from whence also we look for the Saviour, the Lord Jesus Christ: who shall change our vile body, that it may be fashioned like unto his glorious body" (Philippians 3:20,21). The world held little interest for these citizens of heaven. They were homesick for the Father's house, longing to be with their Lord in that eternal haven of rest.

Hated, persecuted, and killed by Rome, the early Church took comfort in the belief that Christ might return at any moment to rescue His followers from their trials. Paul called the anticipation of an imminent Rapture "that blessed hope" (Titus 2:13), and indeed it was for those early believers who went through "fiery trials" and "rejoiced at being partakers of Christ's sufferings" (1 Peter 4:12,13). How they longed to leave this world to be with Him!

As the weary weeks became years, however, and the years multiplied into decades, and finally centuries passed, the vast majority of those who claimed to be Christ's followers gave less and less thought to that "blessed hope." The promise of Christ's return was first neglected and then forgotten. Finally it was lost in the maze of new interpretations and heresies which began to multiply.

Attitudes and outlook changed. Citizenship in heaven had proved to be too nebulous a concept. Something more tangible was desired. Being despised on this earth, hated, persecuted, and killed, as their Lord had been, no longer seemed a necessary accompaniment of true Christianity. Perhaps this world had something to offer after all. Perhaps the church could even take the leadership in political affairs and transform the world, establishing the kingdom in Christ's absence. A more accommodating attitude toward secular society might even make the unsaved more receptive to the gospel—especially if they realized that becoming a Christian needn't mean persecution or even much of a change in one's way of life.

The First "Vicar of Christ"

The steadily worsening apostasy took on a hitherto unimagined dimension with the ascent to power of a new Emperor in A.D. 313. He was a brilliant military strategist and general named Constantine. He also had a genius for political organization and realism. Constantine faced the fact that almost three centuries of persecuting Christians had not stamped out that strange sect. Instead it had only grown until nearly one out of every ten citizens in the empire was among that despised band.

Tertullian's remark that the blood of the martyrs was the seed of the Church, inexplicable though it might be, had proved to be true. People apparently wanted something more than pleasure and profit. Only firmly held convictions worth dying for could make life worth living.

These "followers of the way," as they were called in those early days of the church, even prayed for the Roman emperors and other magistrates and soldiers who persecuted and killed them! Why not take advantage of that exemplary loyalty to kings and kingdoms which seemed to be a part of this strange religion?

The Christians were conscientious, hard workers. They didn't get drunk or rebel against the government. Insurrection was not in their natures. Then why not encourage them, give them full rights? Perhaps their philosophy of industry and fidelity would spread to other citizens. The empire would be much the better for it if the numbers of Christians multiplied. The new policy was a very pragmatic one.

To further this strategy, Constantine himself claimed to have become a Christian, though he continued, as Pontifex Maximus, to head the pagan priesthood and to preside over the pagan holiday ceremonies. Of course, that was his duty as emperor and it was excused in view of his encouragement of the building of Christian churches. A new day of tolerance had dawned.

Worshiped as God, the emperor was the head of the empire's official religion. Now that Christianity was recognized along with the old paganism, Constantine assumed leadership of the Christian Church. In doing so, he took the title Vicar of Christ. Posing as the Church's greatest friend and benefactor, and perhaps even doing so sincerely, Constantine became its destroyer.

Christ had refused Satan's offer of the kingdoms of this world if He would but bow down to him. In a moment of weakness, a Church weary of persecution accepted the same offer from Satan, this time presented through the Roman emperor. It was the beginning of centuries of what would be known as the Church's "Babylonian captivity."

Augustine lamented that those who were now inside the Church were "drunkards, misers, tricksters, gamblers, adulterers, fornicators, people wearing amulets, assiduous clients of sorcerers, astrologers . . . the same crowds that press into the churches on Christian festivals also fill the theatres on pagan holidays." For many Christians, however, it was a welcome change to go from being despised, hated, hunted, and killed, to being popular and even leaders in the world.

Once it had meant almost certain persecution and possible death to heed the gospel. There had been little need to worry about false professions of faith under those circumstances. Now it was just the opposite. False professions were more the rule than the exception.

The Church Marries the World

In the new order of things under Constantine, it had become a great advantage to be a Christian. One had to attend the growing number of Christian churches to get anywhere in business, politics, and even in the military. Conversions of convenience multiplied as church attendance soared.

Corruption quickly reached to the top in the Church. The empire's best-paying jobs with the most worldly prestige and influence were in church leadership. Constantine encouraged the growth of an ecclesiastical system that he could use to his own ends. It attracted men whose ambitions were not to gain reward in the world to come but in the present one.

Many who rose to power within the Church hierarchy were master politicians who knew how to use Christian terminology but knew not Christ. As Will Durant put it in *The Story of Civilization*, the paganism of Rome "passed like maternal blood into the new religion, and captive Rome captured her conqueror. While Christianity converted the world, the world converted Christianity." What a tragic commentary! Such was the birth of Roman Catholicism, which would dominate the scene from that moment on.

The Church that was supposed to be the bride of Christ, awaiting eagerly the return of her Bridegroom to take her to heaven, had tired of waiting for Him and married the world instead. Now occupied with building an earthly kingdom over which she could reign in an adulterous partnership with kings and emperors, the Church lost its hope of heaven and began to look upon itself as the replacement for God's earthly people, Israel. Forgotten were admonitions such as this from the Lord:

> Lay not up for yourselves treasures upon earth, where moth and rust doth corrupt and thieves break through and steal: but lay up for yourselves treasures in heaven, where neither moth nor rust doth corrupt, and where thieves do not break through nor steal: for where your treasure is, there will your heart be also (Matthew 6:19-21).

In disobedience to her Lord, the Church became the wealthiest institution on earth and gloried in her earthly treasures. Much of the wealth was acquired by selling salvation. Every sin had its price for "forgiveness." The greater and more numerous the sins the wealthier the Church of Rome became. Crosses and altars that supposedly depicted the sacrifice of Christ were gilded with gold. Bishops, cardinals, and popes, who claimed to be the successors of barefoot fishermen disciples, lived lifestyles that shamed even secular kings. The perversion of the Church which began with Constantine continued to worsen through the centuries, giving us today's Roman Catholicism.

During the Dark Ages and for centuries thereafter, Roman Catholicism was recognized by secular governments as the only true Christian Church. The Popes had their armies, fought numerous wars (sometimes against each other), made political alliances with princes, kings, and emperors, over whom they gradually asserted their power. Emperors trembled at the threat of excommunication by a pope, for only heretics doubted that outside the Church there was no salvation. To be excommunicated meant eternal damnation without any hope—and that threat gave the Church almost absolute power.

Rome became "that great city, which reigneth over the kings of the earth" (Revelation 17:18). Her rule was not by military might, for the Roman legions were no more. Her power to rule the world was wielded by a religious hierarchy that claimed to have inherited the keys to the kingdom given by our Lord to Peter. For centuries Roman Catholicism was the hand inside the glove of secular authorities, who even executed those whom she pronounced heretics. Thus Rome disclaims any responsibility for the martyrs of the infamous Inquisition, for the actual executions were, in most cases, carried out by the state.

Hope of the Rapture Is Lost

There was no longer any reason for Christ to return. Claiming that Constantine had given them his authority, the popes ruled with an iron hand over what they conceived to be "the kingdom of God" come to earth. To this day the popes proudly bear Constantine's three religious titles: Pontifex Maximus, Vicar of Christ, and Bishop of Bishops.

These titles, together with imperial power, the early popes claimed, had been conferred upon them by Constantine himself. To support that assertion the Church circulated a document known as *The Donation of Constantine*. Today it is recognized, even by Catholic historians, to have been a deliberate forgery. That such a document was needed is more than sufficient proof that the doctrine of papal succession, upon which today's popes rely as proof of their supreme spiritual authority, was a much later invention.

The Rapture is unknown in today's Roman Catholicism. In fact, it is specifically contradicted by the twin Catholic dogmas of purgatory and indulgences. Although down through the centuries there have been many relatively small groups of evangelical believers independent of and persecuted by Rome, they, too, for the most part lost the hope of the Rapture.

Depending upon how much they have suffered in this life, good works accomplished, indulgences earned, faithful Catholics must spend varying and unknown lengths of time in purgatory suffering for the sins for which Christ also suffered. That unbiblical teaching eliminated the promise, "The dead in Christ shall rise first: then we which are alive and remain shall be caught up together with them . . . to meet the Lord in the air" (1 Thessalonians 4:16,17). A simultaneous resurrection of the "dead in Christ" and all living believers caught up together with them in the Rapture would be impossible. All of the dead would not have finished purgatorial sufferings, and the living would not even have been there as yet.

The Reformation did little to recover any hope in Christ's promise, "I will come again and receive you unto myself." The Rapture is generally denied or has little importance among Reformed groups such as Presbyterians and Lutherans. There seemed to be good reason to avoid that teaching due to past fanaticism surrounding it. The best proof that the hope of an imminent Rapture was not biblical was found in the fact that Christ had not yet come.

Unfortunately, when the "blessed hope" of Christ's imminent return has been revived periodically in the last two centuries, the excitement created here and there has usually developed into date setting, causing the Rapture to become an object of derision. Voluntarily divested of their earthly possessions, cruelly deluded, white-robed zealots have more than once waited in vain on hilltop or rooftop while the promised hour came and went. Such fanatical anticipation has always subsided once again into disillusionment and forgetfulness.

An Understandable Apathy

More recently the "blessed hope" became prominent in evangelical thought in the 1970s and early 1980s with the publication of Hal Lindsey's *The Late Great Planet Earth* and other books attempting a biblical treatment of the Rapture. Then came *Eighty-eight Reasons for [the Rapture to occur in] 1988* followed by *Eighty-nine Reasons for 1989*. The flurry of excitement turned to disappointment and disillusionment when Christ failed to Rapture His Church in September of either of those years as the author had assured readers the Scriptures promised.

Most recently a Korean "prophet" declared that the Rapture would occur on October 28, 1992. Many of his followers around the world, but especially in Korea, quit their jobs and gave away their possessions to await the promised event. The day passed with everyone still on earth, leaving the deluded believers embarrassed and ashamed. Shortly thereafter the leader was indicted for converting to his own use about four million dollars of the church's funds. It seemed that he used much of the money to buy bonds whose maturity date far exceeded the day he had set for the Rapture!

In the wake of such excited anticipation and then disappointment, greater disillusionment than ever has now smothered the legitimate hope of Christ's imminent return. The Rapture and Second Coming are now looked upon as topics to be avoided by the vast majority of Christians—and, it would seem, with good reason. The gospel, too, because it was clearly preached by these date setters, has come in for increasing mockery.

Today there are about 1.7 billion people around the world who call themselves Christians and claim to believe God's Word. Most of them, however, as one might suspect after the passage of so much time, give little thought to the Lord's return. His promise "*I will come again!*" is still in the Bible and remains a tenet—if a vague, unimportant, and controversial one—of the Christian faith. That it musters little genuine interest, much less hope, is not surprising considering the fact that 1960 years have passed since our Lord spoke those words.

Who can say how many more years or centuries may go by before that promise is fulfilled? After all, the Bible says that with God a thousand years is like "yesterday when it is past, and as a watch in the night" (Psalm 90:4). By that reckoning, Christ has only been gone a few hours. So it could be thousands of years yet before His return. And what difference does it really make? That is the vital question we must confront in all honesty.

CHAPTER 10

Reconciling Contradictions

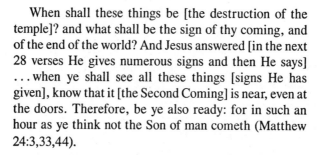

> When shall these things be [the destruction of the
> temple]? and what shall be the sign of thy coming, and
> of the end of the world? And Jesus answered [in the next
> 28 verses He gives numerous signs and then He says]
> ...when ye shall see all these things [signs He has
> given], know that it [the Second Coming] is near, even at
> the doors. Therefore, be ye also ready: for in such an
> hour as ye think not the Son of man cometh (Matthew
> 24:3,33,44).

What contradictions are these! Can it be? On the one hand,
Christ declares that His coming will follow immediately upon
the heels of multiple and unusual signs widely scattered around
the globe: wars, pestilences, famines, earthquakes, a time of
trouble (the Great Tribulation) such as the world has never
known nor ever shall know again. There will be supernatural
occurrences in the sky: a darkened sun and moon and "the sign
of the Son of man," visible to all. These signs will be apparent
to everyone on the earth. There will not be the slightest doubt
in anyone's mind that Christ's coming is at hand, "even at the
doors." No one will be taken by surprise.

On the other hand, Christ with no less clarity declares that
His coming will catch almost everyone by surprise. The contradiction could hardly be more blatant. Quite easy to reconcile, is the answer some give. Only the Christians will heed the

signs. Didn't Paul say, "But ye, brethren, are not in darkness, that that day should overtake you as a thief" (1 Thessalonians 5:4)? Those who are spiritually blind, however, won't recognize the signs, and they are the ones who will be caught by surprise. So goes the argument, but it doesn't fit the Word of God.

Cataclysmic Events That Will Terrorize the World

The signs which Christ and the apostles and prophets mention are not of such a subtle nature that it would take any spiritual discernment at all to recognize them. On the contrary, the signs are so overwhelming that they can't be overlooked or ignored by anyone. The Second Coming takes no one on earth by surprise.

The events leading up to Christ's return to the Mount of Olives are so unprecedented and universally calamitous that the whole world knows the time has come for the prophesied face-to-face confrontation between Christ and Antichrist. The Bible declares that "the beast [Antichrist], and the kings of the earth, and their armies" will gather together at Armageddon to make war with Christ (Revelation 19:19). They know that the fatal hour has arrived for the final showdown.

Consider again the signs of His return which Jesus enumerates in Matthew 24. Then read the terrifying description of the incredible devastation occurring on earth which is mentioned only in chapter 6 of Revelation. Forget the mind-boggling destruction mentioned elsewhere. At this early stage in the Great Tribulation one-fourth of the earth's population has already been killed. That's nearly 1.5 billion people! Natural disasters beyond imagination assault this beleaguered planet. Catastrophic meteor showers rain down upon the earth, accompanied by gigantic earthquakes and volcanic upheavals of such magnitude that "every mountain and island [moves] out of their places." Every person on the earth realizes that God's wrath is being poured out from heaven. Proud leaders are so terrified that they cry out to the mountains and rocks to fall upon them to hide them from God's fierce anger (Revelation 6:15-17).

No, Christ does not warn us to be "ready" because we might otherwise not have the godly discernment to recognize the subtle spiritual signs that will herald His coming. Those signs will be physical and of such magnitude that they can't be overlooked or ignored by anyone, no matter how spiritually blind.

An Inescapable Contradiction

Christ warns us to "watch" for an entirely different reason. He will come at a time when mankind, confident and complacent—and a sleeping church (Matthew 25:5)—will least expect Him: "At such an hour as ye think not the Son of man cometh" (Matthew 24:44). There will have been no signs. For that to be the case, the disasters mentioned above could not yet have occurred. God's judgment is the last thing the world of that day will be expecting. There will be no advance warning. It will be like the calm before a hurricane—but in this case there will be no sense of a storm impending.

Jesus warned that He would come when conditions would be like those just prior to the flood: "They did eat, they drank, they married wives . . . until the day that Noah entered into the ark and the flood came and destroyed them all" (Luke 17:27). His coming will occur at a time of business as usual, of pleasure, of optimism for the future. Just as it was immediately before the flood, the last thing the world will expect is judgment from God.

Surely Christ is not describing the Second Coming in the midst of Armageddon! Normal business conditions, complacency and surprise could only apply to a previous coming—the Rapture. At the time of the Second Coming mankind has endured perhaps four years of God's wrath and is expecting more. This world is in ruins and teetering on the brink of total destruction.

For Christ's coming to be without warning and to catch everyone by surprise it must occur *before* the time of great disaster He refers to in Matthew 24. He comes *before* God pours out His wrath upon earth as described in Revelation. Otherwise He could not say that His coming would be at a time similar to the days of Noah just before the flood.

Yet, just as clearly, He declared that He would come *after* these horrible disasters have wreaked their awful toll and *after* God's wrath has been poured out for several years upon this earth. These catastrophes will be the signs which Christ says will herald His coming. Moreover, His coming will not take place until *all* of these events have occurred, so that no one will have any doubt that His coming is "at the doors."

All of mankind will know that He is about to descend from heaven, because of the unmistakable signs that herald His return. So Jesus declared in unequivocal language. Yet just as clearly He warned that there would be no signs at all to signal His coming. It will occur when conditions on earth make it seem, even to His own, that He surely wouldn't be coming then: "in such an hour as ye think not." That's when He will come!

The contradiction is inescapable: He comes when there have been no warning signs, yet He comes after all of the signs have been displayed to a terrified world; He comes like a thief when no one would expect Him, yet He comes when everyone will expect Him.

Two Separate Events: The Rapture and the Second Coming

How can Christ come immediately following unmistakable signs which are intended to warn of His coming—and at the same time come as a thief in the night when few if any of His followers would expect Him? How can He come "when they say peace and safety" (1 Thessalonians 5:3) and at the same time come in the midst of Armageddon, the most destructive war the world has ever known? How can the saints be *caught up from earth to heaven* to dwell with Christ eternally and at the same time come with Him *from heaven* to execute judgment upon this earth?

How can two scenarios that are so contrary to one another both be true? There is only one possible answer to that question. Obviously, these diametrically contradictory descriptions of His coming cannot refer to the same event.

We saw that what the Old Testament prophets said of Christ's coming could not fit into one time frame and one event. Thus two comings of the Messiah were required, though the prophets didn't say so directly. There was no excuse for Christ's contemporaries not to realize that fact. Likewise it is inexcusable today not to realize that what the Bible says of His return simply cannot fit into one time frame and one event.

There must be two separate comings of Christ, both still future, which occur at two distinctly different periods of time. There is no other possible way to reconcile the otherwise contradictory statements in Scripture concerning Christ's return. According to Christ's own words, the conditions on earth at one coming will be the exact opposite of those at His other coming.

There is no way to combine in one event and in the same time frame an ecstatic catching away of all believers *to* heaven with the descent of Christ and all believers *from* heaven to rescue Israel at Armageddon. The Second Coming takes place *after* the incredible devastation of earth, called the Great Tribulation, which the Bible predicts for that time. The Rapture takes place *before* the Great Tribulation. The whole world will know that the Second Coming is about to take place. No unbelievers, and even very few Christians, will be expecting the Rapture when it occurs.

The Second Coming, which is the climactic event of the Great Tribulation, will occur in the midst of Armageddon. The armies of the world will have conquered much of Israel and will be pressing their attack against Jerusalem. They will be intent upon effecting what Hitler called the "final solution to the Jewish problem"—the enraged extermination of every Israeli and probably of all Jews on planet earth (Zechariah 12).

Threatened with total destruction, Israel, in desperation, will undoubtedly retaliate with nuclear weapons. The entire human race—indeed, all life on this planet—will be in danger of annihilation as this nuclear exchange escalates. Christ referred to that moment with these solemn words: "And except those days should be shortened, there should no flesh be saved [alive]" (Matthew 24:22). He will have to intervene, not only to save Israel, but to preserve life itself on earth. We will come back to those Scriptures later.

Yes, a Secret Rapture!

Clearly, the Rapture and the Second Coming must be two separate events. The Second Coming, occurring at the end of the Great Tribulation and in the midst of Armageddon, will surprise no one. The Rapture, occurring at a time of normalcy and complacency, will catch the world and a sleeping church by surprise.

Millions of Christians—and quite likely all infants—will suddenly vanish from earth, but how or why will not be known by the world. Nor will those left behind believe that Christ has caught away those who have disappeared and taken them to His Father's house in heaven. A seemingly plausible explanation (which we will discuss later), will be provided by the Antichrist, who will take over world leadership at that time. His hypothesis will satisfy the world, but it will be a lie.

Several times Christ's coming is likened to that of a thief who creeps in when all are asleep. Peter writes: "The day of the Lord will come as a thief" (2 Peter 3:10); and Paul adds, "as a thief in the night" (1 Thessalonians 5:2). A thief deliberately comes in such a time and manner that no one is aware of his presence. He secretly takes what he is after and leaves without anyone's knowledge.

In like manner, the Rapture will be a secret snatching away of a prize from this earth. Christ declared: "Behold, I come as a thief" (Revelation 16:15). Secretly, like a thief, Christ will take out of this world His church. The world will not know it is happening until suddenly millions are missing. Those who complain that a "secret Rapture" isn't biblical need to look at such Scriptures again.

No Signs for the Rapture

We are not only asserting that the Rapture (coming *for* His saints) takes place first, followed seven years later by the Second Coming (*with* His saints for Israel). We are also establishing that there will be no signs for the Rapture, no warning that it is about to occur. The signs are for the Second Coming.

When Christ comes secretly to catch His saints up to heaven, the world will be living in self-complacency and pleasure, seemingly on the way to solving its ecological problems and establishing perpetual international peace. Any thought of the Rapture will be widely ridiculed. Even few Christians will expect that long-promised event, although it should be their hope. One could say that such is already the general attitude even in the evangelical Church. How many are eagerly watching and longing for Christ to take them to heaven?

As we shall see in the following pages, many of the signs of the Second Coming are already in the world today. Others are clearly on the horizon, casting their long shadows in our direction. There can be no doubt that the props are being set in place and the curtain is about to rise on the final drama in human history. The principal actors, including the Antichrist, are waiting in the wings, eager to effect their will. In fact, they will play their roles precisely as the prophets have foretold.

The final act, called "the day of the Lord" (1 Thessalonians 5:2), must begin with the Rapture, for that time period is ushered in "as a thief in the night." The Second Coming cannot mark the beginning of "the day of the Lord," for it comes as no surprise. It is essential to understand that all the signs the Bible gives pertain to the Second Coming.

No signs precede the Rapture. It can only be that coming which will take place without warning, when the world and even most Christians least expect it. Everything on this earth will be changed after that event. The Rapture could occur at any moment. That has always been the case.

The reasons to expect our Lord now, however, are more compelling than ever. How close are we? Today's sleeping

Church, sinking ever deeper into apostasy, is one of the primary marks of the nearness of Christ's return. The signs of the Second Coming are building, and the Rapture must precede that event by seven years. Surely we are very close.

CHAPTER 11

Signs of the Times

◇

> When ye see a cloud rise out of the west, straightway
> ye say, There cometh a shower; and so it is. And when ye
> see the south wind blow, ye say, There will be heat; and it
> cometh to pass. Ye hypocrites, ye can discern the face of
> the sky and of the earth; but how is it that ye do not
> discern this time? (Luke 12:54-56).

There can be no doubt that Jesus Christ, who is God, came
to this earth as a man through a virgin birth, lived a perfect,
sinless life, died for our sins, and rose from the dead the third
day. Historically these events are firmly established. We have,
however, an even more powerful witness. That Christ came to
this earth in the past is not only a matter of history. It is also a
matter of fulfilled prophecy. Consider what that means!

Christ's first coming more than 1900 years ago, as we have
already seen, fulfilled dozens of specific prophecies made by
the Hebrew prophets and recorded centuries earlier in the Old
Testament. So will the Rapture of His church and His Second
Coming fulfill even more details of the prophetic blueprint.
Furthermore, these events are not independent of one another,
but part of an overall plan of God. They all fit together like
pieces in a jigsaw puzzle. Each event can be understood only in
relation to the whole.

Here we confront another aspect of the uniqueness of Christ
that sets Him apart from all others. No prophecy foretold the

coming of Buddha, Confucius, Muhammad, or any other of the leaders of the world's religions. Muslims suggest that Christ's statement, "I will send you another Comforter," foretold the coming of Muhammad. However, that claim doesn't fit by any stretch of the imagination.

Christ said that the Comforter would "come from the Father" (John 14:26; 15:26). Yet Muhammad denied that God was a father or had a son. Christ said of the Comforter, "He dwelleth with you and shall be in you" (John 14:17). So the Comforter, who was already with the disciples more than 500 years before Muhammad was born, obviously could not have been Muhammad.

Christ came once, nearly 2000 years ago. The how and where of His coming and all that He suffered and accomplished was exactly as the prophets foretold. He is coming again, and very soon. That coming, too, in every detail, will be exactly as prophesied. It is those prophecies which we will examine in the following pages.

Prophecy Provides Foolproof Identification

Why were such prophecies given? There are at least two fairly obvious reasons. First of all, prophecy indicates that the God who created us has not lost interest in His creatures nor has He lost control of events. He is in charge of history and will see that it works out according to His plan. That plan involves His people, Israel. It also involves the Messiah and the Church. God wants us to know His plan in advance and has revealed it through His prophets.

Secondly, at His comings there must be no doubt as to the identity of the Messiah. Antichrist, as we shall see, will try to pass himself off as the Christ. The deception will be clever and persuasive. Those who know prophecy will be armed in advance with the facts that unmask Satan's most brilliant deceit.

All that was needed to identify Christ at His first advent, and all that will be needed to identify Him when He comes again, has already been stated by the prophets. That overwhelming proof of His identity provides absolute assurance of our salvation. Of equal importance, we can share with the proof prophecy provides. It is the most powerful means of convincing unbelievers and of introducing them to the Savior.

There is another important significance of prophecy which is not as readily accepted. God wants us to know the signs of the times that reveal the nearness of Christ's return. We have seen how neglect and ignorance of prophecy caused both the secular and religious authorities to crucify Christ at His first advent. In view of today's neglect of prophecy, there is every reason to expect a comparable confusion when Christ comes again. To prevent such tragic misunderstandings—for those who are willing to take a fresh look at the Messianic prophecies—is a major purpose of this book.

As we have seen, Israel's religious leaders of that day were blind to the fact that the Messiah would be rejected by His own people and crucified. The same was true, until after the resurrection, of even Christ's closest followers. They were blind also to the fact that when Christ made that solemn promise, "*I will come again*," it was one more proof that He was the Savior.

As we have already seen, a most vital part of the testimony of the Old Testament prophets was that the Messiah must come more than once. Centuries beforehand, the Hebrew prophets had given their stamp of authenticity to the electrifying words which the disciples would find so incomprehensible: "*I will come again.*"

After These Many Centuries—Why Now?

Christ's declaration, however, confronts us with a dilemma. After the passage of nearly 2000 years, He has not come as He promised. Succeeding generations of believers have watched and waited and have gone to their graves without seeing their earnest hopes and prayers realized. Why should we be any more likely than they to see this promise fulfilled in our time?

How close are we? Is it presumption even to ask that question? Some Christians think so. However, since so much has been revealed by the prophets, might it not be that the answer even to this question is contained in the very prophecies which the rabbis overlooked and which we neglect today? Surely the possibility of discovering an answer to that burning question makes the careful study of what the prophets had to say more than worthwhile.

Those thrilling but as yet unfulfilled words, "*I will come again*," must be taken in the context of all of Scripture. Let us not forget that the One who made that promise had come to fulfill specific, detailed, and numerous Old Testament prophecies. Everything He said and did and all that man did to Him was only the culmination of what the prophets had long before declared.

Yet there can be no doubt that Christ left this earth without fulfilling all messianic prophecies. Thus He must return to complete His mission, and He must do so exactly as the prophets have foretold. The disciples' perspective of prophecy was too narrow. There was a much larger picture which they did not comprehend. We must beware of missing it as well. If we are to understand when and why and for whom Christ will return, then we must see His promise to do so in the full context of God's eternal plan.

God had taken great care to inspire His prophets and guard His Word to provide His people with sufficient means of recognizing the time of the Messiah's first advent. Would He not inspire His prophets to give similar insight into the Rapture and Second Coming as well? We believe that He has, and will substantiate that from Scripture.

Jesus indicted Israel's religious leaders for failing to recognize the signs of the times in which they lived: "Ye hypocrites, ye can discern the face of the sky and of the earth; but how is it that ye do not discern this time?" (Luke 12:56). Apparently they were responsible to know the signs given in Scripture, to recognize when they were present, and to conduct themselves accordingly. That same accountability is ours today.

"Signs" of His Coming?

As far as most Christians are concerned, when Christ comes He comes, so why not let it go at that? After all, there's nothing that can be done either to hasten or delay that day. Raising children, holding the family together, earning a living, and preparing for retirement leave little time even to think about an event that will not likely happen in one's lifetime. Fear of repeating past fanaticisms and follies seems reason enough to avoid focusing any attention upon Christ's return. Reason enough, that is, until one reads the words of Jesus more carefully.

One cannot escape the fact that Christ and His apostles gave definite signs to watch for that would herald the nearness of His return. Why give these signs if some generation at some time in the future was not expected to recognize them and know that His Second Coming was, as He Himself said, "near, even at the doors"?

Yes, but if the Rapture occurs seven years prior to the Second Coming, then those signs are not for us. So it would seem. Yet Christ commanded His own to watch for His coming and warned against being caught by surprise at His return— and surprise could only apply to the Rapture. Are we faced again with a contradiction, and this time one that cannot be resolved?

We may be certain that the answers are to be found if we desire to know them and diligently search His Word. Jesus also said, "And when these things begin to come to pass, then look up, and lift up your heads; for your redemption draweth nigh" (Luke 21:28). When these things *begin . . . look up*. The commencement of the signs cannot herald the Second Coming, for that event cannot occur until the signs are all complete. Therefore, with this statement, Christ can only be referring to the Rapture.

When Jesus, in response to His disciples' request for signs of His return, enumerated a long list of events (wars, rumors of wars, pestilence, earthquakes, famines, etc.), He also used that same word, *begin*. He made this interesting comment: "All these are the *beginning* of sorrows" (Matthew 24:8). The Greek word Jesus used for "sorrow" is most interesting as well. It referred especially to a woman's birthpangs.

Jesus is apparently revealing that these signs will *begin* to occur substantially ahead of the Second Coming. They will increase in frequency and intensity like birthpangs. Moreover, it would seem that these signs *begin* prior to the Rapture. Then how could the Rapture come as a surprise? Because these signs when they begin, will by their very nature be phenomena which have always been known on the world scene: earthquakes, famines, pestilences, wars.

There are some peculiarities, however, which have never before been known but which, for the first time in history, could now occur at any moment. We will discuss them in a later chapter.

Fanaticism and date setting are folly. It would seem to be at least equal folly, however, to ignore Christ's warnings about being caught by surprise. We are responsible, as every generation before us has been, to know the signs of His coming and to determine whether they are applicable to our day. No matter that others have misinterpreted Scripture and mistakenly set a time for Christ's return, only to be proved wrong. We are responsible to know the signs and to apply that knowledge biblically.

Though past generations have so consistently misinterpreted the Scriptures, is it possible that we now possess the insight they lacked? Isn't such a suggestion the very height of conceit? It could be, except for one obvious but overlooked fact, which we will also discuss later. As we shall see, ours is the first generation to whom certain special signs Christ foretold could possibly apply!

Christ's Total Mission Is the Key

In our attempt to understand the full meaning of Christ's promise, "I will come again"—and to establish how close we are to that event—we must examine the full range of biblical prophecies. It is not enough merely to look at Christ's own words and the events and teaching of the apostles which followed His departure from earth. The Old Testament prophets foretold not only His first advent, but His Second Coming as well.

It is to the Old Testament, then, that we must first of all turn to begin our investigation. Nor shall we have proceeded far in this careful study until we will be forced to conclude that prophecy is the backbone of God's Word. Without prophecy the Bible would lose much of its uniqueness and power to convince the searching soul.

God has stated unequivocally: "Surely the Lord God will do nothing, but he revealeth his secret unto his servants, the prophets" (Amos 3:7). If we would know God's secrets and understand all that He has planned, then we must study what He has spoken through His prophets. For it is through the prophets that God has declared His eternal purpose—and even the details of how He will work it all out for our good and His glory.

Christ's crucifixion and departure from this earth were not the unfortunate results of an aborted mission but the successful completion of *phase one*. Thus, His promise to return was the pledge to finish the remainder of a task which the prophets had laid out in no uncertain terms. The mission which brought the Messiah to this earth was much larger than His disciples imagined.

Christ's purpose in coming back again will be to bring to a grand conclusion His total objective. Consequently, we must understand God's plan from eternity past to eternity future or we cannot possibly reach a valid conclusion from the Scriptures concerning the timing of His triumphant return in power and glory to the scene of His rejection and crucifixion. Let us turn, then, to the Scriptural account of the origin of evil which necessitated the coming of the Messiah to this earth.

CHAPTER 12

How It All Began

◇

> How art thou fallen from heaven, O Lucifer! . . . For thou hast said . . . *I will* ascend into heaven: *I will* exalt my throne above the stars of God: *I will* sit also . . . in the sides of the north: *I will* ascend above the heights . . . *I will* be like the most High. Yet thou shalt be brought down to hell (Isaiah 14:12-15).

What is evil? From where does it come? Why does it exist? The questions echo down the centuries to haunt us even today. Science, philosophy, psychology, sociology, anthropology—none of these has ever come close to explaining evil and some of them refuse even to recognize it. Inspired of the Holy Spirit, Isaiah draws the curtain aside and gives us a shocking glimpse into evil's awesome origin—an incomprehensible occurrence in heaven in ages past. How long ago it was we don't know.

We are introduced to Lucifer. Behold the most beautiful, brilliant, and powerful being God ever created. Yet, mystery of mysteries, his heart contemplates then boldly plans that which had been for an eternity unthinkable: rebellion against God! This inconceivable and terrifying drama marked the entrance of iniquity into God's perfect universe. In its wake followed inevitable cosmic chaos and ruin which threatened to drag the whole of mankind into the deepest hell. Hence the need for the Messiah to come to earth to rescue our fallen race.

How and why did rebellion against the God who had created him arise in Lucifer's heart? How could selfish ambition obsess a perfect being who had known only God's intimate presence? Here we reach the bounds of human understanding, beyond which we cannot venture. Paul speaks of the "*mystery* of iniquity" (2 Thessalonians 2:7)—a mystery which began with Lucifer's mad passion to "be like the most High." Though evil remains unfathomable, the place and manner of its origin carry implications which teach us much.

Unbelievable though it seems, this grotesque ambition came to birth in heaven itself—and in the heart of one who was "full of wisdom, and perfect in beauty . . . the anointed cherub" (Ezekiel 28:12-15), very possibly heaven's choir director (Isaiah 14:11; Ezekiel 28:13)! Yes, it was in this perfect and blameless creature of apparent innocence, whose future seemed so bright and assured, that evil had its origin. Eons later, planet earth, like the rest of the universe, is still reeling from the horrifying effects of his downfall.

From this preposterous rebellion flows the entire saga of sin and redemption. As a result of his pride and selfish ambition, Lucifer became "the great dragon . . . that old serpent, called the devil and Satan, which deceiveth the whole world" (Revelation 12:9). Though the sworn enemy of God, he is to this day still granted access into the very throne room of heaven. There he continually accuses those who trust and obey their Creator (Job 1:6-12; Revelation 12:10).

Without Satan's rebellion there would have been no need for a Messiah. God's Word declares: "The Son of God was manifested [i.e., Christ came to this earth], that he might destroy the works of the devil" (1 John 3:8). Clearly, then, if we fail to comprehend Lucifer's fall and its consequences for mankind, we cannot understand why Christ came the first time, much less why and when He will return.

The Awful Birth of Self

One cannot overemphasize the devastating effects of Lucifer's rebellion. It introduced sin for the first time into God's creation and is therefore an event of the utmost importance to any understanding of the problem of evil. Five times Lucifer declared with purposeful passion and proud determination, "*I will*." Here was the awful birth of self into the universe. Its devilish offspring—self-image, self-worth, self-esteem, self-love, self-acceptance, self-assertion, self-ad infinitum—are the scourge of today's world and have even entered into the church.

Behold the very heart of evil! Self-determination, the right to set his own standards and to control his own destiny—these were Lucifer's selfish ambitions, for which he will yet be "cast down to hell." For the first time a creature God had made was demanding to have its own way in rebellious independence of Him. God's very right to fulfill His will for His creation was being challenged. What damnable audacity!

How appalling it is to realize that the very self-qualities which are today sought, taught, and highly prized among men were conceived by Satan! The same self-exaltations, which brought about Lucifer's fall, are highly prized as the keys to success in today's world! No wonder John, the beloved apostle, wrote: "The whole world lies in wickedness [literally, in the wicked one, Satan]" (1 John 5:19).

Even more distressing is the fact that a large percentage of the church has bought the same lies. Self-esteem, self-image, and the other selfisms which Satan originated are the pillars of Christian psychology. What a masterful deception!

Lucifer challenged God's right to rule the universe He had created. He was literally demanding equality with God: "I will be like the most High." It was an insolent assault upon God's throne. In one stroke Satan rejected monotheism (the belief in one supreme God) and introduced polytheism (the belief in many gods), exalting himself to godhood. Eve would later embrace the same ambition. Here we discover why Christ requires all who would be His disciples to utterly deny self.

Lucifer's heart had conceived the incredible obsession of tearing God from His throne as sovereign of the universe and exalting himself in his Creator's place. Apparently many angels joined Satan's rebellion and are demons today. Every person on earth faces the same choice: whether to follow the true God, or to claim godhood for himself and thus join forces with Satan. The battle in essence is self against God. Each of us remains on Satan's side until we can with deep conviction declare what Christ prayed as our substitute, "Not my will, but thine be done" (Luke 22:42).

Psychological Theories Don't Fit Lucifer

Inasmuch as Lucifer's fall marked the origin of evil in the universe, it must provide the pattern by which all evil is to be understood. Any alleged explanation for aberrant, antisocial, or sinful conduct that doesn't fit the Luciferian model must be rejected, since he is the originator of such behavior. It is immediately clear that the psychological explanations for wrong attitudes and actions which are so popularly accepted today, both in the secular world and in the church, do not fit Lucifer's case. Therefore these theories must be rejected as false.

No details of Lucifer's background are provided. We can only conclude that such data has no bearing on his case. And if background history is irrelevant to Lucifer's actions, it must be in all cases of wrong behavior, in spite of modern psychological theories to the contrary. Moreover, those who insist upon probing into the past as the key to present conduct will find no comfort in Lucifer. His past life prior to his fall was impeccable.

Certainly Lucifer had suffered none of the childhood traumas, disappointments, deprivations, frustrations, temptations, broken relationships, rejections, or addictions which are now brought forth to "explain" and thereby excuse what the Bible calls sin. No "dysfunctional family" warped his thinking! Instead, his background was perfection itself, for he dwelt in the continual presence and favor of God and His angelic host. If background, environment, and past experiences determine present behavior, then Lucifer should have remained a paragon of virtue to this day. Yet pride took root in his heart and bore its evil fruit.

Certainly Lucifer had not been "abused as a child." Most assuredly he hadn't been the victim of Satanic Ritual Abuse (SRA), yet he would later be its inventor! Nor was he suffering the traumas of "codependency," "Multiple Personality Disorder" (MPD), "Obsessive Compulsive Disorder" (OCD), or Post-Traumatic Stress Disorder (PTSD). These new "explanations" of undesirable behavior, which are now generally accepted even among evangelicals, do not apply in Lucifer's case at all. Therefore they do not apply in any case. For if Lucifer's behavior, which is the embodiment of all evil, needs no such "explanation," then neither does the undesirable conduct of any human being.

It would be absurd to suggest that this angelic creature of seemingly perfect wisdom, talent, and beauty, whose heart was lifted up with pride, suffered from a "bad self-image" or "low self-esteem." Yet Christian psychologists, parroting the humanists, have convinced many Christian leaders and much of the church that a low view of self lies at the root of every evil plaguing society, from drug addiction and homosexuality to pornography, fornication, and abortion. Lucifer's case gives the lie to selfist theories. His problem was quite otherwise: the desire to exalt and assert self.

The highly exalted "son of the morning" needed no training in "self-confidence, self-affirmation, self-development, self-assertion" or in "looking out for number one." These passions were foreign to his nature as God created him—yet they sprang spontaneously from the depths of his being. That Eve so readily embraced these same self-centered desires, and that they come so naturally to all mankind, only confirms Christ's indictment of our race: "Ye are of your father the devil, and the lusts of your father ye will do" (John 8:44).

Nor would psychotherapy or the newer 12-step programs have helped Lucifer. Such recently invented humanistic methodologies are becoming increasingly popular. Yet they cannot solve the basic problem of self-willed evil which originated with Lucifer and now festers in every human heart. On the contrary, most psychotherapies foster and encourage the very selfisms which Lucifer brought to earth so long ago.

Like Lucifer, we are not automatons forced by circumstances to react in a certain way. Temptations and traumas may be rationalized as excuses for retaliating or reacting angrily, vengefully, destructively, irrationally—but they do not "explain" one's behavior. It is the heart, not circumstances no matter how traumatic, that determines one's actions.

One is not compelled to retaliate or nourish resentment when ill-treated, but one decides to do so in defense or promotion of self. Thus we prove ourselves to be the offspring of Lucifer and in partnership with him against God. His rebellion could not be explained, much less excused or justified, as a reaction to some prior mistreatment he had suffered. There had been none. Evil originated in his heart, and environment and past experiences obviously had nothing to do with it. So it is with each of us. We choose to behave the way we do; and psychological theories which attempt to place the blame elsewhere promote a delusion.

Love, Evil, and the Power of Choice

Why would God give mankind the power to choose evil? Why not only the power to choose good? Obviously, choice that is limited is not choice at all. The power to say yes is meaningless without the power to say no. It is not genuine choice if what one is supposedly "free to choose" is all there is. And any being that has the power to choose and is prevented from doing so becomes frustrated, like a wild animal in a cage. Heaven would be a prison for those who were forced to go there.

While evil could not exist without a genuine freedom to choose, neither would love be possible. We all intuitively recognize that real love comes from the heart. Submission to rape at the point of knife or gun is not love. Love cannot be forced. Even God can no more make us love Him than He could commit sin, for to do either would be to violate His very nature.

God loved us so much that He wanted to give us the most wonderful gift possible. That gift was Himself, in a relationship of love. For such a transaction to be possible, however, required that we must have the power of choice. Without genuinely being able to choose, it would have been impossible for us to enjoy that which all recognize as the highest of all human experience: love of God and of one another.

We had to be free to rebel against and even hate God or we could never truly love Him. Love and hate, good and evil, are two sides of the same coin. It was inevitable that the power to choose would open the door to evil and make it possible for Satan to rebel against God and to despoil Eden's innocence. God knew the consequences and provided the remedy before sin ever entered the world. That remedy is in the Messiah, and each of His comings plays a significant part in the destruction of evil.

Love is as much a mystery as is evil. To deny the genuine power of choice is to deny both love and evil. One can neither give love under duress nor be held responsible for what one is forced to do. Such is the problem with all psychological diagnoses: they absolve us of guilt by turning us all into victims who parrot in endless refrain: "It's not my fault. . . . I had no choice . . . I was abused. . . . My family didn't understand me . . . circumstances forced me." Everyone becomes a victim. It's always someone else's fault. On the contrary, a choice was exercised; and until that fact is admitted and responsibility taken for one's actions, there is no real solution.

Conflict of the Ages

We are not told what battles raged across the galaxies in ages past as a result of Satan's rebellion. We are informed only that God and Satan are still locked in deadly combat for control of the universe. We know also that this unimaginable cosmic struggle now centers on planet earth and involves the destiny of mankind. Man has become the prize for which both sides are striving. God's desire is to save mankind; Satan's is to dupe earth's inhabitants into joining his side and thus to share his eternal and abhorrent fate.

In this battle for control of the universe God works through a man, the Christ. Satan, too, is represented by a man, the

Antichrist. This cosmic conflict will reach its climax in an incredible face-to-face confrontation between Christ and Antichrist here on planet earth. We will deal specifically with that event later. The coming of Christ 1900 years ago as well as the Rapture and His Second Coming soon to take place are all part of this titanic struggle between God and Satan, and can only be properly understood in that context.

In some mysterious way that Scripture does not explain (indeed, probably cannot fully explain to finite beings), every human heart is a microcosm of this colossal contest between God and Satan. "Have you considered my servant Job?" God asked Satan (Job 1:8). With that challenge this unsuspecting man's world fell apart and his soul became a raging battlefield between self and God. Job's eternal destiny hung in the balance and depended upon the outcome of that warfare, an outcome that was decided by the choice he made.

Satan was convinced that Job's loyalty to God depended upon the protection and blessings God provided. Take those away, Satan challenged God, and Job "will curse thee to thy face" (2:5). So God responded by allowing Satan to do his worst, short of taking Job's life. It was a test of Job's love and loyalty to God, a test that we must each face, though not necessarily in the same manner or intensity. Whether we pass or fail reveals which side we have chosen to be on in this conflict of the ages and thus determines our eternal destiny. Job won the battle the only way it could be won—by total submission to God's will, even to the point of saying, "Though he [God] slay me, yet will I trust him" (13:15).

Indeed, we must allow ourselves to be slain, "crucified with Christ" (Galatians 2:20) as Paul put it, accepting His death on the cross as our own death, and thereby admitting that was what we deserved. We must give up the rebellious life of self as we would live it, in exchange for the life Christ would live through us, or we remain the servants of sin and Satan forever. Did not Jesus say: "For whosoever will save [hold onto] his life shall lose it: and whosoever will lose [give up] his life for my sake shall find it [i.e., the real life God intended for him]" (Matthew 16:25)?

A Raging Battle in Every Heart

Job, of course, was not the first to be tempted to rebel against God. Having convinced a large number of God's angels to join him, Satan had long before brought his rebellion to planet earth. How long this occurred after mankind was created we do not know. It is likely, however, that Adam and Eve had children before their fall. They had been told to "be fruitful and multiply" (Genesis 1:28). And part of God's judgment upon Eve was to "*multiply* her conception" (3:16). These early offspring of our first parents were likely the "sons of God" who married "the daughters of men" and produced unusual offspring (Genesis 6:2-4).

Unlike Job, who triumphed in his temptation, and to whom God restored even more than he had lost in the battle against evil, Eve failed miserably and lost all. When tempted to put herself and her own desires ahead of God, she fell just as Satan had. In her wake she dragged down the entire human family that has descended from her.

The serpent seduced Eve with the very lie to which his own heart had given birth: "You can become one of the gods" (Genesis 3:5). That the biblical story of the Garden of Eden is not myth but history is evidenced by the fact that each member of the human race is still obsessed with the same Satanic ambition. The universal obsession of mankind is to have godlike freedom to do whatever one pleases and to develop the godlike powers that will enable one to be in control of life and circumstances. It is a fact, too, that the memory of a paradise lost seems to haunt us all. Restoring this world to its lost Edenic bliss, by self-effort rather than submission to God's sovereignty, is still the dream and highest ambition of mankind.

Rescuing our fallen race from Satan's grip, redeeming us from the penalty of sin, and restoring the universe to God's sovereign rule is the task of the Messiah. Our Lord's first advent laid the foundation and His second will be stage two. Nor will the final battle be fought until the end of Christ's millennial reign on David's throne.

Before going into the future, however, we need to take a closer look at this conflict of the ages as it rages in every human heart. This desperate battle between self and God has been the ruin of every person to walk this earth, except for Christ Himself. Consequently, He alone can rescue us. Furthermore, the problem of evil must be solved justly and on a practical level or it cannot be solved at all.

CHAPTER 13

Self and God

―――――――――― ◇ ――――――――――

> For rebellion is as the sin of witchcraft, and stubbornness is as iniquity and idolatry. Because thou hast rejected the word of the Lord, he hath also rejected thee (1 Samuel 15:23).
>
> I can of mine own self do nothing. . . . I seek not mine own will, but the will of the Father which hath sent me. . . . The words which I speak unto you, I speak not of myself: but the Father that dwelleth in me, he doeth the works (John 5:30; 14:10).

What could be wrong with the complete freedom Eve sought to fulfill her own desires? After all, isn't freedom essential to love? Ah, yes, but in exercising her freedom Eve showed no love whatsoever either for Adam or God. Genuine love, made possible by freedom of choice, providentially carries within itself that which holds the reins on the freedom it requires. In contrast, "free love" destroys both freedom and love.

The law could never make us good. It could only tempt us, as Paul pointed out, to do what it forbids (Romans 7:7-11). Love alone is able to restrict our conduct and even cause us to fulfill the law. "Love worketh no ill to his neighbor; therefore love is the fulfilling of the law" (Romans 13:10).

Love forgets self and abandons self-interest in order to please the one who is loved. How incongruous, then, is the very term "self-love." Where demands are made for self and complaints are voiced of not being treated fairly or not being "responded to," one may be absolutely certain that true love is not present, for "love seeketh not her own."

Listen to Paul's beautiful description of genuine love:

> Love suffers long and is kind; love envieth not, vaunteth not itself... seeketh not her own, is not easily provoked, thinketh no evil... beareth all things... endureth all things... love never faileth (1 Corinthians 13:1-8).

Our fallen hearts are not capable of such divine love. It can only be ours through the transformation of the new birth and the empowering of the Holy Spirit.

Love of Self or Love of God

Affectionate feelings and deep passions do not necessarily spring from genuine love. The words "I love you," though spoken with fervor, too often mean "I love me and *want* you." Beware, for lust habitually masquerades as love and has deceived multitudes. When the mask at last has slipped, as it eventually does, the horrible truth is revealed—but so often too late.

Where love's restrictions are not observed and self is not denied so that God can reign supreme, there is no love, no matter how eloquently it may be professed. Satan, being incapable of genuine love, knows not the difference between love and lust. Those who follow him become similarly blinded by their own sensual appetites. Self seeks nothing but its own desires and will protest its fervent and loyal affection to gain satisfaction for its cravings.

True love has no higher joy than pleasing the one who is loved. Jesus gave us the secret of victory in the Christian life when He declared, "He that hath my commandments, and keepeth them, he it is that loveth me... If a man love me, he will keep my words... He that loveth me not keepeth not my sayings" (John 14:21-24). Love delights in obeying God—and in so doing brings blessing to those on earth who are loved as well.

It cannot be emphasized enough that the battle of the ages which began with Satan's rebellion now rages in every human heart. The conflict, as we have already noted, is between self and God. It is *whom* one loves, self or God, that determines one's behavior. The crucial choice we each face a thousand times a day is whether to love and serve self or to love and serve God and our neighbor as ourself. That conflict needs to be settled once and for all so that we are no longer double-minded.

Self-love, which is the very heart of Satan's rebellion, is the partner of lust. The "love" it gives exists only in order to satisfy its own needs by getting something in return. It cannot exist side-by-side with love for God, which must be selfless. One cannot be devoted to God and at the same time be devoted to serving and pleasing oneself, which is what it means to love self. In order to be His followers, Jesus said we must deny this loyalty to and love of ourselves. We must give ourselves to God and others as He gave Himself for us. Even love between husband and wife, parent and child, neighbors and friends, must be selfless or it is not genuine.

Yet "self-love" is sought and taught as an essential good rather than the great evil that it is. One hears the new psychological gospel of self-love, self-esteem, and the other selfisms proclaimed from some of the otherwise best evangelical pulpits. Behold how far the world is from Christ, and how deep the church has sunk into apostasy! In *The City of God*, Augustine's fourth century classic, we read:

> There are no more than two kinds of human society, which we may justly call two cities, according to the language of our Scriptures. . . . These two cities were made by two loves: the earthly city by the love of self unto the contempt of God, and the heavenly city by the love of God unto the contempt of self.

While Satan was the originator of evil in the universe at large, it was Adam and Eve who introduced it to this earth. Eve was deceived, but Adam was not (1 Timothy 2:14). His sin, therefore, was worse than Eve's, for he disobeyed God know-ingly, quite likely because he didn't want to be separated from his wife. Together, they were separated from God, a spiritual death into which we, as their offspring, are all born: "Where-fore, as by one man sin entered into the world, and death by sin; so death passed upon all men, for that all have sinned" (Romans 5:12).

Depravity and the Power of Choice

The many similarities to Lucifer's rebellion and fall which we find in the case of Adam and Eve are, of course, no coincidence. As it was with Lucifer, so with Adam and Eve (and us as well). There was no "explanation"—and thus no excuse—for their willful and rebellious disobedience. Evil remains a mystery, hidden in the depths of the human heart where it was nourished by Satan. The power of choice was part of the image of God in which we were created, and it opened the door to both love and evil.

That Adam and Eve had the power to make a genuine choice is evident from the fact that God commanded them not to eat of "the tree of the knowledge of good and evil" (Genesis 2:17) and held them accountable when they disobeyed. That their offspring, though depraved and enslaved by sin, still have the moral capacity to choose either good or evil is evident by God's continued appeals to mankind to obey Him: "Choose you this day whom ye will serve" (Joshua 24:15).

Revealing his own struggles as a natural man, Paul himself declared: "To will [choose to do good] is present with me" (Romans 7:18). He went on to explain that he lacked the power to put his good desires into practice. It was not the ability to choose to do good that was lacking, but the power to perform.

Obedience is a conscious choice that man has the capacity for and must make from his heart. Disobedience is the choice not to obey. There is no denying that choice is essential to our humanity as God made us. That simple and self-evident fact does away with the foundational precept of Calvinism, "total depravity."

That the theory of *total* depravity goes too far is obvious from the fact that every person does not engage in evil to the maximum. We are all depraved, but we are not all Hitlers. We are immoral creatures, but each of us resists much immorality while falling prey to some. Not everyone has robbed, raped, or murdered. Most of humanity has perhaps never even been tempted to commit such heinous crimes. If we were totally depraved, however, *all* of us would pursue evil without any restraint.

Contrary to Calvin's teaching, the fact is that we have the capacity to choose what is right and to resist what is wrong, and we do so in varying degrees. God gave us each a conscience on which He wrote His laws (Romans 2:14,15). He would have done so to no purpose were we incapable of heeding conscience.

There is a humanistic goodness that cannot be denied. Of course, it falls far short of the glory of God, and is thus unacceptable to Him and even sinful in its self-righteousness. Yet it also falls far short of the wantonly savage, ruthless, lecherous behavior which would most assuredly characterize all those who were *totally* depraved. Such complete abandonment to evil has never been observed. Even Hitler could be loyal to friends, jovial with children, and courtly to women.

Furthermore, it cannot be denied that Adam and Eve were not depraved at all, much less *totally* so. Thus, depravity, whatever it might mean, is no better explanation for sin than low self-esteem, codependency, a dysfunctional background, or some other currently popular psychological theory. None of these newly contrived explanations would have applied to our first parents. Yet it was they who, in the Garden of Eden, originated sin and evil behavior. Today's psychological clichés are attempts to excuse ourselves with alibis that have only recently been invented.

Evil is a choice we still make today as surely as Lucifer and Adam and Eve originally made it. Neither Lucifer nor Adam nor Eve was forced to make an evil choice. Each was created perfect, so we cannot explain their behavior by any built-in bias toward evil as Calvinists seek to explain man's rebellious-ness today. Why we choose evil so much of the time (though not always) is a mystery wrapped in the enigma of the power of choice. At the heart of that mystery is self, which Christ said must be denied. Instead, it is being loved and pampered. Even evangelical leaders are preaching this seductively evil doctrine of self because they have embraced psychology and its "expla-nations" for sinful conduct.

Self-Gratification and the Denial of Self

Adam and Eve were perfect creatures made by God in His image to glorify Him. Though not in God's image, Lucifer, too, was "perfect in all [his] ways until iniquity was found" in him (Ezekiel 28:15). How is it possible that perfect beings living in the paradise of God's presence could rebel against the God who had made them, who had only loved and cared for and given them every benefit His wisdom could devise? It seems inconceivable! That evil could arise in such creatures and under such circumstances points to the mystery of evil that dwells in each of our hearts!

The central role played by the love of self in man's rebellion against God is the reason for Christ's unequivocal command that we must deny self (Matthew 16:24; Mark 8:24; Luke 9:23). This self which must be denied, if we are to cease following Satan and become the followers of Christ, had its awful birth on this planet in the Garden of Eden. Eve's disobedience was motivated by her love of self, which produced and satisfied selfish desires.

Eve's dominant thought was of no one but herself. Visions of self-gratification propelled her toward the forbidden fruit as she gazed upon it in lustful desire. Her selfish disobedience was justified with the thoughts: How beautiful this fruit looks to *me*, how delicious it will taste to *me*, how wise it will make *me*. She needed no training in self-assertion or "looking out for number one." Satan, who had originated these ideas, remains the great missionary of the gospel of self. He had little trouble in converting Eve to abandon her love of God and to begin a more exciting and satisfying worship at the new shrine of self.

In her determination to satisfy her own desires and ambitions, Eve trampled under her feet honor and commitment both to God and to her husband, Adam. Clearly Eve felt no obligation to her Creator who had so graciously provided for her this beautiful environment. Self had been placed ahead of God. Nor did she consult her husband, Adam, but took the leadership into sin, then seduced her spouse into joining her.

The Cult of Self

Here we have the beginning of cultism. Satan's claim that he alone had the correct interpretation of what God had said is the foundation of every cult. Those who join a cult do so because its perverted interpretation of Scripture appeals to them. Appealing, too, is the fact that its leader decides and dictates what each member should believe and do. Cultists mistakenly imagine that by submission to such absolute authority, whether guru, pastor, or pope, they can escape personal responsibility to God. Self-interest motivates the members of any cult. Whoever truly loves and seeks God, however, will be delivered from self-deception.

Not so Eve. She had found a religious leader whose new interpretation of what God had said was exactly what she wanted to hear. God had forbidden the pair to eat the fruit of one particular tree and had warned that disobedience would bring death. The serpent convinced Eve that disobedience would be conducive to self-improvement and self-development. The serpent dismissed God's warnings as restrictive and narrow-minded and assured Eve that liberation from such dogmatic authoritarianism would bring glorious self-fulfillment. It would even turn her into a god such as this shining one had become.

Eve chose to put self ahead of God. There can be no doubt that she loved self instead of God. But is self-love wrong? Did not Christ command us: "Thou shalt love thy neighbor as thyself" (Matthew 22:39). True, but He was not commanding self-love; He was correcting it. Far from indicating that we hate ourselves, or that we fail to love ourselves enough and need to be taught to love ourselves, Christ's command proves that we innately do love ourselves. Surely He was not saying, "Love your neighbor as you hate yourself"—or "Love your neighbor as you insufficiently love yourself."

The fact is that we all innately love ourselves—and far too much. That sentiment has been inherited from Adam and Eve and has firm roots deep within us all. Do we not lavish attention upon ourselves? Is not self-preservation and self-protection our primary instinct? We zealously clothe and feed and comfort and care for ourselves. Christ was simply saying, "Give some of the attention and care to your neighbor that you squander upon yourself!"

But what of those who hate themselves? While some people use such language, that is not what is meant. Paul declared, "For no man ever yet hated his own flesh, but nourisheth and cherisheth it" (Ephesians 5:29). No one hates his or her own *self*. One may hate his job, his salary, his appearance, the way others treat him, but dislike of these things only proves a most fervent self-love. Otherwise why the concern?

Surely if a man really hated himself he would be only too glad to see himself become the victim of an unfair boss, unfair treatment, vicious hatred, ugly features. Instead he complains about those abuses and blemishes. Eve's rebellion in order to satisfy her selfish desires was not the consequence of hating herself, but of loving herself instead of God. And so it is with each of us.

"Self-Image" for a Mirror?

Such bold self-assertion in taking control of her own life was supposed to give Eve what is today declared to be essential: a "good self-image." It takes little reflection, however, to see the folly of this concept. We are made in the image of God. "Image" immediately brings to mind a mirror. Interestingly enough, a mirror's *only* purpose is to reflect an image *of something other than itself*. How absurd for a mirror to try to develop a "good *self*-image"!

If there is something defective about its image, the mirror needs two remedies: 1) to be cleaned so that nothing of self interferes; and 2) to be restored to a right relationship with the one whose image it was designed to reflect. Having been seduced by Satan, our natural bent is to try to develop God's image in which we were made from within self. Such effort can only destroy God's image that we are to reflect. In *The Four Loves*, C.S. Lewis put it well:

> It is easy to acknowledge, but almost impossible to realize for long, that we are mirrors whose brightness, if we are bright, depends entirely upon the sun [Son] that shines upon us. Surely we must have a little—however little—native luminosity? Surely we can't be *quite* creatures?

Like Lucifer, Adam and Eve were not only perfect beings but they inhabited a perfect environment. There was nothing in their past to "explain" their action: no childhood abuse, no poverty, no crying oneself to sleep night after night on an empty stomach in a rat-infested ghetto, no traumatic experiences buried in their subconscious, no disappointments, no rejection, no addiction, no broken relationships, no upbringing in a "dysfunctional family." Not one of the popular excuses that are today being offered for misbehavior applied to Adam and Eve.

As we have already seen in Lucifer's case, it is a great delusion to attach labels to sinful behavior that would not fit Adam and Eve. Nor can these new diagnoses be any more applicable to us than to them. Likewise, today's multiplying experimental therapies are of no more benefit for us than they would have been for Adam and Eve. Certainly God did not prescribe "professional help" for that guilty pair. Weekly visits to a psychological counselor, healing of memories, a 12-step program, discovering one's temperament—none of today's popular remedies would have been relevant to Adam's and Eve's sin and need.

We are no different. The remedy we need is the same as it was for them—our repentance and His forgiveness. The first two sinners on planet earth had willfully disobeyed. The personal responsibility for their sin had to be acknowledged by each of them and its consequences borne. God could not just smile and say, "Let bygones be bygones." Adam and Eve were put out of the Garden of Eden. That penalty was required both by God's justice and His love for this guilty pair.

In love God desired to forgive these rebels and restore them to Himself. It would, however, take more than a bookkeeping entry in heaven. Both love and justice demanded that the full penalty for sin be paid. As finite beings we could never pay that penalty, but would have been separated for eternity from God. By God's grace, Christ, who is both God and man and thus both sinless and infinite, bore the consequences of our sin. As a free gift, He offers full pardon and eternal life to all who will admit their sin and accept His payment of the penalty in their place.

Many parents fail to follow God's example when their children disobey. They back away from discipline, and the child never learns the serious consequences of rebellion. Failure to discipline shows a lack of love, encourages the self-will that dwells in every heart, and courts increasing disaster.

Prophecy Distinguishes Christ from Antichrist

The only remedy for evil is the Christ who was crucified for our sins and rose from the dead for our justification (Romans 4:25). He is the only One who, by His indwelling Spirit, can provide both the forgiveness that delivers from guilt and fear and the power to live the life that God intended for us. It is not the fruit of *therapy*, but the fruit of the *Spirit*, which is described as: "love, joy, peace, long-suffering, gentleness, goodness, faith, meekness, temperance" (Galatians 5:22,23). A prisoner in a penitentiary, one of the many who have become believers behind bars, recently wrote:

> The "selfism" doctrines welcomed by the Church today are being treated as though Christ taught them Himself! . . . Even good, sound Christians are falling for

this humanistic nonsense. It surely is seductive! I'm finding, through biblical study, that the doctrine of "self-forgiveness" is also a fallacy. Our conscience can only be cleansed by the blood of Christ. . . . Real freedom from sin comes only through repentance and faith in the blood of our Lord; not through "forgiving ourselves."

To save us from the penalty, power, and eventually the very presence of sin—to undo what Satan and Adam and Eve had done—was Christ's purpose in coming into the world. Thus He is called the "Savior," and those who accept His "salvation" are described as "saved." But how could this salvation be accomplished? And how would mankind recognize the Savior when He came?

The answer to these two vital questions was communicated by God through His prophets and recorded in Scripture. Moreover, it was done in such a manner that the authenticity of the promise and the credentials of the One promised would be absolutely assured. Without recorded prophecies setting identifying criteria, one could easily mistake Antichrist for Christ. Such is the great value of prophecy. Such, too, is the danger that its neglect poses today as Satan prepares Antichrist to make his appearance.

As we have already noted, the Bible, from which hundreds of fulfilled prophecies can be cited, is unique in this respect. There is nothing comparable in any other scriptures. No prophecies foretold the coming of Buddha, Muhammad, or any other religious leaders. The life, death, and resurrection of Christ alone were foretold. Nor can it be denied that the many messianic prophecies were fulfilled to the letter in His first coming. That fact gives us absolute confidence that the Scriptures foretelling Christ's return will be fulfilled in precise detail as well.

The first coming of Christ was in fulfillment of dozens of specific prophecies. In like manner, His Second Coming must occur on the precise schedule spelled out in Scripture. Even Antichrist cannot be revealed until it is "his time" (2 Thessalonians 2:6).

The precise date of Christ's triumphal entrance into Jerusalem and of His crucifixion was given in Scripture centuries beforehand. Why not the date of His return? In fact, the date of the Second Coming can be determined, as we shall see, but not the date of the Rapture. And there is a difference spelled out in Scripture between these two events.

CHAPTER 14

A Most Amazing Prophecy

———————— ◇ ————————

> In the first year of Darius...I Daniel understood
> ...that [the Lord] would accomplish seventy years in the
> desolations of Jerusalem. Seventy weeks [of years] are
> determined upon thy people [Israel] and upon thy holy
> city [Jerusalem]...to bring in everlasting righteous-
> ness, and to seal up the vision and prophecy, and to anoint
> the most Holy [i.e., for Messiah's reign to begin]....
> From the going forth of the commandment to restore and
> to build Jerusalem unto the Messiah the Prince shall be
> seven weeks, and threescore and two weeks (69 weeks of
> years equals 483 years)...[Then] shall Messiah be cut
> off [i.e., slain] (Daniel 9:1,2,24-26).

Imagine setting the date for Christ's triumphal entry into
Jerusalem 500 years before the event and being accurate to the
very day! Daniel did that. In fact, this and his many other
prophecies are so astonishing that the book of Daniel has been
a chief target of determined skeptics for more than 100 years.
Somehow Daniel had to be exposed as a fraud.

Critics have insisted that Daniel's prophecies must have
been made after the fact. Otherwise, one would have to admit
that God, as Daniel claimed, had given him a personal revelation of future world events hundreds of years before they
happened. Such an admission would be intolerable for any
skeptic to be forced to make.

If the prophecies of Daniel could not be discredited, the cause of atheism would suffer an irreparable blow. Therefore, the book of Daniel has been examined and attacked relentlessly. It has withstood every assault and demonstrated conclusively that it is God's Word. Mankind is left with no excuse for rejecting the Bible and the message it brings.

Daniel's Many Remarkable Prophecies

To deal with the many prophecies of Daniel is beyond the scope of this writing. The four world empires—Babylonian, Medo-Persian, Grecian, and Roman—are foretold, including numerous details concerning each. For example, the succession of the Medo-Persian empire by the Grecian empire and the division of Alexander the Great's Grecian empire into four parts is prophesied (8:20-22). That division is again mentioned in 11:4. The next 16 verses give amazing details of the wars of Ptolemy (the Grecian general who took possession of Egypt after Alexander's death) and his successors against the Seleucids of Syria. That prophecy climaxed with details concerning Seleucid ruler Antiochus Epiphanes (11:21-36), a type of Antichrist. Incredibly, one reads history written in advance!

Daniel, too, in the two legs of the image, foretells the division of the Roman Empire into eastern and western kingdoms (Rome and Constantinople). In its feet and ten toes, signifying ten kings, the revival of the Roman Empire under ten heads in the last days is foretold. Daniel also prophesies the coming of the Antichrist and that he will rule over the revived Roman Empire (9:26). He further foretells that Christ (the "stone cut out without hands"—4:34,44,45), at His Second Coming, will destroy the Antichrist and this last world empire and establish His millennial reign.

Interesting as Daniel's many prophecies are, we must confine ourselves to those which pertain directly to the Messiah's first advent, to the Rapture, and to the Second Coming. So remarkable are this great prophet's insights concerning the coming Messiah that had Christ's critics understood only one verse in Daniel they would have been compelled to change their entire outlook toward Jesus of Nazareth.

As we have seen, Christ's contemporaries, from the rabbis to the disciples, were confused about the kingdom. They imagined that it was to be set up in their time. And because Jesus didn't liberate Israel from Rome and reign as king on David's throne but was crucified instead, even the disciples were convinced, at that point, that He couldn't possibly be the Messiah. John the Baptist suffered from the same misconception. From prison he voiced his doubts that Jesus was the Christ. The reason for those doubts sheds light upon a similar confusion today concerning the kingdom.

A Great Prophet—Yet Ignorant of Prophecy

It seems impossible that John the Baptist could have been so mistaken. This man had been chosen by God for a very special mission, and one which he had completed magnificently. John had even been "filled with the Holy Spirit" before his birth. While still in the womb, he had leaped with joy at Mary's announcement to her cousin Elizabeth that she was with child of the Holy Spirit. Though unborn, John had supernaturally reacted with joy to the news that Mary would give birth to the Messiah, the One whom John was to introduce to Israel.

John knew his mission, and as certainly as he knew his own identity he knew that Jesus was the Christ. When the Pharisees sent officers to ask whether he believed himself to be the Messiah, he "confessed, I am not the Christ. . . . I am the voice of one crying in the wilderness, make straight the way of the Lord" (John 1:19-24). In quoting from Isaiah 40:3, John claimed to be the fulfillment of that prophecy. He not only knew his mission by revelation from God, but he had visible and miraculous confirmation:

> And John bare record, saying, I saw the Spirit descending from heaven like a dove, and it abode upon him [as Christ came up out of the water after John baptized him]. And I knew him not [until that time]: but he [God] that sent me to baptize with water, the same said unto me, Upon whom thou shalt see the Spirit descending and remaining on him, the same is he. . . . And I saw, and bare record that this is the Son of God (John 1:32-34).

This fiery and fearless messenger of God not only knew that Jesus was the Messiah, he revealed insights unknown to Israel's religious leaders into what that meant: "Behold the Lamb of God, which taketh away the sin of the world" (John 1:29). In spite of his calling and knowledge, however, the day came when he sent two of his disciples to Jesus to ask Him, "Art thou he that should come? or look we for another?" (Luke 7:19).

What could possibly have brought this man, who was so in touch with and inspired of God, to the place where he would ask a question evidencing such unbelief? On this very occasion, though John had expressed great confusion, Jesus said, "There is not a greater prophet than John the Baptist" (Luke 7:28). Then how could he doubt that Jesus was the Messiah?

The answer is very simple. John suffered from the same misunderstanding as all the rest—that the Messiah would set up His kingdom and rule on David's throne the first time He came. That being the case (as he thought), why was he, John, in prison about to have his head cut off? If anyone deserved to reign in that kingdom, surely it was he, the one who had proclaimed Jesus to be the Messiah and had introduced Him to Israel. Yet Jesus seemed powerless to deliver him from King Herod, the very monarch who would have to be deposed for the Messiah to take David's throne. It didn't make sense—unless Jesus was not the Christ after all.

Had John known only one of the verses from Daniel to which we have referred, he would have understood that the time was not right for the Messiah to set up His kingdom. That verse also presents one of the prophecies whereby we know for certain that the Roman Empire must be revived. It is the culmination of Daniel's interpretation of Nebuchadnezzar's dream about the strange image with a "head of fine gold, his breast and his arms of silver, his belly and his thighs of brass, and his legs of iron, his feet [with ten toes representing ten kings] part of iron and part of clay" (Daniel 2:31-33).

In the Days of Those Kings

Inspired of God, Daniel explained that the four parts of the image, each of a different substance, represented four world kingdoms:

> Thou, O king [Nebuchadnezzar] . . . art this head of gold. And after thee shall arise another kingdom [Medo-Persian] inferior to thee, and another third kingdom [Grecian] of brass, which shall bear rule over all the earth. And the fourth kingdom [Roman] shall be strong as iron (Daniel 2:37-40).

We see these four world kingdoms again in chapter 7, where further details about each of them are given. There they are depicted as four beasts. The fourth (Roman) has ten horns and we are told what they signify: "The ten horns out of this kingdom are ten kings that shall arise" (Daniel 7:24). That these ten kings pertain to the future revived Roman Empire is evident from the fact that no such division of that empire ever occurred in the past.

The interpretation that the ten toes of the image signify ten kings yet to arise is also clear from the explanation Daniel gives in his interpretation of the image in chapter 2. Finally, he declares in that key verse (2:44): "And in the days of these kings [represented by the ten toes] shall the God of heaven set up a kingdom, which shall never be destroyed: and [it] . . . shall break in pieces and consume all these kingdoms, and it shall stand forever."

Inasmuch as the Roman Empire was never ruled by ten kings or co-emperors, it must be revived under ten heads for this prophecy to be fulfilled. Certainly there were not ten kings ruling the empire in the days of Jesus. Therefore, on the basis of this one verse, the rabbis, the disciples, and so great a prophet as John the Baptist should have known that it was not time for the Messiah to set up His kingdom. Daniel 2:44 is very explicit that the millennial kingdom will not be established except "in the days of these kings." No reasonable interpretation can be adopted to change that simple fact.

That the Roman Empire, as already noted, was divided into two segments, as depicted by the two legs of the image, is a matter of history. The division was also religious and continues to manifest itself to this day in the separation between Roman Catholicism and Eastern Orthodoxy. This breach will more than likely not be healed until the Antichrist inaugurates his new world religion. That we are, however, already moving rapidly in that direction seems evident. It is also clear from numerous Scriptures (which we'll consider later) that religion will play as important a role in the revived Roman Empire as it did in the ancient one. The close partnership between the popes and emperors will of necessity have its parallels in the key role to be played by the Roman pontiff in assisting the Antichrist in his reign.

Seventy Years and Seventy Weeks

Verse 26, quoted from Daniel 9 at the beginning of this chapter, gives another reason why the Messiah would not set up His kingdom the first time He came to earth: "And after threescore and two weeks [adding that to the previous 7 makes 69 times 7 equals 483 years from the command to rebuild Jerusalem] shall Messiah be cut off [i.e., slain]." So Daniel, too, like David, Isaiah, and Zechariah indicated in plain language that Messiah would be killed the first time He came. There was no excuse for anyone in Christ's day who was at all familiar with the Scriptures to misunderstand this oft-repeated prophecy.

Let us take a closer look at these verses. The ninth chapter of Daniel is one of the most amazing passages in Scripture. It begins with Daniel gaining insight (from reading the prophecy of Jeremiah) into a very precise and important date that was immediately on Israel's horizon. The Babylonian captivity was to last exactly 70 years. After that period had been fulfilled, the Jews would be free to return to their land. This was good news indeed for the captives!

The reason for this precise period of 70 years was no mystery. God had made a covenant with Israel, a binding contract that carried a penalty for its violation. Yahweh had done His part, but Israel had failed to fulfill her obligation.

Therefore God's judgment came upon her as He had warned it would from the beginning. He had been patient, but at last the time for judgment had come:

> And the Lord hath sent unto you all his servants the prophets, rising early and sending them; but ye have not hearkened, nor inclined your ear to hear. They said, Turn ye again now every one from his evil way . . . and dwell in the land that the Lord hath given unto you. . . . Yet ye have not hearkened unto me, saith the Lord; that ye might provoke me to anger. . . . Therefore . . . this whole land shall be a desolation [and ye] shall serve the king of Babylon seventy years. And when seventy years are accomplished, I will punish the king of Babylon (Jeremiah 25:4-14).

What had Israel violated? When God first brought the descendants of Abraham, Isaac, and Jacob (Israel) into the promised land, He instructed them: "Six years thou shalt sow thy field . . . but in the seventh year shall be a sabbath of rest unto the land, a sabbath for the Lord: thou shalt neither sow thy field nor prune thy vineyard" (Leviticus 25:1-7). Every seventh year all Hebrew slaves were also to be released and debts owed by Hebrews to one another were to be forgiven. (Exodus 21:2; Deuteronomy 15:12) Jeremiah reminded his people even as the invading armies of Nebuchadnezzar were in the process of executing God's retribution:

> Thus saith the Lord, the God of Israel; I made a covenant with your fathers in the day that I brought them forth out of the land of Egypt, out of the house of bondage, saying, . . . let ye go every man his brother an Hebrew, which hath been sold unto thee . . . when he hath served thee six years, thou shalt let him go free from thee: but your fathers hearkened not unto me, neither inclined their ear (Jeremiah 34:13,14).

For 490 years Israel had failed to obey these ordinances of the seventh-year sabbath. She had neither let the Hebrew slaves go free nor allowed the land to lie fallow. Thus, she owed God 70 years (490 divided by 7) of sabbaths that she had failed to keep. With the Babylonian captivity came Israel's bitter restitution. For 70 years the Jews would themselves be slaves, and the land would enjoy the 70 sabbaths that were owing to God.

Prophecy Is Like the Weather

Upon learning the reason for the Babylonian captivity and how long it would last, Daniel does something that many find strange today. He doesn't "claim" this promise. No "positive confession" from him! Nor does he immediately send word to the captives that their sentence is about to end and that they will soon be on their way home and all they need to do is "claim their blessing." Instead, he addresses God in earnest prayer, confessing the sins of his people and calling upon God to restore them to their land.

Why ask God to do what He has already said He would? Yet isn't that what prayer is all about? It isn't so simple as "claiming" a promise. For God's promises to be fulfilled, we must call upon Him to do so and meet the required conditions. Ask Him to do what He has promised? What else can we ask? Surely we dare not ask God in prayer to do anything that is against His will! Yet how many Christians attempt to use prayer to persuade God to fulfill their own desires!

Daniel's reaction was so unlike what we see among Christians in our time. Judging from today's attitudes, one could say of prophecy what Mark Twain used to say of the weather: "Everyone talks about it but nobody does anything about it!" The purpose of prophecy is not only to tell us in advance what will happen, but to move our hearts to prayer, repentance, and readiness to play our part in its fulfillment.

An important part of the role we are to play is to engage in earnest prayer for God to fulfill in our day the prophecies He has made. Especially we should be in prayer for the return of Christ. "And the Spirit and the bride say, Come. . . . Surely I come quickly. Even so, come, Lord Jesus" (Revelation 22:17,20).

Four Hundred and Ninety Years Once Again

While Daniel is praying, God sends the angel Gabriel to inform him of something that he could not have known from Jeremiah's prophecy: Divine judgment upon Israel will not be complete at the end of the 70 years. The 490 years of disobedience will be paid for in an additional way. That length of time must be endured once more by Israel before the Messiah will set up His kingdom.

Gabriel announced to Daniel that another period of precisely 490 years (70 weeks of years) lies ahead for the people of Israel and for Jerusalem before Messiah will ascend to David's throne. It will include "the time of Jacob's trouble" (Jeremiah 30:7), the climax of God's judgment upon Israel immediately preceding the Second Coming. Thus an understanding of these 70 weeks of years is essential if we are to gain insight into the timing for the Rapture and the Second Coming.

To interpret this prophecy correctly, we must not forget that the 70 weeks of years are specifically stated to be "determined upon thy people [Israel] and upon thy holy city [Jerusalem]." To attempt to apply this 490-year period in any other way than that which is so plainly stated—to the Church, for example—would do offense both to the Bible and common sense.

The Church did not come into existence until 483 of the 490 years had already passed. Thus this period of time and this prophecy could not possibly have applied to the Church. The end of the 490-year period would have come a mere seven years into the Church's history had the last week run its course immediately following completion of the 69 weeks which ended with Christ's prophesied crucifixion. By that reckoning, the 490 years ended more than 1900 years ago and could have no more significance for Israel today than for the Church. The mathematics seem quite simple. Yet Christ did not ascend to David's throne at His first advent, nor has He returned to do so. Nor did the next seven years following Christ's ascension to heaven see the culmination of the prophecies that were to be completed in the last week.

The 490 years could not possibly have ended without the Messiah establishing His millennial kingdom. If it has ended, then a major part of Bible prophecy has been proved false. No Christian can accept that for a moment; not because our faith in the Bible is blind, but because we have carefully examined it and know it to be the infallible Word of God. There can be no mistakes or failed prophecies. We must, therefore, seek another interpretation.

Inasmuch as the relevant prophecies have not been fulfilled, we can only conclude that the 490 years (70 weeks of years), for some reason, have not yet ended. Clearly this important prophetic period was interrupted after Christ's death so that the last week (of years) has yet to run its course. In fact, Daniel does divide the 70 weeks into segments: "From the commandment to restore and to build Jerusalem unto the Messiah the Prince shall be seven weeks, and threescore and two weeks . . . and after threescore and two weeks shall Messiah be cut off." The last week of the 70 is left hanging.

Establishing a Precise Date

So the 70 weeks are divided as follows: 7 weeks, 62 weeks, and 1 week. Why? The first 7 weeks of years (49) is most likely distinguished from the rest because it was that exact period of time (from the beginning of the 70 weeks) until Malachi, in 397 B.C., penned the last of the Old Testament. To understand the 62 weeks (which added to the 7 makes 69) and the one week remaining, it is necessary to go back to the time when these 70 weeks began.

Daniel is very specific. The 70 weeks (490 years) was to be measured "from the going forth of the commandment to restore and to build Jerusalem." So this period begins, not with the rebuilding of the *temple* under Zerubbabel, but from the later authorization Nehemiah received to rebuild *Jerusalem*. The Bible itself establishes for us with exactitude this most important date.

Nehemiah was in the service of King Artaxerxes in the winter palace of the Persian monarchs at Shushan. This was the same place where Daniel received one of his most important visions (8:2). The reconstruction of the temple had been completed about 70 years before, yet nothing had been done to rebuild the city. The people living in its ruins were poor and few in number. Concerned for his homeland, Nehemiah asked some friends who had just returned from Jerusalem how the Jews were faring there. We pick up the story in his own words:

> And I asked them concerning the Jews . . . and concerning Jerusalem. And they said unto me, The remnant that are left of the captivity there in the province are in great affliction and reproach: the wall of Jerusalem also is broken down, and the gates thereof are burned with fire. And when I heard these words, I sat down and wept, and mourned certain days, and fasted, and prayed before the God of heaven (Nehemiah 1:2-4).

Nehemiah determines to petition the king for authorization to rebuild Jerusalem. And he asks God to give him favor with the king to grant this request. That prayer was answered. Nehemiah even tells us precisely when the authorization was granted and thereby gives us the date we need to apply Daniel's prophecy:

> And it came to pass in the month Nisan, in the twentieth year of Artaxerxes the king . . . I said unto the king, If it please the king . . . that thou wouldest send me unto Judah, unto the city of my fathers' sepulchres, that I may build it. . . . And the king granted me (Nehemiah 2:1-8).

There was more than one Artaxerxes, but only one whose monarchy exceeded 20 years. He was Artaxerxes Longimanus and his reign began in 465 B.C. Thus the twentieth year of his rule would have been during 445 B.C. That Nehemiah did not specify another day in the month indicates, as was the custom, that he was referring to the first day. Here, then, is the date: Nisan 1, 445 B.C. Counting 483 years (69 times 7) of 360 days each, the Hebrew and Babylonian calendar of that time (173,880 days), from that date brings us exactly to April 6, A.D. 32. That was the very day when Jesus made His triumphal entry into Jerusalem!

For the investigation of the facts pertaining to both dates and for the calculations of the time elapsing between them we are indebted to Sir Robert Anderson. The data is given in detail in his book, *The Coming Prince*. As head of the criminal investigation division of Scotland Yard, Anderson was certainly a man well-qualified to conduct an accurate investigation into this prophecy.

What an incredible prophecy! The God who watches over history declared 500 years in advance not only that a specific event would occur but that it would happen on a particular day! Try to imagine the many related circumstances and happenings which also had to fit into place! That Daniel foretold 500 years in advance the precise day when Christ would make His triumphal entry into Jerusalem has been fully established. That amazing fact requires the most stubborn skeptic to become a believer. No honest person can deny the evidence.

When Stones Would Cry Out

Why would Daniel's statement "unto the Messiah the Prince" signify Christ's entry into Jerusalem? Why not His birth? There are a number of reasons. His birth was known to very few. Certainly there was no announcement to Israel that the Messiah had been born. It was too soon for that. Even during His public ministry, Christ told His disciples not to reveal that He was the Messiah (Matthew 16:20). The reason for the prohibition is obvious. The Messiah could only be revealed to Israel on the precise day foretold by Daniel and in the manner described by the prophet Zechariah.

Whether Jesus was the Messiah would not be established by a majority vote on the part of the Jews. Nor would it be by the persuasiveness of His disciples. The Old Testament prophecies had to be fulfilled to the letter. On no other basis was the Messiah to be identified. Therefore, the Messiah could not be revealed until the appropriate time and in the manner prophesied. Had Christ allowed His disciples to proclaim Him as the Messiah before that time, it would have been proof that He was in fact not the Messiah!

By the time this special day, April 6, A.D. 32, arrived Christ had fulfilled many of the necessary messianic prophecies. All that remained was the triumphal entry into Jerusalem foretold by Zechariah, to be followed by the cleansing of the temple, His betrayal, crucifixion, and resurrection. Those climactic events would occur in that very week, as Christ alone knew.

As Jesus rode into Jerusalem on a borrowed donkey—something He had never done before—hundreds, perhaps even thousands, of His disciples lined the small, winding road leading down from the Mount of Olives. It was a spontaneous yet prophesied demonstration. Throwing out their clothes for the beast to walk upon, the enthusiasts waved palm branches over Christ's head and hailed Him as the Messiah. To the Pharisees, the cries of the mob were blasphemous.

Never before had Christ been greeted publicly by a huge crowd in this manner. Their unlikely response to His entrance into Jerusalem, not on a white horse and brandishing a flashing sword but on this humble beast, was itself the fulfillment of prophecy: "Rejoice greatly, O daughter of Zion; shout, O daughter of Jerusalem: behold, thy King cometh unto thee: he is just, and having salvation; lowly, and riding upon an ass" (Zechariah 9:9).

Amazingly, the crowd, without knowing it, was doing exactly what Zechariah had foretold. Very likely no one present that day knew Zechariah's prophecy, much less related it to Jesus and what was happening. The Pharisees were scandalized that the people were calling Him the Son of David, which meant the Messiah. They ordered Jesus to rebuke His disciples, to which He replied: "I tell you that, if these should hold their peace, the stones would immediately cry out" (Luke 19:40). This was the "coming of the Messiah the Prince" (Daniel 9:25) on the precise day Daniel had prophesied and in the very manner Zechariah had foretold! Those prophecies were being fulfilled to the letter!

A Passover plot? How much money would it have taken to pay this entire multitude to go through these motions! Had Christ arranged for His friend Lazarus to die and thereby bring Him back to Jerusalem just in time for this remarkable occasion? Following the precise timing of the events of the last few days before the crucifixion as given to us in the Gospels is fascinating.

After messengers came telling Jesus that His good friend Lazarus was sick, "He abode two days still in the same place" (John 11:6) before going to Bethany. It would be largely in response to the resurrection of Lazarus that the crowds would line the approach to Jerusalem a few days later to hail Jesus openly for the first (and last) time as the Messiah. The exact day for that climactic event to occur was of the utmost importance.

So the Bible does set dates after all. The precise day on which the Messiah would reveal Himself to Israel and then be rejected and slain by His own people is only one of the specific dates given in Scripture. As we have already noted, the exact date of the Second Coming can be known as well.

CHAPTER 15

Christ, the Passover Lamb

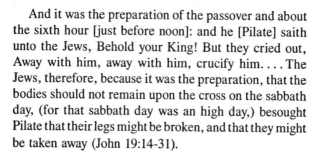

> And it was the preparation of the passover and about the sixth hour [just before noon]: and he [Pilate] saith unto the Jews, Behold your King! But they cried out, Away with him, away with him, crucify him. . . . The Jews, therefore, because it was the preparation, that the bodies should not remain upon the cross on the sabbath day, (for that sabbath day was an high day,) besought Pilate that their legs might be broken, and that they might be taken away (John 19:14-31).

Seeing the multitudes hail Jesus as the long-promised Messiah that first Palm Sunday, and observing His growing popularity over the next few days, who would have imagined that before the week was over He would be hanging on a cross outside Jerusalem! The Pharisees didn't think so. They were in despair of ever stopping this One from capturing the hearts of all Israel. Nor could the disciples have imagined the turn of events. They were on a high of enthusiasm, anticipating their Master's soon ascension to David's throne and their reign beside Him. The prophets, however, knew what would happen. They had foretold it all in detail hundreds of years in advance.

We must pause a moment to contemplate in wonder the unerring reliability of God's Holy Word. Not a phrase is unimportant; not a word that is essential is left out. History is recorded with flawless accuracy before it happens.

Seventy weeks of years were prophesied by Daniel upon the people of Israel and their holy city, Jerusalem. Let us take a closer look at the meticulous precision with which specific prophecies were fulfilled at the climax of the 69 weeks. One can only stand in awe. Again we are reminded that prophecies pertaining to the Rapture and Second Coming will be fulfilled with equal perfection.

Precisely 69 weeks of years (483 years) to the very day after the command (Nisan 1, 445 B.C.) to rebuild the Jewish capital from the ruins left by Nebuchadnezzar's army, Messiah the Prince made His historic entrance into Jerusalem! It was the very day which Daniel had foretold—and in the manner which Zechariah had prophesied.

Christ was not mounted on a prancing white horse and waving a flashing sword, as the people imagined their liberating Messiah, but upon a donkey. What a strange way for King David's successor to present Himself; yet it was exactly as the prophet Zechariah had foreseen (9:9). In fulfillment of that same prophecy by Zechariah ("rejoice . . . [and] shout, O daughter of Jerusalem")—and in confirmation of Daniel's prophecy—He was hailed by the multitudes as Messiah the Prince. They had never acclaimed Him in this manner before, but now they did so on the very day prophesied!

As we have noted, it was Sunday, April 6, A.D. 32. Depending on the date it falls each year in our calendar, that day is now celebrated as Palm Sunday. More significantly, however, it was Nisan 10! Nisan 10? Yes, the very day that the Passover lamb was taken out of the flock (Exodus 12:3-6) and kept for four days under observation to be certain that it was unblemished! Christ was not only presenting Himself to Israel as her king, but as the sacrificial Lamb of God who, rejected by His own, would pay the debt for the sins of the world!

For some time Jesus had been avoiding Jerusalem, because the rabbis were seeking to take Him and kill Him. Now, however, He remained in the vicinity at night and returned to Jerusalem each day. It was as though He, "the Lamb of God" (John 1:29), were placing Himself on display before Israel during those particular four days when all over Israel the Passover lambs, set apart, were being inspected prior to being sacrificed.

The following Wednesday night, betrayed by Judas Iscariot in fulfillment of Scripture as we have already noted, Christ was arrested and taken secretly to the palace of Caiaphas, the high priest. That was Nisan 14, the day of "preparation" when the Passover lamb, after the days of observation to make certain that it was "without blemish" (Exodus 12:5), had to be slain. In A.D. 32, that special day began at sunset Wednesday and ended at sunset Thursday.

In the few hours before sunset Thursday—"in the evening" of Nisan 14—the Passover lambs would be slain all over Israel. *The* Passover Lamb would be slain as well, just as Moses had foretold in that remarkable prophecy (Exodus 12:6). Daniel, too, had declared: "Messiah [shall] be cut off, but not for himself" (9:26). All the pieces were coming together. It was all happening exactly as the God of prophecy, through His prophets, had said it would.

Peter's Failure, Christ's Deity

A sham trial before the Sanhedrin, with hastily called false witnesses, was convened sometime after midnight. Peter, who had timidly followed into the palace at a distance, saw and heard it all with stunned disbelief. It was just before the time of cock crowing that infamous Thursday morning, Nisan 14, and by the Julian calendar, April 10, A.D. 32.

Some of the servants insisted that Peter, because of his Galilean accent, must be a disciple of Christ, and he twice denied that accusation. A relative of the man whose ear Peter had cut off claimed to have seen the bumbling swordsman in the Garden with Jesus. Fearing for his own life, Peter, who had boasted that he would die rather than deny his Lord, "began to curse and to swear, saying, I know not the man. And immediately a cock crowed" (Matthew 26:69-74)—exactly as Jesus had said it would happen.

Christ's revelation that He would be betrayed by Judas and His warning to Peter that he would betray Him three times before the crowing of the roosters had been intended as a final revelation to His disciples of His deity. At the last supper, when Jesus had made these declarations, He had added this significant statement: "Now I tell you [this] before it come [to pass], that, when it is come to pass, ye may believe that I am *he*" (John 13:19). The word "he" is in italics and does not appear in the original. Jesus was declaring once again to His disciples that He was Yahweh, the I AM of Israel—and the way He did so is most interesting.

We have noted earlier that Yahweh, the I AM, identifies Himself as the God of prophecy, the One who tells what is going to happen beforehand and watches over history to make certain that it comes to pass (Isaiah 46:9,10). In those last intimate moments with His own before His death, Christ identified Himself in the same way, attesting that He foretold the future for the same reason: "that ye may believe that I AM."

Here was final evidence to support their faith in Him in spite of His crucifixion. Unfortunately, the disciples did not comprehend until later, when He appeared to them after His resurrection and "opened their understanding, that they might understand the scriptures" (Luke 24:45). Seeing Christ led away, bound and apparently helpless, had shattered their faith in Him because they did not know what the prophets had declared concerning the Messiah. How equally important it is for us today to know what the prophets have said concerning His return!

A Departed Scepter and the Manner of Death

The first pale fingers of dawn were just beginning to creep across the Judean hills. The sun would soon set ablaze the glittering golden pinnacle atop the great white dome of Herod's temple. The sham trial had ended with Christ having been secretly and unlawfully condemned to death by the Sanhedrin. Israel's religious leaders did not, however, have the power to enforce the death penalty. Moreover, they wanted Rome to be involved in case of a backlash from the mobs that were following this Jesus. Again God's prophets had told the story in advance.

As soon as Pilate, the Roman governor, returned from his early morning bath he was notified of the emergency. Hurriedly taken down side streets, the prisoner was received into the citadel at "the third hour" (Mark 15:25), about 9:00 A.M. Rumors began to fly, started by those who had caught a glimpse of Jesus through the surrounding cordons of soldiers. Rapidly swelling in numbers, an expectant crowd milled about between Pilate's castle and the temple.

The prisoner was unknown to the Roman governor. Certainly He was not on the empire's most wanted list. "Take ye him and judge him according to your law," was Pilate's rebuke to the rabbis for wasting his time. "If he were not a malefactor," they insisted, "we would not have delivered him up unto thee.... It is not lawful for us to put any man to death" (John 18:28-32). That right of kings had been taken from them 25 years earlier by the Romans.

Jacob had prophesied, "The scepter shall not depart from Judah, nor a lawgiver from between his feet, until Shiloh [Messiah] come" (Genesis 49:10). After the scepter departed about A.D. 7 it was forever too late for the Messiah to arrive on the scene. Having rejected Jesus, who was born just in time, the Jews await another Messiah in vain. Jacob's prophecy will not allow it. As a result of their rejection of Christ, they will one day embrace Antichrist.

That the Jews could no longer execute criminals meant that the manner of Christ's death would also fulfill Scripture. Only the Roman authorities could exact the death penalty. Had the Jews killed Him, as they had attempted to do on several occasions, it would have been by stoning. But the Scriptures, long before the Roman Empire had come into existence, had declared that the Messiah would be crucified—the Roman form of execution. And so it would be.

Crucify Him!

The machinery of mock justice did its dishonorable work swiftly. The executions of malefactors, particularly cult leaders as popular as this Jesus of Nazareth, were always dangerous events. Anything could set off a riot, particularly on a religious holiday. The Jews were fanatics when it came to their religion.

This was a very special day in Israel, the preparation of the Passover which was to be eaten that night. Jerusalem was crowded and in a state of great excitement. Pilate, knowing the value of public relations, and having no interest in either condemning or releasing Jesus, decided to consult his ever-volatile citizens and let them decide the prisoner's fate.

Incited by the Pharisees, the bloodthirsty mob which always gathered to witness the spectacle of crucifixion turned unexpectedly against the One who had miraculously healed and fed so many of them. Many of those who had waved palm branches and hailed Him as their Messiah four days earlier now joined in the swelling cry: "Crucify him! Crucify him!" The horrifying chant reverberated from the cold stones of the castle and echoed across the temple mount, bringing those who heard it on the run to join the spectacle.

Anxious to curry the favor of these often-unruly subjects he was supposed to keep in order, Pilate released the murderer, Barabbas, and delivered Jesus to his soldiers to do their worst. The prisoner had now been officialy condemned to death by the Roman civil authority. Everything was legal. Rome was satisfied and so were the rabbis. The rabble continued to chant its thirst for blood.

Only the governor felt ill at ease with the obvious injustice. To absolve himself personally, Pilate publicly and literally, in a basin of water, washed his hands of the whole affair. Little did he know that nothing but the blood of that innocent Victim and the admission of his own guilt could cleanse those awful stains. Dante depicted him washing his hands forever in hell. Flushed with its own power, the mob, little realizing what it was saying, shouted contemptuously: "His blood be on us and on our children" (Matthew 27:25).

The Sacrifice for Sin

Shortly before noon the soldiers had finished their vicious, depraved sport. Jesus, scourged almost into unconsciousness and beaten about the face until he was nearly unrecognizable, was led through the frenzied, screaming crowd out of the city to "the place of the skull." A few women whose lives He had touched pushed their way along with the stampeding throng, trying to keep Him in view and weeping loudly. Jesus turned to them and said,

> Daughters of Jerusalem, weep not for me, but weep for yourselves, and for your children. For, behold, the days are coming, in the which they shall . . . say to the mountains, Fall on us; and to the hills, Cover us (Luke 23:28-31).

John would later elaborate further on that prophecy in the account of his remarkable vision of the future (Revelation 6:15-17).

It was not far to the place of public execution just outside the city wall. The site was deliberately located beside a major thoroughfare where passersby could view the hanging, writhing figures and take warning. By high noon, the One whom Jerusalem, in fulfillment of specific prophecy, had the previous Sunday hailed as its long-awaited Messiah and now rejected was hanging naked, in shame and agony, on the center cross between two thieves. Man had crucified his Creator! Angels recoiled in horror and the sun hid its face.

Alone, forsaken even of God (Mark 15:34) while He finished the work which only He could do, Christ "was made sin for us" (2 Corinthians 5:21). The spotless Lamb of God was being sacrificed for the sins of the world. Here was the redemptive act toward which all the sin offerings in the Old Testament had pointed.

The physical shame and agony were eclipsed by the awful burden of guilt and judgment that was laid upon Him as He, with no one who could help or even pity, endured the full penalty that we owed but could not pay to Infinite Justice. The next three hours of that infamous yet grace-abounding and redemptive Thursday afternoon, the sun was obscured to hide Him from human eye. Darkness hung over Jerusalem like a shroud (Matthew 27:45) as God "laid on him the iniquity of us all" (Isaiah 53:6).

A Day and Date Foretold

The day and year of Christ's crucifixion is of the utmost importance. It is not a matter of speculation. The precise date and time as well as the manner of His death had to be exactly as prophesied. Let us go back to take another look at how it occurred.

The rabbis had been plotting to take him for months. As the Passover drew near, however, they agreed among themselves to do nothing until the high holidays of the Feast of Unleavened Bread came to an end. In spite of their decision to the contrary, Christ would be taken on the feast day when the Passover was prepared, for so the prophets had declared.

The rabbis had to be extremely careful, because the people were solidly with Jesus. The raising of Lazarus from the dead a few days earlier had excited Jerusalem. That undeniable miracle was one of the major reasons so many had lined the approach to the holy city and hailed Jesus as the Messiah (John 12:17-19). The mob would not tolerate any threatening move against Him. It would have been particularly dangerous to attempt to apprehend Him during the holidays when Jerusalem was packed with pilgrims and religious feelings were running high. So the council had wisely decided to delay His arrest: "Not on the feast day [passover], lest there be an uproar among the people" (Matthew 26:5), had been the verdict.

Yet He must be crucified on that very feast day, and in this specific year, A.D. 32, for prophecy to be fulfilled. And so it would be. Though He had for some time been avoiding Jerusalem, now Christ, oddly enough, as we have noted, was presenting Himself there daily. Here was a rare chance, and Judas, who had been hoping for such an opportunity, exploited it. The rabbis had been only too willing to change their minds when the traitor explained his strategy of taking Jesus in an isolated area late at night in the absence of the admiring crowds that surrounded Him during the day.

"Christ Our Passover Is Slain for Us"

Here was the order of events. Wednesday at sunset began Nisan 14. This entire 24-hour period ending the following day, Thursday, at sunset, was traditionally also called the first day of unleavened bread. This was the day the Passover lamb was to be slain. That important event had to occur "in the evening" of Nisan 14, which was a short time before sunset on Thursday. The Passover meal itself would follow that night, the beginning of Nisan 15, which also began the Feast of Unleavened Bread. The first day and last day of that annual feast were high sabbaths during which no work could be done.

Shortly after sunset at the beginning of Nisan 14, the disciples had begun to prepare the upper room for the Passover to be eaten there the *following night*. It would only be natural for them, while preparing this room, to eat their pre-Passover supper there as well. In fact, it turned out to be the "last supper" with their Lord, though they did not suspect it would be at the time. The next night, when the disciples had thought they would be taking the Passover together in that same room, Christ's body would be in the grave.

Then why did Christ, when they sat down together that Wednesday night, say, "I have desired to eat this passover with you before I suffer" (Luke 22:15)? The disciples no doubt thought He was referring to the following night, when the preparations would have been completed and the Passover actually celebrated. In fact, Jesus was introducing a new "Passover feast" which would be celebrated weekly instead of annually—and not looking back to the exodus from Egypt but in remembrance of His sacrifice upon the cross.

Thereafter, each Sunday, the day of His resurrection, the disciples would take bread and break and eat it (Acts 20:7; 1 Corinthians 16:2) as a symbol of His body, and share the cup as a symbol of His blood. This they would do in remembrance of the sacrifice of His body and blood for the sins of the world. Today, we, too, continue with this remembrance "until he come" (1 Corinthians 11:26).

Jesus had reasons for beginning the Passover celebration the night before—reasons which the disciples couldn't understand. As we have already noted, to fulfill both Old Testament type and prophecy, Christ's crucifixion had to take place at the very time when the paschal lamb was being killed by households throughout Israel and roasted for eating at the Passover celebration that night. In fact, that was exactly when He died, committing His Spirit into His Father's hands.

No Excuse for Unbelief

There can be no doubt that Christ was the fulfillment of the Passover lamb. Scripture tells us: "Purge out, therefore, the old leaven. . . . For even Christ our passover is sacrificed for us" (1 Corinthians 5:7). Let us summarize what we have noted concerning the celebration of the Passover and Christ's relationship thereto.

The lamb was taken from the flock on the tenth of Nisan and observed until the fourteenth to be certain it was without blemish. On that day it was killed between 3 P.M. and 6 P.M., then roasted and eaten that night (Exodus 12:1-8). As we have noted, Nisan 10 in A.D. 32 fell on Sunday, April 6, the day Jesus was hailed as the Messiah, and fourteenth Nisan came on Thursday, April 10. During those four special days, Jesus deliberately remained in Jerusalem under close observation by Israel, even as the Passover lamb was being inspected to make certain that it was without blemish.

To fulfill the Old Testament type, the Messiah had to be crucified when the Passover lamb was slain. And so it happened. There was a supernatural darkness from noon until 3 P.M. while Jesus hung on the cross. It was therefore shortly after 3 P.M., "in the evening" of Nisan 14, *when the Passover lambs were being slain all over Israel*, that Christ "cried with a loud voice, Father, into thy hands I commend my spirit: and having said thus, he gave up the ghost" (Luke 23:46).

He did not weakly expire as His life ebbed away, but He "cried with a loud voice." For He had said, "I lay down my life, that I might take it again. No man taketh it from me, I lay it down of myself. I have power to lay it down, and I have power to take it again" (John 10:17,18). When His work was finished upon the cross, He cried in triumph, "It is finished" (Matthew 27:50; John 19:30). The debt demanded by God's justice had been paid in full.

In addition to Old Testament type, prophecy also required Him to die at that time. On that first Passover in Egypt, Moses, in explaining the sacrifice of the many Passover lambs, "a lamb for [each] house" (Exodus 12:3), made what must have seemed a very strange statement: "And ye shall keep *it* up until the fourteenth day of the same month: and the whole assembly of the congregation of Israel shall kill *it* in the evening" (Exodus 12:6). Of course not just one but thousands of lambs were slain that day, yet Moses referred to "it."

Here was a prophecy, clearly stated but not understood by Israel, that one day there would be one lamb, the "Lamb of God" (John 1:29), who would be the fulfillment of the Passover. Moreover, this one Lamb would be sacrificed by the whole assembly of Israel—and for the sins of the world.

And so it happened, on the very day and at the very hour foretold by Moses, Daniel, and Zechariah. Those who reject Jesus Christ as Messiah and Savior do so in the face of such overwhelming evidence that they are without excuse.

CHAPTER 16

Forget "Good Friday"

———————— ◇ ————————

> Now before the feast of the Passover . . . supper being
> ended . . . the Jews, therefore, because it was the prepa-
> ration, that the bodies should not remain upon the cross
> on the sabbath day (for that sabbath day was an high day)
> (John 13:1,2; 19:31).

> As it began to dawn toward the first day of the week
> . . . there was a great earthquake: for the angel of the
> Lord . . . rolled back the stone from the door [of the
> sepulcher] and sat upon it (Matthew 28:1,2).

Read superficially, the Scripture account of those important
days from Nisan 10–14 seems to contradict itself. Unless one
has a clear understanding of events, Matthew, Mark, and Luke
seem to indicate that Christ kept the Passover that last night
with His disciples:

> Now the first day of the feast of unleavened bread the
> disciples came to Jesus, saying unto him, Where wilt
> thou that we prepare for thee to eat the Passover. And he
> said, Go into the city to such a man, and say unto him,
> The Master saith, My time is at hand; I will keep the
> Passover at thy house with my disciples. And the dis-
> ciples did as Jesus had appointed them; and they made
> ready the Passover. Now when the even was come, he sat
> down with the twelve" (Matthew 26:17-20; Mark 14:
> 12-17; Luke 22:7-15).

Of course, if Christ and His disciples kept the Passover the night of His betrayal and arrest, then the Passover lamb must have already been slain that afternoon. If that were the case, then His death the following afternoon did not coincide with the killing of the Passover lambs. Yet we know it had to, and it did.

The verses above need some explanation. For example, "evening" sometimes means late afternoon and at other times it means early night. And as we have already mentioned and explain later in more detail, although the Feast of Unleavened Bread began on Nisan 15 when the Passover lamb was eaten, Nisan 14, when the Passover was prepared and the lamb slain was also a time of unleavened bread.

Verses which are not clear need to be understood in harmony with those which are clear. And we do have many very plain statements that the Passover lambs were slain the afternoon following the "last supper," and at the time of the crucifixion. All of the Gospels agree in this regard.

When Was the "Last Supper" and the Crucifixion?

Mark says, "Now when the even [i.e., sunset was approaching] was come [after Christ had died], because it was the preparation [of the Passover lamb], that is, the day before the sabbath [the first day of the Feast of Unleavened Bread, which began at sunset after the Passover lamb had been slain], Joseph of Arimathaea ... went in boldly unto Pilate, and craved the body of Jesus" (15:42,43). Luke agrees: "And that day was the preparation, and the [special] sabbath drew on" (23:54). John gives even more detail:

> Then led they [the rabbis] Jesus from Caiaphas unto the [Roman] hall of judgment ... and they themselves went not into the judgment hall, lest they should be defiled; but that they might eat the Passover [so it hadn't been eaten as yet]. And it was the preparation of the Passover. ... The Jews therefore, because it was the preparation, that the bodies should not remain upon the

cross on the sabbath day (for that sabbath day was an
high day [i.e., the first day of the Feast of Unleavened
Bread]), besought Pilate that their legs might be broken,
and that they might be taken away (John 18:28; 19:14,31).

So, as we noted in the last chapter, the Passover lambs were
indeed being slain at the very time that Christ, the Lamb of
God who fulfilled all of the relevant Old Testament types and
prophecies, died on the cross. How, then, could Christ have
"taken the Passover" with His disciples the night before? He
didn't. The Last Supper did indeed occur the night before the
crucifixion, but it was not the Passover. This often overlooked
fact is clear from John's account, which is a bit more precise.

While the other gospels refer to "the sabbath" drawing
nigh, John alone explains that the sabbath which began at
sunset the day Christ was crucified "was a high day." In other
words, it was not the ordinary weekly sabbath which always
began Friday at sunset. It was, in fact, the first day of the Feast
of Unleavened Bread (the fifteenth of Nisan), of which the first
and last days were special sabbaths during which no work was
to be done (Exodus 12:14-16).

John also clarifies the fact that the "last supper" was not the
Passover: "Now *before* the feast of the Passover, when Jesus
knew that his hour was come . . . supper being ended, the devil
having now put into the heart of Judas Iscariot . . . to betray
him." So the "last supper" actually took place *the night before*
the Passover. How could it have taken place both "the first day
of unleavened bread" and "*before* the feast of the Passover"?

Although technically the Feast of Unleavened Bread began
with the fifteenth of Nisan *after* sunset of the fourteenth (the
Passover lamb was slain just *before* sunset, roasted, and eaten
that night), the days of unleavened bread were also counted
from the fourteenth of Nisan because the eating of unleavened
bread began "on the fourteenth day of the month at evening"
(Exodus 12:18). Though they were two separate feasts, the
Passover and Feast of Unleavened Bread were treated as one
inasmuch as they overlapped. The Passover lamb, though
"prepared" (i.e., slain and the roasting process begun) just

before sunset on the fourteenth, was not eaten until that night, which was then the fifteenth.

What day of the week was Nisan 14? While we refer to Nisan 10 as Sunday, it began on Saturday after sunset when the sabbath ended. Remember, the Jewish day begins at sunset. Thus Nisan 11 began at sunset Sunday, the twelfth Monday, the thirteenth Tuesday, and Nisan 14, the day of preparation, began Wednesday at sunset. The "last supper," then, took place Wednesday night, the beginning of Nisan 14, which was called the day of preparation. The following afternoon, in the "evening" of Nisan 14, the Passover lambs were slain shortly before sunset. Christ was on the cross and "gave up the ghost" at the same time that Thursday afternoon.

Thursday? Not "Good Friday"? Indeed not. A Friday crucifixion doesn't fit the facts. Not only the prophecies but the Old Testament types as well had to be fulfilled. One of those types was known as "the sign of the prophet Jonas [Jonah]." It required Jesus to be in the grave "three days and three nights."

Three Days and Three Nights

Obviously, had Christ been crucified on Friday, He couldn't possibly have spent three days and three nights in the grave by Sunday morning. The verification of that fact is simple. What was left of Friday afternoon can be counted as day one. All day Saturday is day two. Friday and Saturday nights until dawn Sunday total two nights. The period comes up short by one day and one night.

Even counting a few minutes of Sunday morning as the third day would not suffice. There would still be one night missing. Furthermore, no part of the day on Sunday may be counted because we are distinctly told that the angel rolled away the stone "as it began to dawn toward the first day of the week" (Matthew 28:1). The tomb was already empty at that point, so Christ must have risen from the dead sometime prior to dawn. How long before we are not told.

Had the Scriptures simply said "three days," then a Friday crucifixion could have qualified by counting any part of a day as the whole. If Christ were crucified before sunset Friday, then that would be part of the day which began Thursday at sunset and ended Friday at sunset. The second day went from Friday sunset to Saturday sunset, and the third day, which began at sunset Saturday, would be counted as well.

The Bible, however, is precise in its language and quite specific about "three days *and three nights*." The specifications derive from Jonah's experience: "And Jonah was in the belly of the fish three days and three nights" (Jonah 1:17). Jesus Himself declared: "For as Jonas was three days and three nights in the whale's belly; so shall the Son of man be three days and three nights in the heart of the earth [i.e. in that part of Hades known as Abraham's bosom]" (Matthew 12:39,40; Luke 16:22). That specific requirement cannot be met by a Friday crucifixion.

In spite of the undeniable error, the Roman Catholic Church persists in the myth of a "Good Friday" crucifixion. Indeed, Rome has built much of its ritual and dogma upon that obvious falsehood. It is too late for her to change her story now. In this fact alone we have sufficient evidence of the Roman Catholic Church's manufacture and official endorsement of untruth to cast doubt upon everything else it affirms with equal dogmatism. And what can be said for the Protestants by the millions who go along with this lie so willingly in their "Good Friday" special worship services each year?

Does it really matter? Yes! Aren't we just splitting hairs? No, we are not. The day of our Lord's crucifixion is of the utmost importance. Christ said He would be three days and three nights in the grave. If He did not spend that time there, then He lied. Nor is this all. As we've already seen, in fulfillment of numerous prophecies, Christ had to die at the very time when the Passover lambs were being slain all over Israel—and He did. That necessity determined the day of His crucifixion.

What About a Wednesday Crucifixion?

Some scholars claim Christ was crucified on Wednesday. Since it was late afternoon when He died, they don't count that day. So Wednesday, Thursday, and Friday nights give the three nights; Thursday, Friday, and Saturday give the three complete days. It is thus concluded that He must have risen from the dead at *motze shabbat*, the end of the sabbath just before sunset on Saturday. That theory won't work for several reasons.

First of all, the Scripture is clear that the angel rolled away the stone to expose the empty tomb "very early in the morning [Sunday] . . . at the rising of the sun" (Mark 16:2). Why would this heavenly messenger wait so long if Jesus had resurrected the previous afternoon? Why didn't he roll away the stone before sunset Saturday to reveal that the tomb was empty then—if indeed it was?

And why were the Roman soldiers still there guarding the tomb when the angel rolled away the stone Sunday morning? If the three days ended the previous afternoon, Jesus having been dead since Wednesday afternoon, why continue to guard the grave? In fact, they would not. The soldiers had specific orders to guard the grave "until the [end of the] third day" (Matthew 27:64), the period within which Jesus had said He would rise from the dead. When that had expired, let the disciples steal the body if they wanted to. It wouldn't matter any more.

Even if the soldiers had stayed on for one more night, they surely would have sworn that the body had disappeared only after the three-day time limit—too late to claim a "resurrection." Yet no such report was made, as we've already noted. We can only conclude that the three-day period had not elapsed until dawn Sunday.

There are more questions. If Jesus was placed in the tomb Wednesday afternoon, why did the two Marys wait until Sunday morning to come with spices to anoint His body (Matthew 28:1)? In that case, the Feast of Unleavened Bread and the sabbath it brought would have begun at sunset Wednesday. Between the Wednesday sunset to Thursday sunset special sabbath (the first day of the Feast of Unleavened Bread) and the regular Saturday sabbath there would have been a normal work day, Friday, in which to anoint the body. No time would have been wasted to finish that necessary task before the corpse had begun to deteriorate. Time was of the essence, so why wait, as they did, until Sunday morning? It doesn't fit.

Only if He was crucified on Thursday would there have been two sabbaths together (the special sabbath of the first day of the Feast of Unleavened Bread from Thursday evening until Friday evening, followed by the regular sabbath from Friday evening until Saturday evening), thus preventing the women from going to the grave until Sunday morning.

It was very likely failure to recognize that there were two sabbaths together that caused the Roman Catholic Church to declare a Friday crucifixion. It was no doubt assumed that the sabbath which followed Christ's death was the normal Saturday sabbath, when in fact it was the sabbath of the first day of the Feast of Unleavened Bread, which was then followed by the Saturday sabbath. It was a natural mistake and one which could easily be made without a full investigation of the facts. That is no excuse, however, for a church which boasts of its infallibility and requires its members to accept its dogmas without question.

Joseph of Arimathaea had time on the day of crucifixion before the special sabbath began at sunset Thursday to go out and buy the "fine linen" (Mark 15:46) with which he wrapped the body of Jesus when he put Him in the tomb. The women also had time to purchase the spices they needed and to prepare them before the special sabbath. So they would have been ready to go to the tomb immediately after the two contiguous sabbaths ended. Either they were unaware of the fact that Nicodemus brought 100 pounds of spices which he and Joseph of Arimathaea placed on the body as they wrapped it (John 19:39,40), or they thought more was needed. Here is the testimony of Luke:

> And the women also, which came with him from Galilee, followed after, and beheld the sepulchre, and how his body was laid. And they returned, and prepared spices and ointments; and rested the sabbath day according to the commandment. Now upon the first day of the week, very early in the morning, they came unto the

sepulchre, bringing the spices which they had prepared [very likely working late Saturday night after the second sabbath ended] (Luke 23:55–24:1).

The Testimony of Astronomy

In his investigation of the prophecy of Daniel's 70 weeks, Sir Robert Anderson consulted the Astronomer Royal at the Royal Observatory in Greenwich, England. That expert's astronomical calculations determined that in A.D. 32, Nisan 14 was from Wednesday sunset to Thursday sunset. We have already noted, of course, that it had to be on that day in order to conform to the biblical account.

Everything hangs together as it must. It is agreed that Jesus made His triumphal entry into Jerusalem on a Sunday. For the Old Testament type to be fulfilled, that had to be Nisan 10 as we have noted, the day that the Passover lambs were taken for observation. Four more days brings us to the fourteenth, when the Passover lambs were slain, which works out to be a Thursday. For this and the other reasons given above, we can only conclude that Christ was nailed to the cross on Thursday about noon and died shortly after 3 P.M.

The assembly of the congregation of Israel had indeed slain their Messiah and Passover lamb without knowing what they had done. In love and mercy, Christ had prayed while on the cross: "Father, forgive them, for they know not what they do" (Luke 23:34).

Let us count again the days and nights that He was "in the heart of the earth," now that we know from type, prophecy, and astronomical calculations precisely when Christ laid down His life. On Thursday, the nearly three hours left after His death until sundown are counted as day one. Friday and Saturday account for days two and three. Thursday, Friday, and Saturday nights number three. After these three days and three nights in the grave, Christ rose from the dead some time before dawn Sunday morning. No doubt it was shortly, if not immediately, thereafter that the angel rolled the stone back to show that the tomb was empty.

What does all this have to do with the Rapture and the Second Coming? It provides further evidence of the importance of prophecy and the precision with which it is fulfilled. If such has been the case in the past, then we may be certain that future events connected with the coming of Christ will provide an equally precise fulfillment of prophecy down to the last detail.

Why Worship on Sunday?

There is a further value in tracing the timing of events with great care. The day of Christ's resurrection is of enormous importance in our understanding of Scripture. It makes considerable difference whether He rose from the dead on Saturday or Sunday.

Seventh-day Adventists, for example, insist that Saturday is the day on which we should gather to worship Christ because it was the Jewish sabbath instituted by God. Those who claim a Wednesday crucifixion and a *motze shabbat* resurrection late Saturday afternoon believe in worshiping on that day as well. We have seen, however, that He actually arose from the dead early Sunday morning, which is why Christians worship on that day.

It is commonly argued that the Roman Catholic Church changed the sabbath from Saturday to Sunday, thus initiating Sunday worship. The fact is that Rome did not "invent Sunday worship." The early Christians, from the very beginning, met to worship Christ on Sunday. This observance was an established custom centuries before any decrees about worship were issued from a central headquarters after the bishops of Rome began to claim supremacy over the church.

Luke writes: "On the first day of the week when the disciples met together to break bread" (Acts 20:7). This "breaking of bread" did not merely involve taking a meal. That it was a special meal, which included the communion service in memorium of Christ's death, burial, and resurrection as Paul discusses it in 1 Corinthians 11, is clear.

Surely the Christians didn't all come together at every meal; nor did they eat only on the first day of the week. Neither of these possibilities is plausible. On this special "breaking of bread" in remembrance of Christ, the congregation of believers was assembled and Paul preached to them all night. That they gathered together on the first day of the week is reinforced by the fact that Paul instructed the believers to set aside an offering on that day each week (1 Corinthians 16:2). How so, unless the Christians gathered together for worship on that day?

Whatever Rome may have decreed for those in its fold is beside the point. Christians outside Roman Catholicism meet on Sunday for biblical reasons. Not for a moment do they imagine that the sabbath was changed from Saturday to Sunday. Saturday is still the sabbath, but Christians don't keep it for several reasons.

A New Creation

First of all, the sabbath was for the Jews only. It was part of that special covenant, to which we've already referred, between God and Israel involving the land and their relationship with Him. All mankind is, of course, under God's moral law, but not under the Mosaic law. Romans 2:14,15 reminds us that God's moral law, as we all know, has been written in every conscience, including those of Gentiles. Were the sabbath also for Gentiles, then all mankind would have a conscience about keeping it. That sabbath keeping is not written in anyone's conscience is proof enough that it was not intended for anyone outside of Israel.

The sabbath is commemorated as the day on which God rested from His labor in creating the universe. That universe, however, will be destroyed, as 2 Peter 3:10-12 tells us. As Christians, we "look for new heavens and a new earth, wherein dwelleth righteousness" (2 Peter 3:13). It was Christ's death for our sins and His resurrection for our justification that made possible the creation of a new universe to come. Therefore, we celebrate the day of His resurrection. It marks the beginning of God's new creation and points us forward to the new heavens and new earth which we as new creatures in Christ will yet inhabit. We are not of this old world.

Again we see how important the precise timing of prophesied events is. Saturday, which is associated with the old creation, is the last day of the week. It would have been inappropriate for Christ to rise from the dead on that day. He rose from the grave on Sunday, the first day of a new week. He is called "the firstborn from the dead" (Colossians 1:18), and "the last Adam" (1 Corinthians 15:45), the progenitor of a race of "new creatures" (2 Corinthians 5:17), "born-again" people who are "his workmanship, created in Christ Jesus" (Ephesians 2:10). Only these new creatures in Christ will inhabit the new universe.

Christ was born "when the fullness of time was come [i.e., at the time God had foreordained]" (Galatians 4:4). His Second Coming will also take place at the exact time God has decreed. Returning to Daniel, we will discover that he tells us when that will occur as well.

CHAPTER 17

"The Prince That Shall Come"

◇

> And the people of the prince that shall come shall destroy the city and the sanctuary. . . . And he shall confirm the covenant with many for one week: and in the midst of the week he shall cause the sacrifice and the oblation to cease (Daniel 9:26,27).

> And his power shall be mighty, but not by his own power: and he shall destroy . . . the mighty and the holy people . . . And through . . . peace shall [he] destroy many: he shall also stand up against the Prince of princes; but he shall be broken without hand (Daniel 8:24,25).

Precisely 70 weeks of years, beginning Nisan 1, 445 B.C., must roll by to fulfill all that has been foretold by the prophets concerning Israel and Jerusalem. Of course, we are long past A.D. 39 when that period of 490 years of 360 days each should have ended. We know that 69 of these weeks of years (483 years) went exactly according to schedule and ended in A.D. 32. Daniel clearly stated that at that precise time Messiah would come, but instead of reigning He would be slain. And so it happened.

As foretold, the 69 weeks of years were climaxed by Christ being hailed as "the Messiah the Prince"—then four days later being denied His kingdom, mocked with a crown of thorns, and crucified. Thereafter Jerusalem and the temple were to be destroyed once again, this time by the people of the Antichrist, "the prince that shall come." That prophecy also was fulfilled exactly as Daniel declared it. But what of the other prophecies? What happened to the last week?

The climax of these 70 weeks is described by Daniel as "to make an end of sins . . . to seal up the vision and prophecy, and to anoint the most holy" (9:24). That would include, of course, the Messiah reigning as King of kings over His worldwide millennial kingdom from His father David's throne. That seat of authority is in the City of David where God has chosen to place His name (Deuteronomy 12:11,21, etc.; 1 Kings 11:36; 14:21, etc.). Fulfilled at last would be the promises which God had repeatedly made to His ancient chosen people, Israel, through His prophets.

That Christ is not yet physically present and reigning in Jerusalem as promised—that He isn't even reigning there and over this world invisibly—is obvious. There are those who suggest that He is reigning from heaven now and that in this way the promise to Israel has been fulfilled. One need hardly argue that Christ is not in control of this world as the Scriptures promise He will be one day. The daily news attests to that fact, as does our everyday experience. We are, quite obviously, not yet in the millennium, in spite of the claims of the post-millennialists.

It is certain that the 70 weeks could not have expired without the promises all being fulfilled. God would be proved a liar if that were the case. Something has caused a delay. If those weeks had continued one after the other without interruption, they would have ended seven years (one week of years) after Christ's death and resurrection. Obviously they did not. Even the destruction of Jerusalem and the temple which Daniel foretold did not occur within the 70-week period.

The Gap Between the Sixty-ninth and Seventieth Weeks

It is of great importance that 38 years expired after Messiah was "cut off" in A.D. 32 until "the city and the sanctuary" were destroyed in A.D. 70. Had that destruction occurred within seven years (a week of years) of Christ's death, there might have been some excuse for thinking that Daniel's 70 weeks had run their course even though Christ is obviously not yet reigning visibly. No one, however, can dispute the fact that the week of years (seven years) immediately following Christ's death did not see the fulfillment of Daniel's prophecy. Even those who claim all was fulfilled in A.D. 70 must admit a gap of at least 31 years between the end of the sixty-ninth and the beginning of the seventieth weeks, and with no reason for it.

From Daniel's wording it is clear that the last week of the 70 was not to follow immediately on the heels of the sixth-ninth. "The prince that shall come" (i.e., Antichrist) could not be on the scene until after the destruction of Jerusalem. Yet he will be here during the seventieth week. It is, in fact, for that last seven years that he makes "a covenant with many."

We have given many reasons why the seventieth week has not yet become history. For example, far greater tribulation than occurred in A.D. 70 has befallen both Jews and Christians in the past 50 years. Certainly Antichrist has not yet arrived on the world scene to make his "one week" covenant with both Israel and the world ("with many"), allowing the temple to be rebuilt, broken that covenant in the midst of the week as Daniel foretold (9:27), and caused the temple sacrifice to cease.

Surely Nero, who some claim was the Antichrist, did nothing of the kind. Furthermore, the events Christ foretold in the Olivet discourse which were not associated with the A.D. 70 destruction of Jerusalem (the Second Coming, the instantaneous gathering by angels of the "elect" from every corner of earth, etc.), have assuredly not happened as yet. There can be no doubt that the final week leading up to Messiah's reign has not yet run its course.

A Divine Suspension

What has happened to this missing week? We can only conclude that for some reason God has not allowed it to proceed to its prophesied conclusion. The events which Daniel foretold in detail for the 69 weeks all happened right on schedule, but none of those things which were to occur thereafter took place except the destruction of the temple and

Jerusalem. The progress of prophesied events suddenly halted at the end of the sixty-ninth week and has remained in abeyance to this day. Recognizing this fact is extremely important when it comes to determining how close we are to the Rapture and the Second Coming.

We know for certain that if the seventieth week had followed directly after the other 69—or even at any other time since—all of the prophecies of Daniel 9:24-27 would have been fulfilled. In fact, none of the events which were to take place during that final week has occurred. Apparently the seventieth week has been deferred because the time has not yet come for those particular events of that crucial period of God's dealings with Israel to take place. Why that should be the case is of vital concern, as we shall see.

That these events so important to Israel and Jerusalem have not yet occurred cannot be argued. This parenthesis in God's prophetic calendar is undeniable. Thus far the events foretold to take place in that final week of years are all absent from history. We can understand at least one reason for the delay.

Everything that is to occur in that seven-year period revolves around a man who has not yet appeared on the scene. Daniel refers to this central character as "the prince that shall come." Prior to the ascension to David's throne of "the Messiah the Prince," this other "prince" must establish Satan's counterfeit of the Kingdom of God. It is for this denouement that the seventieth week has been reserved.

"The Prince That Shall Come"

Who is this man who, though not the Messiah, will play such a key role in Israel's future? We are given a number of clues. It is said that the people of this prince will destroy Jerusalem and the temple. When Daniel wrote this, Jerusalem and the temple had already, in 586 B.C., been laid in ruins by Nebuchadnezzar. Daniel could only have referred, therefore, to a future destruction. In His day, Jesus also foretold that same devastation after the disciples showed Him Herod's temple and boasted of its beauty: "And Jesus said unto them

... verily I say unto you, There shall not be left here one stone upon another, that shall not be thrown down" (Matthew 24:2).

We know that such a ferocious leveling was executed upon the temple and Jerusalem in A.D. 70 by the Roman armies under the command of Titus. Was Titus, then, "the prince that shall come"? No, because he failed to do what the prophecy ascribes to this prince. Daniels' words are clear: "And he [the prince that shall come] shall confirm the covenant with many for one week." What covenant and what week could this be?

It takes little insight to answer the second part of the question. Since Daniel had just finished relating the events that would occur during the 69 weeks, one can only conclude that this week which he mentioned next must be the seventieth week. Then how could the people who destroyed Jerusalem and the temple more than 1920 years ago be "the people of the prince that shall come," a man who must be on earth during this yet future seven-year period?

A Revived Roman Empire

In the only possible answer to that question, we have one more reason why the Roman Empire must be revived in the last days. It was the armies of Rome which destroyed "the city and the sanctuary." The people of this empire are to be the people of this coming prince. The people of a prince are his subjects; thus he will rule the Roman Empire. Inasmuch as he did not rule it in the past, he must rule it in the future. For that to happen, the Roman Empire must be revived. There is no way to escape this conclusion.

It is clear that, although there will be some important similarities, the Roman Empire will not be revived in exactly the same form in which it existed in the past. We have already noted that it will function under ten kings who will apparently each have control over a part of it. Such a division was unknown to the ancient Roman Empire. This coming prince will be over these ten vice-rulers and will govern the whole empire, for all of its people shall be his people. In fact, this last world empire will encompass all nations, as we shall see.

A Rebuilt Temple

What could be the provisions of this "covenant" to which Daniel refers, and with whom does the coming prince make it? We know it is "for one week," the seven-year conclusion of Daniel's 70 weeks of years. We may also reasonably deduce that it involves sacrifice and oblations, for "in the midst of the week he shall cause the sacrifice and the oblation to cease." One would suspect that this "prince" has guaranteed such worship for the seven years, then goes back upon his word. Other Scriptures confirm this assumption.

Since the entire 70 weeks pertain to Israel and Jerusalem, we can only conclude that this covenant involves the temple in that "holy city," the only place where "sacrifice and oblation" could be offered by Jews. We know definitely from other Scriptures that the temple will yet be rebuilt in Jerusalem. This *will* happen even though it seems next to impossible at the present time due to the Dome of the Rock, Islam's third holiest shrine, being situated on the temple site.

Daniel's statement that the covenant will be made "with many" instead of "with Israel" accurately reflects today's international scene. The entire world is concerned about Jerusalem and through the United Nations is involved in the current peace negotiations between Israel and the Arabs. Any arrangement for the rebuilding of the temple in the future will have to be made with "the many" and not simply with Israel. Again we see the accuracy of prophecy.

The existence of the temple during Daniel's seventieth week is required by a number of other prophecies as well. Take, for example, what Paul declares concerning the Antichrist: "Who opposeth and exalteth himself above all that is called God, or that is worshipped; so that he as God sitteth in the temple of God, shewing himself that he is God" (2 Thessalonians 2:4).

Such blasphemy would surely qualify as the "abomination that makes desolate" (see also Daniel 12:11), which Daniel attributes to the "prince that shall come." Daniel also makes it clear that this coming prince will engage in a final battle with Christ and will be destroyed (8:25). He must, therefore, be the

Antichrist. There are also other reasons for reaching this conclusion.

The Antichrist on the Scene

The Messiah is called the Prince (9:25). This one, then, who takes the designation of prince (9:26), would seem to be a pretender to the title of Messiah the Prince. Does the Antichrist pretend to be Christ? Indeed, he does. In spite of portrayals by Hollywood and even Christian writers and preachers of the Antichrist as an obviously evil ogre, the Bible presents a different picture. Far from being terrorized, the entire world, at least at first, will *worship* him (Revelation 13:8)—surely an indication of genuine attraction and even affection.

The prefix "anti" is derived from the Greek. One ordinarily thinks of it as meaning "opposed to" or "against," which is true. However, it also means "in the place of" or "a substitute for." The Antichrist will indeed oppose Christ, but in the most diabolically clever way it could be done: by pretending to be Christ and thus subverting Christianity while posing as its leader. Anything less would not be worthy of Satan's genius.

Among the last days signs Christ gave that would herald the nearness of His coming, our Lord included this warning: "For many shall come in my name, saying, I am Christ; and shall deceive many" (Matthew 24:5). These numerous counterfeit Christs would seem to be preparing the world for the arrival of the real Antichrist on the scene. Are these claimants rivals? Not really. They present to the world the concept that *everyone* is the Christ. Such a belief, until recently, was largely unknown outside of the Orient, yet it is one of the key notions in today's New Age movement.

The "God" of Atheism

A number of cults, such as Unity School of Christianity and the Church of Religious Science, teach the same lie. They assert that the only thing that distinguished Jesus from the rest of us was His attainment to a "higher state of consciousness" known as "Christ consciousness." Whoever attains this Christ consciousness becomes a Christ just like He was. When enough of mankind—a "critical mass"—reach that state, the world will be transformed. Such is the hope of the New Age.

That the Antichrist will present himself as one who has attained to this state (and he will have the Satanic/psychic powers to prove it—2 Thessalonians 2:9,10) seems apparent from Paul's description of Antichrist's reasons for exalting himself as "God." Paul wrote that this man of lawlessness "opposeth and exalteth himself above all that is called God or that is worshipped." Clearly, he is anti-God. He is, in fact, an atheist. Yet he claims to *be* God. That he is not claiming to be the God of the Bible, however, is quite clear, for he actually rejects the very concept of such a God. He is a humanist who exalts himself as a man (and thus potentially all men) to the place of gods.

The insight Jesus gave us into this impostor agrees with what Paul had to say, as of course it must. Christ spoke of the Antichrist in these terms: "I am come in my Father's name, and ye receive me not: if another shall come in his own name, him ye will receive" (John 5:43). So the Antichrist doesn't acknowledge any relationship to, or dependence upon, the Father as Jesus did. He needs no one but himself and claims to be a self-realized man who has acquired godlike powers. He comes in his own name. His religion is the exaltation of self, which began with Satan (not surprising, since Antichrist is the human embodiment of Satan)—and the world will love him for this celebration of self.

While the Antichrist will be universally worshiped, Jesus tells us that Israel will feel a special kinship with him and will accept him as her Messiah, her Savior. In cryptic terms Daniel explains why. As a result of his covenant with the many, he will apparently bring peace to Israel and through her to the world.

Peace in the Middle East, established by the Antichrist, will become the key to a New Age that will dawn for all mankind, a New World Order. So the world will think, until the bubble bursts.

Chapter 18

The Church Must Be Removed

$\diamond$

And now ye know what withholdeth [prevents] that he [Antichrist] might be revealed in his time. For the mystery of iniquity doth already work; only he who now hinders will hinder, until he be taken out of the way. And then shall that Wicked one [Antichrist], be revealed, whom the Lord shall consume with the spirit of his mouth, and shall destroy with the brightness of his coming (2 Thessalonians 2:6-8).

Though the Antichrist will somehow bring about a peaceful solution to the conflict between Israel and her Arab neighbors, it is a peace which he will himself violate when he leads the armies of the world to attack Israel. Unaware, because of their disregard of their own Scriptures, of what lies ahead, God's chosen people will fall into Satan's trap.

Israel will imagine that this charismatic world leader's ability to establish peace proves him to be the Messiah. Their covenant with this evil one who will turn out to be their deadliest enemy will lead to the time of greatest distress the Jews as a people have ever known. The prophets called it "the time of Jacob's trouble" (Jeremiah 30:7).

Destroyed by "Peace"

Stand on any street corner in Jerusalem these days and ask passersby, "Do you believe the Messiah will come?" Nearly every Israeli will respond with a resounding, "Yes!" Then ask, "How will you recognize Him?" Again nearly every Jew inhabiting Israel will reply with a naivete born of hope, "He will bring peace!"

Most Jews justify their rejection of Jesus as the Messiah by His failure to bring universal peace. After all, the prophets said that the Messiah would establish a kingdom of perpetual peace and reign from David's throne. Jesus didn't do so. Therefore, He couldn't be the Messiah. The lie is as simple as that. It could only deceive those who are ignorant of prophecy.

The world at large is not aware that peace with God, which has definite conditions, is the only basis for peace among men. Blind to the prophecies that the Messiah would first of all die for the sins of the world to reconcile mankind to God, today's Jew is ripe for the false peace of the Antichrist. Israel's leaders are heedless of Daniel's solemn warning: "He shall magnify himself in his heart, and by peace shall destroy many" (8:25).

Israel's Spiritual Blindness

We will come back to consider more carefully the events that must take place in this final seventieth week of that period prophesied by Daniel, and the timing of the Second Coming as affected thereby. For the moment, however, we need to consider why this week has not yet run its course and when it might do so. The answer to these questions is crucial to an understanding of the timing of the Rapture and Second Coming.

We have emphasized the fact that the time period of 70 weeks of years pertains only to Israel, and especially to Jerusalem. It involves God's dealings with His ancient people. The purpose is apparently to bring them to repentance and full reconciliation to Himself and His will so that the Messiah can reign over them. In order for this to happen, the spiritual eyes of these people must be opened.

It is important to recognize, therefore, that the Bible declares that blindness has come upon Israel, and why this is so. This blindness prevents most Jews from realizing that relationship with God enjoyed by Abraham. The apostle Paul, a former rabbi, agonized over Israel's separation from God and from the blessings which God desires for her through the Messiah. We share Paul's deep pain for his people as he confides:

> I have great heaviness and continual sorrow in my heart. For I could wish that myself were accursed from Christ for my brethren, my kinsmen according to the flesh: Who are Israelites; to whom pertaineth...the promises; Whose are the fathers, and of whom as concerning the flesh Christ came, who is over all, God blessed for ever (Romans 9:2-5).

Israel had been in apostasy and heedless of God's warnings through His prophets for centuries before Paul wrote these words. From what Paul, inspired of the Holy Spirit, has to say in this and other epistles, however, it is apparent that a milestone has been passed for Israel. The Messiah has "come to his own and his own received him not" (John 1:11). They have crucified their Creator, crying, "His blood be on us and on our children" (Matthew 27:25). The die has been cast. Something radical has changed between God and His ancient chosen people.

Israel's Fall and World Redemption

Paul calls it Israel's fall. It is not, however, permanent. God is not finished with her. She will one day be restored, but not until the Messiah returns to rescue her at Armageddon. In the meantime, the Gentiles are the beneficiaries of what has happened. Paul puts it like this:

> I say then, Have they [Israel] stumbled that they should fall [permanently]? God forbid: but rather that through their [temporary] fall salvation is come unto the Gentiles. . . . Now if the fall of them be the riches of the world, and the diminishing of them the riches of the Gentiles; how much more their fulness? (Romans 11:11,12).

Since Israel's fall, God has begun to deal directly with the Gentiles in grace and on a grand scale heretofore unimagined.

The prophets "inquired" about this great salvation and even angels don't yet understand it (1 Peter 1:10-12). Most astonishing is the fact that it came about because Israel crucified her Messiah! Nevertheless, she will be held responsible for that infamous deed with which Peter boldly indicted the inhabitants of Jerusalem in his second major sermon:

> The God of Abraham, and of Isaac, and of Jacob, the God of our fathers, hath glorified his Son Jesus; whom ye delivered up, and denied him in the presence of Pilate when he was determined to let him go. But ye denied the Holy One and the Just, and desired a murderer to be granted unto you; And killed the Prince of life, whom God hath raised from the dead; whereof we are witnesses (Acts 3:13-15).

The crucifixion of Christ was a heinous crime for which Israel has been and will be severely punished. Amazingly, however, through her rejection and crucifixion of her Messiah salvation came to the rest of mankind. Christ had to die to pay the debt for the sins of the whole world. The tragedy is that it was His own chosen people who put Him to death. Remember, Pilate found Him innocent and desired to release Him.

Wonder of wonders, the spear that pierced His side drew forth the blood that saves. The blood that flowed from nails contemptuously and wickedly driven into His hands and feet, from thorns mockingly pressed upon His brow—that blood was the price of our redemption (Ephesians 1:7; Colossians 1:14). Israel's rejection of her Messiah brought salvation to the Gentiles. The disciples had a difficult time believing this at first, but eventually they came to understand it.

The Times of the Gentiles

With Israel's rejection of her Messiah, a new era dawned. Jesus called it "the times of the Gentiles"—a time which, He said, must continue until "fulfilled." Only then would Jerusalem be liberated from Gentile influence (Luke 21:24). The duration of "the times of the Gentiles" coincides with the length of time during which Israel will be blind to the gospel and to the fact that she crucified her Messiah. Here is Paul's further explanation:

> For I would not, brethren, that ye should be ignorant of this mystery, lest ye should be wise in your own conceits; that blindness in part is happened to Israel, until the fulness of the Gentiles be come in. And so all Israel shall be saved: as it is written, There shall come out of Sion the Deliverer, and shall turn away ungodliness from Jacob (Romans 11:25,26).

Just before His death, Jesus Christ told His disciples that He was forming a new entity which had never existed before. He called it His Church. In response to Peter's confession that He was the Messiah (Christ), Jesus declared: "On this rock I will build my church, and the gates of hell shall not prevail against it."

Until that time, God's people consisted only of Jews. Their relationship to Him was defined by the Mosaic covenant. After Christ's crucifixion for the sins of the world, there would be an entirely new entity composed of both Jews and Gentiles—the Church. Paul explained it like this:

> Wherefore remember, that ye being in time past Gentiles in the flesh . . . without Christ, being aliens from the commonwealth of Israel, and strangers from the covenants of promise, having no hope, and without God in the world: But now in Christ Jesus ye who . . . were far off are made nigh by the blood of Christ. For he is our peace, who hath made both [Jew and Gentile] one. . . . Having abolished . . . the law of commandments . . . for to make in himself of twain [Jew and Gentile] one new man, so making peace; And that he might reconcile both unto God in one body by the cross. . . . Now therefore ye are no more strangers and foreigners, but fellowcitizens with the saints, and of the household of God; And are built upon the foundation of the apostles and prophets, Jesus Christ himself being the chief corner stone (Ephesians 2:11-20).

Peter's Fallibility

Roman Catholics insist that Peter is the rock upon which the Church was founded. Yes, Jesus did say to Peter, "On this rock I will build my church, and the gates of hell shall not prevail against it, and I will give unto thee the keys of the kingdom of heaven" (Matthew 16:18,19). Out of that simple statement (basically the same as He made to all the disciples in Matthew 18:18,19 and John 20:23) Rome has manufactured a papal office, papal infallibility, apostolic succession, a magisterium which alone can interpret Scripture, a celibate priesthood to whom confession must be made and which alone can administer grace through seven sacraments, and much more. One can examine Christ's statement with a microscope and never find justification for such embellishments.

It is beyond the scope of this writing to engage in a detailed argument against Rome's errors. If Peter was appointed by Christ at that time as the first pope—and if all popes are infallible—one would never have suspected it from Peter's performance. The "first pope" immediately denied the faith! And if Peter did not receive "papal infallibility" from Christ at that moment, then when did he?

Moments after Jesus commended Peter for confessing that He was the Christ, that impetuous ex-fisherman insisted that Christ need not die on the cross. Here was a blatant denial of the central doctrine of Christianity. "Get thee behind me, Satan," was Christ's immediate rebuke. The papal system was off to an incredibly poor start.

In the very next chapter we find Peter, James, and John on the mount, where Christ was "transfigured" before them, thus giving them a glimpse of His coming resurrection glory. Moses and Elijah appeared there with Christ. In another hasty declaration that was far from infallible, Peter lowered Jesus to the level of a prophet, saying, "Let us build here three tabernacles, one for thee, one for Moses and one for Elijah." Immediately God's voice from heaven rebuked this newly appointed "first pope." On this occasion Peter had denied the uniqueness and deity of God's only begotten Son, who is far above any prophet, including Moses and Elijah.

We have already referred to Peter's denial that he even knew Jesus when confronted by servants in the palace of the high priest as Christ was being condemned to death. Rome excuses the sins of the popes (they have included some of the most inhuman monsters to walk this earth) with the trite saying, "There is a difference between infallibility and impeccability." Popes are allegedly infallible when they make a declaration on faith or morals to the entire Church, even though they deny Christ with their lives—a concept unknown in Scripture and the early Church. Yet all three of the grievous denials of truth and of Him who is the truth, pronounced by Peter and which we have just mentioned, pertained to "faith and morals." Most assuredly they were also stated to the entire Church, for they are in the canon of Scripture.

The Only Rock

It is Christ who builds His Church. He is its head and also its foundation. We have already seen how, in the Old Testament, Yahweh makes it very clear that He alone is the Savior. He also declares with equal clarity and finality that He alone is the Rock: "For who is God except Yahweh, or who is a rock except our God?" (Psalm 18:31). Certainly not Peter! All through the Old Testament, Yahweh is called "the rock" of our/my/his salvation. That God is the *only* Rock is reiterated many times: Deuteronomy 32:4; 2 Samuel 22:2; 23:3; Psalm 18:2; 28:1; 42:9; 62:2,6,7; Isaiah 17:10, etc.

Paul argues that Jesus Christ was the Rock of Israel during her wilderness travels (1 Corinthians 10:4), thus claiming that He is Yahweh. Inasmuch as God throughout the Old Testament declares that He is the only Savior, our Lord and Savior Jesus Christ, in order to be the Savior, had to be God come in the flesh. The same is true concerning the Rock upon which the Church is built: It could only be God Himself. Jesus is that Rock, for He is God. Peter could not take that place, nor did he aspire to do so.

Jesus referred the rabbis to the messianic prophecy in Psalm 118:22,23: "The stone which the builders [i.e., Israel's religious leaders] rejected has been made the chief cornerstone."

Christ clearly implied that He was the fulfillment of that Scripture, and the rabbis knew it and hated Him for it.

Peter boldly indicted the rabbis with Christ's crucifixion and then applied this same prophecy to Christ: "Jesus Christ of Nazareth, whom you crucified . . . is the stone which was set at nought of you builders, which is become the head of the corner" (Acts 4:11). Again, in his first epistle, Peter identified Jesus Christ as the "chief cornerstone" upon which the Church is built (1 Peter 2:6,7). In rejecting this stone, Israel has been set aside while God builds something new upon it.

It is over this Rock upon which the Church is built that Israel has stumbled and fallen. Isaiah foretold this fall: "And he [the Messiah] shall be . . . a stone of stumbling and for a rock of offense to both the houses of Israel [i.e., Judah and Israel]" (Isaiah 8:14). Both Peter (1 Peter 2:8) and Paul (Romans 9:33) quote this Scripture and apply it to Christ and to Israel's fall through rejecting Him.

Here we have the two closely related reasons why Daniel's seventieth week has not run its course. The sixty-ninth week ended with Israel's rejection and crucifixion of her Messiah. Out of that rejection came salvation to the world—a salvation which God had planned from eternity past. The way to a new relationship to God was opened to all mankind. Out of Israel's fall, the Church was formed as a composite body of both Jews and Gentiles.

The Church Must Be Removed

Since that time, the Church has been God's focus in this world. She is the instrument of evangelism, bringing the gospel message to all peoples, including Israel. For nearly 2000 years the Church has been the light of the world, calling upon sinners to repent and to be reconciled to God, and warning that a day of judgment is coming. During this time, Israel was set aside, a wandering people without a homeland, scattered among all nations, under God's judgment, but not forgotten by Him.

In 1948, Israel became a nation once again. We have already commented upon what a miracle that was, and upon the even greater miracle that Jerusalem is now the focus of world attention and concern. Has Daniel's seventieth week begun to run its course at last with the restoration of Israel to her land? Obviously not, for she has been there far longer than seven years and Christ has not yet come back to reign in Jerusalem. Clearly the continued presence of the Church on earth stands in the way of Israel becoming the exclusive focus of God's dealings.

Daniel's seventieth week is a period of seven years. Numerous definite prophecies must be fulfilled during that time. When will those events begin to take place? There were two related occurrences which caused the seventieth week to be held in abeyance: 1) Israel's rejection of her Messiah, and 2) the formation of the Church. Suppose Israel turned to Christ. Would that restart God's timeclock? No.

In fact, Scripture is very clear that Israel will not recognize that Christ is her Messiah until the end of the seventieth week, when He appears to rescue her at Armageddon. The prophets were very specific on that point. Therefore we know that, in itself, Israel's continued rejection of Christ does not stand in the way of a resumption of the final week determined upon Israel and Jerusalem.

The presence of the Church, then, must be the hindrance to God's final dealings with Israel. Could the Church be removed, leaving the focus upon Israel once again? Yes, and that is precisely what will happen. One can draw no other conclusion except that the Church, whose formation marked the suspension of the seventieth week, must be removed before those final seven years can run their course. And this removal is exactly what Christ has promised.

Here we have a most powerful argument from Scripture for the Rapture of the Church to take place prior to the beginning of Daniel's seventieth week. A mid-tribulation or pre-wrath Rapture won't do. This last week can't even commence until the Church, whose formation caused its suspension, has been removed. Indeed, she must be removed for a number of other reasons as well.

CHAPTER 19

The Rapture

———————— ◇ ————————

In my Father's house are many mansions. . . . I go to prepare a place for you. And . . . I will come again and receive you unto myself; that where I am there ye may be also (John 14:2,3).

For the Lord himself shall descend from heaven with a shout . . . and the dead in Christ shall rise first: then we which are alive and remain shall be caught up together with them in the clouds, to meet the Lord in the air: and so shall we ever be with the Lord (1 Thessalonians 4:16,17).

Behold I show you a mystery; We shall not all sleep [die], but we shall all be changed, In a moment, in the twinkling of an eye, at the last trump . . . the dead shall be raised incorruptible and we shall be changed (1 Corinthians 15:51,52).

We're soon departing from this old world of sin and sorrow! One glad day Christians will be caught up bodily and alive into heaven! The souls and spirits of those who had previously died believing in Christ, having been consciously with Him in the interim, will come with their Lord from heaven to rejoin their glorious resurrected bodies. Those alive at the time of His return, their bodies instantly transformed as well, will be caught up together with the saints of all ages to meet Christ somewhere above planet earth. From there He will personally escort this innumerable throng into the presence of His Father in heaven, as He promised.

We've read the Bible passages describing this event scores of times and assent to it all in our heads. Unfortunately, for all too many of us, the truth hasn't penetrated our hearts and has little effect upon our lives. Somehow, the breathtaking reality of the Rapture—and the awesome fact that it could occur at any moment—doesn't break through. It all seems like a tale that's been told so often that it has lost its meaning and the power to move and motivate us.

What initial enthusiasm the promise once aroused has been dampened by the realization that Christians have been hoping for centuries for Christ's return to catch them up into heaven and it hasn't happened yet. Why should it occur in our day? Yes, why indeed? There are good reasons.

Christ *could* have come at any moment in the past, but He didn't. However, our generation has indications that no previous one has ever had that our Lord's promised return *must* be very soon. Israel's return to her land after 2500 years and the fact that the nations of the world are at last seriously attempting to bring peace between Arabs and Jews are only two of those new indicators unknown in past generations.

Unique to Christianity

The Rapture is a word to which some critics object because they say it isn't in the Bible. In fact, it is in the Latin translation of 1 Thessalonians 4:17. The Latin *rapturos* means an ecstatic catching away, as does our English word. In any language, that is exactly what the Bible declares will occur when Christ returns to take His own to His Father's house of many mansions. Such was our Lord's promise, and He will not fail to keep it.

The hope of the Rapture is a teaching which is unique to Christianity. On that basis alone, it is a far more important doctrine than most Christians acknowledge. For anything which lessens Christianity's uniqueness weakens its foundation and increases the danger of confusion and compromise.

Prior to Christ's first coming nearly 2000 years ago nothing was known of the Rapture. Paul, therefore, calls it a "mystery" now revealed. Although Enoch and Elijah were caught up alive into heaven, those were exceptional cases which gave no such hope to the average believer in Old Testament times. While Buddhism, Hinduism, Islam, and other world religions offer some kind of heaven after death, none holds out the prospect of being caught up to heaven alive. Christ alone, the Conqueror of death, made that promise to those who would believe in Him.

A Promise Never Made Before

No wonder Paul called the Rapture "that blessed hope" (Titus 2:13). This is not some optional or even peripheral teaching. It is so interwoven with our faith that it cannot be extricated. As we shall see in the last chapter, Paul considered the hope of our appearance with Christ in glory to be the major motivation for godly living. Even in teaching concerning the remembrance of our Lord in His death, partaking of the bread and the cup, Paul noted that it was to be done only "till he come" (1 Corinthians 11:26). This hope lies at the very heart of Christianity.

No, we are not suggesting that one must believe in the Rapture in order to be saved. It is not part of the gospel. We are saved by believing that Christ died for our sins, was buried, and rose from the dead the third day. Those who belong to Christ will be taken to heaven at the Rapture whether they believe in this event or not. But if we do not take seriously Christ's promise to catch us up to heaven, why should we believe anything else He said?

Consider the impact of Christ's words: "I will come again and receive you unto myself, that where I am, there ye may be also"! The promise He gave His disciples at that time was not that they would go to heaven when they died, though that was true. Christ was specifically declaring that the day was coming when He would personally return to take all believers together at one time, the living and the dead whom He would resurrect, to His Father's house in heaven. Such a promise had never been made before!

Paul elaborates upon this unique and mysterious coming event and explains it in more detail. The foundation of this hope, however, remains Christ's personal promise—and the occasion of that promise must be remembered to put it in proper perspective. The promise of the Rapture was made on the night of His betrayal, at the same time and as an integral part of His revelation to His disciples that He was going to the cross. Surely the cross was what He meant by "I go to prepare a place for you." It was not a matter of furnishing heaven for our arrival, but of paying the penalty for our sins so that heaven could receive us.

The Most Thrilling Fruit of the Cross

Heaven is at the very heart of Christianity. Christ didn't come, as some teach, to restore us to the garden paradise that Adam lost, but to prepare us for heaven. He didn't come to remodel this old creation, but to make a new one! Therefore the great task of the Church is not to rescue this world from destruction (it will be destroyed) or to improve society, but to call sinners out of the world to become citizens of heaven who watch and wait for their Lord's return to take them there. Our hope is not in insurance policies and a retirement condominium, but it is eternal in the heavens—from whence we are expecting our Lord to return at any moment and catch us up to meet Him in the air.

Christ's shameful death upon the cross (where He endured not only man's evil but God's judgment upon sin), was not intended to set an example of noble ideals and self-sacrifice for the rest of us to follow as we attempt to avert ecological disaster and return the earth to its Edenic state. Far from it! He redeemed us from the curse of the law—a law which required banishment from God's presence for our sin—and He made it possible for us to enter where Adam had never been! Adam and Eve knew the temporary companionship of God when He came down to walk in the garden in the cool of the evening. We have, through the Holy Spirit's indwelling, a more intimate companionship 24 hours a day, and are to dwell with God in His heavenly home eternally!

Sin entered Eden's paradise. It can never enter God's new universe. Though created perfect and innocent, Adam and Eve could sin and as a result died and brought death upon their descendants. We are new creatures created in Christ Jesus over whom sin and death have lost their power. Adam and Eve could be, and were, expelled from Eden. We will never be expelled from heaven. Our Lord Jesus Christ, who is God and man in one person, brings to us a new and indissoluble union between God and man when He comes to live in our hearts—and He will never leave or forsake us (Hebrews 13:5).

Our catching up out of this world and into heaven is the ultimate goal of our redemption. It is the most thrilling fruit of the cross that Christ could share with His disciples the night of His betrayal. To paraphrase His words: "In my Father's house are many mansions and I want to take you there. That's why I'm going to let them crucify me and bear God's wrath upon sin for your sakes."

The disciples were excited at the prospect of reigning with Him on earthly thrones—and some day they will. He was more concerned, however, for them to understand that He was going to take them to His Father's house in heaven. Only from heaven could they return with Him to rule on the earth in His millennial kingdom. We must all be taken to heaven first, for it is from heaven that the saints come with Christ to rule with Him in His kingdom. Let that fact grip us!

Not of This World

Here again we see a significant difference between Israel and the Church. Those who say that the Church has taken the place of Israel and now has all of the promises that applied to the chosen people (but not their curses!) have really made a bad bargain. Israel was promised a land and a kingdom on this earth. The Church has been promised a home in heaven—and to have the run of the entire universe, a new one which God will make when the present one is destroyed. One perceives the tremendous excitement and joy in Paul's heart as he penned the following verses—a small sample of those which promise this marvelous heritage:

> For our conversation [literally, citizenship] is in heaven;
> from whence also we look for the Saviour, the Lord Jesus
> Christ: Who shall change our vile body, that it may be
> fashioned like unto his glorious body, according to the
> working whereby he is able even to subdue all things unto
> himself (Philippians 3:20,21).

> Therefore let no man glory in men. For all things are
> yours; Whether Paul, or Apollos, or Cephas [Peter], or
> the world, or life, or death, or things present, or things to
> come; all are yours; And ye are Christ's; and Christ is
> God's (1 Corinthians 3:21-23).

Christ spoke continually of heaven. He encouraged those
who were persecuted for His sake, "Rejoice and be exceeding
glad: for great is your reward in heaven" (Matthew 5:12); and
He counseled all of His hearers to lay up treasure not on this
earth but "in heaven" (6:10). To those who would faithfully
follow Him, Christ promised a great reward "in heaven"
(19:21). Clearly heaven was on His heart day and night and the
predominant theme in all He taught. His goal was to take the
redeemed there to be with Him forever.

Heaven was the place from which Christ came and to which
He returned. To the unbelievers He said, "I go my way, and ye
shall seek me, and shall die in your sins; whither I go, ye cannot
come." When they asked what He meant, He replied, "Ye are
from beneath; I am from above: ye are of this world; I am not of
this world" (John 8:21-23). To Pilate He said, "My kingdom is
not of this world" (John 18:36).

To His own Christ declared,

> If ye were of the world, the world would love his own:
> but because ye are not of the world, but I have chosen you
> out of the world, therefore the world hateth you. Re-
> member . . . the servant is not greater than his Lord. If
> they have persecuted me, they will also persecute you
> (John 15:19,20).

And He taught them to pray, "Our Father which art in
heaven" (Matthew 6:9), committing themselves into His hands

and working for His eternal kingdom—a kingdom not of this world.

Exchanging Earthly Rewards for Heavenly

Ours is a "heavenly calling" (Hebrews 1:3). We have been "blessed with all spiritual blessings in the heavenly places in Christ" (Ephesians 1:3); and it is in heaven that God has reserved for us "an inheritance, incorruptible, and undefiled and that fadeth not away" (1 Peter 1:4). Indeed, our hope is in heaven (Colossians 1:5) where our names have been written (Luke 10:20). No wonder, then, that our resurrection bodies are "spiritual" (1 Corinthians 15:44) and "heavenly" (v. 49; 2 Corinthians 5:2), suited for living in God's presence.

The joy in heaven will be so great eternally that we will need new and glorious bodies to appreciate and express it. Heaven is often thought of as a solemn place of pomp and protocol. We forget what David knew: "In thy presence there is fulness of joy; and at thy right hand are pleasures for evermore" (Psalm 16:11).

Christ endured the cross "for the joy set before him" (Hebrews 12:2), a joy He wanted to share with us in heaven. To know that joy, however, we must share the shame and reproach of His cross. Did He not say, "Follow me"? How can we expect to take a different path to heavenly joy than our Lord? The writer to the Hebrews commended the believers for joyfully accepting "the spoiling of your [earthly] goods, knowing in yourselves that ye have in heaven a better and an enduring substance" (10:34).

Why would anyone willingly follow a path leading to persecution and even death unless the reward for doing so was much greater than the loss endured? Surely heaven's reward infinitely surpasses anything earth can offer. Paul understood and wrote: "For our light affliction, which is but for a moment, worketh for us a far more exceeding and eternal weight of glory; while we look not at the things which are seen, but at the things which are not seen: for the things which are seen are temporal; but the things which are not seen are eternal" (2 Corinthians 4:17,18). As the hymn says, "It will be worth it all when we see Jesus; life's trials will seem so small when we see Him!"

Two Distinct Events

In previous chapters we have given a number of reasons why the Rapture and the Second Coming are two distinct events, one occurring at the beginning and the other at the end of Daniel's seventieth week. Christ must first of all come *for* His saints to rapture them *to heaven*, or He could never come *with* His saints *from heaven* to rescue Israel at Armageddon.

The Rapture will occur when least expected; the Second Coming takes place only after all the signs have been given and everyone should know that Christ is about to return in glory and power. The Rapture comes in the midst of peace (1 Thessalonians 5:3); the Second Coming in the midst of war (Revelation 19:11-21). One simply cannot put into one time frame and one event the mutually exclusive statements made in the New Testament about the Rapture and the Second Coming.

"But that means there are still two comings of Christ!" is the protest of many. "Show me in the New Testament where it says there are yet two comings!" The response is rather obvious: "Show me in the Old Testament where it says there are two comings." Of course, it doesn't say so, but, as we have already commented, the conclusion was inescapable. The Messiah was not only going to reign, He was going to be killed. One could not put into one time frame and one event what the Old Testament said about the coming of the Messiah. Failure to understand the two comings caused multitudes to reject Jesus.

The same is true today: There are many who call themselves Christians who will end up following the Antichrist, thinking he's Christ. The reason for their confusion is basically the same as it was the first time Christ came. They will be focusing upon and even seeking to build an earthly kingdom and will be unprepared to be taken to heaven. Failure to understand that the Rapture and the Second Coming are two different events separated by seven years lies at the heart of this confusion.

That these are two distinct events is also clear from Christ's own words. "I will come again and receive you unto myself that where I am there ye may be also" is a personal pledge only for His own. This is what Paul spoke of when he said, "So shall we ever be with the Lord." That is what the Rapture is all about, Christ catching up His bride to present her to His Father. The Second Coming has an entirely different purpose: to rescue Israel in the midst of Armageddon and to destroy Antichrist and his evil world empire.

That longed-for and ecstatic meeting of the heavenly Groom with His bride and His escorting her to His Father's house can hardly take place at the same time He comes with the armies of heaven to destroy the Antichrist and his forces in battle. The promise that we will be caught up to meet Christ in the air and ever thereafter be with Him does not fit the equally valid promise of His descent to the Mount of Olives to rescue Israel. Nor can the intimacy of Christ meeting His redeemed of all ages who already know and believe in Him be confused with the "every eye shall see Him" display of power as He reveals Himself at Armageddon to those who have rejected Him.

The One-Event Theory

Some argue that there is indeed a way for both the Rapture and the Second Coming to be one and the same event. We have already shown that the Rapture comes at a time of peace, the Second Coming in the midst of war; the Rapture comes when one would least expect it, the Second Coming only after all the signs have been fulfilled and there could be no doubt that Christ was right at the door. Thus the two events could not possibly occur at the same time. However, inasmuch as such a belief is growing in popularity among evangelicals (ignoring the reasons we've just given why it can't be true), let us consider the explanation that is given for putting these two diverse events into one time frame.

It is suggested that as Christ is on His way from heaven to the Mount of Olives, He pauses momentarily above the earth and catches us up to meet Him. We then join the armies of heaven and return to earth with Him. In addition to the reasons we've already given, there are a number of other problems with this view, the most obvious being that the language of Scripture doesn't support it.

In the verses quoted at the beginning of this chapter, Jesus promises to "come again" to take us to His Father's house. That is the whole meaning of what He says. One could never extract from this passage that He doesn't return to take us to His Father's house after all but merely catches us up to join Him in the air on His descent to the Mount of Olives. Moreover, this view allows no time for certain events which must take place after the Rapture and before the Church is ready to return to earth with Christ.

Preparing a Bride for War

Surely the first event in heaven after our Lord takes us there will be the Judgment Seat of Christ (2 Corinthians 5:10; 1 Corinthians 3:12-15). We must all give an account to our Lord for every action or failure to act, for every idle word and secret thought. How long that will take we don't know. Certainly it won't take place hovering above earth as a momentary pause on our Lord's descent to the Mount of Olives, but in the presence of the Father.

After the Judgment Seat of Christ has done its cleansing work and He has wiped all tears from our eyes, for there will be tears both of grief and joy, surely the Groom will want to spend some time with His bride, the now glorified Church. He must have much to tell us! It hardly seems the way to treat a bride to catch her up momentarily and then bring her abruptly back into the middle of the most massive and destructive war in earth's history. Bride and Groom will spend time together in the Father's house.

In Christ's day the Jewish bride was taken to the father's house where the two were in seclusion in the honeymoon quarters for seven days. Christ must have had that custom in mind when He promised to take His bride to His Father's house. Here we have that last week again, the seven years of the tribulation period. At the end of that week, in Revelation 19, just before Armageddon, we find the marriage supper of the Lamb taking place. For that event (and clearly as a result of the Judgment Seat of Christ when all that defiled one's life on earth has been purged—1 Corinthians 3:12-15), the bride is clothed "in fine linen, clean and white . . . [which] is the righteousness of saints" (Revelation 19:7-9).

More Compelling Reasons for a Pre-tribulation Rapture

In Revelation 19:11, we find Christ coming to earth at Armageddon to rescue Israel, further described in Ezekiel 38 and 39 and Zechariah 12–14. He is accompanied by "the armies which were in heaven . . . clothed in fine linen, white and clean." We just saw His bride, the Church, identically clothed six verses earlier, so there is every reason to believe that she, composed of the saints of all ages, comprises at least a large part of these armies. There is not a word here about angels coming with Christ (though there is in 1 Thessalonians 1:7), but we are told that "all the saints" accompany Him to the Mount of Olives (Zechariah 14:5).

The saints could hardly be part of the armies in heaven had they never been to heaven. Nor could they accompany Christ from heaven had they not been taken up there previously. Again we find compelling evidence that the Rapture of the Church must take place some time prior to Armageddon. We have already given one powerful reason why it will take place seven years earlier: Since it was the formation of the Church that caused the seventieth week not to follow directly after the end of the sixty-ninth, the Church must be removed from earth for that week to begin to run its long-delayed course.

No less compelling a reason is the fact that without some absolutely unprecedented cataclysmic global disaster the world will never, no matter how great and ingenious the efforts, be unified under one head. Jews and Arabs must be reconciled. Muslims and Hindus must stop their bloodshed; and "Christians" must be united with those of all religions. Ethnic and tribal hatreds and jealousies of many centuries standing must be removed.

What could possibly end nationalism, jealousy among nations, and warring between rival ethnic and religious groups? What could cause the entire world to unite in a new world government and a new world religion and to submit suddenly to the leadership of the Antichrist as world dictator?

To catapult the world into international political, religious, and ethnic peace and unity would take some inconceivable event of cosmic proportions. And that is exactly what the Rapture will be, as we shall see—God's catalyst to usher in Daniel's seventieth week and the final act in the drama of human history.

Consequently, the Rapture must occur before the tribulation period spoken of by Christ and detailed in Revelation. Many arguments are raised against such a view. For example, one of the verses quoted at the beginning of this chapter declares that the raising of the dead and transformation of the living will be "at the last trump." Therefore the Rapture can't take place at the beginning of the seven-year period, for the last trump isn't sounded until near the end (Revelation 11:15). So the argument goes.

First Corinthians 15:52 doesn't identify this "last trump," so we must ask, "The last trump of what?" It could be the last trump of the feast of trumpets (Leviticus 23:24) immediately preceding the Day of Atonement. Such is the belief of many students of prophecy. Or it could be some other "last trump." We aren't told that detail.

At Christ's descent from heaven there could be a series of trumpet blasts, one after the other in rapid and musical succession, as one might expect in announcing such an event. Then one final blast, the last trump, and the dead suddenly arise. The explanation may be as simple as that.

Certainly Paul doesn't identify the "last trump" as the one in Revelation 11:15. Indeed, it can't be, for as we shall see, a pre-tribulation Rapture is the key to the puzzle.

Chapter 20

An Incredible Growing Delusion

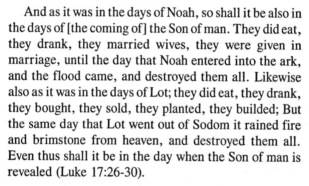

And as it was in the days of Noah, so shall it be also in the days of [the coming of] the Son of man. They did eat, they drank, they married wives, they were given in marriage, until the day that Noah entered into the ark, and the flood came, and destroyed them all. Likewise also as it was in the days of Lot; they did eat, they drank, they bought, they sold, they planted, they builded; But the same day that Lot went out of Sodom it rained fire and brimstone from heaven, and destroyed them all. Even thus shall it be in the day when the Son of man is revealed (Luke 17:26-30).

And take heed to yourselves, lest . . . that day come upon you unawares. For as a snare shall it come on all them that dwell on the face of the whole earth. Watch ye therefore, and pray always (Luke 21:34-36).

Here we have additional evidence which argues powerfully for a pre-tribulation rapture. The coming of Christ will be at a time similar to the days of Noah and Lot. These were times of great wickedness, and in that respect our generation is similar. However, that is not the point being made, for nothing is said about the evil of those days. The emphasis, instead, is upon the fact that life was normal (eating, drinking, buying, selling, planting, building) and the fact that the last thing expected was judgment. So it will be when Christ returns. Jesus Himself said so.

Once again we see that the Rapture and the Second Coming must be two separate events occurring at different times. Surely the verses above do not describe either the economic situation or mood on earth at the time of the Second Coming. Consequently, another event must be the topic.

The Second Coming occurs in Revelation 19. The previous chapters have described the progressive devastation of earth that has at this time reached almost unimaginable catastrophic proportions. Life is not normal at all. Even eating and drinking is a problem, for famine has been rampant (Revelation 6:5-6), a third of the trees and all green grass has been burned up, a third of the ocean has turned to blood, and a third of earth's waters has become bitter and poisonous (Revelation 8:7-11).

Nor is buying, selling, planting, building, or any other part of life normal. More than a billion people have died from plagues and war. There have been cataclysmic upheavals of nature which have left earth pulverized and her inhabitants in desperate straits. Certainly the conditions on earth at the time of the Second Coming are exactly the opposite of those to which Christ refers. In the days of Noah and Lot, judgment from God was unknown and the last thing those about to suffer it would have expected.

Nor is the mood on earth just before the Second Coming at all like the happy-go-lucky, judgment-will-never-come attitude that prevailed just before the flood and just prior to Sodom's destruction. The inhabitants of the earth near the end of Daniel's seventieth week have long since realized that God's judgment is being poured out upon them. As early as Revelation 6:15,16, we read that everyone on the earth is attempting to hide from God and is crying out to the rocks and mountains to fall upon them to protect them from God's judgment.

Christ Could Only Have in Mind a Pre-trib Rapture

When Christ says, "As it was in the days of Noah and Lot," it is absolutely certain that He is not describing conditions that will prevail at the time of the Second Coming. Therefore, these must be the conditions which will prevail just prior to the Rapture at a different time—and, obviously, before the devastation of the tribulation period. A pre-tribulation Rapture is, therefore, imperative.

"Ah, but the symbolism is wrong," objects someone. Christ's statement is put differently in Matthew 24:39. There it says, "And knew not until the flood came and took them [i.e., the wicked] all away." From this it is argued that it wasn't Noah and his family (a picture of believers) who were taken away, but the unbelievers. Thus there won't be a Rapture at all, but the wicked will be taken away to judgment and the righteous will remain upon the earth. So goes the common argument.

Actually, both Noah and those who rejected his preaching were taken away. Noah and his family were taken away by the ark, borne up on the water (a picture, though not a perfect one, of the Rapture), and the wicked were taken away to death by the waters of judgment.

When it comes to Lot, however, the symbolism is crystal clear. He and his family were definitely taken out of Sodom by the angels (a type of the Rapture), and, after their departure to safety, God's judgment fell (a type of the Great Tribulation). The pre-tribulation Rapture could not be depicted more accurately.

Rejection of the Rapture

As clear as the Scriptures are, the truth of the Rapture was largely lost for centuries because of the apostasy and domination of Roman Catholicism. Nor was it recovered at the Reformation, as we have noted. None of the Reformation creeds makes the essential distinction between the Rapture and the Second Coming. They refer only to a coming or return in a general sense. Nor was the Rapture found in the works of some of the most widely read Christian writers. C.S. Lewis, for example, failed even to mention the Rapture when he wrote his famous essay, "The World's Last Night," in which he dealt with the final events in world history.

A surprising number of today's evangelicals are rejecting the Rapture in favor of remaining here to take over the world.

There is an entire movement known as Manifest Sons which rejects the Rapture. It is up to Christians, according to this teaching, to "manifest" themselves as "sons of God" by attaining to sinless perfection and immortality. This, they say, will not happen at the return of Christ, but must be accomplished to bring Him back. Overcomers who manifest themselves as sons of God in this way are then, in that power, to take over the world. When the Church has established the kingdom, Christ will return to earth, not to take anyone to heaven but to rule over the kingdom the overcomers present to Him.

This clearly unbiblical teaching originated in a Pentecostal revival in Canada around 1948. An alleged prophetic utterance gave the divine interpretation of Romans 8:19. If the listeners had simply read the context, verses 14-25, instead of blindly accepting a "prophecy," they would have seen how utterly false this idea was. The "manifestation of the sons of God" comes at "the adoption, to wit the redemption of our body" (v. 23—i.e., the resurrection of the dead and transformation of the living at the Rapture) and with the believer's glorification with Christ in heaven (v. 17).

Though immediately condemned as heresy by the Assemblies of God, and confined to a fanatical fringe for years, this teaching is lately gaining increasing acceptance among Pentecostals and charismatics. In complete disregard for Christ's promise to take us to heaven and for other Scriptures we have already cited, one of the leaders in the movement, writes:

> You can study books about going to heaven in a so-called "rapture" if that turns you on. We want to study the Bible to learn to live and to love and to bring heaven to earth.

Scripture Twisting Par Excellence

Just imagine: *We* are going to bring heaven to earth! What blind pride! Some of the statements by these men are so contrary to Scripture that one finds it difficult to believe that those who make them have even read the Bible. Indeed, they study it and still come to these conclusions. The pastor of a 12,000-member church near Atlanta and author of several books, though denying that he's part of this movement, teaches the same unbiblical doctrines. Note the complete twisting of Scripture in the following:

> We who are alive and remain are left here for one ultimate purpose: to conquer the last enemy, which is death. God has left us here to take dominion over death.

The rejection of clear Biblical teaching could not be more deliberate. This popular author begins the statement with a partial quote from the Bible: "We who are alive and remain." He then substitutes his own words for the rest of the verse, directly contradicting what God has said. The Bible declares: "We who are alive and remain shall be caught up together with them [the resurrected ones] to meet the Lord in the air and so shall we ever be with the Lord." His comment that "we who are alive and remain" are *left here* is the direct opposite of being *caught up*, which the Bible wonderfully promises.

And *we* are going to conquer death? What folly! The teaching of Scripture is very clear. Christ is the One who has already conquered death. There is nothing we must or can do to "take dominion over death." Christ imparts the power of His resurrection to us in the forgiveness of sins and the gift of eternal life. Our bodies, however, remain subject to death until He returns to raise the dead and to transform the living and to catch them all together up to heaven.

Here is the sequence of events presented in 1 Thessalonians 4: 1) the Lord descends from heaven to take His Church out of this world; 2) He shouts and the trumpet sounds and (at the "last trump" per 1 Corinthians 15) the dead are raised incorruptible and caught up to meet Him; 3) the bodies of the living are also transformed into immortality and caught up to meet Christ "in the air"; 4) our Lord takes the saints of all ages to heaven.

Paul elaborates further in 1 Corinthians 15:51-57, telling us that this incredible event will take place "in the twinkling of an eye, at the last trump: for the trumpet shall sound, and the dead shall be raised incorruptible, and we [the living] shall be changed . . . then shall be brought to pass the saying that is written, Death is swallowed up in victory."

The Word of God could not be clearer that the final victory over death takes place when Christ returns, raises the dead and transforms the living. Only then is death "swallowed up in victory." It doesn't happen through our positive confession that we have victory over death, or by believing God for immortality. It is a work of Christ which He does when He returns to catch us up to heaven.

A Church That Does It All Before Christ Returns

Yet this same pastor, whose influence is growing through his books and Christian radio and television and conference speaking, declares: "The Church of Jesus Christ has not yet conquered death but this last enemy will be totally conquered before Jesus's return."[1]

Before Jesus's return? That statement directly contradicts the verses we just quoted! More Scripture perversion follows: "The Church shall be changed in a moment, in the twinkling of an eye, and it will then become the great, glorified Church of Jesus Christ on the earth."[2]

On the contrary, that happens when we are caught up to meet Christ in the air, and He takes us to heaven.

This man will insist that he believes in the Rapture when he is in the presence of those who do, and he will give the false impression that he means what they mean by that term. In fact, however, his "Rapture" has nothing to do with taking the Church to heaven. It is an allegorical term signifying a transformation of the Church into a higher spiritual state with dominion over all disease and death so that she can take over the world. He goes on to say, "I believe that when Christ returns, the Church will have taken such dominion over the earth that rulership will have already been established."

If the Church has taken over the world, Christ, at His coming, would have no need to destroy Antichrist. That teaching would astonish Paul, who specifically declared under the Holy Spirit's inspiration: "Whom the Lord shall destroy with the brightness of His coming" (2 Thessalonians 2:8). Nor does the Lord need to rescue Israel at Armageddon. The Church is in control and has conquered, if not converted, Antichrist. We can do away with Ezekiel 38–39, Zechariah 12–14, Revelation 19, and numerous other Scriptures which these new prophets supersede with their modern revelations. To remove any doubt about what these men believe, this pastor's brother and assistant elaborates:

> For centuries God has waited for His Kingdom to be established [by us] on earth.... God waits to signal His Son's return to earth. But this cannot and will not take place until the Body of Christ, the Church, is mature. ...We [mistakenly in the past] found it convenient to focus our attention on national Israel and ascribe to them the role of "God's timepiece." The scriptures clearly show that we, the Church, have become Israel. God's timepiece is not an identifiable ethnic group. God's timepiece is His Church, spiritual Israel!... But don't expect the "rapture" to rescue you.... If you want to bring Christ back to earth, you can do it... WE CAN DO IT!... We hold the key to His return."[3]

So *we* must establish the kingdom and by doing so *we* can bring Christ back to earth. Nor does Christ catch us up to meet Him in the air and take us to heaven. He comes down to earth to reign over the kingdom we have established for Him, thereby making it possible for Him to return. The Rapture is a delusion, an "escape theory" for those who aren't willing to get involved in changing the world. So this growing movement among professing evangelicals claims.

A Delusion with Serious Consequences

The consequences are rather severe for those who embrace

this deception. The Scripture plainly declares that Christ is going to catch us up to meet Him in the air and take us to heaven. Therefore all those who meet a "Christ" with their feet planted on this earth—a "Christ" who hasn't come to take them to heaven but to reign over the kingdom they've established for him—have been working for Antichrist!

The teaching that the Church must take over the world so that Christ can return to rule it is setting up both the world and a false but professing church to embrace the Antichrist when he comes. His counterfeit kingdom will be established before Christ's millennial reign. Indeed, as we have seen, it is specifically to destroy Antichrist's kingdom that the Second Coming takes place.

It is often argued that belief in a pre-trib Rapture leaves one unprepared to face Antichrist and susceptible to deception. The facts are just the opposite. It is those who deny the Rapture who have set themselves up for the most horrible deception. Antichrist will pretend to be the very "Christ" whom they expect to come to earth to reign. He will congratulate them on the good work they've done in preparing the world for his rule. Hundreds of millions of those who call themselves Christians will be completely deceived.

In actual fact, a belief in the Rapture is the surest way to be kept from deception. Wherever a "Christ" comes from when he arrives on the scene, if he doesn't resurrect all dead Christians and catch them and the living up into heaven, then he is a fraud. That is something which the Antichrist, for all his bag of tricks and lying signs and wonders, will not be able to perform. If one doesn't believe in the Rapture (in being caught up into heaven), it might then be conceivable that the Antichrist could put on such a psychic show of Satanic power that many would think he was Christ. Paul warned of this "lawless one":

> . . . whose coming is after [by the power of] Satan with all power and signs and lying wonders, and with all deceivableness of unrighteousness in them that perish; because they received not the love of the truth, that they

might be saved. And for this cause God shall send them strong delusion, that they should believe a lie: That they all might be damned who believed not the truth, but had pleasure in unrighteousness (2 Thessalonians 2:9-12).

A Strong Delusion From God

Antichrist will do exactly what the Bible foretells. For example, as a means of stabilizing world economies, he'll set up a worldwide system for buying and selling which will employ the number 666 in some way. We needn't speculate about the part that number will play. Those who don't obey him will not be allowed to buy or sell. He will set up his image in the temple—an image which all will be forced to worship on threat of death. How could one witness such events, all prophesied in Scripture and attributed to the Antichrist, and imagine that Christ was doing them?

Paul warns that God Himself will send a strong delusion to those who, prior to the Rapture, refused to receive the love of the truth. Those who reject the clear teaching of Scripture concerning the Rapture and opt instead to take over the world have already demonstrated their rejection of God's truth. They will be completely convinced that Antichrist is Christ and will follow him enthusiastically. He will fulfill all the expectations they had concerning Christ's return.

Won't the disappearance of scores of millions of Christians prove to the hundreds of millions of professing Christians who are left behind that the Rapture has indeed taken place? No. There will be explanations to prove that what occurred was not the Rapture. For example, part of the Manifest Sons teaching is that those who refuse to accept their doctrine and do not become overcomers will be instantly removed to judgment. This is their interpretation of "Then shall be two in the field; the one shall be taken, and the other left. Two women shall be grinding at the mill; the one shall be taken, and the other left" (Matthew 24:40,41).

That those who embrace the Manifest Sons teaching have been left behind will not trouble them at all. Indeed, it will prove that they are the faithful ones. It is the missing, so they will believe, who have been taken away to judgment and who are thus to be mourned. What a setup for Antichrist!

Notes

1. Earl Paulk, *Satan Unmasked*, p. 254.
2. Earl Paulk, Foreword by James Robison, *The Wounded Body of Christ* (K Dimension Publishers, 1985 edition), pp. 97-98.
3. Don Paulk, *Harvester*, June 1984.

CHAPTER 21

Pre-trib—Key to the Puzzle

$\diamond$

Immediately after the tribulation of those days shall the sun be darkened, and the moon shall not give her light. . . . And then shall appear the sign of the Son of man in heaven. . . . And he shall send his angels with a great sound of a trumpet, and they shall gather together his elect from the four winds, from one end of heaven to the other (Matthew 24:29-31).

And it was given unto him [by God] to make war with the saints, and to overcome them: and power was given him [by Satan] over all kindreds, and tongues, and nations. And all that dwell upon the earth shall worship him, whose names are not written in the book of life of the Lamb slain from the foundation of the world. . . . And he [the second beast, Antichrist's false prophet] had power to . . . cause that as many as would not worship the image of the beast should be killed. . . . And that no man might buy or sell, save he that had the mark, or the name of the beast . . . in their right hand, or in their foreheads (Revelation 13:7-17).

The verses from Matthew 24 above present the strongest Scripture for a post-tribulation Rapture. According to the advocates of this view, there simply is no argument against what seems to be stated in the plainest terms: "Immediately after the tribulation of those days . . . shall gather together his elect from the four winds."

The proper interpretation hinges upon the basic argument we have supported with biblical and historical evidence and with logic in so many ways in the previous chapters: There are two comings: 1) the Rapture, which must take place at the beginning of Daniel's seventieth week; and 2) the Second Coming, which clearly takes place at the end thereof in the midst of Armageddon. Yes, there is a coming of Christ "immediately after the tribulation of those days." It is not the Rapture, however, but the Second Coming. The evidence and arguments we have given overwhelmingly support this conclusion. So does the language of the verses above.

There are several factors to take into consideration. The first is that the coming described in these verses takes place after the tribulation and is accompanied by unmistakable signs in the sky which are visible to and recognized by all mankind. Yet the Rapture takes place at a time when conditions are like those in the days of Noah—no tribulation has occurred and the last thing expected is God's judgment. There are no accompanying signs for the Rapture. The whole idea is surprise, which is why Christ warns us to watch and wait lest that day overtake us unawares.

Christ's Language Makes It Clear

Several times we've gone over Christ's "I will come again and receive you unto myself" (John 14:3). This was the wonderful promise He made at the last supper. It is an intimate pledge to His own to catch them up to His Father's house to be with Him forever. What Christ describes in the Matthew 24 passage above sounds altogether different from the Rapture.

Take the previous verse (27): "For as the lightning cometh out of the east, and shineth even unto the west; so shall also the coming of the Son of man be." Obviously the world is deliberately being notified of what is about to occur. The despised and rejected One is coming for vengeance. Christ is about to confront Antichrist face-to-face. Let the world tremble!

Surely the event being described is not the intimate catching away of His bride to His Father's house! One could argue that a miraculous sign in the sky at the time of the Rapture would add terror to the sudden mass disappearance of millions from earth. But Christ is not describing a "sign" that will add significance to a mysterious catching away of millions from earth. He is obviously describing His visible return to the scene of His rejection to execute judgment. He goes on to say, "And they shall see the Son of man coming in the clouds of heaven with power and great glory." It can only be at Armageddon, to the Mount of Olives, as John explained it in more detail later:

> Behold, he cometh with clouds; and every eye shall see him, and they also which pierced him: and all kindreds of the earth shall wail because of him. And I saw heaven opened, and behold a white horse; and he that sat upon him was called Faithful and True. . . . His eyes were as a flame of fire, and on his head were many crowns. . . . And the armies which were in heaven followed him upon white horses, clothed in fine linen, white and clean. And out of his mouth goeth a sharp sword, that with it he should smite the nations: and he shall rule them with a rod of iron: and he treadeth the winepress of the fierceness and wrath of Almighty God. . . . And I saw the beast, and the kings of the earth, and their armies, gathered together to make war against him that sat on the horse (Revelation 1:7; 19:11-20).

Christ came once as the Lamb of God. Like a lamb dumb before its shearers, He was silent before His accusers, for He took our place and we had no answer to make to God's accusation against us. He was meek and submitted to man's hatred and abuse and allowed them to nail Him to a cross. Now He comes as the Lion of the tribe of Judah, in majesty and power, the Lord of glory, Creator of the universe, to execute judgment upon the ungodly. That is why the Second Coming will be like lightning flashing across the sky, visible to every eye.

The language isn't describing the Rapture of saints to heaven, but the visible descent of Christ to earth "with all the saints" accompanying Him. His mission at this time is not to catch up a bride to heaven, but to confront Antichrist upon earth, destroy his evil kingdom, and to set up His own reign of righteousness. This is not the catching up of His saints to the Judgment Seat of Christ in heaven, but the awesome execution of judgment upon the ungodly on this earth.

What About the Elect?

The above may sound logical, is the rejoinder of post-trib advocates, but this passage clearly says that He catches up His elect. That must refer to the church, so this can only be the Rapture. There is the sound of a trumpet, too, just as in 1 Thessalonians 4 and 1 Corinthians 15. It couldn't be clearer: The Rapture takes place in conjunction with the Second Coming at the end of the Great Tribulation.

We have already shown why these two events cannot occur at the same time. Moreover, this passage, from its very language, confirms that fact. Look at verse 31 again and note some contrasts between it and the Rapture passages. In 1 Thessalonians 4 we have "the voice of the archangel and the trump of God"; here we have "a great sound of a trumpet" but no archangel. At the Rapture it is Christ Himself who catches us up to meet Him in the air. Here it is "his angels" who "gather together his elect."

Nor is there anything about being caught up to meet Him in the air. The term "gather together" is altogether different. The gathering together is "from the four winds" or from the four corners of the earth under heaven—obviously to a single location on this earth, not to a rendezvous in the sky.

It is His elect who are being gathered together. Who would they be? That term is used for the Church, but also for Israel: "For Jacob my servant's sake, and Israel mine elect" (Isaiah 45:4). If it were the Church in view here, they would be caught up to meet Christ in the air. Instead, they are being gathered back to their own land for the Messiah's millennial reign exactly as the Hebrew prophets foretold:

> And I will bring forth a seed out of Jacob, and out of
> Judah an inheritor of my mountains: and mine elect shall

inherit it, and my servants shall dwell there. I will rejoice in Jerusalem, and joy in my people: and the voice of weeping shall be no more heard in her. ... And mine elect shall long enjoy the work of their hands ... for they are the seed of the blessed of the Lord, and their off-spring with them. ... The wolf and the lamb shall feed together, and the lion shall eat straw like the bullock. ... They shall not hurt nor destroy in all my holy mountain, saith the Lord (Isaiah 65:9-25).

We can only conclude that "elect" here means the seed of Abraham, Isaac, and Jacob. They are being gathered by the angels from every part of earth and taken to Israel where Christ has arrived to destroy Antichrist, rescue His people, and set up His kingdom. All surviving Jews who have not yet returned to Israel will be gathered there from every part of the earth to meet their Messiah and participate in His millennial reign.

The Rapture is an altogether different event. It has preceded by seven years what is being described in the above verses. In fact, as we shall see, had the Rapture not occurred the Anti-christ could not have come to power. The final events de-scribed in Revelation require the Rapture both to set the stage and as a catalyst to cause otherwise impossible alignments to take place. Moreover, without the Rapture "all the saints" (Zechariah 14:5) would not be in heaven ready to accompany Christ back to earth.

Let's Face the Reality of a Pre-tribulation Rapture

Whether one believes in the Rapture or not, let us suppose for a moment that it actually happened. Here is an event so far beyond anything in history that it staggers the imagination. With no warning—in fact, when prospects are rosy and the world is congratulating itself that "peace and safety" seem assured (1 Thessalonians 5:3)—scores of millions of people from every nation and race and locality instantly vanish from the face of the earth.

Estimates place the number of Christians in Red China at upwards of 80 million, in Africa at 100 million, in the United States at 50 million. These figures may be high, especially in the USA. However, out of an estimated 1.7 billion professing Christians in today's world it would not seem unreasonable to suggest that 250 million truly know the Lord and would leave in the Rapture. That's the entire population of the United States! One cannot even imagine the impact of such a mass disappearance.

Hundreds of millions of people around the world have witnessed the impossible: A relative, friend, neighbor, acquaintance or total stranger—or perhaps a combination of several of them—have suddenly vanished. People have disappeared from escalators in shopping malls, instantly vanished from elevators in high-rise apartments or office buildings, and from airplanes in flight. In some cases the entire cockpit crew has vanished and the plane has crashed. Drivers of automobiles on all kinds of roads and highways have vanished. In sections of some freeways the tangle of wreckage may take weeks to clear for lack of equipment to deal with a disaster on this scale—and for lack of operators of cranes and tow trucks, who have also mysteriously disappeared.

In the United States, unlike most other countries, there are familiar faces missing from top levels of government—from the White House staff, Cabinet, Congress, Senate, Pentagon. The military has been decimated: admirals; generals; colonels; fighter, bomber, and helicopter pilots; those holding key top-secret positions involving cryptography and nuclear arms have vanished by the thousands. Business and industry are similarly stripped of key personnel, from the factory to executive offices.

The United Nations Security Council (except for a few of its members who have vanished as well) is meeting in emergency session almost around the clock. Haggard officials in every city of any size face the same unimaginable chaos. It will take months to unravel the tangle of insurance claims for missing persons, to sort out the credit card and banking confusion of accounts for whom no parties exist either to collect from or to pay.

Effect of a Pre-tribulation Rapture on the World

All of the chaos described above is eclipsed, however, by the horrifying fact that hundreds of millions of infants suddenly vanished as well. If we believe that babies who die are covered by Christ's atonement and taken to heaven, then it would seem likely that at the Rapture all who are too young to be account-able would also be taken. There is scarcely a family anywhere in the world, of any nation or religion that is untouched. Here is the most heartrending and terrifying aspect of this incomprehensible disaster. The fact that missing babies and young children far outnumber adults who vanished gives the event its most ominous tone.

Where did they, the adults and children, all go? Who took them? Is some intergalactic power snatching slaves? Could the missing have been beamed aboard advanced spacecraft and taken off to populate another planet in some bizarre experiment? The inhabitants of earth would feel themselves at the mercy of a power that obviously had no mercy and against which there was no defense. At any moment millions more might vanish. Who might be snatched next?

Beyond the perplexity, mystery, and chaos is the unspeakable terror that grips the world. Here at last would be something large enough and horrible enough to unite every warring faction on earth. The common terror shared by all of earth's inhabitants would unify them in a way that nothing else could. The sudden sense of oneness and mutual dependence experienced by the few survivors of a plane crash on an isolated mountain peak would pale in comparison to the unity created among the survivors of this inconceivable and eerie catastrophe.

Conflicts between Muslims and Hindus in India, between Arabs and Jews in Israel, between Catholics and Protestants in Ireland, between ethnic groups in Yugoslavia or in the former Soviet Union would suddenly have become meaningless. Everything that had seemed so important the moment before—love or hate, war or peace, profit or loss, employment or unemployment, grades in school or salary at work, or whatever it might have been—would have lost all significance. There would be only one reality. The appalling fear gripping every individual would override even the grief of missing loved ones. Stark, raving terror and panic would reign.

Here we have the one event of such magnitude that it could remove all other considerations and unite the world completely as nothing else possibly could. There are those who suggest, for example, that World War III would have that effect and that out of the ashes of a nuclear holocaust would come the necessary unity. That is a doubtful scenario at best. No war yet has had such an effect, nor would it likely be the case for any war in the future. Wars leave deep wounds and fresh hatreds that can only increase division, not bring unity.

Any scenario for uniting the world must deal with one billion Muslims whose allegiance to Allah commits them to ultimate Islamic supremacy as the major article of their faith. No Middle East peace treaty, no pledges, no threats, no deals can ever change that underlying fanatical commitment. Arabs are not even united among themselves but would be at each other's throats had they not a common enemy. The one and only thing that gives the Arab world any semblance of unity is their common hatred for Israel and the passion they share to see her annihilated. Try to think of anything else that could instantly unite Islamic Arabs with the rest of the world. There is nothing else.

The Rapture, and the Rapture alone, would break down every barrier and unite the entire world. Arabs and even the most fanatical of Muslims would now share a common terror with all survivors of this worldwide calamity—a terror so great that even the passion to annihilate Jews would be at least temporarily forgotten.

A Pre-trib Rapture: Perfect Opportunity for Antichrist

Suppose, too, that suddenly in the midst of the terror and chaos a man arises who has an ingenious but sensible explanation for what took place. Moreover, he alone can guarantee that all those who submit to Him as world ruler will be safe from any further threat of disappearance from earth. He is not without unusual credentials that would generate confidence in his abilities and knowledge. Most convincing of all are the apparent miracles he is able to perform. While all is done by the power of Satan, he passes it off as mind or psychic power with the promise that all mankind can develop similar abilities under his guidance.

There are many possible scenarios from this point on. Let us consider only one. Suppose there are massive UFO sightings immediately following the Rapture. Huge spacecraft are seen everywhere, even in broad daylight, so that there can be no doubt as to their existence and power. Earth's military forces are helpless. This man, in a bold attempt at negotiation, consents to being taken aboard a huge spacecraft—or so everyone is led to believe—that hovers over the United Nations headquarters in New York. Of all earth's inhabitants he is singled out by these beings who, though they deny taking anyone from earth, declare that they know which intergalactic power did so and that they can prevent any recurrence in the future. The only man they will work with on earth is this one individual—and through him they guarantee protection if certain rules are followed.

Let such a man arise with an explanation that the world believes and with the apparent power to guarantee safety for everyone on earth, and the world is in his hands. He may even claim to be in negotiation with some intergalactic council for the ultimate return of those who have vanished. Still emotionally unhinged from the mass disappearance (hundreds of thousands have gone insane), those left behind would only be too happy to have Big Brother put his mark on their hand or forehead and know that he was watching out for them, promising that there would be no other such disaster.

There are other possibilities, but little point in presenting them. Whatever explanation may be given for the mass disappearance, and whatever accompanying circumstances may assist, one thing is quite clear: The Rapture is the one catalyst that could suddenly bring into being the New World Order with its one world government and world religion which is foundational to Antichrist's world rule. The Rapture is essential to any scenario for uniting the world under Antichrist and giving him the absolute power which the Bible indicates he will have..

How This Scenario Fits Other Scriptures

We have given many biblical reasons for a pre-tribulation Rapture. We've shown that Daniel's seventieth week can't even start to run its course until the church is removed. We have noted that the saints must have previously been taken to heaven in order to come from there with Christ at the Second Coming. Now we have added a logical reason: Antichrist could not ascend to power without the Rapture terrifying the entire world into uniting under him. The Bible gives at least two reasons which support this view.

First of all is the timing of Antichrist's ascension to power. There are those who suggest that it cannot occur until the middle of the seven-year period. They can't imagine how he could gain control any earlier. Antichrist, however, makes a covenant of peace with the many for that entire week, as we've seen, so he must be in power at the beginning. He breaks that covenant "in the midst of the week," so he can hardly just come to power at that time, since it is a covenant which he has made three and a half years earlier.

The conclusions we've arrived at present a cohesive picture. The seventieth week can't begin nor can Antichrist be revealed until the Church is removed in the Rapture. Yet he must be in full power immediately thereafter in order to make the covenant at the beginning of the seventieth week as Daniel declared. Logically, then, it is the Rapture itself which both allows Antichrist to be revealed and terrifies the world into an otherwise impossible unity and catapults him suddenly into control of the world.

Second, Paul tells the Thessalonians: "You know what withholdeth that he [Antichrist] might be revealed in his time. For . . . he who now hinders will hinder until he be taken out of the way. And then shall that Wicked be revealed" (2 Thessalonians 2:6-8). A Person is preventing the Antichrist from being revealed. Quite clearly He is no ordinary person, for He who prevented Antichrist's revelation in Paul's day 1900 years ago is still doing so today. He is not only timeless but omnipotent, for Satan cannot act until this One is out of the way.

Paul can only be referring to the Holy Spirit. But He cannot be removed from earth because He is omnipresent. Furthermore, there will be many converted through the gospel of the kingdom during the Great Tribulation, and for that to be possible the Holy Spirit must be present to convince and convict them. Then what is the meaning of "until he be taken out of the way"? How could that apply to the Holy Spirit?

The Church is described as "a habitation of God through the Spirit" (Ephesians 2:22). The bodies of all Christians are the "temples of the Holy Spirit" (1 Corinthians 6:19). God the Holy Spirit is present in this world in a unique way that was not true before the Church was formed nor will be so after the Church is removed in the Rapture. When the Church is taken to heaven, that special presence of the Holy Spirit will also be removed, though He will be here as God omnipresent as He eternally is throughout the entire universe.

More Reasons Why the Church Must Be Removed

The true Church would not tolerate the Antichrist for a moment. She would expose his identity, prove it from Scripture, and oppose him. She would actively warn others and stand solidly in the way of Antichrist and his diabolical machinations. Satan's plans through Antichrist cannot go forward until the Church has been removed.

Furthermore, if the Church were present during the Great Tribulation, she would be wiped out by the Antichrist. But that would not be allowed by God. He who protects the Church, who said "the gates of hell shall not prevail against" her, is the same One who gives Antichrist the power to "make war with the saints and overcome [kill] them . . . [and that] as many as would not worship the image of the beast [Antichrist] should be killed" (Revelation 13:7,15).

The only way both to protect the Church and allow Antichrist to kill all saints is to remove the Church. The saints who are killed by Antichrist are those who have not previously rejected the truth and become believers in Christ during the Great Tribulation. They pay for their faith with their blood:

> And I saw under the altar the souls of them that were slain for the word of God, and for the testimony which they held: And they cried, How long, O Lord . . . dost thou not . . . avenge our blood on them that dwell on earth? . . . And it was said unto them, that they should rest . . . until their fellowservants also and their brethren, that should be killed as they were, should be fulfilled. These are they which came out of great tribulation, and have washed their robes and made them white in the blood of the Lamb (Revelation 6:9-11; 7:14).

A post-tribulation "Rapture" would be a classic nonevent. There would be few if any believers in Christ to take to heaven. They would all have been killed, for such is the fate of those who refuse to take the mark of the beast (Antichrist) and worship his image. Submission to Antichrist is the only way to stay alive during that horrible period. For those, however, who take the mark of the beast and worship his image there is an even worse fate:

> If any man worship the beast and his image, and receive his mark in his forehead, or in his hand, The same shall drink of the wine of the wrath of God, which is poured out without mixture. . . . And they have no rest day nor night, who worship the beast and his image, and whosoever receiveth the mark of his name (Revelation 14:9-11).

Finally, a post-tribulation Rapture removes an essential factor involved in the Rapture: imminency. The Bible, as we shall see, teaches that Christ could have come at any time in history. Nor is there anything that prevents Him from coming at this moment.

CHAPTER 22

A Post-trib Scenario

◇

> For yourselves know perfectly that the day of the Lord
> so cometh as a thief in the night. For when they shall say,
> Peace and safety; then sudden destruction cometh upon
> them, as travail upon a woman with child; and they shall
> not escape. But ye, brethren, are not in darkness, that
> that day should overtake you as a thief. Ye are all chil-
> dren of light, and the children of the day. . . . Therefore
> let us not sleep, as do others; but let us watch and be sober
> (1 Thessalonians 5:2-4).

One frequently hears the argument: "There is no record that
the early Church believed in the imminent return of Christ.
The idea of a pre-tribulation Rapture wasn't dreamed up until
the 1830s." No matter how "early" it may have existed, any
church is the wrong place to look for truth. Paul lamented,
"All they which are in Asia be turned away from me" (2 Timothy 1:15). The Church of Paul's own day had already gone
astray in many ways. Most of his epistles had to be written to
correct error that was already in the earliest Church.

Don't be deceived by those who cite some "early Church
father" and suggest that we must accept his interpretation of
Scripture as authentic because he "knew Peter" or "was a
contemporary with the apostle John." Those who lived in the
days of Peter and John had already embraced serious heresies.
Paul had to warn the Ephesian elders, "After my departing

shall grievous wolves enter in among you, not sparing the flock. Also of your own selves shall men arise, speaking perverse things, to draw away disciples after them" (Acts 20:29,30). If the elders at Ephesus whom Paul had trained could go astray, then no so-called "early Church fathers" may be safely looked to as authoritative.

The Word of God is the only sure source of truth. Never mind what some "early Church" did or didn't believe. The New Testament will tell us what the first Christians believed, where they went astray, and what we ought to believe and practice today. Nor can there be any doubt, when one reads the New Testament, that the Church of Paul's day believed in and fervently awaited the imminent return of Christ to Rapture her to heaven. There is no earlier Church to provide an example than that one!

A Troubling Rumor

As we shall see, the early Church believed in and actively watched and waited for Christ's imminent return. Consequently, they must have believed in a pre-tribulation Rapture, though that term is not used. Christ's imminent return is a major theme running throughout the New Testament. It was a "blessed hope" (Titus 2:13) that all were anticipating at any moment. This fact is clear once again from what Paul wrote in his second epistle to the Thessalonians:

> Now we beseech you, brethren, by the coming of our Lord Jesus Christ [Second Coming], and by our gathering together unto him [Rapture], That ye be not soon shaken in mind, or be troubled, neither by spirit, nor by word, nor by letter as from us, as that the day of Christ is at hand (2 Thessalonians 2:1,2).

What was this "day of Christ" to which Paul referred, and why should the believers at Thessalonica be concerned if it had come? The answer to that question has a direct bearing upon our topic. In trying to calm their concern, Paul appeals both to the Rapture and to the Second Coming. Therefore both must have an important relationship to "the day of Christ."

Paul had mentioned that day in his first epistle to the Thessalonian saints in the verses quoted at the beginning of this chapter. He had emphasized that it would come like a thief when the world would not expect it. The Christians, however, would not be caught by surprise if they were watching and waiting for Christ's return. The thought that this day of the Lord was upon them had shaken the believers in Thessalonica. Apparently they had been caught unawares. Their concern, however, went beyond that possibility.

Paul had no doubt discussed the "day of Christ" with them so they knew it was going to be a time of great destruction from God upon this earth. In fact, it would include the Great Tribulation, as Paul reminded them in the opening verses of this his second epistle to the Thessalonians. After commending them for patiently, and with faith in God, enduring "persecutions and tribulations" at the hands of the ungodly, Paul writes:

> Seeing it is a righteous thing with God to recompense tribulation to them that trouble you; And to you who are troubled rest with us, when the Lord Jesus shall be revealed from heaven with his mighty angels, In flaming fire taking vengeance on them that know not God and that obey not the gospel of our Lord Jesus Christ: Who shall be punished with everlasting destruction from the presence of the Lord . . . when he shall come to be glorified in his saints, and to be admired in all them that believe in that day (2 Thessalonians 1:6-10).

The reference is obviously to Christ's Second Coming in power and glory at Armageddon to wreak vengeance upon the godless. "In that day," doubtless refers to the day of Christ, thus attaching that identification to the time of His revelation to the world in the capacity of the Avenger. That day must also have included preliminary events leading up to Armageddon. Otherwise, the Thessalonian believers would not have given rumors that the day of Christ had arrived a second thought, for obviously that huge battle was not even on the distant horizon.

Post-Tribbers Would Not Be Troubled

Other than being caught by surprise, which they shouldn't have been, why would the Thessalonian believers be upset to know that the day of Christ had arrived? There was no reason to be "shaken in mind" if they believed in a post-trib Rapture. There was, however, sound reason for being shaken if they believed in a pre-trib Rapture. Clearly, then, the latter was their view.

If the Thessalonians knew they had to go through the Great Tribulation in order to arrive at the Rapture, which they looked forward to with eager anticipation, then it would not have troubled them to know that the day of Christ had come. Their reaction rather would have been, "Praise God! The time has come for us to face Antichrist and prove our love and faithfulness to our Lord. If we are martyred, we have a special crown. If not, and we endure to the end, then we will be caught up to meet Christ on His descent to the Mount of Olives." After all, the coming of the day of the Lord and the revelation of the Antichrist with the accompanying tribulation was certainly what they had anticipated if they believed in a post-trib rapture. Not exactly a "blessed hope," but surely nothing to be "shaken in mind" or "troubled" about.

If, on the other hand, the Thessalonians were expecting Christ before the tribulation period and it had arrived without their leaving in the Rapture, they had something, indeed, to be "shaken in mind" about! Had they been rejected by Christ? Why hadn't they been taken? And why was Paul still there and all of the other Christians? No one had been caught up to heaven.

If the day of Christ had arrived without Christ taking His own out of the world, then perhaps they had been misinformed not only on this subject but on many others as well. That possibility was enough to shake them.

The point is, the Thessalonians would have had no reason to be "shaken in mind" if they believed in a post-trib Rapture. The fact that they were badly shaken at the thought that they were in the tribulation only shows they had been taught that Christ would Rapture them prior to that horrible time.

Paul, however, did not use the term "Great Tribulation" or even "tribulation." Here he refers to "the day of Christ." Elsewhere he calls it "the day of the Lord Jesus." Both terms are the New Testament equivalent of "the day of the Lord," an expression used many times in the Old Testament.

The Day of the Lord/Christ

That the day of the Lord is not a literal 24-hour day is clear from reading only a few of the references to it. Far too much happens to occur in one day. In fact, as we noted concerning the coming of Christ, so it is with the day of the Lord. Seemingly contradictory statements are made about it that must be reconciled with each other—and which require a far longer period to be worked out than a literal day.

Frequently "the day of the Lord" is referred to as a day of woe, evil, vengeance from God, of indescribable destruction: "the day of his [God's] wrath" (Psalm 110:5); "a destruction from the Almighty" (Joel 1:15); "great and very terrible, who can abide it?" (Joel 2:11); "woe...darkness and not light" (Amos 5:18); "the day of the Lord's anger" (Zephaniah 2:2,3); "that shall burn as an oven; and all the proud, yea, and all that do wickedly, shall be stubble...saith the Lord of hosts" (Malachi 4:1). Such descriptions leave no doubt that the day of the Lord includes the Great Tribulation period.

The Day of the Lord pertains especially to Israel and involves the Messiah coming to her rescue at Armageddon and executing judgment upon those who have mistreated her. That fact is also clear from reading the context of the few verses just referred to as well as from the large number of other passages dealing with this subject.

It is interesting to note how Christ handled the Scripture (Isaiah 61:1,2) that He read in the synagogue of Nazareth on that important day when He declared His mission in coming to earth:

> And he came to Nazareth, where he had been brought
> up: and, as his custom was, he went into the synagogue

on the sabbath day, and stood up for to read. And there
was delivered unto him the book of the prophet Esaias.
And...he found the place where it was written, The
Spirit of the Lord is upon me, because he hath anointed
me to preach the gospel to the poor; he hath sent me to
heal the broken-hearted, to preach deliverance to the
captives, and recovering of sight to the blind, to set at
liberty them that are bruised, To preach the acceptable
year of the Lord. And he closed the book. . . . And he
began to say unto them, This day is this scripture fulfilled in your ears (Luke 4:16-21).

He was, of course, declaring to those in His hometown who
knew Him only as the carpenter that He was the fulfillment of
the passage He had just read, i.e., the Messiah. They were
enraged at such blasphemy and tried to kill Him. Most interesting is the fact that He stopped reading in mid-sentence. The
next phrase, which He avoided, says, "and the day of vengeance of our God."

Again the Necessity for Two Comings

Here we have another example of an Old Testament Scripture with a double meaning which required the Messiah to
come twice. Jesus read that part which pertained to His first
advent and refrained from reading that which pertained to His
Second Coming. "The day of vengeance" is another description of "the day of the Lord." We can now see its intimate
relationship to the Messiah and His Second Coming. Jude, as
already noted, reminds us of Enoch's prophecy that the Lord
(Yahweh) will come "with ten thousands [i.e., an innumerable
company] of his saints, to execute judgment upon all."

So the day of the Lord, this day of vengeance and judgment
from the Almighty, includes the Second Coming. Therefore,
in the New Testament it is called the day of Christ, for it is the
day when He will be "revealed from heaven in flaming fire
taking vengeance upon them that know not God." The Messiah
is the One who will proclaim that day and execute that vengeance; therefore, it is rightly called the day of Christ.

In stopping His reading where He did, Christ was indicating that the day of vengeance was being deferred. Had Daniel's seventieth week followed immediately the consummation of the sixty-ninth, the day of the Lord would have begun right after His crucifixion, but it did not. It has been delayed for reasons we have already discussed.

This day of the Lord, however, includes more than the Great Tribulation ("the time of Jacob's trouble"—Jeremiah 30:7) and Armageddon. It is also a day of great blessing for Israel under the Messiah's millennial reign as Zechariah 14 (and other Scriptures) makes clear:

> Behold the day of the Lord cometh. . . . I will gather all nations against Jerusalem to battle; and the city shall be taken. . . . Then shall the Lord go forth, and fight against those nations. . . . And his feet shall stand in that day [the day of the Lord] upon the mount of Olives . . . and the mount of Olives shall cleave in the midst thereof toward the east and toward the west, and there shall be a very great valley. . . . And it shall be in that day [the day of the Lord] that living waters shall go out from Jerusalem [through the newly formed valley]. . . . And the Lord [Christ] shall be king over all the earth [ruling on the throne of His father David in Jerusalem]: in that day [the day of the Lord] shall there be one Lord, and his name one. [i.e., no false religions allowed]. . . . And it shall come to pass, that every one that is left of all the nations which came against Jerusalem shall even go up from year to year to worship the King, the Lord of hosts [Jesus Christ], and to keep the feast of tabernacles (Zechariah 14:1-4,8,9,16).

There is yet more to the day of the Lord. It also includes the destruction after the millennium of the entire universe by fire and the ushering in of a new universe. Peter confirms Paul's statement about this day arriving as a thief (1 Thessalonians 5:2), then goes on to explain further what John later reconfirmed in Revelation:

> But the day of the Lord will come as a thief in the night; in which the heavens shall pass away with a great noise, and the elements shall melt with fervent heat, the earth also and the works that are therein shall be burned up. . . . Nevertheless we, according to his promise, look for a new heavens and a new earth, wherein dwelleth righteousness (2 Peter 3:10,13).

> And I saw a new heaven and a new earth: for the first heaven and the first earth were passed away; and there was no more sea. And I John saw the holy city, new Jerusalem, coming down from God out of heaven, prepared as a bride adorned for her husband (Revelation 21:1,2).

While agreeing that the day of the Lord begins with the Rapture, the chief proponent of a "pre-wrath Rapture" places it at the end of Revelation 6 just prior to the opening of the seventh seal by Christ. Such a timing is impossible. Six of the seven seals of judgment having already been opened, the world is in chaos, suffering from famine, wars, and unprecedented upheavals of nature.

The opening of the second seal "took peace from the earth" (v. 4). Yet the day of the Lord comes when the world is exulting in having achieved "peace and safety." The whole world recognizes that "the great day of his [Him that sitteth upon the throne and the Lamb] wrath is come" (vv. 16,17) and cries out to the rocks and mountains to hide them from God's wrath. Yet the day of the Lord or the day of Christ comes as a thief, when the last thing the world's inhabitants expect is God's judgment.

We can only conclude that the day of the Lord begins before any signs or warnings or disasters occur. Such are also the conditions at the Rapture. We know that the Rapture marks the beginning of Daniel's seventieth week, which we can now see coincides with the start of the day of the Lord. This scenario agrees with Christ's warning that He would come as a thief (Matthew 24:43; Luke 12:39) when even believers would be caught by surprise (Matthew 24:44; Luke 12:40) and at a time similar to the days of Noah: of eating, drinking, building, marrying, business as usual. Such conditions certainly no longer prevail upon the earth at the end of Revelation 6, much less in the midst of Armageddon.

But What About "The First Resurrection"?

A major post-trib argument is that the Bible teaches a post-trib resurrection, so that has to be when the Rapture takes place. For example, Revelation 20:4-5 declares that the "first resurrection" takes place after the battle of Armageddon, so the Rapture must occur then. Moreover, Christ said, "No man can come to me except the Father which hath sent me draw him: and I will raise him up *at the last day*." The expression "last day" could hardly be referring to the beginning of the Great Tribulation!

First of all, it must be noted that Revelation 20:4,5 is only a partial resurrection. It does not refer to the resurrection of *all* believers, but only to those martyred by Antichrist during the Great Tribulation: "them that were beheaded for the witness of Jesus, and for the word of God, and which had not worshipped the beast, neither his image, neither had received his mark."

One must ask, what about Abraham, David, Peter, Paul, Spurgeon, Moody, and Christians who have died more recently, none of whom were slain by Antichrist? When are they resurrected? It is stated very clearly that they are resurrected at the Rapture: "The dead in Christ [all of them] shall rise first: then we which are alive and remain shall be caught up together...to meet the Lord in the air" (1 Thessalonians 4:16,17).

Therefore, the Rapture, which coincides with a general resurrection of all those who have died trusting in Christ, is another event and must occur at another time. Before or after Armageddon? Obviously it occurs before, because the resurrected saints are already in heaven and accompany Christ from there to Armageddon. Revelation 19:7-9 describes "the marriage supper of the Lamb" involving, of course, His bride, the Church (Ephesians 5:23-32). She is clothed in fine linen, white and clean (v. 8). Next, Christ descends with "the armies which were in heaven...[also] clothed in fine linen, white and clean" (v. 14) to confront and destroy Antichrist at Armageddon. The Church clearly comprises at least a large part of that army.

As we have already noted, Enoch prophesied that Christ would return to this earth "with ten thousands [i.e., an innumerable company] of his saints, to execute judgment" upon Antichrist and his followers (Jude 14,15). Zechariah 14:4,5 states that when Christ comes to earth to rescue Israel and "His feet stand in that day upon the mount of Olives... *all* the saints" come with Him. These are not disembodied spirits waiting to be resurrected! The saints who are present at the marriage supper of the Lamb and who accompany Christ from heaven to reign on earth must be in their glorified bodies—and they must have been taken to heaven previously in order to descend from there with Him at Armageddon.

That this resurrection after Armageddon specifically involves only "the souls of them" who were martyred by Antichrist is, in fact, another argument for a pre-trib Rapture. It indicates that all other saints have previously been resurrected. Then why wait until this late time for these martyrs to be raised? We are told why.

Some of these same souls are seen earlier:

> I saw under the altar the souls of them that were slain
> for the word of God... and it was said unto them, that
> they should rest... until their fellowservants also...
> that should be killed as they were, should be fulfilled
> (Revelation 6:9-11).

Since all Great Tribulation martyrs are resurrected together—and Antichrist kills believers to the very end—their resurrection must await the end of Armageddon.

If the resurrection of believers who lived and died prior to the tribulation took place seven years previously, why is the resurrection in Revelation 20 of those slain by Antichrist called "the first resurrection"? It must be in order to show that these martyrs are part of that company, the Church, which has already been resurrected. It specifically says that they "reign with him [Christ] a thousand years" (Revelation 20:6) as do the saints of all ages.

What about Christ raising all believers "at the last day"? As we have just seen, this "last day" cannot be the 24-hour period in which these martyrs are raised, for there are many more days that follow during the millennium. The "last day" is a reference to what is also called "the day of the Lord [God]" (Isaiah 2:12; Jeremiah 46:10; Ezekiel 30:3; Joel 1:15, etc.) or "the day of Christ" (1 Corinthians 1:8; Philippians 1:10; 2 Thessalonians 2:2), which we have just discussed. As we have seen, it begins with the Rapture and includes Daniel's seventieth week, the millennium, the destruction of this old universe and the creation of a new one.

A Post-tribulation Scenario

Those who believe in a post-tribulation Rapture must place the beginning of the day of the Lord at Armageddon. It can hardly be placed any later, such as the beginning of the millennium, because of the great destruction and judgment upon Israel and all the nations which it unquestionably involves. At the end of the tribulation, however, the conditions are the exact opposite of those that Christ warned would prevail at the time of the Rapture and the beginning of the day of the Lord.

Let us assume a post-tribulation Rapture in order to see that it doesn't fit our Lord's exhortations and warnings. We look in upon a few beleaguered Christians who have gathered together in secret at the risk of their lives. It is the end of the Great Tribulation. They are certain of that fact, because every event Christ foretold in His Olivet discourse and all the events John laid out with such precision in Revelation have happened exactly as prophesied. They have agonizingly witnessed it all.

The Antichrist established his New World Order, recovered from his deadly head wound, continues to perform great signs and wonders, and the world worships his image in Jerusalem's rebuilt temple. All who would not worship him as God have been killed, except for a very few new believers in Jesus who have escaped and are being hunted down by the world police whose informers are everywhere. The natural disasters have followed their course just as foretold. Worldwide television has covered the two witnesses preaching repentance in the streets of Jerusalem. Their execution by Antichrist, resurrection, and ascent into heaven has also been witnessed by the world. There can be no doubt that the seven years of Daniel's seventieth week have gone according to schedule and the calendar is about to run out.

Having gathered together the armies of the world, Antichrist has invaded Israel, and a nuclear exchange has begun. Refusing to go down to defeat like a lamb to the slaughter, Israel opted to use her ultimate weapon as she had warned. Nevertheless, the forces arrayed against her are overwhelming and she is doomed. It is a replay of Hitler's "final solution to the Jewish problem," only this time on a massive scale and engineered by the Antichrist himself.

Our small group of Christians is meeting in a cave deep in a forest somewhere. Having refused to take the mark of the beast, unable to buy or sell, they are destitute, starving. Marked for death for refusing to worship the Antichrist's image, they have managed somehow to escape and barely survive. As they have followed the events of the past seven years, they have noted in the margins of their worn and precious Bibles each time a prophecy was being fulfilled. In that process, they have arrived at Revelation 19 and now mark in the margin that Armageddon is in full execution.

One of their number rises and asks uncertainly, "Do you think it is now time for the Lord to come?" He is hooted down. "Of course not," the others snort. "Look at conditions around you. If there was ever a time when He wouldn't come, this is it. Now let's get some sleep." Such a post-trib scenario is unbelievable.

A Scenario Beyond Belief

The scene above is so far from the "at such an hour as ye think not the Son of man cometh" which Christ described as to be beyond belief. Eating and drinking, buying and selling, marrying and feasting, business as usual, and no expectation of God's judgment just as it was in Noah's day? Those conditions prevailing at the end of the Great Tribulation in the midst of Armageddon? One would have to be mad to imagine such a setting for a post-trib Rapture. The world is on the brink of total destruction! Christ warned that unless He intervened no flesh would be left alive (Matthew 24:22).

A complacent Church sleeping soundly, the wise along with the foolish? Antichrist has had power to kill all Christians for many months—and he and the other world leaders sharing in his New World Order have even turned against the false church and destroyed her (Revelation 17:16,17)! How could Christ come as a thief now, when every sign has been fulfilled so that everyone knows He is "right at the door" (Matthew 24:33)? Even Antichrist and his armies know Christ is coming and have "gathered together to make war against him" (Revelation 19:19).

A post-tribulation coming of Christ? Indeed, there will be, but it will be the Second Coming in power and glory to rescue Israel and destroy Antichrist and his kingdom and armies. The post-trib coming will most assuredly not be the occasion of the Rapture of His bride. She has been in heaven, the marriage has taken place, and now she accompanies Him back to earth to share His triumph.

Don't confuse the Rapture with the Second Coming! When the latter takes place all the signs will have been given and the whole world will know that Christ is about to descend bodily to the earth with heaven's armies. When it comes to the Rapture, however, our Lord is talking surprise and imminency. No signs. No warning. He could come at any moment! One cannot read the New Testament with any understanding at all and come to any other conclusion.

It requires no complicated theological reasoning from obscure verses to realize that a post-trib Rapture couldn't possibly fit Christ's description of a peaceful, prosperous, thriving world and a complacent, sleeping Church. It is as simple and as plain as the meaning of the commonest of words: "Watch! Be ready! At such an hour as ye think not the Son of man cometh!" And that could be at any moment.

CHAPTER 23

Imminency

———————— ◇ ————————

How ye turned to God from idols to serve the living and true God; And to wait for his Son from heaven, whom he raised from the dead, even Jesus, which delivered us from the wrath to come (1 Thessalonians 1:9,10).

And unto them that look for him shall he appear the second time (Hebrews 9:28).

Let your loins be girded about, and your lights burning; And ye yourselves like unto men that wait for their lord . . . that when he cometh and knocketh, they may open unto him immediately. Be ye therefore ready also: for the Son of man cometh at an hour when ye think not (Luke 12:35-40).

Reading the first epistle to the Thessalonians, one can see that Paul was thrilled with the transformation in the lives and with the spiritual growth of those who had come to know Christ in Thessalonica. That ancient Greek city occupied a strategic position at the crossroads of trade routes converging on the Balkan peninsula. Travelers passed through Thessalonica going in all directions, and reports were spreading far and wide about the faith of these former pagans who had "turned to God from idols to serve the living and true God."

Something else was also being reported about them. The information had reached Paul's ears and pleased him greatly. The Christians at Thessalonica, though fairly new in the faith, not only had begun to worship the true God, but they were "wait[ing] for his Son from heaven . . . even Jesus." Paul had obviously taught them this truth and it is equally clear that he considered it to be of great importance.

Waiting for Christ's Return

Paul certainly had not advised them that Christ wasn't coming for at least 1900 years and therefore they shouldn't give much thought to His return. Nor had he told them that Christ wouldn't come until the Antichrist first appeared or until the end of the Great Tribulation. He must have taught them that Christ could come at any moment, or they wouldn't have been *waiting* for Him.

Paul commends the Thessalonian believers for "waiting" for Christ's coming. He reaffirms that such should be the attitude of every follower of Christ—as much the mark of a true Christian as was turning to God from idols. To encourage this anticipation and to reinforce what he had previously taught them, Paul presents in chapter four of this epistle (likely the first one he ever wrote) the clearest description of the Rapture that we have anywhere.

"To wait for his Son from heaven" has an expectant ring. It is much more specific than the general belief in His return expressed in the creeds. It goes beyond accepting the doctrine that Christ will return one day in the distant future. The Thessalonian believers were waiting for Him to return right then. Obviously, Paul had taught them that Christ could come at any moment, or to "wait for Him" would make no sense. One doesn't go to the airport in July to "wait" for Aunt Jane if she has written to say she is coming in November.

"Waiting for Christ" would not have been the attitude of the Thessalonian believers had they been taught by Paul that any signs or events would precede His coming. A person who doesn't believe Christ can come until after the first six seals are opened, or until Antichrist appears, or until the end of the Great Tribulation or millennium would not be "waiting" for Christ.

Belief in a post-*anything* Rapture would eliminate the expectant "waiting" for which Paul commends the Thessalonians. The language of Scripture—waiting, watching, looking for Christ—cries, "Imminency! Christ could come at any moment!"

Imminency and Expectancy in the New Testament

Clearly the Christians Paul commends at Thessalonica did not believe in a post-tribulation Rapture. They would not have been watching and waiting for Christ's return had they been taught that at least seven years lay between them and that longed-for event. Paul's language demonstrates conclusively that the early Christians expected the Rapture as the next event on the prophetic timetable. They did not believe they would be on earth enduring the trials and tribulations of Daniel's seventieth week. No point in watching and waiting for Christ now if He would not come until Israel was surrounded by the world's armies and Armageddon was underway—whenever that might be.

If Antichrist must come first, or if some event must happen before the Rapture, then one would not be watching and waiting for Christ but for that earlier event. If Antichrist must come first, then it would be senseless to watch for Christ until Antichrist had been revealed. Christians would be watching not for Christ, but for Antichrist or for Armageddon or whoever or whatever must precede Christ's coming.

Significantly, there is no record in the New Testament of *anyone* ever watching and waiting for Antichrist. Nor is there any record of *anyone* ever being instructed to do so. Christ exhorted us, His own, to watch for His return—not for Antichrist or some necessary prior event.

Paul ends the Thessalonian epistle with a further reference to Christ's return: "I pray God your whole spirit and soul and body be preserved blameless unto the coming of our Lord Jesus Christ" (5:23). That soon-coming event was much on his heart and is a constant theme in his epistles. Surely such language would be folly if Christ wasn't coming until the end of the millennium! No one was going to live that long.

From even a cursory reading of the New Testament there can be no doubt that it was considered normal in the early church to expect Christ at any moment. Paul greeted the Christians at Corinth as those who were "waiting for the coming of our Lord Jesus Christ" (1 Corinthians 1:7)—again language that requires imminency. He urged Timothy to "keep this commandment without spot, unrebukable, until the appearing of our Lord Jesus Christ" (1 Timothy 6:14). While not demanding imminency, the language includes that as a possibility and certainly implies that the Rapture could occur within Timothy's lifetime. Once again we see the expectancy of the Rapture that Paul himself maintained and encouraged in others.

Indications of such expectancy are found elsewhere throughout Paul's epistles. For example, he begins his epistle to "all the saints in Christ Jesus which are at Philippi" with an expression of his confidence that the One who had "begun a good work" in them would "perform it until the day of Jesus Christ [i.e. the day of His coming]" (1:6). This statement reflects Paul's expectation that these believers could be alive when Christ returned. Paul didn't say, "perform it until you die," which he should have if Christ could not come for hundreds or thousands of years.

That the saints at Philippi (along with Paul, for he includes himself) were definitely expecting Christ's return at any time is again clear from a verse which we have already quoted: "For our conversation [citizenship] is in heaven; from whence also we look for the Saviour, the Lord Jesus Christ" (3:20). The only conclusion one can draw from such language ("we *look* for the Saviour") is that Paul was encouraging the believers at Philippi to expect the resurrection of the dead, transformation of the living, and the Rapture of all together into heaven at any moment. Otherwise it would be foolish to be looking for Christ when He couldn't come until something else occurred first.

The "Blessed Hope"

If, in fact, we must face Antichrist and the Great Tribulation before the Rapture can occur, then Paul is badly misleading us here and in his other epistles. There is never a word of warning about the horrible trials of the Great Tribulation, no encouragement to be strong even though it will mean death for not taking the mark of the beast. Here is a vital topic which should at least have been addressed, if not for his contemporaries, then for us today. Any reference, however, to going through the Great Tribulation, how to identify the Antichrist, encouragement to faithfulness in the face of such unusual deception, and warnings not to take his mark is conspicuous by its absence in all of Paul's epistles and in those of the other apostles as well.

Paul called the prospect of the imminent Rapture "the blessed hope" (Titus 2:13). It would hardly be a blessed hope to know that to experience it one must first endure the Great Tribulation with its devastation of planet earth by war, famine, and natural disasters. Hardly a blessed hope if it couldn't occur until after most if not all Christians had been hunted down and slain for refusing to take Antichrist's mark and worship him as God! Hardly a blessed hope to know that God would give Antichrist the power to kill all Christians (Revelation 13:7) at least three and a half years before the Rapture! Hardly a blessed hope to know that by the time the Rapture occurred in the midst of Armageddon very few if any believers would be left alive for Christ to catch up to meet Him on His way down to rescue Israel! Better to call the Rapture a cruel hoax than a blessed hope if that were the case!

Let us logically consider the meaning of language. A "hope" is something which might possibly occur in time to be of some benefit in an existing situation. For example, a person who finds himself dying in the wreckage of a car might hope to be rescued in time for his life to be saved. Suppose, however, one has been told by a prophet, "You will be among 100 survivors of a plane crash, but the wreckage will lie under 50 feet of salt water slowly seeping inside. No help will arrive to rescue anyone until 98 people have died of injuries and dehydration. At that point an underwater rescue team will manage to save one of those still alive." Would that be a blessed hope?

One could not begin to hope for rescue while there were still 75 people alive, 50, 25, 10. Nor could any Christian who finds himself in the Great Tribulation have any hope of being Raptured until the earth was virtually destroyed and Armageddon was in process. To offer to the Church such a Rapture and to call it a "blessed hope" would be the ultimate deception. It could hardly be what Christ had in mind when He said, "I will come again and receive you unto myself, that where I am, there ye may be also."

If language has any meaning, then one could not possibly call a post-tribulation Rapture "the blessed hope." To do so would be a mockery! Moreover, Paul said that Christians should be "*looking* for that blessed hope" (Titus 2:13)! If the Rapture won't occur until the end of the Great Tribulation, then there is no point in looking for it until then. The fact that Paul tells Christians to be *looking* for that blessed hope right now proves conclusively that no sign or event must precede it.

The Rapture could only be a *blessed* hope if one knew that Christ could come at any moment, right now, tomorrow, or the next day. Only a pre-tribulation Rapture could be a blessed hope. To be a blessed hope one must know that the Rapture will come in time to rescue one from the most horrible devastation and suffering the world will ever see. Such is a blessed hope indeed, and one to wait and watch for at the present time!

Waiting, Watching—Normal Christian Attitude

As with the Thessalonians, the fact that the Philippians were *looking* for Christ certainly indicated that He could come within their lifetime. But it indicated more than that. One doesn't *look* for Uncle George if he has written to say that he may come within the next 20 years. That's too uncertain and possibly distant to actually start *looking* for him. The church we read of in the New Testament was waiting, looking, watching, obviously expecting Christ at any moment. How unlike the church today!

In referring to the Lord's return, the epistle to the Hebrews uses similar terminology—"unto them that *look* for him." Its author, inspired of the Holy Spirit, seems to consider such watchfulness to be the normal attitude of every true Christian. Consider this Scripture again:

> And as it is appointed unto men once to die [no possibility of reincarnation], but after this the judgment: So Christ was once offered to bear the sins of many; and unto them that look for him shall he appear the second time without sin unto salvation (9:27,28).

"Unto them that *look* for him shall he appear." Does that mean that if one doesn't happen to be looking into the sky, or at least thinking of Christ's return when He comes to catch away His bride, he'll be left behind? Surely not. Our going to heaven at the Rapture does not depend upon whether we even believe in that blessed hope much less are *looking* for Christ at that particular moment. Our ticket to heaven is the finished redemptive work of Christ on the cross. If one's faith is in the Lord Jesus Christ as his personal Savior, he will be taken to heaven at the Rapture even if he has never heard of such an event.

If all Christians are included, then why does it say, "Unto them that look for him"? Simply because it is expected of all Christians to be looking for Christ. Reference is not to an elite group of Christians, those who continually look for Christ, as the only ones who will be Raptured. The Bible does not teach a "partial Rapture" of the worthy (however that is defined), leaving the unworthy behind.

To the author of the epistle to the Hebrews (which was more than likely Paul), looking for Christ was clearly considered the normal attitude for every Christian. He didn't even exhort his readers to maintain that expectancy. Rather it is taken for granted. So "unto them that look for him shall he appear" is just another way of saying, "unto all Christians shall he appear." Isn't that redundant? No. He's speaking of the Rapture, and at that time Christ appears only to His bride as He catches her up to heaven.

A "Secret" Rapture?

It is increasingly popular, even among evangelicals in these last days, to mock the idea of a "secret" Rapture. Yet this is the teaching of Scripture and it makes good sense. The world will not see what transpires, for at least two reasons. First of all, the Rapture is an intimate meeting between Christ and His bride and has nothing to do with those who have rejected Him, so why should they be allowed to witness it? They were invited to participate but refused (Luke 14:16-24). Secondly, if all the world witnessed this event, the mystery would be removed and the false explanation that helps Antichrist seize power would not be possible.

It is not God's will for the world to understand the truth about what has happened. From the moment of the Rapture, all those who refused the love of the truth are under a strong delusion from God to believe the lies of Antichrist and Satan. The last thing they would believe, or that God wants them to believe, is that the Rapture has occurred.

Books and newsletters have been written to show that a belief in the secret pre-tribulation Rapture was popularized by Plymouth Brethren founder, J.N. Darby. He presumably picked it up from a false "revelation" related to a Scottish Pentecostal revival and received by a young woman, Margaret MacDonald, in early 1830. A great deal of time and effort and relentless research has gone into establishing this thesis. Much time and effort has been expended in rebuttals as well. Such proofs and disproofs are beside the point.

What Margaret MacDonald did or did not mean by her rather convoluted and vague "revelation"—and what part it played in Darby's thinking—may well be of historical interest for those who have the time to pursue such matters. It has, however, nothing whatsoever to do with the controversy between pre- and post-tribulation Rapture beliefs. That controversy can only be settled by what the Bible does or doesn't say. That is the only issue.

The First Teacher of Imminency

The expectation held by the New Testament Church of Christ's imminent return was not attributable only to the teaching of the apostles. It came first of all from the words of Christ Himself. He taught repeatedly that His coming was imminent.

One could not use stronger language than we quoted at the beginning of this chapter: "Let your loins be girded about, and your lights burning; and ye yourselves like unto men that wait for their lord. . . . Blessed are those servants, whom the lord when he cometh shall find watching." Here Christ urges upon His followers two things: 1) to maintain a high state of *readiness* for His return; and 2) to continue to *watch* for His return. That He is teaching the imminence of and thus a pre-tribulation Rapture cannot be denied.

It is incredible that anyone could read the words of our Lord Himself and conclude that He could not return until the Antichrist had first appeared, or until the middle or end of the tribulation period, much less the end of the millennium! In Matthew 24, we have the same exhortations: "*Watch* therefore: for ye know not what hour your Lord doth come" (v. 42); and "Therefore be ye also *ready*: for in such an hour as ye think not the Son of man cometh" (v. 44).

Would any Christian who had survived the Great Tribulation and saw Armageddon in process possibly be surprised by the Lord's coming, much less say to himself, "I don't think Christ will return now"? Though Christ does come in the midst of Armageddon, surely there must also be another coming at another time that fits the description He gives! Scripture demands, as we have documented, two comings or two stages in Christ's return: the Rapture and the Second Coming. Which one is being referred to is indicated, if not by the description of the event itself, then by the description of the conditions in the world and Church which prevail at the time.

A Complacent, Sleeping Church

In Matthew 25, Christ warns that the Church will likely be asleep when He comes to catch His bride away. Yes, five virgins are wise and five foolish. Apparently because the five foolish do not have oil in their lamps (a symbol of the Holy Spirit) they are not genuine Christians. Be that as it may, the following declaration from the Lord is more than sobering: "While the bridegroom tarried, they *all* slumbered and slept" (Matthew 25:5).

The wise slept along with the foolish! "The bridegroom tarried" and somehow it just didn't seem as though he'd be coming in the next few hours, so they took that opportunity to get some sleep—and that's when he came! Now we see why the Lord coupled His exhortation to *watch* and to be *ready* with the warning that He would come at a time when we wouldn't expect Him—when somehow it just wouldn't seem that He'd be coming then. That description just doesn't fit the end of the Great Tribulation!

Again we have imminency. He could come at any time: Watch, be ready! We also have as clear a presentation as one could ask for of the fact that He won't come at the end of Daniel's seventieth week in the midst of Armageddon. No one would be complacently sleeping then or doubting that it was the right time for Him to come!

A Practical Question About Timing Remains

What about Paul's statement that the dead are raised at the "last trump"? The question comes up again and again. We have commented earlier that the idea of the "last trump" in 1 Corinthians 15 being the seventh trumpet in Revelation 11 is not confirmed in Scripture. Nor does it fit the criteria of a time of complacency, peace, business as usual, and no expectancy whatsoever of God's judgment and Christ's return.

There are many possible last trumps and Paul doesn't give us any criteria for identifying the one to which he refers. Moreover, the timing of the seventh trumpet in Revelation 11 precedes Armageddon by at least several months, so if the

Rapture took place then it would be a separate event from the Second Coming as well. But why then?

There must be a better reason for the timing of the Rapture than to coincide with a trumpet blast! But there is no other reason. It also destroys imminency if the Rapture must wait upon the sounding of this trumpet. Therefore such a theory must be rejected as unbiblical.

There is a growing following for the idea that the "last trump" Paul had in mind is the last trumpet to sound on the Feast of Trumpets. We can now see the fatal flaw in that theory as well. If Christ didn't come at the Feast of Trumpets this year, then we know we have another year before He can come—but that destroys imminency and therefore must be rejected. He might very well come at that time, but we cannot state it as a certainty.

Having made the case for imminency, we know that Christ could return to catch His bride away at any moment. But we still have not answered our question, "How close are we?" One practical problem remains that must be settled first.

Even though there are no preconditions and no signs for the Rapture, there are many for the Second Coming. We know that seven years, the seventieth week of Daniel, separates the Rapture and Second Coming. Is there time for all that is prophesied to take place within that seven-year period without any preparation beforehand? If not, then we've lost the case for imminency after all.

CHAPTER 24

Timing Factors

———————— ◇ ————————

> For then shall be great tribulation, such as was not since the beginning of the world to this time, no, nor ever shall be. And except those days be shortened, there should no flesh [on earth] be saved [i.e., this is a world-wide phenomenon] (Matthew 24:21,22).

> For as a snare shall it come on all them that dwell on the face of the whole earth (Luke 21:35).

> Because thou hast kept the word of my patience, I also will keep thee from the hour of temptation, which shall come upon all the world, to try them that dwell upon the earth (Revelation 3:10).

Let us state our present concern once again. We have arrived at the conclusion that Christ and His apostles taught and the church we read of in the New Testament believed and watched for, a pre-tribulation and imminent Rapture. If we are correct, nothing at any time in history could have stood between the church and the Rapture. There were no signs and no conditions that needed to be fulfilled in the past nor are there any today. Such is definitely the impression one obtains from reading the New Testament.

Have we not, however, given some conditions? For example, that Christ would come at a time when the Church would not expect Him. That statement, of course, could be as much a description of the Church's spiritual lethargy as of conditions in the world. Certainly it was not long before the Church lost its sense of expectancy, so the parable of the sleeping wise and foolish virgins applied throughout history as it does today. How many of those who call themselves Christians around the world are presently really watching, waiting, and looking for Christ's return? A very small percentage!

So this criteria, which has always been met, did not point to a particular time in history during which Christ must come, and thus it did not affect imminency. Instead, as we have seen, it identified the time when the Rapture *could not* occur—i.e., the end of the Great Tribulation. At that time booming business, complacency, no thought of judgment as it was in Noah's day, and surprise are out of the question. Even Antichrist will know that Christ is coming. Thus these criteria, rather than working against pre-trib imminency, actually preserve it by eliminating a post-trib Rapture.

"As It Was in the Days of Noah"

Yes, but what about those criteria: "As it was in the days of Noah"—eating, drinking, buying, building, with no expectation of judgment? Remember, Christ is speaking of conditions worldwide. While there have always been times of famine, war, pestilence, and upheavals of nature in parts of the world, never have these disastrous conditions prevailed worldwide. They will during the Great Tribulation after the Rapture, but not until then. Similar conditions to those prior to the flood have always prevailed in many if not most parts of the world. That fact is supported by the comments of those who remain skeptical of coming judgment even today:

> Knowing this first, that there shall come in the last days scoffers, walking after their own lusts. And saying, Where is the promise of his coming? for since the fathers fell asleep, all things continue as they were from the beginning of creation (2 Peter 3:3,4).

These scoffers insist that world conditions are and always have been as they were in the days of Noah. Yes, many of the

Christians who were being hunted, imprisoned, and killed under communist regimes in Russia, China, Laos, Cambodia, and in Muslim and Catholic countries have at times thought they were already in the Great Tribulation. They had, however, no biblical basis for such fears. The Great Tribulation will be far worse and it will be experienced not only in a few countries but by the entire world all at once as the verses at the beginning of this chapter assure us.

Therefore, this criteria, too, rather than pointing to a special time when the Rapture *must* occur, defines the time when it *could not*—i.e., during and especially at the end of the Great Tribulation, when conditions are anything but like those in the days of Noah.

Unusual Signs Unknown to Previous Generations

In an earlier chapter we mentioned that in addition to the well-known signs of the nearness of His return cited by Christ (wars, pestilence, famine, earthquakes, etc.) there are some other signs unlike anything known to previous generations. Ours is the first generation for which these prophecies, seemingly impossible before, even make sense. Does that mean, then, that we have lost imminency after all? Let us look at some of these peculiar signs.

In the verses quoted at the beginning of this chapter, Christ declared that the Great Tribulation would involve dangers to life unlike anything ever known. So horrendous, in fact, would the weapons be, that "except those days be shortened, there should no flesh be saved." That statement seemed outrageous for more than 1900 years. There were no weapons capable of wiping out all life on this planet. None, that is, until our generation came along. Not only the nuclear arsenals which are now common knowledge fall into that category, but other secret weapons equally deadly have been developed. A major deterrent to the use of these star wars weapons has been the fear that a disaster of cosmic proportions could be unleashed which would make any kind of life on this planet impossible.

How amazingly accurate was Christ's prophecy made more than 1900 years ago! Once again we have confirmation of Christ's deity and of the fact that the Bible is God's Word. Confirmation, too, that these are the last days of which He spoke. In our day, for the first time in history, the fulfillment of Christ's frightening prophecy—a prophecy that seemed impossible for so many centuries—is simply a matter of using existing weapons. This terrifying development in destructive capabilities means that Christ's prophecy could become reality at any time.

This fact, however, confronts us with an important question. If weapons that have only been developed in our generation had to be in existence at Armageddon, did this not prevent Christ from coming in the past? The answer, of course, hinges upon whether or not previous generations might have been able to develop such weapons during the seven years between the Rapture and Armageddon.

Would it have been possible for a previous generation to go from knights in armor, for example, to nuclear arms in such a short period of time? That particular leap in technology may not have been necessary. There may be other weapons more ingenious and far more horrible which could have been developed and used more simply and quickly. No one can dogmatically rule out such a possibility. Human genius is unpredictable.

"That No One Might Buy or Sell [Without] . . . the Mark"

Revelation 13 declares that Antichrist will control all banking and commerce in the entire world. Once again that concept seemed unbelievable in the past. Then along came our generation and developed the computers and communications satellites with which to fulfill this prophecy. We are rapidly heading toward a cashless society for reasons of efficiency and crime control. Holdups, kidnapping, extortion, drug dealing, and money laundering as well as counterfeiting and cheating on income tax could all be eliminated by doing away with cash and requiring that all transactions be electronic. For these reasons such a system is inevitable.

The one smart card, however, could be stolen, lost, or forgotten. A tiny computer chip painlessly and quickly implanted just under the skin in hand or forehead will likely become the means of fulfilling this prophecy. We already have the technology and equipment for implementing such worldwide control at any time. Certainly Antichrist's mark involving 666 and the purpose for imposing it upon the world will not seem to be evil but something overwhelmingly beneficial which our generation has conceived and produced.

Again we must ask whether such sophisticated electronics could have been developed, for example, by a feudal society. Moreover, this system for controlling all buying and selling would have to be in place long before Armageddon, so there would only be the first few years of Daniel's seventieth week in which to complete the task. Could it have been accomplished by previous generations?

Once again, while admitting that such a feat would not seem likely under ordinary circumstances, one cannot say it would have been impossible. There may well be some other more ingenious method of accomplishing more simply the same end which could have been developed quickly had the Rapture occurred at any previous time in history.

It is certainly possible that some former generation, with incredible genius, *could* have developed within seven years or less the weapons and technologies necessary to fulfill all prophecies concerning Daniel's seventieth week. That simple possibility preserves imminency. The Rapture could have come at any time and these developments followed immediately and swiftly, perhaps with techniques even more ingenious than our generation has used.

The Rapture did not occur in the past. Today we are confronted with a solemn reality. Unlike previous generations, ours is the first one which *already possesses* everything necessary to fulfill all remaining prophecies. Moreover, the fact that this unusual and necessary capability has suddenly developed within a generation adds to the sense of expectancy. Why now? Surely for a reason!

While the Rapture could have come at any time, its occurrence in the past would have necessitated some rapid developments. These essential preparations have suddenly occurred in our generation. Today the props are all in place on the stage ready for the final act. Thus it is not only *possible* for the Rapture to occur at any moment, as it always has been, but now it is highly *probable*—certainly more probable than at any time in history!

What About the Temple?

A major factor, of course, is the necessity for Israel to be back in her land, where last days prophecies place her, immediately after the Rapture. This is required by the fact that Antichrist makes a covenant involving Israel at the very beginning of Daniel's seventieth week. Would that not mean, then, that the Rapture could not occur until Israel had once again become a nation? If so, we have lost imminency.

In fact, it would not be necessary for Israel to be back in her land before the Rapture. Suppose Antichrist had risen to power with Jews still scattered around the world without a homeland. Part of the covenant He makes with "the many" would have been to create that homeland and the nation of Israel immediately—which is no longer necessary, for Israel is already in her land.

Prophecy also indicates that the Jewish temple must be rebuilt in Jerusalem. Not *if* but *when* this will occur remains the only question. As we noted in an earlier chapter, Antichrist will seat himself in the temple of God and declare that he is God (2 Thessalonians 2:4), so it must be in existence at that time. He will also "cause the sacrifice and the oblation to cease" (Daniel 9:27), which again tells us that during Daniel's seventieth week (the seven-year tribulation period) the temple must be in existence and functioning with sacrifices being offered.

More than likely, as part of a Middle East peace treaty immediately following the Rapture, Antichrist will allow the Jews to rebuild their temple. According to Daniel, Antichrist will "confirm [this covenant] for one week" (obviously Daniel's seventieth week). Then, in the midst of that week, he will go back on his word. It may be at this time that he unveils his image in the temple and requires that it be worshiped in conjunction with his claim that he is God. These events start the world on the road to Armageddon.

Today the barriers standing in the way of the temple being rebuilt seem insurmountable. Islam's third holiest shrine, the Dome of the Rock, occupies the place where the temple once stood. Try to move that! It was allegedly to this rock, Al-Aqsa, over which this shrine has been built, that Muhammad journeyed from Mecca and from which he ascended to heaven on his magical horse. That claim, however, was the invention of Yasser Arafat's uncle, Haj Amin el-Husseini, during the 1920s when he was Grand Mufti of Jerusalem. Haj Amin worked with the Nazis for the extermination of the Jews. In order to arouse Arabs against any Jewish presence in Jerusalem, he invented the idea that the Dome of the Rock had been constructed over Al-Aqsa.

The Dome of the Rock

That the rock over which this shrine was built was not considered at the time to be the fabled Al-Aqsa is clear. Sura 17:1, the only verse in the Koran to mention Al-Aqsa, is conspicuously absent among the many Koranic scriptures inscribed inside the Dome. In fact, the rock under the Dome, being the highest point of Mount Moriah, was very likely, as tradition holds, the place where Abraham offered Isaac (Genesis 22). David later purchased it from Ornan the Jebusite and built an altar there (1 Chronicles 21) and it was upon this site that Solomon built the first temple (2 Chronicles 3:1). The Arabs' original purpose, then, in building the Dome of the Rock (and in maintaining its presence there today) was to prevent the Jews from rebuilding the temple. The idea that this was Al-Aqsa was not even dreamed of in those days. Remember, the Koran doesn't even mention Jerusalem.

It is believed by some Jewish archaeological experts that the Holy of Holies in the original temple was directly over this rock. Other experts believe it was adjacent. Whatever the precise location when it is finally established, the Dome of the Rock would have to be moved in order for the Jewish temple to be rebuilt. Impossible? No. Suppose the Arabs should discover what Islamic leaders would agree was the true Al-Aqsa. The Dome of the Rock, in that case, could very well be moved to that site. The Jews have the technology and are prepared to move it piece by piece wherever necessary. There are other possibilities which we need not explore.

In any event, given the catalytic force of the sudden mass disappearance of hundreds of millions at the Rapture, Antichrist could bring about the relocation of the Arabs' third holiest shrine. That would open the door for the peaceful reconstruction of the Jewish temple at its authentic site on temple mount.

Many Orthodox Jews believe that only the Messiah can point out the proper location of the temple and oversee its rebuilding. The accomplishment of that feat would seem to validate Antichrist's claim to be the Messiah. If he brought peace to the world, had the Dome of the Rock moved, pointed out the precise site for the temple, granted permission, and very likely even financed much of the construction, most Israelis would be convinced that he was the Messiah.

However it happens is a mere detail. The fact is that the temple will be rebuilt and swiftly, most likely immediately after the Rapture. According to Jewish experts involved in plans for the reconstruction, it could be accomplished in a matter not of years but of months. So again we have no hindrance to imminency. At any time in history Christ could have Raptured his Church, the nation of Israel could have been born immediately, and the temple built very quickly thereafter.

Here again, however, our generation is the first one in history to see Israel already established in her land and preparations for rebuilding the temple finalized. That this essential ramification occurred within the same generation that has seen the development of the technology necessary to fulfill all other prophecies can hardly be a coincidence. Once more, though the *possibility* remains the same, the *probability* that Christ will return momentarily has increased greatly.

Ready to Be Rebuilt

Some Jews today are not in favor of rebuilding the temple. They feel no religious need and are concerned that its construction would only further alienate Israel from the world community. Nevertheless, for most Jews, only with the rebuilding of the temple will Israel finally be functioning in her land and able to fulfill her divine calling. While this sense of destiny may have more to do with a commitment to tradition than with genuine faith in God, it runs deep and strong in Jewish consciousness. Its connection to the temple is most amazing.

One need only recall the intense emotion among Jews worldwide when the temple mount was recovered. Israeli paratroopers took the holy site on the fourth day of the Six-Day War in June 1967. These hardened soldiers wept uncontrollably and found themselves unable to leave the mount, as though some mystical force held them there. However, because of diplomatic pressure, Israeli Defense Minister Moshe Dayan gave the administration of the mount back to the Arabs, who control it to this day. In fact, by Jewish law no Jews are allowed to enter the mount because of the sacredness of the site and the uncertainties surrounding the exact location of the Holy of Holies.

In the meantime, plans have been meticulously laid to erect a third Jewish temple. It will replace Solomon's, built about 950 B.C. and destroyed by Nebuchadnezzar in 586 B.C., and Zerubbabel's temple originally completed in 515 B.C. Remodeled and enlarged by Herod beginning in 20 B.C., the second temple was destroyed by the Roman legions in A.D. 70 and has lain in ruins for 1900 years. Today, however, there is an awakening among Jews that the time has come for the long-anticipated recovery of their spiritual center.

The extent of preparations both for construction of the temple and for reinstitution of animal sacrifices which one discovers by a visit to Jerusalem is astounding. The corner-stone has been quarried, temple garments have been manufac-tured, the instruments to be used in connection with the sacrifices have been fashioned, and the priests are being trained. Even the ancient harps necessary for the singing that accompanies worship are now being handmade in Jerusalem. Everything is in readiness.

An Incredible Phenomenon

Here we are in the last decade of the twentieth century. Ours is an age of space travel, computers, nuclear weapons, and highly advanced technology. It seems incredible, therefore, that today's modern Jews, who are among the best-educated and most scientifically minded people on earth, should have a passion to see the temple rebuilt—and even insist upon the precise location which it occupied in the past. Why? Few Israelies are religious. Most are sophisticates, agnostics, humanists, atheists, New Agers. The masses seldom if ever attend sabbath religious services. What could move these people to desire with such passion the reinstitution of the ancient temple worship?

Why this return to the past? The temple ceremonies date back to Moses and the fantastic (for most Jews) claim that he received the instructions for these rituals directly from God. These are ancient, archaic, strange practices involving incense and anointing oil whose formulas date back thousands of years. At the heart of the temple ceremonies are rituals which involve thousands of animal sacrifices. What will the animal rights activists say to that!

These highly symbolic ceremonies all looked forward to the sacrifice of the Jewish Messiah who, as the Lamb of God, would bear away the sins of the world. What other meaning could they have, especially to a people so irreligious? The rituals they are reviving will be performed by a priesthood that wears archaic garments whose design was given to Moses on Mount Sinai about 3500 years ago. The priests and their garments must be purified in ceremonies which require the ashes of a red heifer. It all seems so empty if the true meaning is missed—yet Israel is aflame with the passion to see the temple rebuilt!

On the one hand it seems incredible that intelligent modern people would involve themselves in such an ancient and formal religion at the end of the twentieth century. Tradition seems inadequate to explain this phenomenon. On the other hand, it is not surprising, for it must happen in order to fulfill prophecy.

So the temple will be rebuilt. How long would it take? Herod was 46 years in building the last temple (John 2:20). We are told by Israeli temple designers and builders that this latest temple, with the modern technology and construction methods of today, could be built in a matter of months. Here again we have an essential criteria that can be satisfied within the seven-year period and does not hinder imminency. Christ could have come at any time in history and the temple could have been rebuilt and functioning in the early part of Daniel's seventieth week in fulfillment of prophecy.

What About Ezekiel 38 and 39—
World War III?

Many students of prophecy believe that the next event on the calendar is World War III, and that only thereafter can the Rapture take place. It is commonly taught that this conflict is foretold in Ezekiel 38 and 39. Based upon these two chapters, and long before the Soviet Union became a world power, students of prophecy declared that Russia would lead a coalition, which would include the Arab nations, in a devastating attack upon Israel and be defeated by God.

The recent collapse of the Soviet Union, rather than weakening this scenario, seems to have strengthened it. Significantly, Russia remains the largest entity to come out of this breakup of the Communist empire. The new independent Russia retains the nuclear warheads and the military manpower to fulfill Ezekiel's prophecy. Furthermore, several of the now-independent former Soviet republics are largely Muslim. Their independence has made it possible for a closer alliance between them and Iran, Iraq, Syria, and other radical Islamic regimes which are determined to annihilate Israel. The collapse of communism seems to have moved the players on the stage much closer to this great battle.

Some Christian leaders are convinced that only out of this global conflict and the miraculous defeat of Russia can the Roman Empire (which they conceive of as ten nations in Western Europe) be revived with Antichrist at its head and take its place as the dominant world power. Once again, if this interpretation is correct and this great war must precede the Rapture, then we have lost imminency. Let us examine these two chapters in Ezekiel briefly to see whether this is the case.

We lack the space, nor is it necessary, to go into detail concerning this conflict. As one reads these two chapters one is impressed with the finality of the language used in some of the verses. The following are a sample:

> It shall be in the latter [last] days, and I will bring thee against my land [Israel], that the heathen may know me (Ezekiel 38:16).

> Surely in that day there shall be a great shaking in the land of Israel; So that the fishes of the sea, and the fowls of the heaven, and the beasts of the field . . . and all the men that are upon the face of the earth, shall shake at my presence, and the mountains shall be thrown down (38:19,20).

> And I will be known in the eyes of many nations, and they shall know that I am the Lord (38:23).

> So will I make my holy name known in the midst of my people Israel; and I will not let them pollute my holy name any more: and the heathen shall know that I am the Lord, the Holy One in Israel (39:7).

> Speak unto every featnered fowl . . . assemble yourselves . . . ye shall eat tne flesh of the mighty, and drink the blood of the princes of the earth (39:17,18).

> And I will set my glory among the heathen. . . . So the house of Israel shall know that I am the Lord their God from that day and forward (39:21,22).

> Neither will I hide my face any more from them
> [Israel]: for I have poured out my spirit upon the house of
> Israel, saith the Lord God (39:29).

The language in these two chapters makes it very clear that this battle is Armageddon and not some earlier conflict prior to the Rapture. Note the magnitude of the shaking of the earth and the fact that the destruction is directly attributed to the presence of the Lord. It sounds like the description of Armageddon in Zechariah and Revelation when Christ Himself comes with the armies of heaven. The call to the fowls (39:17,18) is too similar for coincidence to the same invitation at Armageddon "to all the fowls that fly [to] eat the flesh of kings . . . captains . . . and of mighty men" found in Revelation 19:17,18.

The principle objection to this being Armageddon is the fact that the weapons of the defeated armies will be burned as fuel for seven years. It sounds like a neat fit if this should come at the beginning of the Tribulation—otherwise the burning and the purifying and burying of corpses goes on into the millennial reign of Christ. Why not? Fuel will be used during the millennium. Nor will the earth be suddenly and miraculously cleaned up by God. Men will have much work to do. So this objection cannot be sustained, particularly in view of the language used concerning the heathen and Israel knowing God as a result of this conflict.

The repeated declaration that all the heathen will know that God has done this deed, that He has rescued Israel, and that they are His people is conclusive. The phrase "from that day forth" or similar words are used several times. Israel ever after knows God and that she belongs to Him. Moreover, Israel will never again pollute His holy name and can never again be forsaken of God.

Such language could not be used of anything except Armageddon, for God would have to violate this pledge to allow the destruction of Israel by Antichrist. Thus such a transformation in Israel and pledge from God could not come before Armageddon but only as a result thereof. At Armageddon, as described in Zechariah 12–14, we find the people of Israel, for the first time, realizing who Christ is and returning to God. Yet that is described as happening as a result of the conflict in Ezekiel 38 and 39. These chapters must therefore be a description of Armageddon and could not be referring to some earlier battle.

Imminency Remains

In summary, then, there are certain unusual prophecies which pertain to the last seven-year period known as Daniel's seventieth week or the tribulation. If any of these elements could not be developed within a seven-year period immediately following the Rapture of the Church, then we would have lost imminency. Something would have had to occur prior to the Rapture.

In fact, all of these unusual signs of the Second Coming could have developed within the seven-year period no matter at what point in history the Rapture might have taken place. The great battle described in Ezekiel 38 and 39, too, is clearly Armageddon and not some earlier conflict which must precede the Rapture.

Most interesting is the fact that now, for the first time in history, the means for fulfilling all of these unusual prophecies are already fully in place. Furthermore, this unique capability has come about rather suddenly within the same generation that has seen Israel back in her land. That these developments have rapidly converged on our generation could hardly be coincidence.

Everything necessary for the fulfillment of last days prophecies is now in place. Why should it be held in readiness far ahead of time? All of the signs indicate that the Rapture and the commencement of Daniel's seventieth week will very soon, and without further warning, be upon us.

CHAPTER 25

Israel, the Messiah, and the Church

◇

> And there appeared a great wonder in heaven; a woman clothed with the sun, and the moon under her feet, and upon her head a crown of twelve stars . . . and behold a great red dragon, having seven heads and ten horns. . . . And the dragon stood before the woman which was ready to be delivered, for to devour her child as soon as it was born. And she brought forth a man child, who was to rule all nations with a rod of iron: and her child was caught up unto God. . . . And the woman fled into the wilderness. . . . The dragon persecuted the woman . . . and went to make war with the remnant of her seed, which keep the commandments of God, and have the testimony of Jesus Christ (Revelation 12:1-6,13-17).

Although the book of Revelation is almost entirely about the future, there is, in the passage above, a brief recapitulation of history. The woman can only be Israel. The man-child, of course, is the Messiah. The red dragon is none other than Satan himself. Indeed, later in this same chapter he is described as "the great dragon . . . that old serpent, called the Devil, and Satan, which deceiveth the whole world." The picture is of Satan's past and future determination to destroy first of all the Messiah, and having failed that, to destroy Israel and all Christians as well.

Satan waited long and apprehensively for the virgin birth of the promised One. Here was the Messiah who would be his antagonist in the battle for control of the universe. As we have already seen, that inconceivable cosmic warfare began with Lucifer's rebellion against God eons ago. The Messiah's coming was first promised by God to Adam and Eve immediately after their sin and just prior to their expulsion from the Garden of Eden. Interestingly enough, it was to Satan, who had communicated to Eve through a serpent, that God spoke on this occasion:

> And I will put enmity between thee [the serpent] and the woman, and between thy seed and her seed; it [the seed of the woman, i.e., Messiah] shall bruise [literally crush] thy head, and thou shalt bruise his heel (Genesis 3:15)

Our introductory verses from Revelation 12 depict Satan down through history, waiting, watching for the birth of the Messiah, poised to destroy Him. One such Satanically inspired attempt was made upon the child Jesus by King Herod when, after learning of His birth, he sent his soldiers to kill all the male infants in Bethlehem and the surrounding countryside (Matthew 2:16-18). That slaughter of the innocents fulfilled yet another prophecy by Jeremiah (31:15). There is no mystery about these prophecies if we allow the Bible to speak for and to interpret itself.

Self-Serving "Translations"

Here we must issue a word of caution. Unfortunately, some cults have tampered with the biblical text in order to promote their own peculiar doctrines. Obviously, any teachings that require an alteration of God's Word for their support are not authentic. The Jehovah's Witnesses are an example. They deny so much biblical doctrine, including the deity of Christ and salvation by grace through faith, that they have found it necessary to produce their own *New World Translation*. It is not, however, a translation from the Hebrew and Greek manuscripts, but a self-serving perversion, as a comparison with numerous other more widely accepted translations will quickly reveal. Their proprietary "Bible" was specifically designed to support their peculiar heresies.

The Catholic Douay Bible is another case in point. In its attempt to glorify Mary, it has long rendered this passage from Genesis as follows: "I will put enmities between thee and the woman, and thy seed and her seed: she shall crush thy head, and thou shalt lie in wait for her heel." So Mary, not the Messiah, is presented as the one who will destroy Satan. The marginal note says, "In art Mary is frequently pictured with her foot on the head of a serpent."

Demonic Apparitions of "Mary"

Indeed, in one of numerous demonic impersonations embraced by Roman Catholics, "Mary" appeared to Catherine Laboure in November 1830, in Paris as the "woman clothed with the sun, and the moon under her feet, and upon her head a crown of twelve stars" (Revelation 12:1). This apparition substituted Mary for Israel. Moreover, this counterfeit "Mary" appeared standing with her foot upon a serpent's head which she was crushing beneath her heel. The vision gave seemingly miraculous support to Rome's dishonest rendering of Genesis 3:15. While some modern Catholic translations have in recent times corrected this verse, the teaching that Mary is the one who crushes the serpent's head remains solidly entrenched in Roman Catholicism.

Catherine Laboure's vision has been preserved in a medal minted in 1832, to be worn by the Roman Catholic faithful around the neck for protection. The medal depicts "Mary" as Catherine saw her, crushing the serpent's head. Obviously the apparition, now known as "Our Lady of the Miraculous Medal," was not the true Mary of the Bible, for it perverted the Scripture and gave to Mary a power and a work that belong to Christ alone.

Whether Catherine hallucinated, made up the whole story, or was deceived by a demon impersonating Mary is irrelevant. The fact is that this heretical picture of Mary is honored as the truth by the Roman Catholic Church to this day. This favorite medal, to which many miracles have been credited, has been worn by scores of millions of Catholics around the world. It continues to rank in popularity and official Church recognition next to the rosary and the scapular of "Our Lady of Mount Carmel."

Of course, the Bible gives no such honor to Mary, nor did the real Mary claim it. There are no prophecies in the Old Testament about the coming of the woman, but there are scores of prophecies concerning the coming of the "seed of the woman," i.e., the virgin-born Messiah, as we have already seen. He has come once and defeated Satan by dying for our sins upon the cross. He must come again. This time He will confront Antichrist face-to-face and destroy this Satan-empowered impersonation of evil and his worldwide kingdom (2 Thessalonians 2:8).

Antichrist and the Dragon

In Revelation 13, John makes it clear that the dragon (Satan), is the real power and the Antichrist is his puppet. He puts it like this:

> All the world wondered after the beast [Antichrist]. And they [the whole world] worshipped the dragon which gave power unto the beast: and they worshipped the beast. . . . All that dwell upon the earth shall worship him (Revelation 13:3,4,8).

This time of "great tribulation," as it is called, will be the most horrible period the earth has ever experienced or ever will thereafter (Matthew 24:21). The scourge of Nazism and communism and the unspeakable terror and devastation that numerous evil dictatorships with their death camps have brought to the earth will pale by comparison.

The description of the dragon with seven heads and ten horns, presented at the beginning of this chapter, is most instructive. In Daniel 7:7, we also meet a beast with ten horns. We are told that it represents the fourth world empire, which was Rome. Verse 24 declares that the ten horns "are ten kings that shall arise." These are the same ten kings encountered in Daniel 2 and represented by the ten toes on the image. Since they did not reign over the ancient Roman Empire, they must be involved with it in its revived form. It is specifically "in the days of those kings" that Christ will return to earth to destroy Antichrist and the revived Roman Empire and to establish His millennial kingdom on David's throne.

In Revelation, chapters 13 and 17, we meet this beast again, there described more fully as having seven heads as well as the ten horns. That beast, as we shall see, represents both the Antichrist and the revived Roman Empire, over which he will rule. His power, we are told in Daniel 8:24, is not his own. It comes from Satan according to Revelation 13:2. This fact is reinforced by the similarity in the description of the Dragon (Satan) and the Beast, both of whom have seven heads and ten horns. This striking similarity tells us that the Antichrist and his kingdom will be controlled and empowered by Satan.

Israel's Strategic Role

Getting back to Revelation 12, the dragon, having failed to destroy the man-child, hates and persecutes the rest of her seed—i.e., Christians and Jews. We have noted that there has been, down through history, an unmistakably diabolical element in the persecution of Jews around the world. There can be no doubt that Satan has attempted to inspire their enemies to destroy them so that the Messiah could not come into the world.

That the Jews, because of their physical relationship to the Messiah, would have to be preserved unto the "last days" and brought back to their land is at the very heart of most prophecies in the Bible. Unfortunately, in spite of their preservation to this day, the prophets with one voice warned that the worst time for Jews around the world lies ahead. It will be even worse than the holocaust in Nazi Germany—the time of "Jacob's trouble" (Jeremiah 30:7) to which we have already referred. Only a remnant will survive.

Revelation 12 presents a picture of God's preservation of that remnant of Israel for "a time, times and half a time" (three and a half years) during the last half of Daniel's seventieth week, called the Great Tribulation. Daniel 7:25 speaks of this "time and times and the dividing of time" as the period during which the Antichrist controls the world. Satan will actually be in control, for he is the one who gives this beast of a man—yes, the Antichrist is shown as a beast—his power.

Suppose Satan had succeeded in exterminating the Jews. Couldn't God have started over with another people? No, that would be impossible. The forces of darkness would have remained in control of this earth.

God had committed Himself to bring the Messiah into the world through the descendants of Abraham, Isaac, and Jacob, through the tribe of Judah and specifically from the line of King David. The prophets had declared that it would be so. If those prophecies were not fulfilled, God would be a liar. Moreover, it would have been proved that God had lost control of history and of His universe. Satan would have been the winner by default. No wonder Jews have been persecuted and attempts made to annihilate them, not only by Hitler but at other times in history as well!

It takes little insight to recognize in past and present events the fact that Satan is still determined to destroy Israel. Why? What good would it do now after Christ has come and has defeated Satan on the cross? Here we discover one of many reasons why one cannot, as is becoming increasingly popular, declare that God is finished with Israel and that the Church has taken her place.

The Necessity of Israel's Survival

Christ is coming back, is He not? That was His clear promise and it is the subject of this book. But if God is finished with Israel, what would be the purpose of Christ's return to the earth? He has promised to take the Church out of this world to heaven, so what further interest would Christ have in this earth if Israel no longer had any part in prophecy?

Of course, Christ is coming to confront and destroy the Antichrist. But why? He comes to destroy Antichrist's kingdom and to set up His own millennial reign. Where will His throne be? New York? Washington, D.C.? London? Paris? Berlin? Moscow? Indeed not. It will be in Jerusalem, where He will reign on the throne of His father David over the people of Israel.

The Jewish people scattered all over the earth must have survived as an identifiable ethnic unit and must be together in the promised land when the Messiah returns. It can't be otherwise. The prophets have declared it unequivocally and repeatedly.

The survival of the Jews as a national and ethnic group brought back into their land in the "last days" is absolutely essential to Christ's Second Coming. And so it will be. The Jews have been preserved as God promised. Hitler failed in his "final solution to the Jewish problem." The Arabs have failed repeatedly to wipe out Israel.

The attempts will continue, for if Satan can succeed in destroying the Jews, he will have achieved at least a stalemate with God. The Bible's major prophecies, which all pertain to Israel back in her land when Messiah returns, could not be fulfilled. God would be proved a liar who had lost control of His universe. Thus, the fulfillment of the prophecies concerning Israel is crucial for God in His battle with Satan.

Replacing Israel

In spite of the clarity of the prophecies we have mentioned, there is a growing movement even among evangelicals today to deny that Israel any longer has any part in prophecy. Yes, it is allowed, the Jews may come to Christ for salvation and become part of the Church just as Gentiles may—but as a nation they have no place any longer in God's program. They have been rejected and cut off because they crucified their Messiah.

So goes this diabolical theory. By that reasoning, there is no significance whatsoever to the fact that the nation of Israel exists once again in her own land and that Jews are gathering there in unprecedented numbers from around the world. We have been robbed of a major verifiable evidence for the existence of God and that the Bible is His Word.

The further consequences are equally devastating. Thousands of verses must be ripped out of God's Word, leaving it mutilated beyond recognition. "Spiritualizing" the prophecies concerning Israel in an attempt to make them apply to the church is no better, for it strips Scripture of its literal application and thus of its strength.

Nearly every prophecy concerning the Second Coming is directly tied to Israel as a nation and to the land she must inhabit when her Messiah returns. The angels said that Jesus would come back to the Mount of Olives. When and why? Certainly not at the Rapture. He doesn't come there to catch away His bride, which is composed of the redeemed from every nation scattered all over the earth.

Neither the Mount of Olives nor the land of Israel has any special significance for the Church. Christ would have no reason to return to Israel unless His people were there and unless He intended to occupy the throne of David and rule over them from Jerusalem. That He would do so was stated repeatedly by the prophets as a solemn promise from God. Those prophecies must and will be fulfilled at the Second Coming— and are unrelated to the Rapture.

The Importance of the Land of Israel

Those who insist that the Church has replaced Israel often argue that there are no references in the New Testament to Israel restored to her land, and therefore such promises from the Old Testament are no longer of any effect. That statement simply isn't true. When he told Mary that she would give birth to the Messiah, the angel Gabriel declared explicitly that this One would reign "upon the throne of his father David." Here is a New Testament reference to Israel restored to her land and a reaffirmation of the promise to David concerning the messianic kingdom.

Other New Testament references to Israel's future in her land concern Armageddon (Revelation 16:16; 19:17-21) and Christ's rescue of Israel. Moreover, Christ, who is acknowledged as "the King of Israel" by His disciples (John 1:49;

12:13), promised the twelve that they would reign with Him over "the twelve tribes of Israel" (Matthew 19:28; Revelation 20:4, etc.)—obviously in the land of Israel.

The message of the angels at Christ's ascension, to which we have referred, was another New Testament reference to the land. They declared that it would be to the Mount of Olives just outside Jerusalem that He would return. That statement was a reaffirmation of Zechariah 14:4, which is all about the land of Israel. Furthermore, promises such as Jeremiah 31:35-37, which we have earlier quoted, hardly need to be reaffirmed!

Why does Jesus come back to the land of Israel? Surely it is not because the Church inhabits that land! He comes to rescue Israel at Armageddon. For that to be the case, God's ancient people must have been reestablised there. How, then, dare anyone say that Israel's national presence in her land today means nothing!

An Unbelieving Israel Must Be in the Land

Yes, Israel is back in her land in unbelief, but that is exactly what the Bible said would be the case. Israel as a whole will not believe in her Messiah until she sees Him come in power and glory to rescue her. At that time those who have rejected Christ will look upon Him whom they pierced and believe (Zechariah 12:10). That event will also fulfill two New Testament prophecies, one by Christ, the other by Paul: "But he that shall endure unto the end, the same shall be saved" (Matthew 24:13) and "all Israel shall be saved" (Romans 11:26).

There are those, both Jews and evangelicals, who argue against the presence of Israel in her land from a slightly different point of view. While admitting that the Jews will be returned by God to their land someday, they insist that this return to Israel cannot take place until after the Messiah has come. It takes little reflection to realize how utterly unscriptural such a view is.

The Messiah doesn't come to a land that is empty of inhabitants, or that is crowded with some other people who must be put out to let the Jews in. He comes back to a land that is occupied by His own people who rejected and still don't know Him. They are surrounded by the armies of the world determined to exterminate them.

Christ comes both to rescue His people at Armageddon and to reveal Himself to them. Where is Armageddon? It is in Israel. Why is this battle going to be fought? Because the Jews occupy that land. It is to His people, back in their land, that Christ comes! If they are not there, the Second Coming has no meaning and cannot even occur!

Israel's Central Role in the Kingdom

During the exciting 40 days that Christ spent with His disciples after His resurrection, He conversed with them "of the things pertaining to the kingdom of God" (Acts 1:3). He undoubtedly corrected their previous misunderstandings. One question remained, however, and the disciples asked it: "Lord, wilt thou at this time restore the kingdom to Israel?"

The wording of that question revealed the disciples' basic understanding of the teaching they had just received from Christ concerning the millennial kingdom: 1) that the kingdom would indeed be restored to Israel; 2) that the kingdom had not yet been established; and 3) that Christ, not the Church, was the only One who could restore it. Had any of these assumptions which are implied by their question been false, Christ surely would have corrected them. That He did not, leaves these three points intact.

Certainly He didn't say, as some teach today: "Don't you realize that since they crucified Me God has excommunicated the Jews? Israel no longer has any special place in God's plans. She has nothing to do with the kingdom. It all pertains to the Church now!" Instead, He simply replied: "It is not for you to know the times and seasons, which the Father hath put in his own power" (Acts 1:6).

Serious Consequences

We have noted some of the consequences of asserting that while God chose Israel and gave her special promises in the past, He rejected her when she crucified her Messiah. The most obvious logical deduction from this belief—and it is a growing teaching even among evangelicals—is that Israel, in spite of scores of prophecies to the contrary, has no more right to the land she now possesses than do the Arabs. That teaching makes God a liar.

Nor, according to this reasoning, is the land where God put His name (1 Kings 11:36) and which He said He would never forget (Leviticus 26:42), in spite of Israel's sins, any longer of any significance in God's plans. The Church, according to this doctrine, is now spiritual Israel, and all the promises God gave to Israel belong to her. The land, however, is an obvious exception.

The Church, being composed of scores if not hundreds of millions of people living around the world, has no need of the land of Israel. Indeed, the entire Church couldn't possibly all live in that tiny area. Therefore, the land no longer has any significance. This teaching is a direct denial of scores of prophecies promising the land to Israel forever.

Blessings and Curses

Of course, those who identify the Church with Israel are only interested in claiming her blessings, while leaving Israel with the curses God pronounced upon her. Such an approach encounters two major problems: 1) Most of the blessings God gave Israel, by their very nature, could never apply to the Church; and 2) the curses and the blessings go together, so that the Church cannot claim the one without accepting the other also.

Israel's greatest blessings, in fact, come in the restoration of that which she lost because of the curses of God that resulted from her disobedience. That fact alone makes it clear that Israel and the Church are two distinct entities.

No one tries to apply God's curses upon Israel (to be removed from her land and scattered throughout the world) to the Church, for they so obviously don't apply. Then the blessings that result from the undoing of those curses could not apply either. Yet almost every blessing that lies ahead for Israel is of that nature, and thus could not possibly be claimed by the Church.

Two Distinct Destinies

It is clear from even a cursory study of the prophecies pertaining to the Church and Israel that distinct destinies lie ahead for each. For example, the destiny of the people of Israel is to be brought back into their own land from every place where God has scattered them. The Church never had a land of its own, was never removed from it, and certainly can't be brought back to it. Her destiny is in heaven.

Both Israel and the Church play significant roles in the last days and specific prophecies pertain to each. Failure to distinguish between the two results in a serious distortion of biblical prophecy, especially that which pertains to the Rapture and the Second Coming of Christ.

The distinctives which separate Israel and the Church make inapplicable to the latter, for all time, the promises which God gave to Israel as recorded in numerous places in the Bible. The very nature of God's promises to Israel requires that they pertain to a specific ethnic group of people who lived in a particular location on the earth, were scattered from it, and returned thereto in the last days. In contrast, the Church, which was not in existence when these promises were made and isn't even mentioned in the Old Testament, far from being a single, ethnically identifiable people, is comprised of multitudes from "every kindred, and tongue, and people, and nation" (Revelation 5:9).

It cannot be stated too strongly that if we are to understand the Rapture and the Second Coming, then we must distinguish Israel from the Church. Otherwise we will confuse the distinct roles which each is to play. If we substitute the Church for Israel, then we will be hopelessly confused on prophecy and will not be able to discern the times in which we live, which are described in Scripture as "the last days."

CHAPTER 26

"This Generation"

———————— ◇ ————————

> So likewise ye, when ye shall see all these things,
> know that [my coming] is near, even at the doors. Verily I
> say unto you, This generation shall not pass, till all these
> things be fulfilled (Matthew 24:33,34).

Christ here seems to be giving criteria by which His coming could possibly be dated, at least approximately. There is a generation which will not pass away until everything He has prophesied for the last days has been fulfilled. We know that all must be fulfilled also at the end of Daniel's seventieth week, so this should help us to discover when that will occur. Obviously what Christ has to say here is of great importance in our attempt to discern how close we are to His return.

There are, as always, some problems. To whom is Christ speaking—to Israel or to the Church? Is He referring to the Rapture or to the Second Coming? Who or what does He mean by "this generation"? Furthermore, as we have noted in an earlier chapter, the above statement seems, at least upon its face, to contradict verses 42 and 44: "For ye know not what hour your Lord doth come. . . . For in such an hour as ye think not, the Son of man cometh."

A time was coming when all the signs of which He spoke would have been fulfilled before the eyes of a particular generation. On that basis they would realize that Christ's coming was right at the door. Yet at the same time He declares that no one will know when He will return. In fact, even those who are watching for Him are likely not to think that He is coming when He really is. Of course we know that both of these seemingly contradictory statements from our Lord are true and that there is no contradiction.

We have already pointed out that there is only one rational and Scriptural way to reconcile these two statements. Christ can only be referring to two different events: the Rapture and the Second Coming. There are no signs for the Rapture, which will take almost everyone by surprise. The signs are all for the Second Coming—which is why those who heed His Word would know exactly when He is right at the door about to enter the world scene once again. This time He comes not as a lamb to be led to the slaughter, but in power and glory and to take vengeance upon the enemies of God.

Two Opposing Views

Which generation will know exactly when the Second Coming is about to occur? Before whose eyes will all these signs be visibly fulfilled in such a way that they cannot mistake them? Since we know that these things must take place during the seventieth week of Daniel, the generation alive at that time is the one to whom Christ refers. But which generation is that?

As for the latter question, there are two major opposing views. They are held by preterists on the one hand and by futurists on the other. Preterists believe that all of the prophecies of the Olivet discourse and of the book of Revelation through midway into chapter 20 have already been fulfilled (most of them around the time of A.D. 70). Consequently, they consider "this generation" to refer to the generation of those who were alive at the time Christ spoke these words in A.D. 32. If we consider the length of a generation to be 40 years, then it would seem that the date of A.D. 70, when the temple and Jerusalem were destroyed, would support this view.

The futurists, while accepting as fulfilled those prophecies which can definitely be identified in that manner (such as the destruction of Jerusalem in A.D. 70), believe that most of these

Scriptures just mentioned are yet to be fulfilled in a future period of time known as the "last days." They therefore believe that by "this generation" Christ referred to a future generation yet to live on earth.

Some futurists simply say that Christ was indicating that when these signs began to occur they would all take place within the lifespan of one generation. It seems unlikely, however, that Christ would be indicating that view. Daniel had already told us that everything would have to be fulfilled within a shorter period of time—the seven years of his seventieth week. Christ would certainly not extend that seven-year period to a generation, for to do so would contradict Daniel.

A Disappointing Interpretation

Other futurists hold the view that "this generation" refers to the generation alive when Israel returns to her land. Therefore, all the prophecies will have been fulfilled within a generation from 1948, when Israel became a nation again. Unfortunately, some futurists, calculating that 40 years represented a generation, predicted that all the signs would have come to pass with the end of the Great Tribulation, Armageddon, and the Second Coming in 1988. Those who believed in a pretribulation Rapture subtracted seven years from that date and arrived at 1981 as the year of the Rapture.

Of course, the Rapture didn't occur according to that schedule. Even the post-tribbers were disappointed, because the tribulation didn't arrive nor was the Antichrist revealed. The only option left for those who held this view was to suggest that a generation could be much longer than 40 years. One verse that is given to justify a much longer period as the length of a generation is Genesis 15:16. God tells Abraham that his descendants will come into the promised land of Canaan "in the fourth generation." Since Exodus 12:40 declares that the children of Israel spent 430 years in Egypt, "one generation," by that reckoning, would be more than 100 years.

While we still have more than 50 years to wait to see whether the latter view is correct, it takes no time at all to demolish the preterist position. It is irrefutable that all of the signs and events of which Christ spoke in Matthew 24 had not occurred by A.D. 70. One wonders how anyone could hold to this position. Yet many do. Let us mention just a few of the reasons why the preterist view is a serious misperception.

A Past Fulfillment of All
Can't Possibly Be True

In verse 21, Christ declared that a "great tribulation" was coming, "such as was not since the beginning of the world to this time, no, nor ever shall be." It is that last phrase, "nor ever shall be," which destroys the preterist view. The destruction of Jerusalem and slaughter of Jews at A.D. 70 may indeed have been the greatest tribulation until that time, but there have been some since which have been far worse. One need only mention the Nazi Holocaust to prove the point.

Verses 29-31 tell us that "immediately after the tribulation of those days shall the sun be darkened, and the moon shall not give her light, and the stars shall fall from heaven . . . and then shall appear the sign of the Son of man in heaven . . . and all the earth . . . shall see the Son of man coming in the clouds of heaven with power and great glory. And he shall send his angels . . . and they shall gather together his elect from the four winds, from one end of heaven to the other."

These events are very spectacular and would certainly be observed by the whole world, yet they are all conspicuous by their absence from recorded history. Obviously none of them had happened by A.D. 70, nor have they occurred to this day. That fact is not surprising inasmuch as the Great Tribulation which they are to follow has not taken place either.

One scarcely need mention the plagues and devastation foretold in Revelation that will strike over the entire earth—none of which had occurred by A.D. 70—to provide further evidence that by "this generation" Christ did not mean the one living at the time He spoke these words. The Antichrist hadn't appeared (Nero, as we've seen, certainly didn't qualify), the Roman Empire hadn't been revived (it hadn't even been destroyed by A.D. 70)—and on and on we could go. These prophecies and many more are yet future and will run their course, as we have seen, in that seven-year period of great tribulation that coincides with Daniel's seventieth week and awaits the Rapture of the Church before it can begin to be fulfilled.

Is there any alternative at all to waiting another 50-plus years to see whether everything has been wrapped up by 2048? Yes, there is another interpretation of what Jesus meant by "this generation"—a view which the writer always held and perhaps others have held it as well. This view is clearly supported by Zechariah 12.

"This Generation"—An Oft-used Phrase

The Olivet discourse was not the only time Jesus made reference to "generation." In fact, on numerous occasions He was rather specific in His description of a particular generation, the one I believe He had in mind in the prophecy in question. Twice He used the term "this generation," first of all in Matthew 11:16. There He seemed to refer to those alive at the time, for He made specific mention of their rejection of, and complaints they had voiced about, both John the Baptist and Himself. All other references to "generation" have a different quality about them.

The second reference to "this generation" would seem to be an unreasonable statement if He meant only those living at the time:

> That upon you may come all the righteous blood shed upon the earth, from the blood of righteous Abel unto the blood of Zacharias son of Barachias, whom ye slew between the temple and the altar. Verily I say unto you, All these things shall come upon this generation (Matthew 23:35,36).

The Zacharias to whom Christ refers was no doubt the priest named Zechariah who was stoned in the temple court when, in the days of King Joash, he called upon the people of Judah to repent (Zechariah 24:20,21).

That the full punishment for all the righteous blood shed upon earth, from Abel's death in at least 4000 B.C. to a priest's death by stoning about 1000 B.C., would all come upon one generation of Jews which was not alive at either time hardly makes sense. Thus we confront the probability, indeed, the necessity, that Christ had a larger meaning for "this generation."

Two verses earlier (23:33), we get a hint from these words of Jesus: "Ye serpents, ye generation of vipers, how can ye escape the damnation of hell?" Peter explained the only escape in his sermon at Pentecost; and his use of the same word hints further at a larger meaning: "And with many other words did he testify and exhort, saying, Save yourselves from this untoward generation" (Acts 2:40).

Characteristics, Not Time Period

An "untoward [perverse] generation" or a "generation of vipers" identifies a group of people not by the time in which they lived but by their characteristics. Certainly anyone living at any time who exhibited the same evil tendencies would also be part of that "generation of vipers." In fact, Christ used the same expression earlier and similar expressions often. Here are some of them, all from Matthew:

> 12:34—generation of vipers
> 12:39—evil and adulterous generation
> 16:4—wicked and adulterous generation
> 17:17—faithless and perverse generation

Jesus repeatedly linked the words *evil, wicked, adulterous, perverse,* and *faithless* with his use of the word *generation.* Certainly the generation to which He spoke was characterized by these adjectives of rebuke. However, Jesus also linked His hearers in their sin and unbelief to previous generations of Jews, whom He called the "fathers." In fact, Jesus does exactly that in the process of calling His hearers a "generation of vipers":

> Woe unto you, scribes and Pharisees, hypocrites!
> because ye build the tombs of the prophets, and garnish
> the sepulchres of the righteous. And say, If we had been
> in the days of our fathers, we would not have been
> partakers with them in the blood of the prophets. Where-
> fore ye be witnesses unto yourselves, that ye are the
> children of them which killed the prophets. Fill ye up
> then the measure of your fathers. Ye serpents, ye genera-
> tion of vipers, how can ye escape the damnation of hell?
> (Matthew 23:29-33).

It is quite clear that Christ indicts His hearers with the sins
of their fathers. Why? Because they are related not only
physically but by their evil hearts. If His hearers are a generation of vipers, then so must have been their "fathers" who
lived before them and with whose sins He indicts them.

In his bold and convicting speech to those who were about to
stone him, Stephen indicates that all the generations of Israel
in the past have been idolaters and rebels against God and
murderers of His prophets. One must read his entire brilliant
discourse to savor the power of his argument, but we can't
quote it all here. At the end he indicts those to whom he speaks
with being the children of their fathers—i.e., resisting God
and killing the prophets as the entire perverse and unbelieving
generation of Israel has done since the beginning:

> Ye stiffnecked and uncircumcised in heart and ears,
> ye do always resist the Holy Ghost: as your fathers did, so
> do ye. Which of the prophets have not your fathers
> persecuted? and they have slain them which shewed
> before of the coming of the Just One; of whom ye have
> been now the betrayers and murderers: who received the
> law by the disposition of angels, and have not kept it (Acts
> 7:51-53).

It is clear from what both Jesus and Stephen said and from
the record of Scripture that Israel has always been a perverse
and evil generation of vipers. They have persistently rebelled

against God and rejected and even killed the prophets He sent to them. The attitude of the Jews in His time toward Jesus was nothing new, nothing that had not been prophesied, nothing that was not to be expected—and it would continue.

What Jesus was saying, then, was that this same attitude among the Jews would persist until all was fulfilled. The generational sins of Israel would manifest themselves perpetually until the very end (though many individuals would repent and believe in their Messiah and thereby become part of the Church). The chosen people would remain resistant to God in their blindness and perversion until the very moment when Christ would appear in the midst of Armageddon to rescue them. Indeed, this is exactly what Zechariah prophesied as we have already noted:

> For I will gather all nations against Jerusalem to battle; and the city shall be taken. . . . Then shall the Lord go forth, and fight against those nations. . . . And his feet shall stand in that day upon the mount of Olives. . . . And I will pour upon the house of David, and upon the inhabitants of Jerusalem, the spirit of grace and of supplications: and they shall look upon me whom they have pierced, and they shall mourn for him, as one mourneth for his only son, and shall be in bitterness for him, as one that is in bitterness for his firstborn. In that day there shall be a great mourning in Jerusalem. . . . In that day there shall be a fountain opened to the house of David and to the inhabitants of Jerusalem, for sin and for uncleanness. And one shall say unto him, What are these wounds in thine hands? Then he shall answer, Those with which I was wounded in the house of my friends (Zechariah 12:10–14:4).

A Generation That Won't Pass Until All Is Fulfilled

One hears the complaint increasingly voiced among Christians these days: "Those unbelieving Jews don't deserve to be in that land! They are a bunch of atheists, agnostics, Christ-rejectors. It's merely a coincidence that they happen to be there. God's blessing can't possibly be upon them!"

Ah, yes, they don't deserve to be in that land any more than we deserve the forgiveness of our sins that has come by God's grace through the redemptive work of Christ. Nor are they there because they are worthy, but because of the promise which God made to Abraham, Isaac, and Jacob to bring their descendants back to their land in the last days.

Today's Jews are simply following in the footsteps of their fathers, proving that they are part of that same stubborn and unbelieving generation to which Christ referred. Their ancestors throughout history continually disobeyed God, yet He brought them into the promised land and patiently endured their perverseness for hundreds of years before finally casting them out. So what is new? And how else could the Messiah return to Jerusalem and find His people there being attacked by the armies of the world and have them repent when He rescues them. They *must* have returned there in unbelief? That "generation" could not have passed away.

Jesus said that "this generation" of perverseness and unbelief would not pass away until all was fulfilled. Exactly as He foretold, Israel remains a generation of unbelievers. Paul wrote, however, that all Israel would be saved. When will that take place? Not until "all these things be fulfilled," as Jesus said. When will that be? At Armageddon when Christ comes to rescue Israel.

Armageddon is the last event of the seventieth week. By this time all of the signs Christ gave have been witnessed on earth. Israel is surrounded by the armies of the world intent upon annihilating her. At that point, all signs having been fulfilled, anyone who has studied the Bible would know that the Second Coming was about to occur. Even Antichrist knows Christ is coming and goes out to do battle with Him. We've already covered the Scriptures which assure us of this fact.

When they see the Lord Jesus Christ, whom they have rejected, coming to rescue them, all of Israel that have survived will at last know the truth and believe in Him. Only then will that generation of unbelieving rebels have passed away, but not until then.

While this chapter hasn't brought us any closer to knowing when the Second Coming will occur, it has dealt with a key element in understanding prophecy which we can't ignore. It is necessary to know what Christ meant by "this generation," lest we come to false conclusions concerning the timing of the Rapture.

CHAPTER 27

What About the Kingdom?

——————— ◇ ———————

> And this gospel of the kingdom shall be preached in all the world for a witness unto all nations; and then shall the end come (Matthew 24:14).
>
> Now this I say, brethren, that flesh and blood cannot inherit the kingdom of God (1 Corinthians 15:50).
>
> Verily, verily, I say unto thee, Except a man be born again, he cannot see the kingdom of God (John 3:3).
>
> Fear not, little flock; for it is your Father's good pleasure to give you the kingdom (Luke 12:32).
>
> Wherefore we receiving a kingdom which cannot be moved, let us have grace (Hebrews 12:28).

Many evangelicals believe that Matthew is declaring in the first verse cited above that the gospel must be preached to every tribe and tongue—and even, as some suggest, to every person on earth—before the Rapture can take place. If so, then Christ has set a precondition for His return which denies imminency. Surely He would not have said, "Let your loins be girded about, your lights burning; and ye yourselves like unto men that wait for their lord" (Luke 12:35,36) if He could not return until the gospel had been preached to every person on earth! Nor would Paul have encouraged the early Church to look, watch, and wait for the Lord's return. Therefore, such an interpretation cannot be accepted.

In fact, Christ is not setting a condition for the Rapture. That "blessed hope" should rather be called "the beginning" than "the end," for it ushers in the Day of the Lord and Daniel's seventieth week. It is "the end" which cannot come until the gospel of the kingdom has been declared to all nations. One must ask, "The end of what?" And what is meant by "witness unto all nations"?

Restoring God's Sovereign Rule

Since some preliminary end is not specified, Christ must mean the final end of Satan's and mankind's rebellion and the ushering in of God's new universe. That "the end" coincides with the final establishment of the kingdom of God in its eternal fullness is confirmed by Paul:

> Then cometh the end, when he [Christ] shall have delivered up the kingdom to God, even the Father; when he shall have put down all rule and all authority and power (1 Corinthians 15:24).

By "the end," Paul obviously means the consummation in final victory of God's battle with Satan and a full recovery, through Christ, of God's rightful rule over His universe. Christ destroyed Satan on the cross (Hebrews 2:14,15) and conquered death through His resurrection. He must yet rule over earth from David's throne, bringing the benefits of His victory to God's chosen people in fulfillment of prophetic promises. Ultimately, He must put down the final rebellion instigated by Satan at the end of the millennium. Thereafter, God will rule supreme over His eternal kingdom in a new universe into which sin and rebellion can never enter.

It is widely taught and thought that the "kingdom" in Scripture is the millennium. This is only partially true. The millennial reign of Christ is a temporary and earthly manifestation of the eternal kingdom. That the millennium, however, is not the ultimate kingdom is clear. The millennium is of limited duration and ends in a war, whereas the kingdom embodies endless peace. Obviously, the millennium does not measure up to the following descriptions of the kingdom:

> Thy kingdom is an everlasting kingdom (Psalm 145:13; Daniel 4:3; 2 Peter 1:11).

> Of the increase of his government and peace there shall be no end, upon the throne of David and upon his kingdom, to order it and to establish . . . for ever (Isaiah 9:7).

> Flesh and blood cannot inherit the kingdom of God (1 Corinthians 15:50).

> Except a man be born again, he cannot see . . . [much less] enter into the kingdom of God (John 3:3,5).

If God's true kingdom is eternal, then the "gospel of the kingdom" prepares those who receive it, not for the millennium, but for eternity. Then what is the millennium?

What Is the Millennium?

In contrast to the above, the millennium is not eternal, its peace is terminated by a war, and many flesh-and-blood people who have not been born again inhabit the earth during that time. They are the ones who will rebel against Christ when Satan is loosed after 1000 years of imprisonment in the "bottomless pit" (Revelation 20:2,7).

Christ's thousand-year reign upon David's throne is the fulfillment of God's promises to Abraham, Isaac, Israel and to David—but it is more than that. It is the final proof of the incorrigible nature of man's sinful heart. Christ is present in Jerusalem, ruling the world, and the saints of all ages in resurrected bodies administer the kingdom righteously under His direction. All evil is prohibited and punished immediately. Even Satan is locked away so that he cannot in any way influence mankind.

The earth becomes an Edenic paradise again, and it lasts for 1000 years. At the end of that time, Satan is released and is given access to earth once more. Incredibly, he immediately deceives multitudes of those who have known the benevolent rule of Christ, have experienced only peace and plenty, and who have until then been kept from demonic temptation. They follow Satan!

There has been no child abuse for 1000 years, no "dysfunctional families," no poverty or deprivation. None of the reasons given today for wrong behavior are present, yet evil lurks in the human heart and springs forth when it has the opportunity. This final rebellion of mankind against God will constitute the ultimate proof that the theories of the sociologists and psychologists, which blame evil upon environment and circumstances, are false.

Of course, the folly of such theories had already been fully demonstrated in the Garden of Eden. At the end of the millennium, however, it will no longer have been only Adam and Eve, but millions of their descendants who, in a perfect environment, nevertheless turn against God and give their allegiance to Satan. Morever, these millennial rebels will have had the full proof of sin's destructiveness and God's love and redemption—for the crucified and resurrected Christ has been reigning and living among them. The futile attack upon Jerusalem to tear Christ from His throne is the final attempt by Satan to take control of God's universe.

Clearly, these rebels, though they experienced Christ's millennial reign of perfect peace and righteousness, were never part of His kingdom. They had never believed the "gospel of the kingdom." What is that gospel?

There is only one true gospel. It offers eternal life as a free gift of God's grace through faith in the Lord Jesus Christ. Truly believing that He died for one's sins brings a new birth into God's family. That transformation brings one into loving submission to God's sovereign will throughout all eternity—a new life that will never end.

What did Christ mean that the gospel of the kingdom must be preached in all the world for a witness to all nations before the end could come? Surely, that gospel will be proclaimed in the fullness of its truth and power by Christ Himself during the millennium, and by us, the redeemed, reigning with Him in our resurrected, glorified bodies. But it will also be proclaimed in a most unusual and powerful way during the tribulation.

A Powerful Proclamation to the World

Christ is certainly not saying that this gospel must be preached to *every person*. Millions have already died without hearing it. Rather, it must be proclaimed in "all the world *for a witness to all nations*." That phrase sounds as though the day is coming when not only individuals but all the nations of the world will be powerfully confronted by the gospel and the consequences of rejecting it. John seems to have been shown such a time in his vision:

> And I will give power unto my two witnesses, and they shall prophesy a thousand two hundred and three-score days [1260 days, three and a half years] clothed in sackcloth.... And if any man will hurt them, fire proceedeth out of their mouth, and devoureth their enemies. ...These have power to shut heaven, that it rain not in the days of their prophecy: and have power over waters to turn them to blood, and to smite the earth with all plagues, as often as they will (Revelation 11:3-6).

What a dynamic and compelling message from God these two amazing evangelists will bring to "all nations"! No one can write them off as crazies, for they display incredible supernatural powers and defy the Antichrist and his underlings to stop them. No doubt they will be seen daily on international television in every corner of the earth as they warn mankind of God's coming judgment. The world police and even the military will be powerless to silence them. Anyone who attempts to stop them from preaching is instantly destroyed. Even Antichrist's Satanic powers are no match for these two fearless and God-empowered preachers of truth.

There can be no doubt that these two witnesses will have the attention of the entire world! Their message will be a declaration to all the nations on this earth to repent and to acknowledge that Jesus Christ is the world's rightful ruler. The three and a half years of their compelling preaching would seem to coincide with the first half of Daniel's seventieth week. Many will believe the gospel they proclaim and will thereafter refuse to worship the Antichrist or to take his mark—and will be martyred for their faith.

At the end of 1260 days, Antichrist will at last be allowed by God to slay these two witnesses. Their dead bodies will lie in the street in Jerusalem for three and a half days—one day for each year of their incredible testimony. Then, in the sight of a stunned and watching world, they will be resurrected and caught up to heaven.

At this same time ("in the midst of the [seventieth] week"—Daniel 9:27) Antichrist breaks his covenant with Israel, causing the temple sacrifice and worship to cease. He then sets his image in the temple and demands to be worshiped as God. From that time, his evil empire begins to unravel under the outpouring of God's wrath as the world moves ever closer to all-out war against Israel.

The Great Tribulation

Thus commences the last half of Daniel's seventieth week, known as the Great Tribulation. Antichrist's betrayal of Israel marks the beginning of a period of worldwide persecution of Jews which is far more intense than anything they have experienced in the past. Jeremiah calls it "the time of Jacob's trouble" (30:7). Israel will not take this lying down. The growing conflict will engage all nations and culminate at last in Armageddon.

Most likely at this same time Antichrist is given authority by God "to make war with the saints and to overcome them" (Revelation 13:7). If the Church has been raptured, who are these "saints"? They can only be those who had not heard the gospel before the Rapture but who, during the tribulation period, hear it for the first time and believe in Christ. Those who have previously heard and rejected the gospel—"received not the love of the truth that they might be saved" (2 Thessalonians 2:10)—will be given a "strong delusion that they should believe [Antichrist's] lie" (v. 11). Apparently, no one in this category will any longer have the opportunity to believe the truth. Instead, God will help them to believe the very lie they have wanted to believe in rejecting the gospel.

Inasmuch as those who believe the gospel during the tribulation and become followers of Christ will be killed, a post-trib Rapture would be a classic nonevent. There would be few if any believers to catch up to heaven, all of them having been slain by Antichrist for refusing to worship him and to receive his mark (Revelation 13:15). Multitudes will believe the gospel and be true to Christ during Daniel's seventieth week and will pay for that faith with their lives:

> I saw under the altar the souls of them that were slain for the word of God, and for the testimony which they held: And they cried with a loud voice, saying, How long, O Lord, holy and true, dost thou not judge and avenge our blood on them that dwell on the earth? And white robes were given unto every one of them; and it was said unto them, that they should rest yet for a little season, until their fellowservants also and their brethren, that should be killed as they were, should be fulfilled. After this I beheld, and, lo, a great multitude, which no man could number, of all nations, and kindreds, and people, and tongues, stood before the throne, and before the Lamb.... These are they which came out of great tribulation, and have washed their robes, and made them white in the blood of the Lamb ... and they loved not their lives unto death (Revelation 6:9-11; 7:9-14; 12:11).

The "Gospel of the Kingdom"

What is this "gospel of the kingdom" which the two witnesses and the 144,000 Jewish evangelists (Revelation 7:3-8) will proclaim and which leads to the martyrdom of those who believe it? Many evangelicals distinguish between the gospel of Christ which we now preach, and the gospel of the kingdom which Christ and His disciples announced at the beginning and which will be proclaimed during the tribulation period. They suggest that those who believe this "gospel of the kingdom" are not part of the Church, but will be allowed to continue on earth into the millennial reign of Jesus Christ.

Allegedly, this gospel pertains only to the millennial kingdom and was offered by Christ exclusively to the Jews. In other words, the gospel of the kingdom presumably called upon Israel to recognize her Messiah and to submit herself willingly to Him as the One whose right it was to rule over her from David's ancient throne. When Israel rejected and crucified Christ, the gospel of the kingdom ceased, the Church was born and began to proclaim the gospel of the grace of God. Such a "dispensational" view, however, cannot be sustained from Scripture.

Mark 13 is the passage parallel to Matthew 24. It gives the same statement by Christ about the gospel being preached throughout all the world prior to the end, but leaves out the phrase, "of the kingdom." Mark simply says, "And the gospel must first be published among all nations" (13:10). Which gospel? There is only one. It is called "the everlasting gospel" (Revelation 14:6).

"The gospel of the kingdom" was the only gospel which Christ preached: "And Jesus went about all Galilee . . . preaching the *gospel of the kingdom*" (Matthew 4:23). It must therefore have been the gospel of which Christ spoke when He told His disciples to "go into all the world and preach the gospel" (Mark 16:15). There is no indication that He meant any other gospel than the one He had been preaching and which He must have trained them to preach as well. Clearly, it was the only gospel the disciples knew, even after the resurrection (Acts 8:12). It was also the gospel Paul preached:

> And now, behold, I know that ye all, among whom I have gone preaching the kingdom of God, shall see my face no more [Paul to the Ephesian elders] (Acts 20:25).

> And Paul dwelt two whole years in his own hired
> house [during his imprisonment in Rome], and received
> all that came in unto him, Preaching the kingdom of God
> (Acts 28:30,31).

"The gospel of the kingdom" is an expression which occurs only five times in the Bible (Matthew 4:23; 9:35; 24:14; Mark 1:14,15). Nowhere in the New Testament is there any hint that it differed from the gospel we preach today. Nor is there any indication of a time when a transition was made from a gospel which brought hearers into the kingdom to a gospel which brought hearers into the Church.

The question arises, however, how, prior to the death and resurrection of Christ, the disciples could preach a gospel which included those truths when they did not as yet understand them. The fact is that every promise of salvation in the Old Testament, either to Israel or to the Gentiles, depended for its realization upon the coming Messiah and His redemptive death upon the cross. That He would be rejected and die for our sins in fulfillment of the Old Testament sacrifices was foretold by the prophets, as we have seen. Although the disciples did not understand these truths, nevertheless they pointed their hearers to the One whom they believed to be the Messiah.

That the "everlasting gospel" has not changed from the beginning is clear from the fact that Paul could take the Old Testament and preach from it the same gospel we preach today. The Bereans checked Paul's preaching against the Old Testament and found it biblical (Acts 17:11). Paul preached what He called "the gospel of God, which he promised afore by his prophets in the holy scriptures, concerning his Son Jesus Christ our Lord" (Romans 1:1-3). It was preached according to the progressive revelation available at the time. Today, we enjoy the full revelation of its meaning.

If we do not preach this gospel in its fullness—the very same gospel which Paul preached—we are cursed (Galatians 1:8,9). Is it the "gospel of the kingdom"? Indeed it is, for only those who believe it can be made new creatures in Christ Jesus and inhabit the new universe God will one day make. That

ᴇrnal state in which the redeemed of all ages will
dwell in loving submission to God is the promised

True "Apostolic Succession"

If the gospel of the kingdom was what Paul and the apostles preached both to Jews and Gentiles, then it must be the very gospel which we are to preach today. If ours is a different gospel from that preached by Christ and His disciples, how were we to learn about this new gospel and when were we commissioned to preach it? There is no answer to such questions in Scripture.

Just as Christ discipled the 12, so they were told to make disciples. These new disciples were to be instructed to observe everything which Christ had taught and commanded the original twelve to observe. Christ's disciples were commanded by our Lord to pass on to their converts everything He had taught them during those three-plus years when they had been under His discipline and instruction day and night: "Teaching them to observe [obey] *all things* whatsoever I have commanded you" (Matthew 28:20).

How could the disciples' converts obey everything Christ had commanded the original 12 unless they received the same authority and power to do so? If words mean anything, then all powers and responsibilities which Christ conferred upon His original disciples were to be passed by them to their converts. These new disciples, in turn, were to make more disciples, who would likewise be taught to obey all that Christ had commanded the original 12. Here was true "apostolic succession"!

Apostolic succession does not bestow (as the Roman Catholic Church falsely claims) privileges, responsibilities, and powers upon a select class of clergy, priests, bishops, and popes. No, these blessings accrue equally to every person who becomes a disciple of Christ. This chain of command from Christ through His disciples to their converts and on to their converts' converts has come down to every Christian today. By

God's grace, we have been given the same obligation and privilege of preaching in all the world the same gospel of the kingdom which the original apostles preached, for we are the disciples of those who were made disciples by them. Every true Christian is a successor to the apostles!

Confusion concerning the kingdom has relegated many of Christ's teachings, such as the Sermon on the Mount, to Israel and the millennium, causing Christians today to miss much of value for their own lives. Some evangelicals go so far as to say that the four Gospels are only for Israel and the millennium, while the epistles are for the Church. Yet, it was in the Gospels that Christ founded His Church, and it is there that we find the foundational truths.

At the other extreme are the Reconstructionists, the Reformed or Covenant theologians and the Kingdom Now Dominionists who take for the Church what belongs to Israel. These generally imagine that we are in the millennial kingdom right now and that the Church has the responsibility to establish this kingdom by progressively taking over the world in the name of Christ. Some even teach that Satan is locked up, though one would certainly not suspect it. Some of the leaders in these movements even suggest the use of *violence* to accomplish their misguided takeover of the world.

Are We Already in the Kingdom?

Speaking to a group of Pharisees who were questioning Him, Christ said, "The kingdom of God is within you" (Luke 17:21). Unfortunately, the King James rendering, though generally the best, needs improvement here. Surely, the kingdom of God was not within the *Pharisees*. Yes, the kingdom of God is established in the hearts of those who believe in Jesus, and He begins to reign as Lord in their lives. But Christ was speaking to unbelievers in whom He did not dwell. The Greek also means "in your midst" or "among you," which was no doubt what Christ meant. He, the King, was in their midst, but they were going to reject and even crucify Him.

While the kingdom is here now, it only exists invisibly in the hearts of believers where the King already reigns. There is as yet no outward, visible manifestation of the kingdom taking authority over the ungodly and even animals living at peace with one another and mankind as there will be when Christ personally rules upon earth. That He will do so is promised repeatedly by Old Testament prophets and is also declared in the New Testament. The angel Gabriel told Mary:

> And behold, thou shalt conceive in thy womb, and bring forth a son, and shalt call his name Jesus. And he shall be great, and shall be called the Son of the Highest: and the Lord God shall give unto him the throne of his father David: And he shall reign over the house of Jacob for ever; and of his kingdom there shall be no end (Luke 1:31-33).

God's promises to Abraham, Isaac, and Jacob concerning the future of Israel are repeated and reaffirmed both in the Old and New Testaments, and cannot be annulled. Yet Reformed or Covenant and Dominion theology replaces Israel with the Church. As a corollary, it denies the personal reign of Christ in a future millennium. Covenant theologians insist that God's visible, worldwide kingdom is in place now and that He is reigning over it from heaven through the Church. This rejection of a future kingdom for Israel and application to the Church of prophecies meant for Israel has created a popular and dangerous teaching among many of today's evangelicals— a teaching which could not be more in opposition to Scripture.

A Dangerous Delusion

The Bible declares that when Christ resurrects the dead saints He simultaneously catches up all living Christians together with them to meet Him in the air and to escort them to heaven. The language concerning the resurrection and the Rapture, which we have quoted already, could not be clearer:

> For the Lord himself shall descend from heaven with a shout . . . and the dead in Christ shall rise first: then we which are alive and remain shall be caught up together

> with them in the clouds, to meet the Lord in the air: and
> so shall we ever be with the Lord (1 Thessalonians
> 4:16,17).

Nevertheless, as we have already noted, it is being taught that at His return, rather than taking Christians to heaven, Christ joins them upon earth to rule over a kingdom which the Church has established for Him. While this is not Reformed theology, it is closely related thereto, and those of Reformed persuasion, especially Reconstructionists, often identify with the charismatics and Pentecostals who promote the "Kingdom Now" teaching.

The irreconcilable contradiction between such beliefs and the Bible could not be more obvious nor could the consequences be more serious. While we have earlier referred to these consequences, the warning bears repeating.

The real Jesus Christ will catch us up to meet Him in the air and take us to heaven. Then what of those who look forward to meeting their "Christ" with their feet planted upon earth—a Christ who has arrived to take over the "kingdom" they've established for Him? They have been working for Antichrist! His counterfeit kingdom will be established upon earth through a great peace-and-unity movement which will eliminate all political and religious differences worldwide. It is that new world order which Christ will destroy at His Second Coming (Daniel 2:44; 2 Thessalonians 2:8).

"Reformed" and "Dispensational" Views

The system of belief which includes a pre-trib Rapture and a distinction between Israel and the Church is broadly called "dispensationalism." This systematic way of interpreting the Bible has been attributed to J.N. Darby and C.I. Scofield, among others, and is widely taught among evangelicals and at such dispensationalist institutions as Dallas Theological Seminary. There are, however, several variations within dispensationalism—distinctions of which it is not necessary to take note.

The major opposition to dispensationalism among evangelicals comes from "Reformed" or "Covenant" theology. Again there are variations within these views which we don't have time to discuss, so we will be speaking broadly. Proponents of Reformed theology claim that its view of eschatology (post-millennial or amillennial) is the majority view today and that it held sway throughout history until the early 1800s, when Darby popularized dispensationalism. Indeed, post-millennialism or amillennialism (the small distinction between the two is unimportant to our discussion) did dominate the religious scene because they were Roman Catholic doctrine and anything else was punished as heresy.

It seems odd for those who claim a Reformation heritage to defend their views by saying that they were always held by the Roman Catholic Church! Indeed, when it comes to eschatology, Reformed theology is poorly named. It retained Roman Catholic views which had developed as a result of Rome's apostasy. Claiming to be the true Israel, the Roman Catholic Church became obsessed with taking over the world and lost the hope of the Rapture.

Following in Rome's footsteps, Luther and Calvin made their alignments with the secular powers of this world. Reformed theology retained the Catholic view that we are in the millennium now, that the Church is in the process of taking over the world and even that Satan has already been locked up. Imminency is rejected. Christ is allowed to return only at the end of the millennium.

Revelation 20 twice declares that the saints reign with Christ over the earth for 1000 years and that this reign follows a future battle of Armageddon. Nevertheless, such Scriptures are not taken literally by those of Reformed persuasion. Instead, the millennium is already present and will last not a literal 1000 years but for an indefinite period of time—perhaps many thousands of years.

While some Covenant theologians claim to believe that a rapture will occur at the end of their indefinite and very lengthy "millennium" (or non-millennium, as the case may be), it is certainly not what is described in 1 Thessalonians 4:13-18. Rather they propose simply a final judgment followed by the commencement of the eternal state. Nor does a rapture of any kind that far in the future have any motivating effect upon us today.

Armageddon, rather than being a future literal battle involving earth's armies in an attack upon Israel as the prophets testify, is seen as symbolic of the ongoing spiritual conflict between Christ and the forces of darkness. The fact that the resurrection clearly takes place before the millennium begins (Revelation 20) is again ignored. Whatever doesn't fit their theories is spiritualized to bring it into harmony with the Reformed, Covenant, or Dominion view.

Loosely Handling the Word of Truth

There is no recognition that Daniel's seventieth week has not yet run its course. Instead, it is vaguely assumed that all 70 weeks have come and gone without accounting specifically for the events which were to have occurred within that time frame. Daniel 2:44 is taken to mean that the kingdom will be established during the days of the ancient Roman Empire, thus supporting the teaching that it began when Christ was here the first time. That this verse specifically states that the kingdom will be established when ten kings (the ten toes) are reigning is ignored. Thus, there is no need for the Roman Empire to be revived at all, much less under ten heads.

Amazingly, the unscriptural view that the Church must gradually take over the world for Christ and in this manner establish the kingdom is growing in popularity. Yet the prophecies clearly indicate a cataclysmic inauguration of the kingdom by Christ's personal intervention. Surely the "stone cut out without hands" (a type of Christ, the Rock) which smashes Nebuchadnezzar's image and fills the whole earth indicates a sudden destruction of the kingdoms of earth and the establishment of God's kingdom by Christ's intervention. The same is true of the account in Revelation 19 where Christ comes to intervene at Armageddon, as well as the parallel account in

Zechariah 12–14 and other passages. All of these are generally spiritualized or explained away in Reformed, Covenant, and Dominion eschatologies.

Christ's statement, "All authority is given me in heaven and earth" (Matthew 28:18), becomes the basis for the claim that Christians are therefore, in the strength of that authority, to take over the media, the schools, and the government until they reign over the world for Christ. Most Reformed theologians are Calvinists, so there is no room for human choice and thus no explanation for varying degrees of evil in the world. Everything depends upon how much "irresistible" and "common" grace God provides. As He apportions more and more, the world will gradually improve and the percentage of Christians will grow. Why God has not extended such grace in larger quantities and earlier is not explained.

The simple fact is that God has always been sovereign. Even so, His supreme authority did not prevent the rebellion of Satan in heaven, nor the disobedience of Adam and Eve on earth. They each made their independent choice just as men are doing today. Yet with God's authority the Church is expected to do what God Himself hasn't done—take over the world. Anyone who is not willing to exercise Christ's authority for that purpose is considered a defeatist.

Seemingly forgotten is the fact that Christ and His apostles were all slain by the ungodly. The cross was Christ's great triumph. Those who are victorious over Antichrist die as martyrs at his hands: "And they overcame him by the blood of the Lamb, and by the word of their testimony; and they loved not their lives unto the death" (Revelation 12:11). Here is true victory, the way of the cross!

God's kingdom is made possible through the cross of Christ. Evil is not conquered by bluster and force, but by submission to God's will. And that means accepting His remedy for sin. Only then can paradise be restored fully and eternally.

Paradise Restored

When Adam and Eve were cast out of the garden for rebellion, the Tree of Life was guarded by the flaming sword of

God's judgment. Mankind fled that sword, for its piercing would bring eternal death. The world has alternately cowered, complained that such judgment was too harsh, and even denied that it was real. But there was no way around that sword. Mankind must die and be reborn into God's family.

One day a perfectly sinless man who was, in fact, God and man in one Person, walked up to that sword and took its deadly blow in His heart for us. His blood quenched its flame and thus gave access to the Tree of Life. He is "the way, the truth and the life" to all who believe that He took God's just judgment for them.

Amazingly, the world rejected Him and plunged its own sword of hatred and pride through His heart. For to accept His sacrifice one had to admit one's sin, that God's penalty was just, and that restoration to fellowship with God could only come as a free gift of His grace through Christ's death in our place. Pride has prevented that admission for multitudes and robbed them of God's gracious forgiveness and the eternal life He gives.

Kings and priests, gurus of religion and humanism, ecologists, anthropologists, psychologists, sociologists, revolutionaries, and political leaders of all stripes have offered their solutions. There was, after all, so they promised, a way around that sword. Paradise could be restored if we would all get together, cooperate, love one another, share equally—and especially follow them. But their self-improvement programs miserably failed. Evil masqueraded as good and the world grew worse.

God is patient, but His judgment comes at last. Evil was so great in Noah's day that finally God cleansed the earth with a flood. The wickedness of Sodom and Gomorrah became such a stench that God destroyed them with fire. Today's Sodomites have become a favored class wielding great power. They educate our children in our schools, propagandize through the media, hold public offices, and even preach from our pulpits.

God is not mocked. His patience wears thin. Babies are murdered in the womb by the millions; marriage is ridiculed;

sex, science, success, and pleasure are worshiped. Perversion of all kinds is flaunted in God's face. Judgment must fall upon a world that is at least as wicked and probably more so than the world of Noah and Lot. How close are we?

Paradise will be restored. A new universe will be created. But the cleansing of judgment must come first. That righteous retribution cannot be delayed much longer. Praise God, He has promised that the Rapture comes before God's wrath is poured out in vengeance upon this earth. We must be very close indeed to that most wonderful event—and unfortunately, to the horror for unbelievers that will follow!

CHAPTER 28

How Close Are We?

———————— ◇ ————————

> But and if that evil servant shall say in his heart, My Lord delayeth his coming. . . . The Lord of that servant shall come in a day when he looketh not for him (Matthew 24:48-50).
>
> While the bridegroom tarried, they all slumbered and slept. And at midnight there was a cry made, Behold the bridegroom cometh; go ye out to meet him. . . . Watch therefore, for ye know neither the day nor the hour wherein the Son of man cometh (Matthew 25:5,6,13).

Let us summarize briefly the conclusions we have reached from carefully comparing Scripture with Scripture. In the preceding chapters we have noted a number of seeming contradictions in what Christ and the apostles said about His return: He comes at a time of peace and yet in the midst of war; He comes when no one would expect Him and yet He comes when all of the prophesied signs have been displayed to the world and even Antichrist knows He is about to descend to earth; He comes when judgment is the last thing anyone on earth would expect, yet He comes to a world very much aware that God's divine wrath and judgment are being poured out upon it.

We have found that the only possible way to reconcile these contrary statements is to recognize that they are referring to two separate events: the Rapture and Second Coming. The differences may be simplified in this way: 1) At the Rapture,

Christ comes *for* His saints at a time of peace and business as usual before the tribulation; whereas 2) at the Second Coming seven years later, He comes from heaven *with* all of His saints (they must have previously been taken there) to rescue Israel in the midst of Armageddon at the end of the Great Tribulation

Two Solemn Warnings

There are two solemn and related warnings which Christ gave concerning His coming again. First of all, He repeatedly and earnestly declared that He was coming very soon and should be expected at any moment. That He hasn't come in more than 1900 years, far from discrediting that promise, makes it all the more urgent that we heed it in our day. By heaven's reckoning Christ has been gone a very short time; and His coming is nearer now than it ever was.

He told His disciples 1900 years ago, "Let your loins be girded about, and your lights burning; and ye yourselves like unto men that wait for their lord" (Luke 12:35,36). If that was to be their attitude, how much more should we be anticipating His momentary coming in our day! Christ's words are clear and to the point. They cannot be reinterpreted to fit one's theories. In the plainest, unmistakable language He told us to expect Him at any moment. Dare we ignore His command?

Yet most Christians live as though Christ never made such statements. It is almost frightening to see and hear those who claim to believe in the Rapture deny it with their lives and lips. Christian businessmen become absorbed in long-range programs stretching all the way to retirement. Pastors enthuse over their five-year and ten-year building programs and re-hearse their meticulous plans for future church expansion. Housewives and students have their long-range dreams as well—all involving this present world.

We are not suggesting that plans should not be made, but only that recipes for one's future on this earth should always be contingencies *in case* the Rapture should not occur. One's expectation of Christ's return should be greater than one's expectation of remaining here upon earth. Sadly it seems to be the opposite. The qualifier, "If the Lord tarries and spares us," is scarcely heard as Christians talk and even boast of what they expect to be doing tomorrow, next week, next year, and on into the future.

The Second Warning

Secondly, He warned us about preoccupation with the things of this life. Christ knew the attraction which the pleasures and ambitions of this world, wicked though we realize it to be, can have for each of us. So He warned us that unless we kept the thought of His return fresh in our hearts at all times we would be caught by surprise at His coming.

He warned that He would come when the Church would be characterized by sleepy complacency and when many would even be entertaining wishful thoughts of a delay to His return. It would be at a time when He was least expected and even His own were in danger of being caught by surprise. Such warnings, which could not apply to Israel, clearly tell us that the Gospels, contrary to what some teach, are not only for Israel but for the Church as well.

Most dispensationalists insist, for example, that the Rapture is not in the Gospels. Specifically they say it isn't to be found in the Olivet discourse, which they claim is only for Israel. Obviously that can't be true. What coming will catch Israel by surprise? Surely not the Second Coming to rescue her at Armageddon, for all the signs have been displayed and even Antichrist knows Christ is about to descend from heaven to confront him.

Surely the complacency Christ warned about and the desire for the Messiah to delay His coming would not fit the Jewish situation when Christ comes to rescue Israel. It will be just the opposite. Far from sleepy and complacent, Israel will be in desperate straits under all-out attack by the armies of the world's most powerful nations.

Seeing the Vital Distinction Again

Undergoing destruction by overwhelmingly superior forces

and about to suffer total defeat, Israel's only possible hope would be the immediate appearance of the Messiah to effect a miraculous rescue. It is, therefore, inconceivable that any Jew at that time would be hoping for a delay in Messiah's coming. On the contrary, Israel's inhabitants will be desperately crying out for Him to appear—not necessarily out of any real faith, but driven by the hopelessness and horror facing them.

Here we see again the clear distinction between Israel and the Church and between the Rapture and the Second Coming. Christ's warnings in Matthew 24 and elsewhere about complacency and surprise at His coming and even desiring it to be delayed could not apply at all to Israel in the midst of Armageddon. None of the statements by Christ quoted at the beginning of the chapter could possibly apply to Israel and the Second Coming.

Such language could only apply to the Church and the Rapture. We are forced to conclude that Christ did not have the Second Coming in mind when He warned that He would come like a thief when His followers would be complacently establishing themselves in the world and making long-term plans. "Watch, therefore . . . lest coming suddenly he find you sleeping" (Luke 13:35,36) is an exhortation that would certainly be unnecessary in the midst of Armageddon!

It is, however, a warning which Christians need to hear and heed. Moreover, there is an even more solemn forecast from our Lord. Complacency and finding one's hopes and joys in the world are bad enough. Yet Christ warned that He would come when the Church would not only be sleeping, but would be convinced that He was *not* coming: "Therefore be ye also ready: for in such an hour as ye think not the Son of man cometh" (Matthew 24:44).

It seems inconceivable that any Christian could ever think or say, "I don't think Christ is coming now." Jesus declares that He is coming at precisely such a time. How that warning should stir our hearts to watch and wait and to be ready for His return at any moment!

A Day Which Anyone Can Date

We discover another contrast between the Rapture and the Second Coming. Concerning the former, Christ declared unequivocally: "But of that day and hour knoweth no man, no, not the angels of heaven, but my Father only" (Matthew 24:36). How do we know He's referring to the Rapture and not the Second Coming? Very simply, because the day of the Second Coming can and will be known.

Daniel, who gave the precise date Jesus would enter Jerusalem and be hailed as the Messiah, provides similar data for calculating the exact day of Christ's return in triumph to the City of David. He tells us that Antichrist will break his covenant with Israel "in the midst of the week . . . [and] cause the sacrifice and oblation to cease" (9:27). One need, therefore, only count three and a half years (1260 days) from that event to know the very day of the Second Coming at the end of Daniel's seventieth week of years.

The book of Revelation gives additional data confirming this timetable. The two witnesses are killed 1260 days into the last week of years—i.e., "in the midst [middle] of the week" (Revelation 11:3,7). Again, one need only count, from that event as well, 1260 days to arrive at the date of the Second Coming. As we have already seen, the woman of Revelation 12, obviously a symbol for Israel inasmuch as she gives birth to the Messiah "who was to rule all nations with a rod of iron" (v. 5), is persecuted by Satan for 1260 days (v. 6). She is protected by God for "a time [one year], times [two years], and half a time" [a total of three and a half years].

Thus, Revelation tells us in more than one way that three and a half years into the tribulation period ("in the midst of the week"—Daniel 9:27), when Antichrist breaks his covenant and stops the temple worship, he will begin to persecute Israel. At this point, the period known as the Great Tribulation begins. It will last for another three and a half years or the last half of Daniel's seventieth week. Using this criteria also, one need only count 42 months from Antichrist's image being placed in the temple to arrive at the end of "the time of Jacob's trouble" (Jeremiah 30:7) and the Second Coming.

Of course, the date of the Second Coming cannot be known as yet. Everything hinges upon the Rapture (which cannot be dated) and is calculated from the moment of that event. Once the Church has gone, whose formation stopped God's time clock concerning Israel at the end of 69 weeks, and whose continued presence perpetuates that hiatus, Daniel's seventieth week will begin to run its course. Counting seven years from that time, the day of the Second Coming can be determined and even double-checked by following the fulfillment of the other prophesied events mentioned above.

Why the Day of the Rapture Must Remain Unknown

It takes little thought to realize why God must keep the date of the Rapture as His secret. Suppose, for example, that the Bible indicated the date of the Rapture to be 1996, as some prophecy students are now claiming. What a discouragement it would have been for believers during the 19 centuries leading up to this time! And what an encouragement to carnality and worldly living it would have been to know that the Lord couldn't come at any moment and catch one by surprise doing, perhaps, those things that no Christian should. Much would have been lost by giving the date of the Rapture—and nothing would have been gained.

If 1996 (the most popular date at the moment) could have been calculated from Scripture as the time for the Rapture, the early Church would not have been waiting and looking for Christ, as indeed she was. The "blessed hope" could not have been a hope at all, even for us today, for one doesn't "hope" for something to happen if he knows exactly when it will occur. Of course, "hope" for the Christian has an element of confidence as well, for he is assured of its realization. But if the event couldn't take place for many years, then hope would be lost until that time arrived.

Hope purifies: "Everyone who has this hope in him purifies himself even as he is pure" (1 John 3:3). Yes, we know this event will occur eventually. However, the major impact of that hope in its purifying effect would have been lost to the Church through the centuries had a date been given for either the Rapture or the Second Coming. Nor would the Church today have that "blessed hope" (Titus 2:13) of being raptured at any moment if Christ could not come until some future date or until after Antichrist's appearance, or after the tribulation or some other event or until some prior condition was met.

Of course Christ has always known exactly when He would rapture the Church. He knew that more than 1900 years would go by before His return. Why, then, would He urge His saints to watch for His coming when hundreds of millions would be watching in vain? Ah, no one watches in vain. The expectation of Christ's imminent return is the major motivation for godly living. Christ did not want to rob His own of that purifying expectancy.

How close are we? The Rapture could always have been—and still could be at this moment—only a heartbeat away. To wish to know the date of Christ's return, however, is to wish for that which He will not give and which would not be for our good. If we knew that He wouldn't come until a year from now, we would have lost the hope that He could come at any moment. Lost, too, would be that hope's motivating power which comes from knowing that we might not have another day and so must live and witness for Him as though each day were our last.

Such is the problem with the thesis, now gaining increasing acceptance, that the Rapture will occur when the last trump sounds at the Feast of Trumpets. Christ may indeed rapture His bride at that time. However, if that were clearly stated in Scripture, then each time that date passed with hope unfulfilled, one would know that His return would be delayed for another year. That knowledge, as Christ makes very plain, would not be in the best interests of the Church, but would most assuredly foster evil.

How Close Do You Want It to Be?

How close are we? Christ could come at any moment—before I finish writing this page, or before you finish reading it. Does that thought bring joy or regret—perhaps even fear? The honest answer to that vital question reveals one's spiritual condition and the measure of one's love for Him.

Whether or not we truly long for Christ's return and are ready for Him to come at any moment will obviously affect how we live. To awaken each morning with the joyful anticipation that this could be the day when Christ will catch away His own from earth to heaven transforms our daily lives as nothing else could. The firm conviction that Christ could come at any moment—and the desire for Him to do so—is surely the secret to victorious and holy living.

Such is the message which Paul conveys in Colossians 3. One cannot find another chapter in the Bible which contains a more complete description of what the Christian life ought and ought not to be. And the key to victory which Paul presents is the hope of Christ's return.

Verse 5 begins by telling us to put to death the deeds of the flesh. The list goes on for several verses: "immorality, impurity, passion, evil desire, and greed . . . anger, wrath, malice, slander, and abusive speech and lying." Verses 12-25 list the Christlike virtues we are to embody as He lives through us: "a heart of compassion, kindness, humility, gentleness and patience; bearing with one another, and forgiving each other . . . as the Lord forgave you, so also should you . . . and put on love and let the peace of Christ rule in your hearts."

A key word in verses 5 and 12 was deliberately left out in the paragraph above. The word is *therefore*. It takes us back to the first four verses in the chapter. Here is what they say:

> If ye then are risen with Christ, seek those things which are above, where Christ sitteth on the right hand of God. Set your affection on things above, not on things on the earth. For ye are dead, and your life is hid with Christ in God. When Christ, who is your life, shall appear, then shall ye also appear with him in glory. Mortify *therefore* your members. Put on, *therefore*, as the elect of God.

Imminency: Its Purifying and Motivating Power

In other words, the life which we live as Christians draws its incentive and strength from the realization that we are dead to sin, self, and this world, and draws equally from the hope of momentarily seeing Christ and of being eternally in His presence. All that we say and do is with the sure knowledge that our life is hid with Christ in God and that when He shall appear we will appear with Him to God's glory. That hope inspires us to mortify the deeds of the body and to put on the virtues of Christ.

Contrary to what the critics say, the hope of Christ's imminent return doesn't lead to spiritual lethargy or an escapist mentality which shuns responsibility and trial. Rather it causes us to witness more earnestly and to live holier lives, knowing that very little time for doing so may remain.

Such was the impact this hope had upon the early Church, a motivating and purifying influence which has been largely lost and surely needs to be recovered. Paul himself indicates that the love of Christ's appearing was the driving force of his life:

> For I am now ready to be offered, and the time of my departure is at hand. I have fought a good fight, I have finished my course, I have kept the faith: Henceforth there is laid up for me a crown of righteousness, which the Lord, the righteous judge, shall give me at that day: and not to me only, but unto all them also that love his appearing (2 Timothy 4:6-8).

What has been the result of rejecting imminency? It could not help but foster a more worldly orientation. It surely has not increased the love Christians have for their Lord. Nor has the tragic loss of imminency fostered holy living or an increased sense of urgency in spreading the gospel. Instead, Christians have set their hope and affection on the status, security, pleasures, and possessions offered by this evil world.

Not expecting, until they die, to leave the earth they love so much, and hoping to delay the inevitability of death as long as possible, Christians have become as earthly minded as the worldlings around them. Building an estate, a bank account, trusting in insurance policies, and planning for retirement, have preoccupied a Church that no longer hopes for Christ's imminent return to take her to heaven. Believers have become much like the rich man to whom God said, "Thou fool, this night thy soul shall be required of thee: then whose shall those things be, which thou has provided?" (Luke 12:20).

Hoping for Heaven—But Not Yet

For most Christians heaven is a place they desire to reach eventually, but not until they have lived out their full days on earth. Their hopes, ambitions, and interests, contrary to what Christ taught and the early Church lived, are really bound up in the life they aspire to live in this world. Heaven is a distant and unreal destination they reluctantly expect to reach at the end of life, but it is not desired before then. To be suddenly raptured to heaven would be, for most Christians, an unwelcome interruption of their earthly plans and ambitions.

Unfortunately, such an indictment applies even to many who intellectually believe in the pre-trib Rapture. Though mental assent is given to the doctrine, the truth of imminency has not gripped them. The awesome reality of suddenly at any moment being caught up to meet Christ in the air has not affected their lives. Instead, the Rapture is like a tale that has been told, something they believe in theoretically but which they have little if any expectation of experiencing in their lifetime.

Tragically, even those who claim to believe in the imminent return of Christ often do not live as Christ said they should, with "loins girded about and lights burning . . . as men who wait for their Lord when he will return" (Luke 12:35,36). Only if His imminent return is our constant hope will we live as true followers of Christ—those who live as citizens of heaven and who are looking for their Lord to catch them up to His Father's house at any moment.

Was there ever a bride truly in love who didn't eagerly anticipate the wedding day when she and her fiance could be united and begin to share their lives together? One longs to be with the one loved; and if that possibility is not a distant or vague hope but one which could be realized at any moment, then love is strengthened by it. To know, however, that one cannot see or be with the one loved for many years does not help the relationship.

The Choice: Heaven or This Earth

Let us be reminded that Christ always equated the thought of a delay in His coming with evil. Not only the first two verses quoted at the beginning of the chapter but others as well reiterate this same sober rebuke. What a convicting reprimand He gives to those who hope for a delay in His return! Nor could any stronger argument for imminency be given, for Christ's reprimand is always accompanied by the warning that He will return at a time when He is least expected:

> But and if that servant say in his heart, My Lord delayeth his coming; and shall begin to beat the menservants and maidens, and to eat and drink, and to be drunken; the Lord of that servant will come in a day when he looketh not for him (Luke 12:45,46).

There are some who desire the Rapture to be delayed, and many who think they have biblical reasons for believing that it cannot occur until after Antichrist appears, or the Great Tribulation has ended, or even until the end of the millennium. Yet Christ says that such thoughts are the first step in the wrong direction. It is always an "evil" servant who imagines his Lord won't come just yet and therefore he has time to live for self.

The very words John uses—"everyone who has this hope in him purifieth himself"—argue for imminency. If he is simply referring to some distantly future coming in which we could not possibly participate, such as a post-millennial coming, then there is no hope at all and thus no purifying effect. Nor would a post-tribulation Rapture, as we have already seen, qualify as a purifying "hope" for the reasons which we have given.

It is argued that John was referring to the confidence shared by all Christians of meeting the Lord at one's death. In a sense that is true. John must, however, have had more than that in mind, for who hopes for death? He must be referring to something which has an even more powerful purifying impact than the thought of death. It can only be the hope of the imminent return of Christ to rapture His bride to His Father's house of many mansions.

John is not, of course, recommending a fanatical, other-worldly mindedness that foolishly ignores any common-sense provision for this life. We are to live as those who long to leave this earth and who expect to depart at any moment, yet who also make contingency plans in case the Rapture is delayed. One must prudently plan and provide for this life without resting one's hope or placing one's affection upon it.

The pre-trib Rapture goes to the heart of the battle between God and Satan for the souls of mankind. The choice we each face, surprisingly, is not heaven or hell. If that were the case, who would not choose heaven? The real choice we must and do make—daily, hourly—is between heaven and this earth. Only the possibility of an imminent Rapture confronts us with that choice.

Our attitudes and actions continually reflect our unconscious answer to the question: "Am I willing to leave this earth right now for heaven, or is there something that holds me here and thus something of earth which stands between my Lord and me at this moment?" When we honestly face that choice, we begin to understand why Paul exhorted, "Set your affection on things above, not on things on this earth."

The Real Question

The battle that is fought in man's heart began as a choice between two worlds—the world as God made it and the world which man, as a little god in partnership with Satan, intended to make. Adam bartered the world God made for another world which man, as the new presiding deity, would fashion to his own liking. In fact, we are in the process of destroying this world in spite of programs for ecological salvation and promises of a new world order.

One day God will "destroy them which destroy the earth" (Revelation 11:18) so that Christ can rule in righteousness. At the end of His millennial reign, following man's final rebellion, God will destroy this doomed universe and create a new one for "new creatures in Christ"—a perfect and eternal universe into which sin will never be able to enter.

Make no mistake, the actual choice we all face moment by moment is between man's new world and God's. Moreover, the real test is whether we truly long to make that exchange *now*, when life is vibrant, exciting, enjoyable. Of course, everyone wants to exchange sickness, death, hell for heaven—but do we, *right now*, want to exchange the best this world offers for God's presence? Such is the unique challenge of the imminent Rapture!

How close are we? The real question is, rather, how close we desire the Rapture to be. Such is the heart-searching impact of imminency and of Christ's many warnings to watch and wait and to be ready for His return at any moment.

Is the Rapture something we really want right now, or do we wish for a delay? Yes, our hearts are torn because we long for unsaved friends and loved ones to receive Christ before it is forever too late. But nothing must stand in the way of our love for Him. May the hope of His imminent return become our passion and produce its purifying fruit in our lives—and, through us, impact many others before it is forever too late!

ACKNOWLEDGMENTS

I dedicate this volume of homilies, which I have written over the years, to the people whom I have been privileged to serve. I mention especially all of the people of Saint John Parish in Winona, all the people of Saints Peter and Paul Parish in Hart, all of the people of Queen of Angels Parish in Austin, all the people of the Cathedral of the Sacred Heart Parish in Winona, all the people of Saint Joseph Parish in Owatonna, all the people of Saint Augustine Parish in Austin, and all of the people of Saint Pius X Parish in Rochester. These people supported me, encouraged me, and inspired and challenged me to give my best for their spiritual nurturance through preaching and teaching. They, in turn, taught me, nurtured me, and enriched my life in a profoundly happy manner. I am humbly thankful.

Fr. Paul E. Nelson

CONTENTS

FOREWORD

Welcome to Grandoc Publications' second book by Fr. Paul Nelson. As I mentioned in the forward of the first book, *A Priest From the Prairies of Minnesota,* I am very honored to be Fr. Paul's friend and publisher. Very few people have contributed to the well-being of the people of southern Minnesota more than has he.

I must say we were thrilled by the tremendous reception of Fr. Paul's first book. I think our decision to make the present book a separate volume instead of adding it onto the first as an appendix was a good one. We now have no space constraints, and can present you with a much larger number of Fr. Paul's very valuable homilies.

I think one of the many reasons Fr. Paul is so well known in the southern Minnesota area is his homilies. In this written form, they are a source of reflection, mediation and inspiration. I am certainly better for having read them, and it is my hope that you will be, too.

Wherever possible, we added footnotes to the many literary references, and I would encourage the reader to make use of them. Doing this will expand your appreciation of the work.

After all, there is just so much one can say in the short time allowed for giving a homily. Most of us have access to a computer these days, and so whenever possible I tried to find references on the Internet because they are immediately available and free.

Some editorial notes regarding format: I have not dated the homilies unless I saw a specific need to do so, which was usually when Fr. Paul mentions specific events for which a date to place them in context seemed necessary. Otherwise, I see his thoughts as being more or less timeless, fitting for any year in which the homily is presented. Most, but not all, of the homilies begin with quotes from the Biblical readings of the day.

Also, several times we have included more than one homily for the same Church calendar day. In such cases I have inserted numbers after the titles to separate them. Finally, the reader may notice that not quite all Sundays of the Church year are included. Everyone needs a vacation-even Paul!

May God bless you all!

John Graner, MD
Grandoc Publications
February 2, 2012

PREFACE

This book is composed of some of the homilies which I have researched, written and delivered to congregations one or more times over the past several years. I chose these homilies, as a sample of the various themes presented by the scriptures for our reflection, as an example of the many emphases which are present in scriptures, and as an indicator to me as presenter, and to you the reader and listener, that we must pay attention to the truth in its many forms, arriving through many channels, as the truth leads us, forms us, reforms us, challenges us, and leads us into deeper life where we find new peace and happiness each day.

I also hope that reading these homilies will help you to come to know better what I have learned ever so slowly over my fifty years as a priest, teacher and preacher: that we are touched most completely, memorably, and effectively though the telling of and the hearing of stories. Jesus' entire life, as presented in the four Gospels which we use, was a teaching life through stories and parables.

Theory, lecturing, dry narrative, put students and all of us to sleep, or, at least put us off being able to listen. I have tried in each of my homilies to use stories, in an effort to demonstrate a truth.

Writing homilies has been a weekly task for me for over fifty years as a priest. This responsibility has been a blessing for many reasons. I have had to learn again and again that I had to continue praying, studying, and reading, every day of my life. I have learned over the years of writing and delivering homilies, that while the scriptures are rich sources of truth, other forms of literature are also important and essential to help flesh out the gospel teachings. I have used biography, poetry, fiction and the daily press a lot over the years. The lives of famous people, the poetry of the gifted artists, the yarns of fiction, and the everyday news happening around us are profound sources of inspiration, information, and expression of a dimension of the truth.

Another medium which I have engaged very frequently while reflecting on and writing down my homilies has been the world of music. Classical music, modern day music, the music of African Americans, Country music, and many other forms have been contributors to my thoughts, emotions and expressions over the years. The stories about how music developed in all cultures, about the composers who were able to dig deep within to find the beauty that orchestras, bands and artists of all types bring to our ears are inspiring and helpful for me to appreciate scripture, faith, hope and charity.

These media help me to learn again and again that every dimension of our human nature must be engaged in order to find the Christ, the Mystery of God in the Gospel. My hope is that reading some or all of these homilies will unleash in you new creativity, new curiosity, new inspiration and hunger for the ultimate meaning of our lives, the search for and the rich participation in *the truth*!

Advent & Christmas

FIRST SUNDAY OF ADVENT*

ISAIAH 63: "No ear has ever heard, no eye has ever seen, any God but you."

PSALM 80: "Lord, let us see your face and we shall be saved."

1 COR 1: "In Christ Jesus, you were enriched in every way, with all discourse and all knowledge."

MARK 1: "Jesus said to his disciples, 'Be watchful! Be alert!'"

As we begin a new Advent in 2005, perhaps it is something like all of us beginning to read a new book. We have all read books. We have liked some. Others have bored us. Some books deepen us and other books we tolerate. But all books change our lives and lead us on. Advent, as we begin and enter it sincerely, will change our lives and lead us on.

Advent is a new beginning. New beginnings are essential to life for all of us. We begin new weeks fifty-two times a year.

---

* Editor's note: This homily was originally presented on 11/27/05.

We begin new days 365 times a year. We begin new grades in school from a few times to twenty and more times. We begin new chapters in life frequently, moving from infancy to childhood, from childhood to adolescence, from adolescence to adulthood, and in adulthood, we experience many seasons, all giving us a new perspective, a new opportunity, a new challenge.

Advent is about that newness. And our scriptures give us inspiration, invitation, challenge for change in our lives and for moving on, as we begin again to listen to the Word of God each week, and as we begin again to contribute to, to receive from and to participate in, the Eucharist each week. These two gifts give us a tremendous stage upon which to act out a new dimension of life, a deepening experience of life, a richer involvement in life, the life of Christ and the very life of God. To begin again and to experience newness again gives us energy and inspiration.

The prophesy of Isaiah, from which we read today, inspires us to use our energy to hear God and to see God. "No ear has ever heard, no eye has ever seen, any God but you." Advent, through Isaiah, instructs us to refocus on the truth of God, the centrality of God, the life of God within us. We are reminded that God is the absolute foundation to any meaning, peace, happiness, success in life. Isaiah fundamentally tells his contemporaries and us to "get it right." Put God where God belongs, at the center and foundation of our life, of all life.

Psalm 80, our response today, says, "Lord, let us see your face and we shall be saved."

This is a beautiful and simple prayer, asking God to enable and empower us to see God in all of creation. God's face is seen in the sunset, in the face of a child, in a moment of emotion, in the power of imagination, memory, thought and reflection. Prayer is any human movement which enables us again to approach the throne of God where we see God's face.

St. Paul, to the Corinthian people, reminds us of the truth that richness is to be in the Lord. He says, "In Christ Jesus, you are enriched in every way, with all discourse and all knowledge." To speak with God, and to listen to God, is sacred discourse, rich dialogue, inspiring prayer. And this activity and willingness lead to all knowledge of God. To discourse with God leads to the most beautiful knowledge the human is capable of, the knowledge of the source of life, the sacredness of life, the infinity of life. We share deeply in the very knowledge of God, in the life of God, in the infinity of God. This is what we refer to as eternal life. Paul says that we find it simply in humble prayer, simple dialogue, open hearts before our Creator.

And, finally, Mark's Gospel quotes Jesus as telling his followers to, "Be watchful! Be alert!" Basically, Jesus tells us to pay attention to the most important aspect of our existence, which is our involvement with and dedication to, the very life of God, which is within each of us. But God's life is within us to be welcomed, to be used, to be accepted in the most human way, that is, thoughtfully, sincerely, constantly, and thoroughly. God's life within is the most important and rich aspect of our existence. It is where happiness lies.

Advent is the door opening again for each of us, to prepare for Christmas, to deepen our appreciation of life, to enrich our experiences, to find our way to happiness and peace of heart. Advent is a rich gift for all.

FIRST SUNDAY OF ADVENT (2)

JEREMIAH 33: "I will raise up for David a just shoot; he shall do what is right and just in the land."

PSALM 25: "To you, O Lord, I lift my soul."

1 THES 3: "Brothers and Sisters: May the Lord make you increase and abound in love for one another and for all."

LUKE 21: "Beware that your hearts do not become drowsy from carousing and drunkenness, and the anxieties of daily life."

Perhaps you have heard the old dictum that goes something like this: "When one is three years old, one DOES NOT KNOW what people think. When a person is twenty-three years old, he or she WORRIES about what people think. When you hit forty-three years old, you WONDER about what people think. And when we hit the plateau of sixty-three years of age, we DON'T CARE what people think. I don't know if or how true this analysis is, but it is an effort to address the growth of people through the various stages of per-

sonality, moral, intellectual and social maturing and development.

As we begin Advent and another Liturgical Year, our scriptures invite us to consider how we have grown, are growing,
and are planning to grow as the days, weeks, months and
years continue to unfold for us. Personal and social development is a responsibility for each of us as individuals, families, and as participants in society. World peace, social justice, harmony among various people, depends on our commitment to, and willingness to make efforts to grow spiritually, personally, morally, socially.

SECOND SUNDAY OF ADVENT[*]

ISAIAH 11:   "The Spirit of the Lord shall rest upon him: a spirit of wisdom & of understanding, a spirit of counsel and of strength, a spirit of knowledge and of fear of the Lord, and his delight shall be fear of the Lord."

PSALM 72:   "Justice shall flourish in his time, and fullness of peace forever."

ROMANS 15:   "Brothers and Sisters: Whatever was written previously was written for our instruction, that by endurance and by the encouragement of the scriptures we might have hope."

MATTHEW 3: "John the Baptist appeared, preaching....Repent, for the kingdom of heaven is at hand.....Prepare the way of the Lord, make straight his paths."

A week ago I heard a man interviewing children who were standing in line to speak with Santa Claus. He was asking

---

[*] Editor's note: This homily was originally presented on 12/5/04.

them if they had been, throughout the last year, naughty or nice. The first two children said that they had been nice. The third child, a boy, hesitated ever so briefly before he said, "Well, kind of nice and kind of naughty, kind of in the middle." When I heard this, I thought, "This is a kid after my own heart," because I believe that his answer was a pretty good description of the way I have lived most of my life – kind of in the middle. And I would suspect that many of you can relate to the wisdom and honesty of that little boy, because, throughout life, we live many times somewhere in the middle.

This being the case, we need the scriptures, as we were told today, to inspire us to wisdom and to be our instruction as to proper living, recovering from sin, mistakes and loss, and that we might have *hope*. Advent liturgy is intended to inspire us to honesty with self, as that little boy demonstrated; to empower us to embrace again the gifts of the Holy Spirit, as described in Isaiah, *wisdom, understanding, counsel, strength, knowledge* and *fear of the Lord*. Isaiah says we do not judge by appearance, but by reality, not by our standards, but by God's. All of nature, all of creation, exists not arbitrarily but by the eternal and certain plan of God. We humans are not exempt from that standard, but are immediate and essential participants in it.

Psalm 72, our response today, reminds us that *justice* flourishes in God's time, and that *fullness of peace* is from God. Paul's letter to the Romans references *instruction, endurance* and *encouragement*. And Matthew's Gospel speaks of *repentance* and *preparation*.

What wonderful gifts, powers, virtues, and ideas the scriptures hold up for our study and renewed appreciation today: Hope, wisdom, understanding, counsel, strength, knowledge, fear of the Lord, justice, fullness of peace, instruction, endurance, encouragement, repentance and preparation. But to access these gifts we must have the truth, simplicity, maturity and reality of the little boy who can admit the big truth: We are kind of naughty, kind of nice, kind of in the middle. We are indeed, human beings in search sincerely of our God, or we are lost, we are on the wrong road, we are confused as to what life is and what life is about.

USA Today, in its December 1, 2004 edition, stated that the population of the United States of America was on this last Tuesday, November 30, 2004 at 294,877,547. The article also stated that there is a birth of a baby every seven seconds in this country, and that there is a death of a person every twelve seconds in this nation. Our population is growing, births are outstripping deaths as we live longer. This is another dimension of truth for all of us to ponder as we listen to the scriptures today. Our responsibility for society, for integrity in our governmental, church, industrial, commercial, legal, medical, educational and all social institutions continues to be so very important for each of us. And this second Sunday of Advent, using the scriptural wisdom of the ages, clearly advises us to enter again into the health and illness of our society, and to have an idea, to make a contribution, to offer a suggestion, to courageously make our thoughts available for scrutiny, for dialogue, for possible healing and growth for the life we all share together in culture.

The agenda offered for us today is full, challenging, and reassuringly clear. Each of us is needed to manage our individual lives, and each of us is essential for the health and peaceful continuance of our way of life. We can recommit ourselves as we worship together today.

SECOND SUNDAY OF ADVENT (2)[*]

ISAIAH 40: "Comfort, give comfort to my people, says the Lord... A voice cries out: 'In the desert, prepare the way of the Lord.'"

PSALM 85: "Lord, let us see your kindness, and grant us your salvation."

2 PETER 3: "We await new heavens and a new earth, in which righteousness dwells."

MARK 1: "A voice of one crying out in the desert: Prepare the way of the Lord, make straight his paths."

Two years ago, I visited the sight of the World Trade Center, which had been blown up on 9-11-01. The city has built a viewing pavilion at the sight which can accommodate several thousand people at once, in order to view the huge hole in the ground, that resulted from cleaning up the debris of the sight. The day I visited, there may have been two thousand people present. As we viewed the sight, there was almost absolute silence among all the people. Those who spoke did so in a

---

[*] Editor's note: This homily was originally presented on 12/4/05.

whispering tone of voice. The silence was profound, reverent and filled with respect for the thousands of people who had died there.

Several years ago, I visited the federal building sight in Oklahoma City, Oklahoma, where several people died in that terrorist attack on the building. As I walked the perimeter of the sight, several hundreds of people were present, and again, there was almost total silence among all of us viewers, in respect for the people who had died there.

On this Second Sunday of Advent, the Scriptures exhort us to the gift, the posture, the stance of silence. Silence is the absolutely necessary condition for listening, for hearing, for learning, for becoming aware of more truth than I possessed before the silence. We are asked to sit in silence, to befriend silence, to wait in silence, that we may hear the important message of God.

Isaiah, our first reading, asks us to, "Comfort, give comfort to my people...." To comfort another, we must learn to be in silence, so that we can know how to comfort, what the comfort must consist of, what comfort is needed. Noise dissipates energy and attention. Silence empowers us with focus, with energy, with attention, with the best of our human potential. Silence welcomes God Almighty, and therefore, God's creatures.

Psalm 85, our response, states, "Lord, let us see your kindness and grant us your salvation." We cannot see God or the spirit of God or the presence of God without silence. Again, silence is the essential ingredient enabling us to see God and the movements of God's Spirit.

St. Peter states, "We await new heavens and a new earth, in which righteousness dwells." Righteousness is reality, holiness, the condition of growth, the foundation of peace of mind, the essence of happiness. It comes only through silence, silence of mind and soul and emotions. We must learn the art, the discipline, the practice of silence, if we want to enter in to the presence and kingdom of God. Noise and distraction and confusion and dissipation of energy, are the conditions of death of Spirit. Silence nurtures our spirit with focus and attention, which sets the stage for seeing newness in life, in the reality of life on earth, the possibilities involved in the experience of heaven, because, in silence, we develop our potential, our humanity, our hopes and aspirations. Silence enables us to see new heavens and new earth and new righteousness all around.

And, finally, Mark's Gospel quotes Isaiah and tells us to be quiet enough to prepare the way of the Lord, and to make straight his paths. The power of silence is the power of Isaiah's word, which has lasted almost three thousand years. This word blesses us as we listen to it, but only if we listen. We cannot listen if we are not silent.

Wendell Berry, an American poet, speaks of silence:
> "What must a man do to be at home in the world?
> There must be times when he is here as though absent,
> Gone beyond words into the woven shadows...
> And he hears the silence of the tongues of the dead..."[†]

Advent's invitation into silence is a difficult and rich moment to be welcomed and practiced by all who hear the silent murmur of the Spirit of God. Silence is one of the ways to a richer and happier life. Silence is one of the gifts of Advent.

---

† Berry, Wendell. *The Collected Poems of Wendell Berry, 1957-1982.* San Francisco: North Point, 1985, p. 111.

SECOND SUNDAY OF ADVENT (3)[*]

ISAIAH 11: "The spirit of the Lord shall rest upon him:
a spirit of wisdom and of understanding,
a spirit of counsel and of strength,
a spirit of knowledge and of fear of the
Lord."

PSALM 72: "Justice shall flourish in his time, and
fullness of peace forever."

ROMANS 15: "Whatever was written was written for our
instruction."

MATT 3: "The prophet Isaiah said: 'A voice of one
crying out in the desert, prepare the way of
the Lord, make straight his paths.'"

I watched a professional football game last Sunday evening.
The most enjoyable moment of viewing was not a football
play. It was a commercial, involving seven or eight nine-
year-old boys, having lunch in a school lunch room. The
story begins by one of the boys turning to his friend, as he is
eating. He says, "So, how is the family?" His friend re-

---

[*] Editor's note: This homily was originally presented on 12/9/07.

sponds, rather whimsically, "Oh, my dad still thinks that social security will be there for him when he retires." And the conversation goes on with all of the boys giving their two cents worth about their parents' naivety when it comes to retirement income. And, the commercial concludes with them naming the money management company that will solve this problem, involving the naïve position of their parents. It truly was a keeper commercial. It showed the nine year olds having the wisdom of the forty year old parents who were not with it at all. The commercial concludes with one of the boys showing his milk mustache, and asking his buddies, "Does my mustache make me look wiser?"

On this Second Sunday of Advent, the scriptures, I think, ask us to be attentive, aware and wise, as nine year olds when we are nine years old, as forty year olds when we are forty, and as seventy-five year olds when we are seventy-five. In other words, part of the scriptural message today is to be age-appropriate, to be mature, to continue to grow, as life is given.

Isaiah beautifully describes the spirit of the Lord that is upon each of us, the spirit of wisdom and understanding, the spirit of counsel and strength, the spirit of knowledge and of fear of the Lord. What power and strength for peace and happiness these dimensions of soul give to us! We are reminded that these energies are to be renewed during these Advent days within each of us and among us all.

Psalm 72 states again for us the foundation of all peace, that is, Justice. "Justice shall flourish in his time, and fullness of peace forever." All the days of our life, we are to be peace people. Perhaps you remember the woman here in America who was known as "Peace Pilgrim." She walked the length and breadth of this country, speaking when she was invited to do so, and wearing a sign on her person that encouraged all people to work for peace through justice. Tragically, she was killed in an accident after spending, I think, twenty-seven years crisscrossing this country on foot with the message of peace through justice. She was a dramatic peace pilgrim. Each of us is called to be a peace pilgrim in our own way. Psalm 72 reminds us of that fact again today.

St. Paul reminds the Roman people and us that the Scriptures are written for our instruction. Each time the Christian Community gathers in worship, in all denominations around the world, we read from the scriptures, to be reminded, to be informed, to be inspired, so that, hopefully, we can continue to grow in the spirit of life, in the spirit of justice and peace, in the Holy Spirit of God.

And our Gospel account concludes the lesson today by stating that we are not only to hear the word, but we are to make it happen, we are to give the word flesh, and energy, and presence in our world. We are to be the voice crying out in the desert, "Prepare the way of the Lord, Make straight his paths."

THIRD SUNDAY OF ADVENT

ISAIAH 35: "They will see the glory of the Lord, the splendor of our God."

JAMES 5: "Be patient, Brothers and Sisters, until the coming of the Lord. See how the farmer waits for the precious fruit of the earth being patient with it until it receives the early and the late rains. You, too, must be patient."

MATT 11: "Jesus said, 'Go and tell John what you see and hear: the blind regain their sight, the lame walk, lepers are cleansed, the deaf hear, the dead are raised, and the poor have the good news proclaimed to them.'"

In the current issue of *Weavings* (January-February 2005, p. 11), the following statement is made: "The evidence that deep prayer and meditation actually change both mind and body (or more accurately, our seamless body-mind) has been accumulating for over forty years. When consciousness shifts from what one psychiatrist calls 'instrumental' to 'connective' mode, changes abound: heartbeat may slow, the flow of blood to the capillaries increases, the lace-like electrical patterns on the skin run more smoothly, and muscles relax, as inwardly the mind becomes less agitated, more still and focused. More than that, what we radiate outward is also changed in ways that can become discernible, transforming the atmosphere of human gatherings, because it changes how people are present. PRESENCE IS HARD TO DEFINE BUT EASY TO EXPERIENCE."

Advent time is human time, reflective time, prayer time. Our scriptures today define prayer as seeing the glory of the Lord (Isaiah & Matthew's Gospel) and as patience (James). Prayer life certainly is about these two experiences, seeing and patiently waiting. Prayer is the power to progressively see the truth – about the universe, about the self, about all relationships with persons, properties and possessions, about perspectives, about the mysteries of God, eternity, life, death, meaning, destiny, history.

As the article from *Weavings* states, prayer has been researched and studied in its effects on our body, mind, soul, spirit, relationality for more than forty years. Prayer affects us as unitive, living, growing beings. Prayer, meaning reflection and communion with truth, is essential to health, peace of mind, body function, and social relationships.

Prayer is a discipline which needs time, patience, effort, and practice. Prayer is part and parcel of human experience, of social stability, of cultural richness. Worship, communal prayer, meditation, private prayer, spiritual imagination, mental awareness, emotional involvement, these and other human experiences and practices are needed to deepen our appreciation, our awareness, our strength, to continue to grow throughout life and through death. The need to practice prayer is as essential as the need to practice eating, drinking, toileting, exercising the body, and balancing the emotions. Prayer is a function which informs the whole person, as surely as breathing informs the body with health and energy needed to continue life.

Prayer gives accuracy and stability to the whole person, renewing our body, informing our soul, bringing peace and calmness to our emotions. Prayer is intimacy with the transcendent, with the mystery of life, with the mystery of God. Prayer empowers us to love, to forgive, to be present to life in responsibility. Prayer takes selfishness out as the discipline of prayer teaches us to know our place in the universe, and to take our rightful place in the universe, not as its center, but as a grateful participant in the grand mystery of existence and life.

When one thinks about prayer and praying, we are taken to the depths of what and who we are. Words, ideas, thoughts, concepts cannot satisfy our hunger for what prayer is, for why we should pray, for an appreciation of where the spirit we call prayer comes from. Perhaps this is so because, in the experience and expression we call prayer, we are attempting to approach God; we are seeking the beyond, we are plumbing deeply into the meaning of all life. In prayer journeying, we travel roads not often visited, in confidence, in calmness, in security. Prayer remains a challenge to us much of our lives because it is so important to complete what we are, that is, persons with eternal connections and with eternal destinies.

On this Advent day, we joyfully recommit ourselves to pursue the way of prayer, the practice of prayer, the life-enriching discipline which unites us to ourselves, to society, to all of creation and to God.

ISAIAH 61: "The spirit of the Lord God is upon me.....
I rejoice heartily in the Lord, in God is the joy
of my soul."

1 THES 5: "Rejoice always...Give thanks...Do not
quench the spirit."

JOHN 1: "A man named John was sent by God. He was
not the light but came to testify to the light."

Most of us have experienced the joy and peace of holding a
small child who smiles at us. Most of us have known the
deep feeling of visiting a funeral home to greet a grieving
family, at the loss of their loved one. Most of us have been
touched when we have looked into the eyes of a person who
is weeping, and have offered a supporting hug. Most of us
have stood in awe, as we looked into the nighttime sky and
pondered the immensity and infinity of what we share on this
earth as we live. And most of us have known moments of
kindness and support of others, giving us the confidence to
take one more step into the challenges of life.

These experiences are what this third Sunday highlights for us as we come to pray, to listen and to grow in spirit. Isaiah tells us today that we can experience deeply because we share in the very spirit of God. Our first reading started by confidently stating, "The spirit of the Lord God is upon me." And we are further instructed in the same reading, "I rejoice heartily in the Lord, in my God is the joy of my soul." We have been richly endowed, and part of our responsibility in life is to develop that wealth of spirit, by prayer, by thought, by meditation, by the best behaviors.

St. Paul, in our second reading, gives life-giving advice: "Rejoice always...Give thanks...Do not quench the spirit." To develop a spirit that is happy, contented and peaceful, is a difficult and life-long discipline. Each of us knows what bitterness inside feels like. Each of us has had the times of discouragement, depression, confusion and defeat. Each of us probably knows the ease with which we can give up, stop trying, enter into self-pity, and to say that life is unfair. Each of us, through neglect, laziness and listlessness, can find our world coming apart, our spirit sinking, our future bleak.

The antidote to this spirit is found in Paul's exhortation to, "Rejoice always," and, "Give thanks," and, "Do not quench the spirit." This is a Gospel discipline. This is a way of life to be chosen. This is the way to peace. Life is not automatically, magically, a happy experience. Life needs to be earned every day, by good and healthy and holy attitudes, decisions and practices. A happy life is a life of effort. A happy life is a life which we choose to make. To allow defeat and discouragement to break our confidence is a sin, and it leads to more and more bitterness, blaming, scapegoating and misery. The scriptures clearly teach that we have a responsibility to seek happiness, to generate peace, to strive for a life of meaning and contentment. No one owes these gifts to us. God has given us the nature, the intelligence, and the strength to accomplish this spirit. It is our choice.

And, finally today, the Gospel of John tells us of a strange, strong, humble and virtuous man named John, John the Baptist, the cousin of Jesus. John came, we are told, not to be light, the center of attention, but to show the way to and to testify about the light of the world, Jesus. John found his life by doing what he was sent to do. He is a wonderful example of a mature, responsible person, who learned what his role was, and who carried it out beautifully. John identified what he was to be about, and then threw his energy into accomplishing that vocation.

Each of us will find happiness where we are, or we will not find happiness. I am to find happiness and joy in being a priest, and in doing what a priest is called to do. Each of you is finding happiness now by identifying and doing what you are currently called to. As an example, if you are a student, find your happiness in being a good student. If you are a truck driver, find life in driving truck; if you are a parent, find joy in nurturing your children. We find a happy life where we find ourselves. Wishing away the life we have leads only to frustration, defeat, and bitterness.

To find a happy life, we must find ourselves, we must find our God, we must find our energy and determination. John teaches us that the raw material given by God to each of us is the stuff out of which we are to find life, a happy life. It is up to each of us.

THIRD SUNDAY OF ADVENT (3)

ZEPHANIAH 3: "Shout for joy, O daughter Zion. Sing joyfully, O Israel! Be glad and exult with all your heart."

ISAIAH 12: "Cry out with joy and gladness, for among you is the great and holy one of Israel."

PHILIPPIANS 4: "Rejoice in the Lord always. I say it again. Rejoice!"

LUKE 3: "John the Baptist said in reply, 'Whoever has two cloaks should share with the person who has none. And whoever has food should do likewise.'"

In the December 11, 2006 issue of *America* Magazine, an author by the name of Maryann Cusimano Love, who is a Professor of International Relations at Catholic University in Washington D.C., wrote an article entitled, "Kneeling at the Cradle."* The subject was poverty among children in the United States. The article begins, " Last year as we set up our

---

* Love, Maryann Cusimano. "Kneeling at the Cradle." *America The National Catholic Weekly*, December 11, 2006.

nativity set, our then two-year-old daughter asked why so many of the figures were kneeling. Plopping baby Jesus in the manger, she quickly answered her own question, 'Oh. To better see God.'"

Seeing God in the richness of creation is the hunger of every human heart, in one way or another. And to see God in any function, exercise, posture, movement or experience, demands the development of at least two human powers, those being discipline and perseverance. If a child wishes to become educated, he or she must develop discipline and perseverance in study and research. If one wishes to become an effective athlete, artist, sculptor or musician, the individual must exercise discipline and perseverance in practice and refinement. If an adult wishes to become a capable and responsible parent and mentor to his or her children, they must find discipline and perseverance.

It should not come as any surprise then, that if we wish to find joy in life through peace of mind, we must work at discipline and perseverance. The old saying that we must make our living every day is true. It is true financially, socially, professionally, morally, and spiritually. If we wish to be happy, we must work at it. This is the message of the scriptures today, on this Gaudete Sunday.

To be happy sometimes is hard work. Happiness and joy demand the utilization of our best human resources. Happiness is not automatic, magical, nor does happiness spring from luck. Happiness is the fruit of human endeavor. The prophet Zephaniah exhorts, "Shout for joy, O daughter Zion, Sing joyfully, O Israel! Be glad and exult with all your heart." Isaiah says, "Cry out with joy and gladness, for among you is the great and holy one of Israel." Paul's letter to the Philippians encourages, "Rejoice in the Lord always. I say it again. Rejoice!" And in Luke's Gospel, John the Baptist is quoted as saying, "Whoever has two cloaks should share with the person who has none. And whoever has food should do likewise." In Luke, we have the social and sharing aspect of becoming and remaining happy. We are only happy in a rich social setting of family, work, school, society.

The scriptures given for our consideration today span several thousands of years, and come from various settings, and they all speak of discipline, perseverance and sharing. To be happy, it is good to think about these aspects of human life, human growth, human nature.

Happiness and joy also demand growth, movement, and change. There is a spiritual and psychological principle that states, "You cannot say hello to the new dimension and stage of life until you say goodbye to the previous one." One must say goodbye to childhood, if that person hopes to find happiness in adolescence, and one must move from adolescence to young adulthood for the same reason. And so we move throughout our lives. Happiness demands that we focus on the present condition and circumstance of life, no matter what those circumstances and conditions are. I see many happy people, for example, in rest homes, because they have come to own the fact that they are there and that is where they are going to live. I see others in rest homes who are miserable, because they cannot, or will not, own the fact of their situation. Biblical teaching and our Christian tradition teach clearly that happiness and joy are the fruit of discipline, perseverance, ownership of life situations and conditions. Happiness is not an accident. Happiness is a choice.

FOURTH SUNDAY OF ADVENT*

ISAIAH 7:   "Therefore the Lord will give you this sign: the virgin shall conceive, and bear a son, and shall name him Emmanuel."

PSALM 24:   "Let the Lord enter; he is king of glory."

ROMANS 1: "Through him we have received the grace of apostleship, to bring about the obedience of faith."

MATT 1:   "The angel appeared to Joseph in a dream and said, 'Joseph, do not be afraid to take Mary, your wife, into your home.'"

The day of the year which holds for us in the northern hemisphere the fewest hours and minutes of sunlight is in 2004 the 21st of December, next Tuesday. On this day, the earth will stop leaning to the north and begin slowly and certainly to return to the south, giving us each day a few more minutes of sunlight, until June 21, 2005, when the journey begins again. This mystery of existence is but one manifestation of

---

* Editor's note: This homily was originally presented on 12/19/04.

the universe's ability to perform, as God made it to do so, guaranteeing us continued life.

In Christian history, the feast of Christmas was situated on December 25, marking the return of light, as we celebrate the birth of the son of God, the light of the world. Our scriptures today speak, in Isaiah, of a sign. How can the winter solstice not be a profound sign of God coming for us? How can this phenomenon not deepen our awe, reverence and appreciation of the simple and constant presence of God in the powers of the universe, which we call home?

Psalm 24, our response, exhorts us to, "let the Lord enter. He is the king of Glory." Our hearts and souls and minds are enriched as we reflect on God present in our world through all of reality, in this instance, in the winter solstice. And Romans, the second reading, speaks of bringing about the obedience of faith. We are reminded that our powers of intelligence, awareness, intuition, and decision are to be engaged obediently, as we acknowledge the profound mystery of existence, and of our part in it.

Matthew's Gospel tells the story of Joseph being confronted with the huge reality of an unplanned and misunderstood pregnancy, involving his wife. And through a strange medium, the dream, which we still do not understand much, Joseph was exhorted to not be afraid, and to obey. Life lessons these things are.

To stand in awe and wonder before all that is, is the responsibility of each of us, as Isaiah teaches. The Psalm response asks us to learn to allow and to welcome God in all times, places and conditions of life. Romans commands obedience, which is the guarantor of life for all of us. And Matthew's Gospel holds out for us the call to be courageous in face of the difficulties of life, to trust God through nature and its functions.

In the current issue of *National Catholic Reporter* (12-17-04), an article on spirituality is printed for the reader, and it is entitled, "After talking about God, learning to talk to God." The article states, "We talk about God from the enclosure of our own ideas. Talking to God, we grow. We become." The winter solstice this week is a profound invitation to talk to God, not only with our thoughts and words, but also with our appreciation, our sense of awe, our reverent acceptance of all that is part of our life. While the goal of the spiritual life is not special experiences, this event has the power to inspire us to new depths of life. We can engage our spirit power with new enthusiasm, with a willingness to grow and change and become. These dark days here in the north offer the chance to be quiet, to be reflective, to be responsive, to be in awe and wonder of our God. Prayer can flow from every moment of life, but this solstice experience is a wonderful turning of the earth, of our awareness, of opportunities for growth.

As we conclude the liturgical observance of Advent for this year, let us rejoice in the fact that we are deepened by being here, that we are inspired by participating, that we are enriched through developed awareness of God's presence, of God's creation, of God's power in all that is.

FOURTH SUNDAY OF ADVENT (2)[*]

2 SAMUEL 7:   "I will fix a place for my people Israel."

PSALM 89:   "Forever I will sing the goodness of the
              Lord."

ROMANS 16:   "To him who can strengthen you...be glory
              forever and ever."

LUKE 1:   "Behold, I am the handmaid of the Lord.
              May it be done to me according to your
              word."

As we gather in prayer and worship today, we conclude the
official Advent observance for 2005. We are approaching, in
three or four days, the shortest daylight day of the year here
in the Northern Hemisphere. And we will be joining millions
and millions of people of many religions in celebration of
light and love and life. But our celebration, as Catholic Christians, will be focusing on God becoming one with us in Jesus
Christ, as we celebrate His birth.

---

[*] Editor's note: This homily was originally presented on 12/18/05.

50

The birth of Jesus has defined the calendar of the world, and his teaching has revolutionized the human approach to justice, truth, and charity. His teaching demands dignity for every human being and reverence for all of creation. Throughout the history of the Jewish People, who are Christ's family, their literature developed into what we call the Old Testament. Our first reading today is part of the history of the Jews, and speaks of King David's home, the home he wanted to build for the Lord, and the home God was giving to the Jewish People.

The Jews had a deep reverence for their homeland, for all of creation, and that respect was shown frequently in their literature, and has become the backbone of the teachings of Jesus Christ. All of creation, physical, spiritual, energy, space, relationality and time – all dimensions of our existence are to be held in highest honor and care. It is that lesson that we reflect on as we conclude Advent. Life is gift. The Universe is gift. The earth is gift. We learn again that we are part of all of this life-gift, and we are responsible to keep it safe, unsullied, and as God gave it to us. We are, in short to be intelligent ecologists and wise stewards of the gifts of God.

In our response psalm, we react to this renewed realization and we proclaim, in the words of Psalm 89, "Forever I will sing of the goodness of the Lord." We pray in thanksgiving as we conclude Advent, and prepare to observe the feast of gifts. Romans, our second reading, continues the refrain, as

St. Paul reminds the Roman People, "To Him who can strengthen you…be glory forever and ever."

We continue from Old Testament to New Testament history by the beautiful story from Luke's Gospel. The story continues to expand our vision as to the power, immensity, and the infinite expressions of God's creation and gifts. God's creation involves angels, communication between the angel Gabriel and Mary, new life, through the mystery and miracle of human fertility, gestation and birth. God's intention is that we are to assist each other, as did Mary and her cousin Elizabeth did in this difficult time for both of them. The power of life shown by Mary and Elizabeth through faith, obedience, and acceptance of responsibility, inspires us to that same intention and behavior before God. This story of the Annunciation summarizes so simply and so well, the creative power of God Almighty through all manifestations of life on our earth and in the presence of God.

Advent is a rich time for us. Advent invites us to deepen our heart and soul through silent reflection, prayerful consideration, and attentive listening. Advent challenges us to generosity in all dimensions of our living. Advent is a new call each year to realize a bit more of the beauty and profound goodness of life. As we embrace Advent, our soul matures and becomes more of what God intends each of us to be, a rich manifestation of God's very life within us, with and for one another. This is a wonderful preparation for Christmas.

The last line of Luke's Gospel, which we heard today, is a rich expression of what life for each of us can be: "Mary said, 'Behold, I am the handmaid of the Lord. Be it done onto me according to your word.' Then the angel departed from her."

CHRISTMAS*

Gatherings such as this one, of which each of us is a part, are coming together all over the Christian world today. Some estimate that in the United States today, more than fifty million Catholics will share in the Mass. Millions of people are gathering around dinner tables to enjoy good food, and family and friendship conversation. Gifts are shared, and in Minnesota and Wisconsin most television sets are glowing with football of the purple and white, green and gold variety.

On this Christmas, prayer will be offered, hymns will be sung, stories will be told, scriptures will be reviewed, expletives will be uttered under the breath concerning football performance and officiating, peace will be offered in liturgy, and Holy Communion will be shared simply, quietly, undramatically, solemnly, profoundly.

The question is, "Why all of this?" The short answer is, "A baby is born." A more accurate answer is that on a day in history on planet earth, some 2000 years ago, an event came to be which involved God and humanity, an unmarried couple and the birth of their child, shepherds and kings, the rich and the poor, sheep and cattle, angels and heavenly singing, trav-

---

* Editor's note: This homily was originally presented on 12/25/04.

eling wise men and a moving star, a stable and a manger, a swaddling garment for the newborn, gifts offered by strangers of gold, frankincense and myrrh, and a king frightened by the power of birth mystery, which resulted in the deaths of the martyrs we call the Holy Innocents, the little boys whose lives were taken by King Herod, in his frantic search for the one baby, named Jesus.

The answer as to "Why?" is a long one. For two thousand years, the mystery has been pondered, the history has been researched, the birth has been celebrated, the observance has been constant every year. The name of Jesus is uttered in more languages and in more settings than any other name in history. Christmas trees, Christmas cribs, Yule logs, Advent wreaths, candles, liturgical art, music, and vestment enrich liturgies of all kinds in celebration.

The answer to "Why?" continues to challenge us in 2004. In our current world of space travel, inner-planetary probes, instantaneous world-wide communication through e-mail and satellite, constant air travel by millions of people and space station living for long periods of time, the reality of Christmas is considered and celebrated as richly and enthusiastically as ever in history.

On this day, we go deeply into meaning and mystery. On this day, we ponder our God in humanity, and humanity as God's creation and love. On this day, the birth-mystery intrigues us and inspires us and challenges us to deeper human goodness, more generous human behavior, more clear and just thinking, to more appreciation of our world and of our place in this world.

The God-mystery touches us tenderly and deeply, and calls us to grow, to change, to become. Christmas is a celebration of the best that is in us – generosity, forgiveness, respect for creation, willingness to enter spirit more completely.

The feast of Christmas renews our confidence that we are prayer people, capable of pondering truth which is way beyond us and which, at the same time, is part of us. Christmas is about our human potential to live, and to die, all in the hand of God. The Christmas observance is a comprehensive and beautiful review of the human journey, and of the truths which go beyond history, cultural evolvement and technical advancement. Christmas is about the timeless meaning of God being here always, and reminding us annually that God's safest home is in the heart of each one of us. God comes again today as a baby that cannot be fully explained, but who is so real and so present, so in need of us, and so inspiring and reassuring to all who stop to acknowledge the beautiful child.

Our Christmas prayer is a wonderful teacher, because it is experienced through people and food, through liturgy and silence, through word and song, through greetings and laughter. Christmas prayer involves each of us and all of us together, our thoughts and feelings, our convictions and our questions, our sin and our salvation.

Christmas simply speaks to us that God is here, that all is well, that we are participants in a grand reality called life, on earth and in heaven, in time and unto eternity.

CHRISTMAS (2)[*]

AMAZING PEACE
A Christmas Poem
By
Maya Angelou

Maya Angelou read a Christmas Poem she wrote on December 1, 2005 at the White House in Washington D.C., at the lighting of the National Christmas Tree. I am choosing to share portions of the poem with you as we reflect on Christmas. She wrote:

We clap hands and welcome the Peace of Christmas.
We beckon this good season to wait a while with us.
We, Baptist and Buddhist, Methodist and Muslim, say come.
Peace.
Come and fill us and our world with your majesty.
We, the Jew and the Jainist, the Catholic and the Confucian,
implore you to stay awhile
With us so we may learn by your shimmering light

---

[*] Editor's note: This homily was originally presented on 12/25/05.

how to look beyond complexion and see community.[†]

As we gather this day in worship, we are called to look beyond complexion to see and find community, as Maya Angelou suggests in her poem. Christmas is an annual invitation to peace, in our hearts, in our families, in our neighborhoods, in our world. The meaning of this holy day is found only if we rededicate our lives to peace. And peace can exist only if we are willing to work at community, being one earth, one people, respecting, helping, forgiving, serving each other.

Imperfect as it is, the gift of love, which we celebrate today, is still the power that saves and rules our world. In the crib of porcelain figures, in the tabernacle of sacramental bread, in the spontaneous and free gathering of this congregation, we see and experience the love of God in each other.

Soren Kierkegaard, the great Danish Philosopher-Theologian, had the following to say about Christmas: "Christmas speaks to us each year because we know that this child (Jesus), once an adult, would ask only for sacrifice, humility, service. His was a Gospel of love – love with all its terrifying demands and consequences – a love that would bring justice. The Gospel has not died after 2000 years. And why? Because he has not died. He is risen and so his Gospel continues."

[†] Editor's note: This poem may be found at http://aseekingspirit.wordpress.com/2007/12/07/amazing-peace-a-christmas-poem-maya-angelou/.

Our Christmas gift to the world is to embrace that Gospel again this Christmas, knowing that we will not live it perfectly, but that we believe it to be the only authentic and certain way to truth and light. Today serves as a beacon for all who are willing to look and listen, and this day shows a way to depth, richness, human development, intellectual awareness, and soul peace which no other experience gives.

Christmas gives us another look at God Almighty in the simplicity of human gestation and birth, in poverty and naturalness, in animals and humans and angels, in a baby and in parenthood. Christmas is an annual comprehensive lesson in paying attention, in focusing energy, in developing our potential, in knowing more of our dignity. Christmas is the path to peace, to joy, to happiness, because it takes us again into simplicity and nature and mystery and awe.

Christmas gatherings, Christmas décor, Christmas music, Christmas prayer, Christmas spirit, draw us again to the possibility of growth and enrichment. It is in this setting that we recommit to becoming more of the person we have the potential to be. Christmas is the teacher that tells us to look again at silence and simplicity and serenity, in order to find truth beyond comprehension, appreciation beyond understanding, richness and meaning in mystery. Christmas is about finding life in charity, love, kindness, forgiveness and reconciliation.

Maya Angelou, late in her Christmas Poem, says, "It is Christmas time, a halting of hate time. On this platform of peace, we can create a language to translate ourselves to ourselves and to each other." And she concludes the poem by saying, "Peace. We look at each other, then into ourselves, and we say without shyness or apology or hesitation: Peace, My Brother, Peace, My Sister, Peace, My Soul."

A very Blessed Christmas to each of you!

CHRISTMAS (3)*

Today the world is blessed and renewed by the annual celebration of the most powerful and life-giving movement of all time, the birth of Jesus Christ, the development of the Gospels, and the living of the Christ Way. The gift to the world of this movement is forgiving love. Jesus Christ is the deliverer of this essential and life-giving blessing of forgiving love to all the nations, to the ends of the earth.

This gift of forgiving love makes us human, demands that we grow, and crucifies us in its practice. The gift of forgiving love inspires us and empowers us and protects us. Each of us needs forgiving love, and each of us must mature enough each day to offer forgiving love. Forgiving love is the glue that keeps society going and growing in peace. Forgiving love is the greatest gift the world has ever known. Christmas is the annual celebration of forgiving love.

Many of us have heard the story of the Roman Catholic Nun who has, for years, worked with the men on death row in the prisons in the South of this country. A movie was made about parts of her work with these people. I believe the movie is

---

* Editor's note: This homily was originally presented on 12/25/06.

entitled, "Dead Man Walking."† This nun has said that on death row she has dealt with men who were grade school drop-outs, and with men who had Ph.D. degrees. She worked on death row with Blacks, Whites, Hispanics, and people of other national and racial origins. She found men on death row who came from extreme wealth, and others who came from dire poverty. The men on death row were as diverse as any other cross section of the American population.

She has indicated that the only thing these men on death row have in common is that they in their childhood never felt forgiven by their parents, and by those adults who had authority over them. Their hearts became tortured and twisted and hardened because of a lack of forgiving love, and perhaps this is a big piece of the reason that they ended up on death row.

The gift of Jesus, forgiving love, is absolutely necessary for individuals to develop healthy, balanced and good spirits of mind, soul and emotions. And this gift of forgiving love is essential to societal health, balance and peace, which enables us all to be safe in our cultures.

As we celebrate this great feast again this year, we are reminded through our faith practice that the spirit behind the many wonderful gifts we offer and receive is forgiving love,

---

† Editor's note: The film *Dead Man Walking* was released in 1995, directed by Tim Robbins. Sister Helen Prejean is played by Susan Sarandon.

authentic forgiving love, the forgiving love of Jesus Christ. Christmas helps us to remember what Jesus told Peter, when Peter asked Jesus, "What if my brother hurts me? Must I forgive him seven times?" Jesus, we are told, said only, "Seventy times seven times." Forgiving love is the heart of the Gospel, the soul of Christmas.

This past week gave us a news story that perhaps some of you heard. It is the story about the new Chief of Police for Washington D.C. Washington D.C. has 3900 Police Officers. Washington, D.C. is a predominantly black city. The city government has been going through the process of choosing the new Chief for some months. The thought was that because Washington, D.C. is a mostly black community, that the new Chief would be a black man. This past week the choice was announced, and a thirty-nine year old woman was chosen to be the new Chief, who will take over on January 2, 2007. She dropped out of high school when she was a sophomore, because she was pregnant. She had her baby and has been a good single mother in raising that child. She currently holds two Master's Degrees, lives with and cares for her aging mother, and has been a police officer in D.C. for 19 years. This woman, because she knew forgiving love, overcame almost overwhelming odds to become a national leader in police work.

Christmas is truly the "Feast of Forgiving Love." Let us today renew our willingness to receive this gift as often as we need it, and to offer this gift as often as others need it. A very peace-filled Christmas to each of you.

THE BLESSED VIRGIN MARY, THE MOTHER OF GOD[*]

NUMBERS 6:   "The Lord said to Moses:… 'This is how you shall bless the Israelites.'"

PSALM 67:   "May God bless us in his mercy."

GALATIONS 4: "When the fullness of time had come…"

LUKE 2:   "All who heard it were amazed by what had been told them."

Blessing, fullness of time, and amazement are the three dimensions of human encounter and experience that are offered today for our renewal and consideration. The blessing is the opening of our human experience into mystery, into truth that is bigger than we are, into truth that captivates us and challenges us and leads us further into our potential. Uncovering mystery is our way of living through faith.

The fullness of time is each moment offered. Each moment of life is full with potential. Thomas Merten[†] taught that each

---

[*] Editor's note: This homily was originally presented on 1/1/04.

[†] Simsic, Wayne. "Learning to See," *Weavings,* Jan/Feb 2004, p. 6.

moment plants seeds of spiritual dynamism in our lives. Fullness of time also reminds us that life comes in the ordinary dailiness.

Amazement is the movement of the human being into richer life, deeper encounters, fuller appreciation. Amazement is the great motivator.

These gifts enable you and me to live fully. Realizing that we are blessed releases our fullest potential for rich living. The blessing is positive and empowering. Fullness of time, paying the best attention to each moment, bringing our mind home – these are disciplines which enable us to grow. And realizing repeatedly that we are blessed, and paying attention to the NOW, to life present, is how we reach amazement in life.

New Years is a grand opportunity for us to be once again blessed, focused and amazed. Great gifts.

THE HOLY FAMILY

SIRACH 3:   "God sets a father in honor over his children; a mother's authority God confirms over her sons."

PSALM 128:   "Blessed are those who fear the Lord and walk in his ways."

COLOSS 3:   "Put on, as God's chosen ones, holy and be-loved, heartfelt compassion, kindness, humility, gentleness, and patience, bearing with one another and forgiving one another...
As the Lord has forgiven, so must you also do."

MATT 2:   "When the Magi had departed, behold, the angel of the Lord appeared to Joseph in a dream and said, 'Rise, take the child and his mother, Flee to Egypt, and stay there until I tell you.'"

Today, the first Sunday after Christmas, we Catholics observe as Holy Family Sunday. It is an excellent time to review this fundamental and most basic unit of society, and to reconsider our role in the family, our attitude toward the family, our commitment to contributing health and holiness and happiness to the family unit.

We belong to many families. We belong to the family of the world, which now numbers about seven billion persons. We belong to the family of the United States, which has a population, according to recent statistics, of 295 million persons. We here at St. Pius X are a family which numbers just over 3,000 persons. Our biological family is the most intimate experience of unity, and demands the most immediate and responsible involvement on our part. We also know and participate in work families, school families, social families, and other units which have a definite identity and which contribute to the welfare of our society.

Our scriptures give us simple and clear advice as to how we can be family. Sirach speaks about the parent-child interaction. Psalm 128, our response, reminds us that we belong to the family of God and that we must always revere our God. Paul's letter to the Colossians speaks of the virtues which are crucial to family unity, peace, happiness. We must discipline ourselves to compassion, kindness, humility, gentleness, patience and forgiveness. These are difficult virtues to practice and live consistently, but it is, we know, the formula for family unity and happiness and peace.

The Minnesota Catholic Bishops are releasing today, a Pastoral Letter on the Family. They recall with us the fact that we must hold marriage in high regard, that we must honor our bodies with sexual integrity and restraint, so as not to endanger life. This feast reiterates the truth that we must work for adoption of unwanted babies, and must do all that we can to stop the scourge of abortion.

We reflect again on this Feast of the Holy Family, that we must continue to learn a vocabulary, develop a maturity, and practice the art, as parents and teachers and priests and mentors, all of whom have a serious responsibility to speak with our children and our youth about the profound power, beauty, and nature of our sexuality. We need to inform them with truth, in the most respectful fashion, and with appropriate and mature and wise goodness regarding the mystery and gift of sexuality. Secular culture and the disgusting presence of pornography is a prevailing and ever-present option for our youth. We Catholic adults must be a stronger and clearer and more persuasive presence in this war for the hearts and minds of our children and youth. This is the essence of family life responsibility.

A final thought: Many families, good families, have experienced the pain of divorce among their ranks. We, as American Catholics, must continue to hold high the ideal of marriage, but we must also, for our divorced Catholics and their children, develop a more compassionate and welcoming attitude. Government statistics tell us now that currently two-thirds of our children in the United States will not begin kindergarten and graduate from high school with both biological parents in the home. We, as a Church, must do more in this difficult and important area of life. We must continue to form, inform and reform our culture through the basic unit of the Christian family.

THE FEAST OF EPIPHANY

ISAIAH 60:   "Rise up in splendor, Jerusalem. Your light
               has come, the glory of the Lord shines
               upon you."

EPHES 3:   "The gentiles are coheirs, members of the
               same body…"

MATTHEW 2: "They opened their treasures and offered him
               gifts of gold, frankincense, and myrrh."

Today the story of Jesus opens another chapter. Little Bethlehem and Judea are invaded by the powers of the world. The
wise men, the kings of earth arrive, bringing gifts and seeking knowledge, comprehension and appreciation of this mysterious event. The word has traveled and curiosity has been
piqued. Times are changing and the plot is thickening.
Neighborhood expectations, prevailing philosophies, national
interests are being touched and impacted.

The Jesus story also shows us another dimension today. Different people have different gifts. All are called to share those
gifts, and all are instructed to accept new and different gifts,

than habit has taught us. This feast is one of manifestation of the new and different. It speaks of opening our hearts to each other, even to the gentiles among us. Epiphany does not allow us to close down, exclude others, and selfishly pull the world in behind us. Epiphany clears our minds, opens our souls, challenges our tendency to selfishness. This feast truly does bless us with growthful discomfort, and with a willingness to be welcoming to others.

Epiphany in 2004 reminds us that we must be involved in such opening movements as globalization, instant worldwide communication, international concern for the environment, the just distribution of wealth. Epiphany talks about the knowledge explosion which is taking place, about competition vs cooperation on world issues, about restructuring of organizations and governments to accommodate changing world conditions, politics and movements.

Epiphany asks us to have confidence in our gifts and humility in being willing to share them. This feast instructs us to be informed, to be involved, to be interested. We are to give of our insights, our judgment, our concern. The Epiphany says that each of us and that all of our gifts are important and necessary for the best world. The gold of the king and the instruction of the shepherds and angels were essential at the time of Jesus' birth. Your gift and mine must be in play today to make Jesus live effectively.

Epiphany also reminds us that there is a Herod in each of us that needs to be dealt with on a regular basis. This feast does give us homework, but it also promises results if we get aboard.

THE FEAST OF EPIPHANY (2)

ISAIAH 60:   "Then you shall be radiant at what you see.
             Your heart shall throb and overflow."

PSALM 72:   "Lord, every nation on earth will adore you."

EPHES 3:   "Brothers and sisters, you have heard of the
             stewardship of God's grace...."

MATTHEW 2: "Magi from the east arrived in Jerusalem,
             saying, 'Where is the newborn King of
             the Jews? We saw his star at its rising
             and have come to do him homage.'"

Today is one dedicated to SEEING, HEARING, APPRECI-
ATING. The very word, "Epiphany" means "a showing
forth." We are invited to look to the commonplace reality of a
birth of a boy-child in a humble setting to learn again and
better that we find God in the most simple and humble of circumstances and happenings. The Feast of Epiphany calls believers to see beyond bodily vision and to hear beyond what
the ear can respond to. This feast invites us in to the world of
appreciation, which is able to comprehend much more than
limited brain power can deal with.

William Stafford (1914-1993), an American Poet, gives a beautiful example of what Epiphany vision is about in his poem, "Up a Side Canyon." He writes:

> "They have trained the water to talk, and it
> prattles along a stone trough…
> Following its instinct, unafraid of rock or of
> anything but rest.
> It never decides, 'This is the place.'"*

The nature of water as always moving is a call for us to see movement, life, transcendence, mystery, the beyond the obvious into the possible. God gives life to millions of living species and to billions of human expressions, and these realities also are always changing, becoming, moving. The human heart is for growth and being in its constant becoming through life until death. And beyond death, we do not understand and cannot comprehend what will be. We can only trust that it happens in the hand of God, and it is not important that we cannot comprehend it all.

The 60th chapter of Isaiah, our first reading today, tells us that we will be radiant because of what we see. We are told that our heart will throb and overflow. To experience this power, however, we must engage our total powers, and pay attention and focus our energies. Isaiah speaks what modern psychology is teaching us today, that the greatest source of peace and happiness is *concentration*, the direction of our mind, soul

---

* Stafford, William. "Up a Side Canyon," in *Even in Quiet Places*, Lewiston: Confluence Press, 1997, p. 46.

and spirit to the present moment, where life exists. Epiphany asks us to see clearly, thoroughly, as completely as possible, the presence of life, the presence of God, the presence of peace.

Psalm 72 states, "Lord, every nation on earth will adore you." The human heart has the capacity to see so much and so deeply. It is a delightful realization that every person alive, of every religion, and of every culture, can see the depths of truth and beauty. For us Christians, we have a profound presence of the teaching about this deep truth in Jesus Christ and his Gospel. The story in Matthew today reiterates the fact that the wise men were from far away, and saw a strange happening and were open to its possibilities. This teaching is good for us to open our hearts and souls again to growth and change and development.

There is a sadness which the world feels this week after so many people died and were rendered homeless by the Tsunami. We cannot understand why but we can band together all around the world to help simply, to pray fervently, to speak especially to our children about this human calamity, and to vow to continue to try to live our precious lives as richly and with as much integrity as possible. The Epiphany empowers us to life. The Epiphany points us to life. The Epiphany calls us to deepen the gift of life every day, through every circumstance, through every emotion, feeling, insight and question. We thank God for the gift of this new call to openness to life on this Epiphany Sunday.

THE FEAST OF EPIPHANY (3)

"Epiphany" is a Greek word, and it means, "The showing forth," the showing forth of life, of truth, of mystery. It is an effort to declare a dimension, a possibility, an appreciation of truth in life. Epiphany is like a beautiful picture frame that shows forth the intended picture in the most magnificent fashion. It is akin to the care we take when we take a picture of the family at a First Communion, or at a fiftieth wedding anniversary. Epiphany is what happens every time we click a camera, or pose for a picture of an event in life that means something to us. We are aware of the fact that, in some fashion, our life makes a difference.

Epiphany also reminds us that we do not always have to calculate or measure, or even be aware of how we show forth the truth and beauty and direction of life. At a recent funeral, at which I was the celebrant, a brother-in-law of the deceased person gave a eulogy, in an effort to express the contribution that the deceased had made in life. He began his remarks with, and I quote, "Unlearn the idea that our unique mission must consist of some achievement which all the world will see – and learn instead, that, as the stone does not always know what ripples it has caused in the pond, whose surface it impacts, so neither we nor those who watch our life, will always know what we have achieved by our life and by our mission. It may be, that by the grace of God, we helped bring about a profound change for the better in the lives of other souls around us, but it also may be that this takes place beyond our sight, or after we have gone on. And we may never know what we have accomplished, until we see God face-to-face, after this life has passed" (Richard Bolles). Epiphany, then, for us followers of Christ, is to live authentically, and in this way, show forth the truth of life.

On this Epiphany, in our first reading, Isaiah (60:1-6) states, "Rise up in splendor, Jerusalem! Your light has come." We are to rise up and show forth the gift of God within. Our Psalm response, (Psalm 72) states, "Lord, every nation on earth will adore you." Somehow, the beauty of the Lord is everywhere, every place, every time of life. Epiphany is partly experienced as we open our souls to the present place, the present moment, the present experience. In joy and in sorrow, in pleasure and in pain, in success and in human failure, the Lord shines. Our challenge is to learn to see, to appreciate, to ponder, to humbly accept, what life presents.

Paul's letter to the Ephesians (3:2-6), reminds us, "...you have heard of the stewardship of God's grace....that the mystery was made known." Epiphany is about deepening our soul so that we walk with the mystery, so that we are intuitively aware of the mystery, so that God is welcome in our being by our deliberate choice, every moment of every day, while we live consciously, while we sleep, while we focus energy on work or play, while we converse with others. We, through entering Epiphany, live more and more what St. Paul says in another writing, "I live now, not I, but Christ lives in me."

Matthew's Gospel (2:1-12) today, tells the story of the opposite of Epiphany. It is the story of the self-focus and paranoia of King Herod, the most powerful king, who was closed to, and afraid of, the baby Jesus, because Herod had heard of this new King of the Jews. Epiphany leads to new life, welcoming new people, enjoying the process of living, aging, becoming wise through life experience, and sharing the total mystery of being alive in the Lord. Herod's life of selfishness, of control and abuse of others, of dishonest and secret dealings under the table, led to the murder of several little boys in the region of Bethlehem. A king murdering babies! How crazy is that? Matthew says, "Then Herod called the magi secretly, and ascertained from them the time of the star's appearance. He sent them to Bethlehem, and said, "Go, and search diligently for the child." The magi knew he was dishonest, murderous, sick, because he was selfish. They knew that he was not about the Epiphany, being open to, and searching for, the truth of life, the truth of Jesus, the truth of God's goodness. Herod was the opposite of Epiphany.

Thomas Merton was a Catholic Monk in Gethsemane, Kentucky, about 50 years ago. He died in a tragic accident in Thailand, while working with Buddhist Monks to open the mystery of God as Catholic Christians and as Buddhists saw the presence of God. He helped change the bigotry of our world into Epiphany, although not many people knew it at the time, fifty years ago. He said of the mystery of Epiphany:

"The Lord travels in all directions at once.

The Lord arrives from all directions at once.

Wherever we are, we find that he has just departed.

Wherever we go, we find that he has just arrived before us."[*]

Basically, this wonderful feast reminds us to open our minds, to open our souls, to open our lives, to truth, to mystery, to love and life. It is there always that we find God.

---

[*] Chopra, Deepak, *How to Know God The Soul's Journey Into the Mystery of Mysteries.* New York: Three Rivers Press, 2000, p 293.

THE BAPTISM OF THE LORD

ISAIAH 42:   "Here is my servant whom I uphold...upon whom I have put my spirit."

ACTS 10:   "God shows no partiality. Rather, in every nation whoever fears God is acceptable to God."

LUKE 3:   "You are my beloved Son; with you I am well pleased."

Probably every person here today has been baptized into Christ Jesus. Most of us were very young when this happened. Most of us did not ask to be baptized. Most of us do not remember anything about the day or the experience of being baptized. Perhaps some of us do not even know who our Godparents are. Then, why is baptism such an important moment and experience in our Catholic tradition and practice?

This ritual partially defines who we claim to be. Baptism identifies us with a people, with a spirit, with a movement. Baptism points us in a direction for life, through sacraments and prayer, and ritual and observances, which significantly color who we are and who we come to be. Our marriages, our funerals, our confirmations and first communions, our celebrations of reconciliation and anointing all flow from the fact that we are united in Baptism.

To be baptized sets our moral codes. We believe in truth, life, charity, justice, peace and forgiveness. We believe in family, and in the disciplines which are needed to make family happen, to make family heal, to make family persevere. We believe in community, and in the free movement toward each other in ways that make church happen.

Baptism teaches us how to be responsible parents, grandparents, adults. It shows children through church how to become disciplined toward community, generosity and peaceful living. Baptism is a call to the fullness of our human potential, to maturity, to change and growth. It is an experience of the transcendent, and it enables us to see beyond the obvious, through mystery, to life beyond the grave, to the communion of saints, to the very life of God.

Baptism demands of us that we grow through prayer, contemplation, reflection. Baptism is the basis for our orderly and deliberate growth in spiritual dimensions, appreciations, directions. Baptism is an institution, an experience, a communion between us that is cause for pondering the greatest truths. It challenges us frequently throughout life to rise up, to regroup, to try again, to be human, and Christian and Catholic.

To share baptism with others is to reconfirm our commitment to decency, to humanity, to nature, to God. Through reflection on this piece of our life, we are called to dignity, to rise above excuses in life, to engage our very best. Baptismal thinking and pondering is of our best, takes us to the brink of mystery, empowers us to be in God's presence.

As a priest, it has been my privilege in the last 43 years to baptize 1500 to 2000 infants, babies of young parents. Most of these parents, bringing their children for the sacrament of Baptism, were married; some were divorced, still others were single and unmarried parents. I do not think I ever once had a parent, no matter what his or her circumstance martially might have been, who did not approach this moment with respect, wonder, awe. They came with conviction that this was an important thing for their child, for themselves, for the extended family, for the ongoing health of the community.

In experiencing the joy of grandparents, great-grandparents, aunts and uncles and cousins and friends at the baptism and at the party following is truly an expression of rich faith, willing hope and kind charity. The baptismal moment brings forgiveness to family hurt, healing to family brokenness, patience to all of our tendencies to be judgmental and self-righteous.

This wonderful sacrament, which we reflect on today in liturgy, is a society builder through us. This sacrament invites all of us to simplicity and sincerity about babies, water, prayer, ourselves, sin and grace. Baptism is the glue which makes us one as families, as parishes, as Christians. We pray that each of us can live this reality to the best of our ability today and to death.

THE BAPTISM OF THE LORD (2)

Isaiah 42: "I have formed you and set you as a covenant of the people, a light for the nations, to open the eyes of the blind, to bring out prisoners from confinement and from the dungeon, those who live in darkness."

Psalm 29: "The lord will bless his people with peace."

Acts 10: " Peter spoke, 'In truth, I see that God shows no partiality.'"

Matthew 3: The Baptism of Jesus.

Today we are invited into our identity, into our conviction, into our commitment as baptized people. We remember that we are one with Jesus Christ, our God-Brother , and one with all of His and of our brothers and sisters. Our dedication, our willingness and readiness to be a Christian and a Catholic are under review. How does this reality change our lives? How does this Baptismal identity direct our lives?

Saint Teresa of Avila (1515-1582) is probably the most influential female saint in the western world. In a poem she writes, "I said to my Lord, 'This Holy Place I have entered-is your name the only key to this?'" Baptism in the name of the Father, and of the Son, and of the Holy Spirit, God's holy name for us Christians, is the key to our way of life as we accept and/or continue the life of Baptism.

Baptismal life, for Jesus, was to commit to all of us, and baptismal life for John the Baptist, for you and for me, is to commit to Jesus, and to live his life each day. This means, among other things, that we are willing to grow, to change, to become more the Christian man, woman, young person every day.

Baptism is about reverence for God and for all of creation, and for all people. Baptism is about openness to God, to creation and to other people. Baptism is about worship for God and service and forgiveness for each other.

As baptized people, we have a new dignity, a strong identity with the Lord and each other, a rich inheritance for the possibility of growth in happiness and peace as we journey through life. Baptism is empowerment to goodness, to justice, to kindness, to peace, to patience and forgiveness.

Baptism is a call and a response to go beyond ourselves, beyond our selfish will, beyond our comfort zone. Baptism is about maturing and maturity. We read throughout the scriptures of the goodness of God, and we experience through our living the goodness of God, and we are gifted by nature within us, around us and between us, the goodness of God. Baptism, lived, embraced, enthusiastically accepted, is our response in goodness for God and one another.

Baptism, we believe, gives us the power of the Holy Spirit, the life of God. We are able to be, as baptized people, prudent, just, courageous, and temperate. We learn these qualities as the Cardinal Virtues (Prudence, Justice, Fortitude and Temperance). We are given the power to believe, to hope, to be kind. We call these goods the Theological Virtues (Faith, Hope and Charity). In baptism we commit to the Decalogue, which we call the Ten Commandments. As baptized people, we believe in and dedicate our lives to living the Eight Beatitudes, and as baptized people, we commit to the Corporal and Spiritual works of mercy: (Corporal Works of Mercy) Feed the hungry, give drink to the thirsty, clothe the naked, shelter the homeless, visit the sick, visit the imprisoned, bury the dead; (Spiritual Works of Mercy) Counsel the doubtful, instruct the ignorant, admonish the sinner, comfort the sorrowful, forgive injuries, bear wrongs patiently, pray for the living and the dead.

This should be enough of an agenda for each of us for the coming week, but if you should run out of things to do on this list, please do not call me. Have a good week, and relax!

Ordinary Time (1)

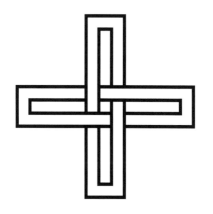

SECOND SUNDAY IN ORDINARY TIME

ISAIAH 49: "I will make you a light to the nations, that my salvation may reach the ends of the earth."

PSALM 40: "Here I am Lord, I come to do your will."

1 COR 1: "You who have been sanctified in Christ Jesus, called to be holy."

JOHN 1: "Behold the Lamb of God, who takes away the sin of the world."

The American Poet, William Stafford, has written a magnificent poem entitled, "Being a Person."* He concludes the short, but expressive poem with the following words: "How you stand here is important. How you listen to the next things to happen. How you breathe." His point is that person is important, life is important, How I view life is important.

Our scriptures today emphasize this same message. Isaiah sets the standard high by stating that God has made each of us to be a light to the nations, so that salvation may be ex-

---

* Editor's note: The works of Mr. Stafford may be found in many places on the internet, including at poemhunter.com.

tended to all. Psalm 40, our response, answers for us the call of Isaiah, stating, "Here I am Lord, I come to do your will." Paul's first letter to the Corinthians reiterates and upgrades Isaiah, saying about us, "You have been sanctified in Christ Jesus, called to be holy." And John's Gospel, in the first chapter, tells us how to see, how to perceive and how to pay attention, telling us to look always for God, in every moment and circumstance, "Behold the Lamb of God...."

The development of our mindset, of our attitudes, of our emotional atmospheres, is a very important part of life. As the poet William Stafford, and as our Scriptures tell us today, "How you stand here is important." Our spirituality, the quality of life for each of us, depends on how we establish, correct, and redirect our spirit each day. Mind and soul management and growth are important. We do not become deeper persons by magic or by accident. We grow because we engage our human potential, by knowing our place in this world, by taking our place in this world, and by being sacredly in touch with the Lord, with God's creation and with God's people, our brothers and sisters.

We are by nature, intelligent, social, spiritual beings. We have a destiny, in which we are personally and responsibly involved. We are sinners, who need to own this dimension of our history, and we are empowered to grow through all of what and who and where we are, to increase in the light of Christ, to be and become the light of Christ.

The condition and color of our soul is in our hands, in our minds, in our dispositions, in our choices, in the total way in which we address each and every day of life. To be healthy spiritually, we must work at physical, mental, emotional, social health. We are one with our body and soul, one with our surroundings, one with our relationships, and each of these dimensions of life needs our continued and continuing attention. To be healthy is to be holy, and to be both of these demands the conscious willingness to grow, to change, to direct, to mature, to be advancing. This means we stop blaming other people, the circumstances of life, luck, fate, God. We assume, each day, total responsibility for self, and for the way self acts, reacts, and lives.

The spiritual life includes all dimensions of existence, presence, and the conditions of our being. The spiritual life is the container of our happiness. The condition of our spiritual life determines the quality of the life we have on any given day. Rumi, the greatest mystic poet of Islam, was born in 1207 in what is now Afghanistan.[†] In one of his poems he states, "The real work of religion is permanent astonishment." We must engage our entire being to live in astonishment before God

There is an old saying that each of us must earn a living. Usually, this means in our conversations that we must get a job so that we can make enough money so that we can live.

[†] Editor's note: The poetry of Rumi may be found on the Internet at rumi.org.uk.

But, truly, making a living goes way beyond the money we make. Making a living means that we manage our body, mind, soul, spirit and relationship with all things and people in as healthy and complete and responsible a way as possible.

In short, to be a light for the nations brings us joy, happiness and peace. And to be light for the nations demands maturity, discipline, commitment, conviction, and a spirit of fairness to God, and to all of creation. The way we stand here is most important.

SECOND SUNDAY IN ORDINARY TIME (2)

1 SAMUEL 3: "Samuel was sleeping in the temple of the Lord where the ark of God was. The Lord called to Samuel, who answered, 'Here I am.'"

PSALM 40:8: "Here am I Lord; I come to do your will."

1 COR 6: "Brothers and Sisters: Do you not know that your bodies are members of Christ?"

JOHN 1:35: "John was standing with two of his disciples, and as he watched Jesus walk by, he said, 'Behold the Lamb of God!'"

Four different authors from antiquity speak to us today in the scriptures of our tradition. They all describe a portion of our relationship with God, and all four are coming from a different place in life, and are experiencing a different condition of life. Samuel is a young man, and he admits to sleeping in church, and he is totally bewildered when he realizes that God is calling him, even while he is sleeping, and doing so in church.

The Psalmist, who is a singer, like Tony Bennet or Barbara Striesand, is praying to the Lord in a song, committing to do God's will. The song goes, "Here am I Lord; I come to do your will." This is a serious love song, if we have ever heard one.

St. Paul is a teacher. He reminds his students that they are members of God, in Jesus Christ. "Brothers and sisters: Did you not know that your bodies are members of Christ?" This is an important truth, placed directly and clearly before those who heard him, and it is a big challenge for those who accept. We belong to the Lord, and so the message is, "Behave yourself!"

And John, the fourth of our authors is today, a sight-seer. He is watching people. "John was standing with two of his disciples, and as he watched Jesus walk by, he said, "Behold, the Lamb of God!"

And so today, we hear from a sleeper, a singer, a teacher, and a sight-seer. Each points us toward the Lord, and each at least implies that we must commit to the Lord if we wish to live happily. Each of us knows this truth at some level of consciousness, and each of us accepts this truth.

Today we, the people of the Catholic Church, begin the period in our worship called "Ordinary Time." For the next seven weeks we observe Ordinary Time, and then we go in to Lent and Easter. Picking up again, after Pentecost, we continue Ordinary Time until next November, when we begin Advent again.

This Ordinary Time, which lasts for thirty-four weeks, is the time when we hear a review of Jesus' teachings about God. The ordinary lessons for life are presented for our review and updating in life during Ordinary Time. We observe and appreciate the Gospel differently at different stages of growth. When we are five years old, we see Jesus differently than when we are fifteen, or thirty-five, or eighty years old. Ordinary time presents basic beliefs, practices and ethical demands which give us a road map, in an updated fashion, as to how to negotiate the conditions, turns and circumstances of life.

This time is like the basic study of the school curriculum, only this is about peace of mind, health, holiness and happiness. This is about service, forgiveness, caring, helping, growing. We hear about the demands of justice and fairness. We look again at respect for all of creation and at reverence for our parents and children and family and neighbors. We are challenged anew to take care of the prisoner, the orphan, the elderly, the sick and the starving people.

Our humanity is again held up for us to see. We are asked to take a new and good look at the various dimensions of life which affect us and those around us and all of creation. Ordinary time will give us the images of the birds of the air, the lost sheep, the lilies of the field, the prodigal son, the good thief, the widow of Naim, the lepers, the scribes and the Pharisees, and many other pictures of life, which contribute to the life that each of us is called to develop, for our own happiness, for the service of others, and for the glory of God. We humbly ask the grace of God, as we begin this life lesson in Ordinary Time again.

THIRD SUNDAY IN ORDINARY TIME

JONAH 3:1:   "God saw by their actions how they had turned from their evil way."

PSALM 25:   "Teach me your ways, O Lord."

1 COR 7:   "For the world in its present form is passing away."

MARK 1:   "The kingdom of God is at hand. Repent, and believe in the Gospel."

The scriptures today mark out a place of wisdom to be studied. The truths presented are very clear, simple, and essential to human growth, peace and salvation. The two concepts given for our consideration today are, number one, the present moment, and number two, repentance.

Jesus, in all of his teaching, brings his way, his truth, his life, in to the present. The verbs Jesus used are all present tense. He adamantly taught that the kingdom of God is among you. Our attention is always focused on life now, and here and as it is. We are to love the neighbor who is present. We are to feed the hungry person at our door now. We are to forgive now, and not be tied to the past. We are to live now, and not be anxious about the future. Jesus taught that we should not let our hearts be troubled. Jesus taught that we should look at nature and let it teach us. Look at the birds of the air, and the lilies of the field, and learn to live now, because now is the only way we can live.

A wonderful recent book, entitled, *The Power of Now* by Eckhart Tolle*, reiterates what Jesus taught. Live authentically and richly, by living in the present moment. The author basically says that the two most debilitating thieves in all of life are the past and the future. Worrying about the past and agonizing about the future, rob us of the only life stage we have, and that is the present. We live now, or we do not have a life.

Our spiritual life is totally tied to the present. Each moment, each emotion, each experience comes, significantly beyond our control, and paying attention to the now, to the present, is what empowers us to appreciate life, to live life richly, and to grow in our ability and capacity to enter more deeply in to life. The Gospel teaches this way of living constantly and consistently. Today, in Mark's Gospel, Jesus is quoted as teaching, "The kingdom of God is at hand." Our Psalm response draws us to the present, when it states, "Teach me your ways, O Lord." And Paul's letter to the Corinthians reminds us that, "the world in its present form is passing

---

* Published by Namaste Publishing, 1997; ISBN 1-t7731-152-3.

away." Each moment comes once. There is an ancient Latin phrase, *Carpe Diem*, translated, "seize the day," seize the moment, or forever lose it.

The second concept offered for consideration today is repentance. In the first reading, from the Book of Jonah, we hear, "God saw by their actions how the people had turned from their evil way." Turning from evil is called repentance, and it is the possibility in life for every single one of us. We are all sinners, and have the need to own that piece of truth about ourselves. The virtue of hope is found in repentance. We can change, grow, correct failures, reverse sins, and choose new directions in life.

One of my favorite poets is Maiya Angelou.[†] She is, as you may know, a black American poet. I love her poetry and I respect her candor and honest and humble spirit. A few years ago, I saw a television interview which she gave. The young woman interviewing her, at one point in the exchange, said something like the following: "Ms. Angelou, I have been told, that in your young life, you were a prostitute for a time." Maiya looked simply and confidently at the camera, and said humbly and directly, "I did then what I knew how to do. Now, I know better; now I do better."

What a beautiful and profound example of repentance, and of life change. Ms. Angelou did not deny her past, she did not

---

[†] Editor's note: Learn more about Ms. Angelou at mayaangelou.com.

condemn herself, she did not justify her actions. She owns her soul and corrects her path and redirects her life. That is repentance. That is the path to peace of mind, that is the way to salvation.

Repentance acknowledges the fact that God never condemns a sinner, and so, neither should we condemn ourselves or others. But God calls us continually to repentance. If we can find the wisdom and the humility of Maiya Angelou, we find new life, hope, peace of heart, and a rich spirit, knowing forgiveness. This has been the path of a majority of the Saints who have been canonized in our Catholic tradition. Repentance, humility, truth, total ownership of soul equals repentance.

FOURTH SUNDAY IN ORDINARY TIME*

ZEPHANIAH 2: "Seek the Lord, all you humble of the earth who have observed his law; seek justice, seek humility."

1 CORINTH 1: "Consider your own calling, brothers and sisters. Not many of you were wise by human standards, not many were powerful, not many were of noble birth."

MATTHEW 5: The Beatitudes.

As we come together today in worship and care for one another, we do so in a world which seemingly is accelerating in violence, history, experience and potential. As we gather, the Iraqi people are voting for the first time in their history, in the midst of violence. During the past week, the United Nations held a memorial moment acknowledging the millions of people who were killed 60 years ago at Auschwitz and other places in Europe – another instance of violence in the history of humanity. The sadness of all who are made aware of the train wreck in California, and the helicopter crash in Iraq, killing many people in each experience, is fresh in reminding

---

* Originally presented on January 30, 2005.

us that peace and health of soul are a decision, a choice which has to be responsibly made each day.

Healthy decisions are the fruit of a healthy mind and soul and spirit. Zephaniah speaks to this health and to us, saying, " Seek the Lord, all you humble of the earth who have observed his law. Seek justice, seek humility." Paul's letter to the Corinthians reminds us, "Consider your own calling, brothers and sisters. Not many of you were wise by human standards, Not many were powerful, not many were of noble birth." And the beatitudes equate health of heart, soul and mind with poverty of spirit, mourning, comforting others, meekness, hunger for truth and righteousness, mercy, cleanliness of heart, peace-making and acceptance of suffering.

The scriptures today all instruct us to be disciplined, informed, aware, accurate in our assessments of self-importance. To be instruments of peace, justice, and dignity, to be Christ-bearers, we must shoulder the burden of being healthy, caring, redeeming, present to suffering in life. Life among us human beings demands constant growth, attentiveness, a willingness and readiness to be the whole Christ to the continuous flow of life in our world.

Today, we celebrate Catholic Schools. We reflect on this approach of our church to offer the Gospel and the life of Christ to our children and youth. Our culture is in need of the sincere offering of a variety of approaches to the formation of youth, and for the continuous renewing of society. Our

Catholic Tradition of Faith has, for centuries, operated schools at all levels of formal education in the United States. Catholic Schools offer a most effective option to the Public School which we, as Americans, subsidize and operate to ensure education for all children. The freedom which Catholic Schools enjoy enable the Church to offer formation of minds, souls, persons in the spirit and way of Jesus Christ. This Christian emphasis is essential to continued health, renewal, reformation of education in general. As friendly competitors with Public Schools, our Catholic Schools serve an essential presence in the formation and education of our youth, even as we, as Catholics, continue to support and renew our Public Schools through the payment of just taxes and through concerned oversight as to quality, human decency and ethical integrity.

Today, as we give thanks for Catholic Schools, we can renew our dedicated interest in all schools, in Rochester, in Minnesota, in America, in the entire world. Our youth are the future of this planet. We, as citizens, as Catholics, as participants in the mystery of life, are obligated to have interest in, to financially support, and to sincerely monitor our schools, educators and systems which so importantly touch the hearts and minds of our children and young people. Schools give birth to new dimensions of living as surely as parents give birth in conceiving, bearing and developing their respective offspring.

This observance gives us an opportunity to thank our educators, administrators, teachers, service people, counselors – all who help our children and youth continue to grow to become responsible, generous, healthy and happy citizens of our world.

FIFTH SUNDAY IN ORDINARY TIME

ISAIAH 58: "If you bestow your bread on the hungry, and satisfy the afflicted; the light shall rise for you in the darkness, and the gloom shall become for you like midday."

PSALM 112: "The just man is a light in darkness to the upright."

1 COR 2: "I resolved to know nothing…except Jesus Christ, and him crucified, …that your faith might rest, not on human wisdom but on the power of God."

MATT 5: "You are the salt of the earth…you are the light of the world."

The mystery of God is found in the details, so say the scriptures today. The details like giving bread to the hungry, helping the afflicted, being a light in darkness for self and others, resting our faith, not on humans, but on God, being salt and light. Wonderful, and difficult details, demanding growth, generosity, courage and dedication.

Joseph Priestly, an English amateur chemist, in 1772, proved that plants breathe as they grow. In 1772, Joseph Priestly enclosed a growing plant in an airtight chamber, and found that it suffocated and died, just as surely, if not as quickly, as an animal sealed in a similar container. But much more surprising and wonderful was his famous subsequent experiment of enclosing a plant and animal in the same airtight container, and discovered that both could live. This was a seeming miracle that was soon to show that the breaths or gases of plants and animals are different. These gases were soon to be named oxygen and carbon dioxide. The animal inhaled oxygen and exhaled carbon dioxide, while the plant did just the opposite. This was a first step in discovering photosynthesis.[*]

The behaviors of plants and animals have built into them the power to live in a natural, God-given setting, as do we humans. The difference of course is that we humans can choose; indeed, we must choose the right thing to give life now and forever. The natural law directs animals and plants in the integrity of their nature. The natural law directs us humans in the integrity of our nature. Plants and animals have no choice but to follow the power of God within to live. We human *must* choose to follow the power of God within, if we wish to live.

Isaiah today reminds us that the power of God within us must learn to see the hungry and feed them. This is a choice. We

---

[*] Murchie, Guy. *The Seven Mysteries of Life*. Boston: Houghton Mifflin Company, p. 50, seq.

are to educate, form and inspire our hearts to recognize the afflicted, and then offer to help them. This is a choice. Psalm 112, our response, teaches that we must give good example to each other. This is a choice. We are to be light in darkness. This is a choice. St Paul, in 1 Corinthians, tells us to place the basis of our faith on the power of God, not on human wisdom. This is a choice. And Jesus tells us, as quoted in Matthew's Gospel, to be creative, that is salt, and to be true, that is light. And this is choice.

We are learning more and more in this twenty-first century, that all of God's Creation is *one*, and that each creation must function according to its nature, totally, always, or it must die. We cannot have it our way, if it is not predicated on God's Law. This is why we come together to worship frequently, so that we can learn to purify our choices. This is why we try so hard to give our children the seeds of faith, so that they can learn to purify their choices. This is why we remain good friends to some that we can encourage each other to life, so that we can continue to purify choices. Salvation and eternal life are operating now, and for us humans, these dimensions of our journey depend on clear thinking, valid choosing, emotional health and continued spiritual development. We are different when we are seventy years old than when we were seven or seventeen or thirty-seven. God expects us to change, to become, to grow, to move on in this experience and journey which we call *life with God*.

Lent begins this coming Wednesday. This period of life is an excellent opportunity to choose something small, and possible, and challenging which can renew our discipline, and enable us to give healthy direction to life. Perhaps a small and doable plan is the best way to come to Wednesday, and Lent, and the rest of our lives.

FIFTH SUNDAY IN ORDINARY TIME (2)

ISAIAH 6:   "Then I heard the voice of the Lord saying, 'Whom shall I send? Who will go for us?' 'Here I am,' I said, 'Send me.'"

PSALM 138:   "In the sight of the angels, I will sing your praises, Lord."

1 COR15:   "Therefore, whether it be I or they, so we preached and so you believed."

LUKE 5:   "When they brought their boats to the shore, they left everything and followed him."

A good friend gave me the following story: The lunch buffet line in a Catholic school was all laid out for the children. The first food item in the line was a big bowl of apples. The Nun in charge of the lunch room had printed nicely a sign which lay on the table in front of the apples, and it read, "One apple per person. God is watching." At the far end of the food line was a big plate of cookies. When an enterprising fourth grader got there, he quickly tore a page from his notebook, and wrote, "Take as many cookies as you want. God is watching the apples."

The scriptures today offer us a lesson in the beauty of God's Word, and without explicitly saying so, teach us about how to read the sacred texts. The teaching church, through encyclicals and other documents, asks us to read scripture as we read any other literature, contextually, with open hearts and minds, seeking to deepen our spirit in truth. It is a dangerous thing to draw a box around a passage of scripture, extract its meaning, and post that meaning on the wall as an absolute truth. The Bible has to be read like other books-as a whole, each passage understood in the context of what came before, what comes after.[*]

A story can help us to appreciate this truth. In mid-nineteenth-century America, Baptist layman William Miller, carefully computing as he read his Bible literally, concluded that the exact date of Christ's return could be predicted. His calculation of October 1844 was widely accepted by members of Baptist, Presbyterian, Methodist and Campbellite churches, some of whom abandoned their farms, sold their homes, and left their employment to propagate the Gospel of the last days. In the wake of the "great disappointment" of Christ's apparent failure to return, the Millerite movement spawned a number of new religious groups, among them the Jehovah's Witnesses and Seventh-day Adventists, who reinterpreted and continued to make Adventist prophesies central to their faith visions.[†]

---

[*] See *Weavings,* July/August, 2006, p. 8.

[†] See *Weavings,* November/December, 2006, p. 34.

Still today, every now and again, some fundamentalist religious group, reading the Bible literally, predicts the end of the world, and each time, when nothing happens there is religious fallout and spiritual confusion among some sincere, but misguided people.

Scripture is intended to be a living path to truth, which has to be interpreted carefully, and continually in community. No one individual has a corner on what the scriptures mean. This is why we say that teachers and preachers are to proclaim the scriptures, and not explain them tightly and in a closed manner. We stand before the Word of God humbly, simply, openly, allowing the Word to form us, inform us, reform us in the moment. Times change, people change as we go and grow, and the Word of God is the truth, which can continuously empower us to spiritual growth and continuous maturity in Christ.

The Scriptures are wonder gifts. The Scriptures are powerful spiritual guides. The Scriptures are living companions for all of us, for the entirety of our journey. The Scriptures, read humbly, nurture our hearts and souls onto eternity. We thank God for the gift of the Word, which is free for the taking all the days of life.

SIXTH SUNDAY IN ORDINARY TIME

JEREMIAH 17: "Thus says the Lord, 'Cursed is the one who trusts in human beings….Blessed is the one who trusts in the Lord, who hopes in the Lord.'"

1 COR 15: "Christ has been raised from the dead, the first fruits of those who have fallen asleep."

LUKE 6: "Blessed are you…"

There is an old line from the lore of the oceans and sailors. It exhorts the people as to the course of action to be taken in the event of storms, ship wrecks, difficulties of any kind. And it says, "Look to the heavens, and row toward shore." The meaning, it seems to me, is to trust in the providence of God and do what you can to solve the situation. The scriptures today point us in that same direction. Trust God in all things, and times and circumstances. This may sound easy at first glance, but it is a difficult posture to take. The second part of the formula, that is, to do what one can to correct the situation, is also a demanding dimension of life – to be responsible in the moment in which we find ourselves. This, too, demands the best of our human nature.

Jeremiah makes a strong statement when he says we are cursed if we do not trust God, the flow of life, the changes in life, the mystery of life. St. Paul, in a different scripture from that which we hear today, states that when he was a child, he thought like a child, spoke like a child, behaved like a child, but that as he grew, he knew that his responsibility also grew with him. Luke's Gospel today advises us to deal with the whole of life, the good and the easy, and also the difficult, the defeating portions, with living, succeeding, suffering and, ultimately, dying. Trust the Lord in all of this – this is a lifetime job.

To be a Christian demands that we be a human being totally and always. To be a Christian makes us to grow, to mature, to change, to become more of life every day that we live. To be a Christian demands that we pay attention to life, and to life's demands always. And to be a Christian, we are pulled out of ourselves to each other. We are social by nature, we are brothers and sisters, we are to assist and help each other, we are to live for each other. We are to be a blessing through involvement with and for each other. We are to avoid the curse of selfishness, self-focus, inordinate self-concern.

To have this kind of spiritual strength and depth, the scriptures and the spiritual literature of our constant tradition over the centuries tell us that we must constantly and perseveringly grow, and be willing to change, in our minds, in our perceptions and assessments, in our prejudgments and prejudices. We are challenged to have the most complete and comprehensive view of our nature possible. That is, we need to be able and willing to see within ourselves the beauty and the beast, our strengths and our weaknesses, the positive and the negative, the peaceful and the uncontrolled. We need to be able to be aware that we are capable of beautiful and positive contributions, and that we are equally able, sometimes, to be selfishly negative. This is a fairly accurate historical description of our human nature and its conditions,

In our own time, Mother Teresa, when she was being praised by a young admirer, said, "I am fully aware that there is a Hitler in me." Blessedness and woefulness, as today's Gospel reminds us, depend on our choices, made either with proper information and spiritual integrity, or based on half-baked and ill-informed positions.

Happiness or sorrow, then, to a great degree, flow from the choices we make about the life situation that comes down the road toward us. Wishing, refusing to courageously grow and change, and ducking our share of responsibility are always a guarantee of failure, sadness and defeat. Trusting in God, changing and growing, and facing reality each day is the best chance we have of peace and life.

SIXTH SUNDAY IN ORDINARY TIME (2)*

LEVITICUS 13: "If someone has a sore of leprosy on his skin, he shall be brought to Aaron, the priest…"

PSALM 32: "I turn to you, Lord, in times of trouble."

1 CORINTH 10: "Avoid giving offense, whether to the Jews or the Greeks or the church of God.."

MARK 1: "Go, show yourself to the priest, and offer for your cleansing what Moses prescribed."

As most of you know, I was on vacation with my college classmate and good priest-friend, Charles Quinn, during the past ten days in Ft. Lauderdale, Florida. While there, during the past few years, we have stayed at the same small motel. It was, as was most of South Florida, severely damaged by the hurricanes this past Fall. The owners are a couple from Trinidad originally. They came to the United States many years ago as day laborers, and worked hard for many years, and now own the motel, and run it wonderfully. They are strug-

---

* Editor's note: This homily was originally presented on 2/12/06.

gling to recover from the storms, and go on. To make things worse, the husband has been seriously ill for over two years, unable to work. Each morning and each afternoon while we were there, Fr. Quinn and I sat near the pool and prayed morning prayer and night prayer. The husband was watching one morning, and later he asked what we had been doing. We explained that we were praying morning and evening prayer. He did not realize that we were priests, and was surprised when we told him we were. He told us that he and his wife were Hindu people, but he asked for us to bless him in his illness, so both of us prayed over him for a moment. Like the people in the scriptures today who were ill, he wanted the blessing of God. He was very thankful for our blessing, so we asked him to pray for us.

He promised that he would pray for us, and then, he asked us if we would like to hear some of his Hindu prayer. We said that we would like that, so he went and got a tape recorder, and came to our room so that he could plug the recorder in to electricity, and for the next forty-five minutes, he played what would be the equivalent of our Psalms, that is prayer in song. The prayers were sung in the Hindi language, and he would stop the recording from time to time, to translate for us. The prayers were beautiful, and spoke mostly of the inner spirit of God present in all of us. He was so proud of his prayer, and so respectful of us and ours.

He again thanked us for the blessing, and we thanked him for sharing some of his prayer with us. It was a wonderful moment, an enlightening moment, a moment of growth for all three of us men. In sickness and in health, in life and in death, both the Hindus and we Christians believe that God is deeply and richly present, and we believe in welcoming the God of all people, and of all traditions, into life.

The scriptures today are descriptions of sickness, exclusion, going to the priests, who represent the entire community and God, as in Leviticus, our first reading, and as in Mark's Gospel. Psalm 32, our response, says, "I turn to you, Lord, in times of trouble." And the second reading from Paul to the Corinthians exhorts us to quote, "Avoid giving offense, whether to the Jews or the Greeks or the church of God." As I read the scriptures for today, I realized that those attitudes and behaviors were in play between our Hindu friend in Florida and ourselves, and it was the Hindu who asked for the prayer and sharing. Jesus always spoke of the need to include all people, and he scolded his Apostles only when they wanted to exclude, or worse still attack, those people who did not walk according to their way.

I want to address the young people who are here today as our Confirmation Candidates. You young people are inheriting a world of division, hatred, prejudice, exclusion, war and violence. Your commitment to accept Confirmation in your faith practice is an experience of hope for this war torn world. You are willing to continue to struggle to grow in the spirit of healing, the spirit of peace, the spirit of justice for all, the spirit of welcoming each person as brother or sister. We adults give you respect, care and love as you continue the journey of Christian growth and maturity.

In closing, I want to share another story about vacation last week. I was standing outside by the swimming pool, speaking with a couple from Montreal, Canada. As we spoke, I looked out to the sidewalk, and noticed there, walking along at a brisk pace, a young Hispanic man, probably in his mid twenties. He was looking at me very attentively and had a big grin on his face. As he continued to walk along, he pointed at me with one hand and placed his other hand on his head, and he said, in broken English, "Shiny." So, I shouted after him, "That is why I need your cap to protect this shiny head." He kept laughing and continued down the street twenty more paces. He then abruptly stopped, turned around, took his cap off, and started to come toward me, all the while with this big smile on his face.

When he got to me, he pushed his cap toward me, and very kindly said, "Take my cap…for you." I said that I was only kidding but he insisted that I have his cap. He said, "I have two caps…this one for you." What a moment for me. A young Hispanic man who was financially very poor, offering to an old Caucasian man, his cap, well worn, not the cleanest, but a profound gift to me, and a most generous and kind gesture from him. That is Christianity in the works.

SEVENTH SUNDAY IN ORDINARY TIME

1 Samuel 26: "The Lord will reward each person for his justice and faithfulness."

1 COR 15: "It is written, the first man, Adam, became a living being, the last Adam, a life-giving spirit."

LUKE 6: "Be merciful, just as your Father is merciful..."

In a recent periodical,* a beautiful little meditation was offered, entitled, "What to do in the darkness," by Marilyn Chandler McEntyre. It appears to be an exhortation to the reader as to what to do when one experiences depression, anxiety, defeat, failure, darkness of any kind in our spirit, in our life. The brief offering reads:

" Go slowly......Consent to it......But don't wallow in it......Know it as a place of germination......And growth......Remember the light......Take an outstretched hand if you find one......Exercise unused senses......Find the path by walking it......Practice trust......Watch for dawn."

---

* *Weavings*, March-April, 2004, p. 27.

This would seem to be excellent advice for any one of us when things are frightening and painful and dark. This is a road map for the times of trial. This coming Wednesday is Ash Wednesday, the beginning of Lent. This is a period of time which we observe each year, in which we are aware of the need to be responsible, in which we ponder pain, sorrow, loss, suffering in life. This is an opportunity to reflect on how we handle the darkness that is simply part of our journey.

This time of Lenten observance is a wonderful chance for us to review our own spiritual emphasis and practices. We are given increased opportunities to renew the spirit within us and within our families. Lent is a community-wide observance because we need each other for encouragement and perseverance in living the Christ life. Lent is a time to renew the discipline needed for growth, peace and happiness. Lent tells us again that peace and happiness just don't happen. These qualities of life must be earned by each of us each day that we live. Life does not serve up free lunches to anyone. The first reading today from I Samuel, reminds us of this truth – "The Lord will reward each person for his justice and faithfulness." Life is costly if we want life to be rich, meaningful, and filled with hope. Each of us is called to earn our lives every day.

Lent also speaks the truth which we hear today in the Gospel. Other people sometimes hurt us, and each of us knows that sometimes we hurt others. To offer the other cheek, to return a blessing for a curse, sets the bar pretty high. To continue to grow as a sincere Christian, I must learn continuously how to deal with the darkness within myself and within the people and the world around me.

Lent is an excellent opportunity, a new invitation, to re-establish a closer relationship with our old and absolutely necessary friend, *discipline*. Life demands discipline, and most of us do not remain totally faithful to this dimension of our existence. We are not called by the Gospel during Lent to berate ourselves, to be discouraged about failure in this regard, but we are called again to begin, to renew effort to manage and discipline life, the body, the mind and the spirit. We are given the boost needed to try a bit harder to be and to become the person God made each of us to be.

Lent is a time for an honest appraisal of our condition in life at this moment, for an honest appraisal of the direction in which our life is moving. We can together look anew at weakness and failure, at strength and beauty, at the potential that is waiting to be unfolded within each of us. Jesus calls us through the various behaviors described in today's Gospel to get better on the path of our Christian commitment, by striving anew to try to love those we do not like, by striving for compassion and patience with self and with others, and by struggling not to be so judgmental sometimes toward others, or even toward ourselves. Lent asks us to renew effort in seeking the truth of Christ, the mercy of Christ, the justice of Christ, the love of Christ.

Lent is, in short, a second or third or 75th chance at what we all believe in and accept as our way of life. As we accept ashes on our foreheads on Wednesday to begin this new Lent, each of us can again embrace our cross with Jesus, each of us can renew our courage in our darkness with Jesus, and each of us can recommit to be persons of kindness, peace and love. This is our glorious call.

Lent & Easter

FIRST SUNDAY OF LENT*

Our strongest convictions are rooted in our life-experience. The ancient Jacob (Genesis 28:16) discovered that, "The Lord is in this place, but I knew it not." Lent offers us each year, the opportunity to review our convictions, rooted in our life-experience, as to the fact that the Lord is in this place of life, but, in speedy distraction, we too often know it not, as was the case with Jacob.

Lenten observance is a powerful time. We are enabled to practice listening again – listening to the earth and universe around us. Listening in short to the sounds of our home which is the earth and the universe. And we renew our listening to our family, the chosen intimacy of our days, where most of our peace or impatience is engendered.

We listen these days to our body for its wisdom to teach us about quality of life. And, we listen to our depths, our being, our nature, our soul. It is there that we find new meaning, deeper appreciation, richer realization as to who we are, where we are heading, and as to what is most important to our destiny.

---

* Editor's note: This homily was originally presented on 2/29/04.

It is in listening to these settings and persons that we find a new appreciation of the presence of God. We come, more and more, to realize that God is in this place, this relationship, this moment of existence. Our souls expand and breath, stretch and become more aware of God-presence, other-presence, self-presence, and of our essential union with and participation in the life of the universe and earth.

Lenten observance is also rich in offering us lessons in how to see, how to engage our curiosity, ingenuity and intuitive energy so as to enrich our own lives and the lives we touch each day. The power of our soul is potentially increasing, expanding and unfolding every day of life. Lent is a wonderful chance to be aware of our opportunities and abilities to become deeper and happier people.

We are all aware that the John Jay University audit report on clergy sexual abuse of children and minors came out in the public press this past week. This report points up the sad truth that we have, as a clerical church, kept this terrible problem covered up for so long. Hopefully, with the efforts of this audit, the opening of supervision beyond bishops and priests to include lay men and women, and with a new awareness of human frailty and the need for sufficient training, this problem will be history and finished. If any person has questions or concerns about this, please contact our parish staff or the Bishop of the Diocese of Winona.

GENESIS 2: "The Lord God formed man out of the clay and blew into his nostrils the breath of life, and so man became a living being."

PSALM 51: "Be merciful, O Lord, for we have sinned."

ROMANS 5: "Through one man sin entered the world."

MATTHEW 4: The temptations of Jesus.

Recently I read a story. A lady was picking through the frozen turkeys at the local grocery store, but couldn't find one big enough for her family. She asked a stock boy, "Do these turkeys get any bigger?" The stock boy replied, "No Ma'am, they're dead." The scriptures today speak about living and growing, or about sin which brings us to death as surely as butchered turkeys.

Temptation, sin, redemption are three big pieces of Christianity which appear throughout the biblical stories, and throughout Christian history. Triumph and tragedy are forever present in the context of temptation and sin and redemption. The Biblical story finishes with the life, teaching, suffering and death of Jesus Christ, coming to save all of us from sin through forgiveness and renewal of spirit, which results in eternal life.

One of the most important realities that must be taught, learned, appreciated, and frequently revisited in life, if one hopes to have a happy life, is the fact of human potential and human sin. We must constantly teach our youth about the wisdom found in humble acknowledgment of human weakness and sin. And all of us, without exception, must be constantly vigilant as to our attitudes, wants, desires, and behaviors.

The Islamic Poet, Rumi* (1207-1273) explored in his poetry the aspects of the extreme, gorgeous drama of the soul's journey to God. In his poem, entitled, "The Torrent Leaves," he describes the journey of a mountain stream, and says, "The torrent knows it can't stay on the mountain." It is the very nature of the stream to flow down the mountain. So it is with human nature. We are broken and we must acknowledge that truth and appreciate it at the deepest level, or we betray our nature and fail. Sin is inevitable and demands attention, or we are lost in it. Like the stream that tries to stay on the mountain, a human being denying sin frustrates nature and will be wounded and lost in the process of this lie.

---

* Editor's note: The poetry of Rumi may be found on the Internet at rumi.org.uk.

Sin is a denial of truth in some manner or capacity. Sin is the breaking with the plan, as God has presented it. Sin is, in short, against nature, against truth, against goodness. If we do not comprehend this reality, it leads us to confusion, disruption, failure, and death. That is the story found repeatedly in the Scriptures. Sin manifests itself in our lives, when we allow our souls to get lazy, selfish, undisciplined and blinded to the needs of others. When we allow the delicate balance between self, others, creation and Almighty God to get out of whack, we fall into sin. This is why, over the centuries, our forbearers learned the wisdom of the rhythms of life, and gave us this season of Lent.

Balance of soul, integrity of heart, conditioning of mind and body happen when we exercise these dimensions of life, according to the plan of God. That is, when we think, consider, ponder, plan, and behave with integrity, wisdom, prudence, and a clear vision, we avoid sin and find life. This path takes a discipline and a direction which we call our spiritual life. It is in practicing faith, worshipping God, serving others, and developing a Christian plan that we live in the Lord.

The first reading today gives the story of temptation and sin. Adam and Eve did poor thinking, dishonest calculating and selfish behaving. That is sin. Psalm 51 is the story of King David, after he had committed adultery with his friend's wife, and cried out acknowledging his sin, selfishness, and destructive behavior. Paul, in writing to the Romans, tells us of forgiveness, redemption, peace brought by Jesus Christ, and made available to all.

And Matthew's Gospel gives us a plan, a format, a recipe for success in living a life free from sin, filled with integrity, and able to offer us peace of mind and happiness. Jesus faced the temptations, named them, and addressed them with thoughtful courage. This is the plan for human growth. This is the plan for defeating evil. Thinking, naming and being thoughtfully courageous are within the scope of each person's ability. Hope is all around when we address temptation and sin directly and immediately.

THE FIRST SUNDAY OF LENT (3)

GENESIS 9:   "God said to Noah and to his sons with him: 'See, I am establishing my covenant with you and your descendants.'"

PSALM 25:   "Your ways, O Lord, make known to me; teach me your paths."

1 PETER 3:   "Beloved, Christ suffered for sins once, the righteous for the sake of the unrighteous, that he might lead you to God."

MARK 1:   "The Spirit drove Jesus out into the desert, and he remained in the desert for forty days. Jesus came to Galilee proclaiming the Gospel of God: 'This is the time of fulfillment. The kingdom of God is at hand. Repent, and believe in the Gospel.'"

Today we observe the first Sunday of Lent. Each year during the forty days of Lent, all Christian people are invited to move a bit deeper into our souls, for a good look at what we are doing with our lives, how we are spending our time, how we seek the mystery of God, and how we hold respect for our God, ourselves and our neighbors.

We are invited and encouraged to review our spiritual life, our moral stances, our total response to life, as we are experiencing it. Lent is also a time of discipline. Our body, our mind, our soul and spirit, all need a calm and steady discipline, in order to grow in an optimal way. *Life, happy life, is a deliberate choice.* We never just stumble into happiness. We deliberately choose to be happy, and this choice demands discipline.

The Gospel which we hear every Ash Wednesday teaches us to do three simple, life giving disciplines: pray, give alms, and fast. And in that Gospel account, Jesus promises us, that if we do these three things, that we will find continuous life unto eternity. The good life is not indulgence of all of our hungers. The good life is the result of disciplining our time, attitude and behavior in such a fashion that our human dignity and nature is developed and enhanced.

The three disciplines that Jesus teaches are possible for, and available to, and the responsibility of, every single Christian person. No one else can do these things for you or me. Praying, giving alms and fasting is the work of each of us, if we are to develop our soul and spirit. Let's look briefly at each of these disciplines.

Prayer is opening our mind, heart, attention, and intention to the mystery of God. We can experience prayer through listening, through shared prayer, through speech, through meditation, through contemplation, through silence. We can experience prayer through music, listening to scripture and uplifting literature; we can experience prayer through sadness, sorrow, grief, and we can experience prayer through joy, laughter and blissful experiences. We can experience prayer by teaching children to pray. We Catholics are blessed with wonderful experience of prayer called the Sacraments and Mass. Prayer can be experienced in all the circumstances of life.

Almsgiving is fundamentally and basically generosity. The Gospel exhorts us to use all the gifts God has given to us, for self, for others, and for the glory of God. Generosity teaches us that all we are given is to be shared. We are, in this discipline, asked to share generously, our time, our talents, our energy, our health, our possessions, our money. We are to remember that our lives are not for ourselves alone. Each life is for others, for God and for self. We are social beings. Christ gave us the great commandments. Love God above all. Love neighbor and self always. In other words, be generous always. It is largely through giving to others that each of us finds happiness.

Fasting is the last of the three disciplines given to us. Fasting includes monitoring and controlling all of our passions, emotions and hungers. Fasting means that we watch and limit what we eat and drink. Fasting means that we behave properly in our sexuality. Fasting means to control our temper, our language, our attitudes, toward each other and toward self. Fasting strengthens our self control, helps us maintain dignity, empowers us to develop our life to the maximum. Prayer, almsgiving and fasting truly are our friends, and Lent invites us to be renewed through them.

THIRD SUNDAY OF LENT

EXODUS 3:   "Moses was tending the flock of his father-
               in-law, Jethro. An angel of the Lord
               appeared to Moses in fire flaming out of a
               bush. God said, 'Moses, come no nearer!
               Remove the sandals from your feet, for the
               place where you stand is holy ground.'"

PSALM 103:   "The Lord is kind and merciful."

1 CORIN 10:   "Do not grumble like some of your
               ancestors, who suffered death
               by the destroyer."

LUKE 13:   "Sir, leave the fig tree for this year, and I
               shall cultivate the ground around it and
               fertilize it. It may bear fruit in the future. If
               not you may cut it down."

The scriptures of this third Sunday of Lent tell us again the
story of Moses tending his father-in-law's flocks, his experience of the mystery of the burning bush, and the further mystery of God's voice telling him not to get closer, and to take
his shoes off, because he was standing on holy ground. Psalm

103, our response, reminds us that God is kind and merciful. St. Paul, to the Corinthians warns them and us not to be grumbling; there are dire consequences to grumbling. And Luke's Gospel tells us again of the fig tree that was not producing and the gardener begging the boss to let it live for a year, so that he could care for it and fertilize it to see if it would produce. If not, after a year of care and effort, it would be cut down. There is much to think about here.

Henry David Thoreau (1817-62) concluded his masterpiece, *Walden*, with an account of his two-year long experiment of living alone in the woods where he went to confront "the essential facts of life, and see if I could not learn what it had to teach." From his experience, he gained a vibrant belief in resurrection and immortality.* In his writing about this experience, he included a true story which has gone the rounds of New England, of a strong and beautiful bug which came out of the dry leaf of an old table of apple-tree wood, which had stood in a farmer's kitchen for sixty years, first in Connecticut, and afterward in Massachusetts, from an egg deposited in the living tree many years earlier still. The bug was heard gnawing out of the table leaf for several weeks, hatched per chance by the heat of an urn placed on the table. This story touched Thoreau deeply. It helped him find belief in resurrection and immortality.

---

* Beckness, Thomas: *Of Earth and Sky: Spiritual Lessons From Nature*. Minneapolis: Augsburg Fortress, 2001, p. 103.

This third Sunday invites us to read the scriptures as purely, calmly, and authentically as possible. God is never described as comprehensible or conquerable by the human brain in the Scriptures. Images, metaphors, stories are offered for our consideration. All of human effort, human knowledge, human understanding, does not equal God, expose God, or enable us to be in the know about God. Joseph Campbell, perhaps the leading mythologist in the entire world of the last century, sums up our search for God by saying something like, "Those people who think they know God do not know God; those people who know that they cannot and do not know God, know."

Moses today in Exodus gives us some beautiful insights. He was doing his job, herding his father-in-law's animals, when he experienced mysterious things, like the burning bush, which was not consumed by the flames. He heard a voice telling him to be reverent because creation is holy, and he was told not to try to conquer God. "Come no closer, and take your shoes off." Be who you are, a creature, and stop trying to be in control of God. We worship God, we do not comprehend God. We stand in awe before the mystery of God, we are not in control of the mystery.

Psalm 103, our response, asks us to trust the mercy and kindness of the Lord. St. Paul warns that we are not to be self-focused and grumbling. That spirit does nothing to enable us to appreciate the mystery of God. Luke's story of the fig tree invites us to be who we are, to cultivate our potential, and live according to the nature God gave us. It is really a story about authenticity. We are to be, to become who we really are, God's creatures, God's people, God's worshippers; we are not to be God's controllers, comptrollers, managers. This third Sunday of Lent tells us to live humbly, naturally, reverently before God.

Today's message was succinctly captured in the prophecy of Micah, chapter 6, verse 8, where it says, "You have been told, O man, what is good, and what the Lord requires of you: only to do the right and to love goodness, and to walk humbly with your God."

FOURTH SUNDAY OF LENT

JOSHUA 5: "The Lord said to Joshua, 'Today I have removed the reproach of Egypt from you.'"

COR 5: "Whoever is in Christ is a new creation: the old things have passed away; behold, new things have come. And all this is from God."

LUKE 15: The prodigal son story.

Several years ago, I worked with prisoners in a prison at Faribault, Minnesota. I would go there to hear confessions and to offer the Mass for the prisoners. One night, after Mass, as I was about to leave, a prisoner asked me if I would do him a favor. I responded that I would if I could. He asked if I would go to his mother to tell her how sorry he was, and to ask her forgiveness. Shortly after he made the request, I contacted the mother and went to see her. When I told her that I came to express, for her son, how sorry he was, that he had caused her such pain, and that he wanted me to ask her to forgive him, she threw up her arms, and said, "Oh, I forgave that boy years ago, and so many times. God has forgiven that boy absolutely. All that is left to do is that he forgive himself."

Self-forgiveness, the forgiveness of others, God's forgiveness, the difficulty of forgiveness, the humility needed to ask forgiveness, the absolute need of forgiveness to accomplish world, community, family and personal peace; these are the issues discussed for and with us today in the scriptures.

In our first reading, the prophet Joshua asks the Jews to move out of Egypt in their minds. They had physically been out of slavery for years and years, but they were stuck in hatred, unwillingness to forgive, and they were not ready to choose peace and to move on. Joshua says that God has removed this. Now it is their turn.

In Paul's letter to the Corinthians, our second reading, we are reminded that Christ makes all things possible. We are forgiven and made new. We can forgive and make new. In a human world, there is both sin, pain-causing behavior and brokenness, and there is the God-given power to neutralize the sin, the pain, the break. It is called reconciliation through forgiveness.

Healthy humanity demands the continued growth into a forgiving spirit. Without the discipline of learning, every day, about forgiveness, about forgiving, about being forgiven, we get sick and hard and stuck – in negativity, in hate, in bitterness. Forgiving is the movement which continually renews life to be possible, to be peaceful, to be an experience of hope and goodness.

In the story of the prodigal son, we get again three dimensions of the mystery of reconciliation. We have the Father who shows the best in each of us, that is, the willingness to forgive totally. When we are at our best, we can do this.

We have the younger son, who has to mess up life almost beyond repair, and who has to struggle with pride, self, shame, guilt, in order to find the humility necessary to come home and to say, forgive me, I have sinned. It would seem that if we try to live in forgiveness and with a forgiving spirit, we can have the humility at those moments in life when we need to be forgiven.

And in the older son, we have the spirit which is self-righteous in each of us, when we hug our pride, our way, our self at the expense of all others. Unforgiving hardness becomes paralyses when clung to for any lengthy period of life. Refusal to forgive is hell. Refusal to forgive is the destruction of the human heart. Refusal to forgive brings deep bitterness, relentless revenge, and a deadening of the human spirit which leads to destruction of person, of family, of community.

Pope John Paul II taught the world when he went to the prison which housed Ali Agca, the man who had stabbed the Pope, trying to kill him. The picture of the Pope and Ali sitting in the prison cell while the Pope forgave Ali has become an icon of the last century.

And Maria Ghoretti's Mother of a hundred years ago was a great example of forgiveness. A man had raped and killed her daughter Maria in Italy. For all the years that the rapist-murderer was in prison, the Mother wrote to him, visited him and prayed with him. When, years later he was released from prison, the mother took him in to her own home where he lived until his death.

Forgiveness is our vocation. No one is exempt from needing forgiveness or from giving forgiveness. Jesus reminds us that the way we forgive is the way we will be forgiven.

FOURTH SUNDAY OF LENT (2)*

2 CHRONICLES 36: "Early and often did the Lord, the God of their fathers, send his messengers to them…But they mocked the messengers of God."

PSALM 137: "Let my tongue be silenced if I ever forget you."

EPHESIANS 2: "God…brought us to life with Christ… that in the ages to come, He might show the immeasurable richness of his grace in his kindness to us in Jesus Christ."

JOHN 3: "The light came into the world, but people preferred darkness to light because their works were evil."

On last Monday, just after noon, the Northern Hemisphere experienced the Vernal Equinox, the beginning of Spring. We have been seeing the signs of the rebirthing of the earth and all of its plants and creatures. Robins are returning, tulips are

---

* Editor's note: This homily was originally presented on 3/26/06.

coming out of the ground, insects are beginning to appear and move about, grasses and plants in warm spots near home foundations are turning green. The miracle of new life comes again, giving food to all creatures, empowering the trees to produce again the earth's supply of oxygen, and enhancing our happiness, as we experience the rich beauty of new colors, new smells, new expressions of life in millions of species.

Given this setting for our reflection, the scriptures assigned for today challenge us all to consider again our attitudes toward the earth, the creatures of the earth and our fellow human beings. We are invited to renew our hearts and minds and spirits, just as the earth and the forces of physical nature are giving again new life in so many ways.

The Old Testament, Second Book of Chronicles, reminds us, "Early and often did the Lord, the God of their fathers, send his messengers to the people, but they mocked the messengers of God." God's messengers come not only as human beings, but through all of creation. The earth, with its millions of expressions of life, is the greatest messenger of the Lord. We all, as infants and babies, are taught by the earth, long before language becomes the medium of much communication. We must continue to be aware of how we treat the earth, so that we do not take it for granted, or worse, so that we do not pollute, abuse and destroy Mother Earth. God forbid that the generations yet to be born will look back at us and accuse us of mocking the messengers and the message of God, regarding the earth.

We all know that much of our industrial behavior takes place at the expense of the health of the earth. The health of the earth is the precursor of our human health. As the earth is polluted, human health begins immediately to suffer. Chronicles today reminds us that "early and often" the earth sends us messages of proper behavior toward her. We Americans, as the greatest consumers of the people of the earth, do have the responsibility and obligation to look carefully and critically at the how we live, consume, pollute and waste the resources of the earth.

John's Gospel today states, "The light comes into the world, but people prefer darkness to light, because our works are evil." The world community of science, research and ecological studies has told us for fifty years that we are, by our behavior, diminishing the ozone, that our glaciers are melting at an unprecedented rate, that the earth is warming, that deserts are expanding. The United States, because we are primarily focused on the economy, is continuing to refuse to sign on with the major ecological agreements put forth by the vast majority of the world's countries. We Americans, through our governmental leaders, are arrogant, and love the darkness much more than the light in this regard, because money has been, and continues to be, our god. We care much more for money and power, for the economy, than we do for the health and integrity of the earth. We are on a suicidal path, according to the best knowledge that science and ecology can give us. We, indeed, love darkness more than light.

Spring coming is a good opportunity to look again at our attitudes, our convictions, our beliefs, our blindness, our mental habituation with regard to the earth, the source of all life in God's creative plan. Without the earth, there is no life. Without a healthy earth, there is no health in life.

FOURTH SUNDAY IN LENT (3)*

1 SAMUEL 16: "Not as man sees does God see, because man sees the appearance but the Lord looks into the heart."

PSALM 23: "The Lord is my shepherd; there is nothing I shall want."

EPHESIANS 5: "Brothers and Sisters: You were once in darkness, but now you are light in the Lord. Live as children of the light."

JOHN 9: "As Jesus passed by, he saw a man blind from birth."

On this fourth Sunday in Lent, our scriptures invite us to reconsider how we see with our eyes, with our mind, with our imagination, with our heart. A provocative story about seeing differently is contained in the March 3rd issue of *America* Magazine, the Jesuit weekly dealing with moral, philosophical, theological and spiritual issues. In an excellent editorial, entitled "The Green Isle," Maryann Cusimano Love, a professor of International Relations at Catholic University in

---

* Editor's note: This homily was originally presented on 3/2/08.

Washington, D.C., writes about the efforts of the people and government of Ireland to see the waste problem in that country differently.[†]

Municipal waste increased over 65% in Ireland since 1995. The Irish are currently putting programs into place to reduce waste. We, in America, are still focusing on recycling waste. A practical example of waste prevention in Ireland, according to this article, is the so-called "plastax." Five years ago, Ireland began to tax plastic bags, the scourge of modern consumer life.

Around the world over a billion of these "free" plastic bags are given away in shops and markets every day. That amounts to over one million plastic bags a minute, according to reusablebags.com. Only one to three percent are recycled. Ireland has come to see that they must see this issue with new eyes, or very quickly destroy their Green Isle.

Life for all of us needs to be renewed each day through new, more complete, and more responsible seeing. When I was born, there were fewer that one-half of the people on the earth as there are today. Obviously, we have to look differently at life issues today than we did in 1935. Our scriptures are a wonderful perennial reminder to see with new eyes.

[†] Editor's note: This article may be found at http://www,americamagazine.org.

Our first reading, I Samuel, reminds us, "Not as man sees does God see, because man sees appearances, but the Lord looks into the heart." Samuel exhorts us to look again, more deeply, more thoughtfully, more comprehensively, more responsibly. Our response psalm, the famed twenty-third, says in effect, "Look again!" The Lord is my shepherd; there is nothing I shall want.

Paul tells us through Ephesians that, "We were once in darkness, but now we are in the light." He says further that we are to be people of the light. In many ways, we are still in the darkness in this country and around the world. We walk in darkness in the world of ecology. We continue to walk in the darkness as we poison our earth, water, air and environment. We walk in darkness of war, hatred, racism, classism. We walk in the darkness of much injustice, especially as it relates to the uneducated, the impoverished, the little and forgotten people. We have a long way to go before we can confidently say that we are people of the light.

And, finally, we have the story of Jesus curing the man of blindness since his birth. As Catholic Christians, we want to clear up the blindness of humanity with good education, with renewed discipline, as individuals, and as a society. We want to eradicate blindness with social policies that are just, wise, inclusive, and life-giving. We want to eliminate the blindness of prejudice and exclusivity. We will continue to make good efforts to live as people of the light.

FIFTH SUNDAY OF LENT

JEREMIAH 31: "I will place my law within them and write it upon their hearts; I will be their God and they will be my people."

PSALM 51: "Create a clean heart in me, O God."

HEBREWS 5: "Son though he was, he learned obedience from what he suffered."

JOHN 12: "Unless a grain of wheat falls to the ground and dies, it remains just a grain of wheat; but if it dies, it produces much fruit."

Today the scriptures give us a very rich menu for consideration and application to life. Jeremiah quotes the promise of God: "I will place my law within them and write it upon their hearts; I will be their God and they will be my people." Psalm 51 quotes King David after he committed adultery with Bathsheba, the wife of his army general, while the husband was at war protecting David's kingdom; and David, after coming to his senses, says, "Create a clean heart in me, O God."

St Paul, in the Letter to the Hebrews, reminds us, "Son though he was, he learned obedience from what he suffered." And finally, John's Gospel quotes Jesus as saying, "Unless a grain of wheat falls to the ground and dies, it remains just a grain of wheat, but if it dies, it produces much fruit."

Jeremiah helps us to understand and appreciate anew that God has given us the law and the spirit of God in a deep manner in our souls. We experience God's law more deeply than knowledge only. God's law is sum and substance of our lives. God's law moves us, and calls us, and protects us, unless we place an obstacle in the way. What a profound gift this is, to know God in our knowledge and intuition, in our feelings and imagination, in all the movements, experiences and awarenesses of our journey! To be deeply imbued with God's law is part of the gift of our very nature and this is a rich dimension of being human.

Psalm 51 is the greatest prayer of repentance in the Old Testament. King David, the King and Religious Leader of the people commits adultery, and then when he is found out, he places Uriah, the husband of Bathsheba, with whom he had committed adultery, into the heart of the battle, where Uriah was certain to be killed; and he was killed. So David's adultery led to a cover-up, and then lies, and then murder. When David finally owned his sins, he went into despair and begged God to give him a new heart. As you know this story, please read Psalm 51 in it's entirety. It is powerful.

St. Paul, in the Letter to the Hebrews, tells us that Jesus learned obedience through suffering. This is a good and saving lesson to learn. None of us likes obeying another person, and yet, obedience is essential to personal happiness, to social stability, and to organizational functioning. Without obedience there is anarchy and confusion, which leads to death. Obedience is not a function we perform or a behavior we practice. Obedience is an essential part of our well-being. Obedience is our sharing in the spirit of God at the deepest and most saving level.

John's Gospel references dying to self. The entire message of Jesus involves sacrificial love and forgiveness, which cannot happen unless the Christian has in place the willingness to die to self in various ways. Lent is about penance, not for penance sake, but to give us the opportunity to practice dying to self: self will, self indulgence, and all forms of selfishness, which is a tendency for all of us. To remain healthy and balanced all through life, we need to die to self to some degree, or more and more selfishness takes over. Dying to self is like eating, breathing, bathing, exercising, sleeping. We need some of it every day or soon we are off balance and sick.

Discipline is an essential for living and for preparing for dying, dying to self each day, and dying to our body one day. Discipline gives us strength that nothing else can give. The wisdom of the gospel, the message of Jesus, is found in dying to self.

FIFTH SUNDAY OF LENT (2)

ISAIAH 43: "See, I am doing something new! Now it springs forth, do you not perceive it?"

PSALM 126: "The Lord has done great things for us; we are filled with joy."

PHILIPPIANS 3: "…the supreme good of knowing Christ Jesus my Lord."

JOHN 8: "Let the one among you who is without sin be the first to throw a stone at her."

Story: Forgive us our trespasses…Lead us not into temptation.

In the last few weeks, the priests of the Rochester area have been hearing a lot of confessions, especially of children in Faith Formation programs and in our Catholic Schools. This is joyful work for us priests because we see the very best that is in people, the spirit of the Lord present in each person, and the innate desire to grow, become a deeper person, a better Christian. Perhaps we are never closer to being the human being God wants us to be and to become, than when we are in the stance of repentance, in the spirit of reconciliation, in the act of confession of our sinfulness. A beautiful power is released in this prayerful admission of my selfishness, and a renewed hope and spirit of determination and encouragement is renewed.

This past Wednesday, we priests heard confessions at Lourdes High School from 8:00 A.M. until 12:00 Noon. We heard one class at a time and we finished the morning with the Seniors. This was a beautiful moment for me, as a human being and as a Confessor. The Seniors are at a point in their young lives where they stand at the threshold of adulthood, as they come to realize that they will be leaving the safety and taken for granted security of their entire lives at home with their parents, and with almost everything provided for them. They are awakening to a new realization of the profound sacrifice of their parents, and their hearts are grieving that they have taken so much for granted, and that they have not been as grateful as they could have been, and probably should have been, toward their parents and families. They are aware that they have not said thank you to their parents and families often enough, if at all. Several of the students who came to me for the sacrament voiced something of that sentiment. I tried to affirm for each one that that was another step in maturing, in growing up, in crawling out of that self-focus that can incarcerate us all along the road of life.

In one commentary on today's scriptures, the author stated that the focus of biblical wisdom today is, "On Becoming

Human." Not only the high school students, but all of us need to stay in this school of becoming human all the days of our lives. This is the way we grow, develop morally, spiritually, emotionally, socially and humanly. This is the road to maturity, to peace of mind and heart and soul. Developing our humanity is our moral responsibility, is the Christian challenge, is the road to peace among individuals, societies, and nations.

In our first reading, Isaiah reminds us of the Lord saying, "See, I am doing something new. Now it springs forth. Do you not perceive it?" Each person is a manifestation of God's newness springing forth. We are to show to one another God's goodness to us, thus encouraging each other, helping each other, inspiring each other.

Psalm 126, our response, tells us, "The Lord has done great things for us, we are filled with joy." We are called to practice joy and gratitude in our human development and deportment. Paul's letter to the Philippians reflects on the power in our faith development of being aware of "the supreme good of knowing Christ Jesus as my Lord." Balance in life is achieved by the practice of being in Christ. The Gospels tell us that Jesus is the vine, and that we are the branches, and that it is only in that union and communion that we find life, and find it abundantly.

And finally, our Gospel account from the eighth chapter of John tells us that the crowning glory of Christian and human development lies in the lesson graphically presented in the story of the woman caught in adultery. The questions jump at us. Where was the male adulterer? Who gave the elder the right to judge her, and her alone? Why did Jesus not give a lecture about chastity and about not being judgmental? Everything about that story and about our human development is summed up in Jesus' simple and calm statement, "Let the one among you who is without sin be the first to throw a stone at her."

FIFTH SUNDAY IN LENT (3)

EZEKIEL 37:   "I will put my spirit in you that you may live, says the Lord."

PSALM 130:   "With the Lord there is mercy and fullness of redemption."

ROMANS 8:   "You are in the spirit, if only the spirit of God lives in you."

JOHN 11:   "Jesus cried in a loud voice, 'Lazarus, come out.'"

A story is told about the Supreme Court Justice and author, Oliver Wendell Holmes. He was well known for his great knowledge of Constitutional Law, and he was also well known for being forgetful. He was traveling on a train. The Conductor came by for the tickets. Holmes could not find his ticket. So the Conductor, knowing who the Supreme Court Justice was, said, "OK, just send it to the railroad when you find it." Holmes said, "Oh no, you do not understand the gravity of the situation. I need the ticket to tell me where I am going!"

Most of us do not need to worry about Constitutional Law, but all of us need to know where we are going, in the short and in the long runs. As we grow up, and come to increasing self-awareness, self knowledge, self control, and self-assurance, we Christian people have a great tool at hand. And that tool is the comforting and defining knowledge that we have the very spirit of God within us, around us, and among us.

Ezekiel speaks the most comforting and encouraging words, coming from our God, "I will put my spirit in you, that you may live." Psalm 130, our refrain, reassures us, "With the Lord there is mercy and the fullness of redemption." Romans says, "You are in the spirit, if only the spirit of God lives in you." And John's Gospel tells us the story of Lazarus.

The biblical message is clear. We do not find happiness, joy, lasting peace in property, possessions, or public adulation. We find happiness in living the Holy Spirit of God, the spirit of life given to each of us. The pursuit of happiness works as we manage, develop, redirect and protect the spirit of God within us each day. Our vocation is to live in the present always, focusing on the peace that comes from union with God, union with God's creatures, and union with all of creation.

Robert Coles was a Professor of Psychiatry, and an accomplished author at Harvard University. He and his wife, also a psychiatrist, spent the better part of their lives studying children all around the world. They studied what makes children happy, mentally, emotionally, spiritually, morally. They studied what makes children stable, confident, civilized, productive in peaceful societies.

In his book entitled, *The Moral Life of Children**, Robert Coles has a rich story of the qualities of impoverished barrio children in Lima, Peru. His research found that these children, living in dire poverty, filth, and unsanitary conditions, were able to develop five essential qualities or conditions: 1. A subtle intelligence, 2. A compassionate regard for others, 3. An alert sense of humor, 4. A stubborn persistence, and 5. An ever-present modesty.

It strikes me that perhaps a reason that these children can develop this kind of personal, moral, spiritual, emotional health, is that they are not, and never in their lives had been, bogged down with property and possessions. Poverty is an evil and demeaning condition, but so is the danger of over-indulgence in things, comforts, and selfishness. This is a world that can so easily distract and confuse us.

We pray today that the spirit of God, which each of us richly possesses, can and will be the spirit which enlivens us each day. It seems really true that what Jesus said is the absolute truth. "If one wants to find our life, we must lose it in the spirit of God."

---

* Coles, Robert: *The Moral Life of Children.* New York: First Atlantic Monthly Press, 1986, p. 103.

HOLY THURSDAY

EXODUS 12: "This day shall be a memorial feast for you, which all generations shall celebrate with pilgrimage to the Lord, as a perpetual institution."

PSALM 116: "Our blessing-cup is a communion with the blood of Christ."

1 COR 11: "Brothers and Sisters: I received from the Lord what I also handed on to you, that the Lord Jesus, on the night he was handed over, took bread, and, after He had given thanks, broke it and said, 'This is my body that is for you. Do this in remembrance of me.'"

JOHN 13: "Then Jesus poured water into the basin, and began to wash the disciples' feet, and dry them with the towel around his waist."

I recently watched a wonderful documentary on public television on the subject of elephants. The man who filmed and narrated this program has spent over twenty-five years watching and studying elephants. A family of elephants was watched on this particular program. As one of the elephants neared her death, the rest of the family gently took her child away with them, to allow the mother to die in peace. The mother elephant did die. After a significant period of time the family returned to the death sight, and very reverently smelled the remains, gently touched the remains, and quite obviously knew that this had been their family member, the mother of the young elephant, and after this tender ritual, the elephants continued on their journey of life. This was an awesome and touching story for me. It demonstrated the deep power of nature and the power of knowledge of God's creatures, in this case, the family of elephants.

Our celebration this evening, as a family of humanity, is observing reverently the sacred truths, mysteries all, of death, continuing life, service of one another, and of the nurturing of our bodies and souls with the body and blood of Christ, the profound mystery of God being present to us in a body-spirit fashion. We do tonight in a human reverence, what the elephants did according to their nature.

In our scriptures, the Old Testament book of Exodus reminds us, "This day shall be a memorial feast for you, which all generations shall celebrate with pilgrimage to the Lord, as a perpetual institution." Psalm 116 inspired us with the refrain, "Our blessing-cup is a communion with the blood of Christ." The institution of the Eucharist is simply and beautifully described by Paul in the first letter to the Corinthians: "Brothers and Sisters: I received from the Lord what I also handed on to you, that the Lord Jesus, on the night he was handed over, took bread, and, after He had given thanks, broke it and said, 'This is my body that is for you. Do this in remembrance of me.'"

And finally, John's Gospel depicts for us the Servant Jesus, as it states, "Then Jesus poured water into the basin, and began to wash the disciples' feet, and dry them with the towel around his waist."

This night is truly an inspiring and inviting experience of faith, seeking truth. The deepest mysteries of living and dying, of addressing our God, in service and care of one another, and in the ancient and constant institution of the Mass, are reviewed as we gather to pray, to ponder, to look and to listen. Our dignity is renewed in this worship experience. Our faith is deepened in this moment.

This Liturgy helps us to know that faith is an openness to truth, truth comprehended, truth addressed in humility, truth searched for in mystery, truth that continues to set us free as we experience life. Faith empowers us to learn again that nobody knows what the fullest truth is, what it means, what it has been, what it forever will be. We are treated, in the faith journey, to a lesson: to be creatures, to be responsible and accountable, to be vulnerable, to be open. Without that disposition we are in paralysis- humanly, as Christians, as creatures. Tonight's observance helps us to know again that we walk the spiritual path, with direction from family, from church, from life experience, from thought, intuition, reflection, prayer and wonder, from our deepest center. We thank God for this beautiful gift of communal worship, of faith search, of service to one another, of experiencing redemptive love and forgiveness.

GOOD FRIDAY

The cross is a murderer. The cross is sacred. The cross is a universal symbol. The cross belonged to Jesus, and it is the property of each one of us, whether or not we want one. Take up your cross every day and follow me, was Christ's invitation to all followers.

Good Friday is a call to the cross in life. We are educated again as to the value of the cross, the saving nature of the cross, the inevitability of the cross in life. We are humbled by this sign and reality, and become more human each time we embrace our cross. Good Friday invites us through focusing on the cross to deal with life on life's terms, to grow up and to mature in our mortality, our human limits. The cross teaches us to help carry each others' crosses. The cross invites us in to the more difficult aspects of this human journey. We are strengthened by the cross if we embrace it.

The cross also has the power to crush us in bitterness, self-focus and resentment if we try to avoid it. St. Paul exhorts us to "bear our share of the cross," as a way to goodness, holiness, healing and strength. Today we will have the opportunity to reverence the cross later in this service. As we approach it, we recommit ourselves to the cross of Christ, to our own suffering and to charity in assisting each other at the foot of the cross.

We have read the Passion today. Just let it walk quietly with you for the rest of the day. We will soon pray for all the world's people. We recommit ourselves to help the world's poor as we can, to lighten their crosses.

We conclude our prayer today by sharing in Holy Communion. This unites us as closely as possible with the Lord of the Cross, and of Life. We are strengthened to go forth in the fullest way into the life God offers us from now until our death.

The message of Christ is for us to help carry the cross for each other. *Perhaps the greatest charity we can offer or experience is in helping with the burdens of others and allowing them to assist us.*

Most of our crosses are the result of sin. Good Friday asks us again to look at the power of sin in our lives. Freedom comes, and the cross is removed to some degree, as we identify our sin, face our sin, deal with our sin. Courage grows in proportion to our willingness to do this.

As we look at the large crucifix in our sanctuary, as we wear the symbol of the cross as jewelry, as we sign ourselves at the door of the church with holy water, we quietly acknowledge that we are willing to deal with the cross in life. The cross is a stern, but life giving teacher. We pray to be able to pay attention to its call.

GOOD FRIDAY (2)[*]

As we gather this evening, we come to a serious and deliberate pause in the agenda of life, to consider, to ponder, to appreciate the spirit, the emotion, the wonder that surrounds suffering and pain and death in life. Each person must learn the path of suffering, and each person must develop an awareness and willingness to deal with suffering in his or her own life, and in the lives of the people they love and care about. This is a difficult matter, but it is a blessing to stop together and enter into the liturgical observance of pain, suffering, and death, in communion with Jesus, our God and our brother.

The Liturgy of Good Friday unfolds gently and somberly to help us consider the pain, suffering and death of Jesus, of ourselves, of our family and friends. The priest and ministers enter the church in silence, and when they reach the altar, the priest lies on the floor, face down, for a brief time, to signify and represent death. Then the collect prayer gathers the attention of the worshipping community, preparing us to hear the word of God, and to participate in the proclamation of the passion of our Lord.

---

* Editor's note: This homily was originally presented on 4/6/07.

Then follows the reading of the Word, and the proclamation of the Passion of our Lord. This story, of course, is also in some way our story. We prepare for this suffering and dying through the discipline and practice of prayer, acceptance and courage. On Monday of this week the Bishop led the people of the Diocese in consecrating the oils for Sacramental use. The oils are the Oil of Catechumens, which is used for Baptism; the Oil of Chrism, which is used for Confirmation and Ordination; and the Oil of the Sick, which is used for the anointing and preparation for times of suffering and of preparation for death.

When I got home Monday evening I called a good friend, and brother priest, who is preparing for death. His name is Father Dan Dernek.† He has been a priest of this Diocese for 45 years. He has been a gift to thousands of people, many of whom knew deep suffering. Dan and I had the most wonderful talk about his dying, the emotions surrounding this experience, and the discipline Dan is engaging to live until he dies. He said that he lives in the present moment, and practices the peace of Christ in his heart, and that empowers him to live each day that the Lord is giving him. Dan is courageous and a wonderful example of the Passion of Christ in his own life. He blessed me with that conversation, with new courage, strength, and willingness to face my own sufferings and eventually, my own death. This is part of the gift of Good

---

† Editor's note: Fr. Dernek died on June 5, 2007. An obituary may be read online at www.winonapost.com.

Friday, when we together face and consider these moments of our existence.

Next in our liturgy are the prayers for all the people of the world, and this is followed by each person having the opportunity to venerate the cross, which is positioned here as we see it. Each person is welcome to come to the cross to venerate by briefly touching the cross, kissing the cross, or reverently bowing before the cross. We conclude our liturgy by receiving the Body and Blood of the Suffering Christ, and leave when we choose to go, in silence. We ask God to gift us with new courage to carry the cross of suffering, pain and death, in, with and through Christ.

EASTER SUNDAY[*]

ACTS 10:   "God anointed Jesus of Nazareth with the
                  Holy Spirit and power."

PSALM 118:   "This is the day that the Lord has made; let
                  us rejoice and be glad."

COLOSS 3:   "If you were raised with Christ, seek what
                  is above."

JOHN 20:   "Then the other disciple also went in; he
                  saw and believed."

A Baptist friend told me a story about new life coming, the
resurrection if you will, for a twenty dollar bill and for a one
dollar bill. The two bills were standing in line to be shredded
because they were old and worn out, and after the shredding
they would become new bills. So as they are standing there,
to make conversation the one dollar bill says to the twenty,
"So tell me about your life. Where have you been?" The
twenty dollar bill responded, "O, I have had a very exciting
life. I have been to Vegas several times, I have been to Hollywood a few times, I have been to Paris and to Venice, to

[*] Editor's note: This homily was originally presented on 3/23/08.

name a few." Then the twenty dollar bill asked the one dollar bill, "And, you, where have you been?" The one dollar bill thought for a moment, and then said, "Well, I have been to the Catholic Church, the Lutheran Church, the Methodist Church, the Baptist Church." Now don't think about this story when collection time comes today!

We celebrate the Resurrection of Jesus Christ today, with over a billion Christian People around the world. We think of new life, of deeper life, of eternal life. We are invited through our scriptures and through this observance to explore richer life in every dimension of our being as humans.

In our first reading, Acts, we are told, "God anointed Jesus of Nazareth with the Holy Spirit and with power." We believe that we are one with Christ, and that we too are anointed with the Holy Spirit and with power. We have a tremendous capacity for new life, in our body, in our soul, in our mind, in our emotions and passions, in our imagination. Through the power of memory and intellect and by the power to choose and make decisions we can bring new life to self, to others, to the earth which is our home.

Psalm 118, our response today, reminds us where we find new life, as it states, "This is the day the Lord has made; let us rejoice and be glad in it." We are taught again the basic truth of the power of now, of the power of the present moment. The past and the future are thieves, which by engaging worry, regret, and anxiety, rob us of the only raw material we have to make new and deeper life, and that is the present moment. The ancient psalmist knew the deep wisdom of bringing the mind home, again and again, to find life in abundance.

In our second reading, Paul to the Colossians, we are exhorted, "If you were raised with Christ, seek what is above." Life has the potential to always be better, to always have new richness, to always be able to change, but we must seek those conditions, we must choose those conditions. Self-focus, self-pity, chosen bitterness, holding on to resentments and anger, these are the killers of life. The scriptures remind us early and often to "Choose Life!" This is indeed our vocation: to choose new life every day.

And finally, our Gospel Story is a story about believing. John's Gospel says, among other things, "Then the other disciple also went in to the tomb. He saw and believed." The fabric of world unity is based on our ability and power to choose to believe. National governments can only work if the citizens are willing to believe each other. Social structures and all kinds of institutions and groupings only work if there is mutual belief. The virtue of Hope is predicated on our ability to choose to believe. Vows and personal relationships are based on the ability and willingness we have to believe. Life, in all its dimensions, demands every moment of every day, belief.

The disciple went into the tomb, saw, and believed. Easter asks us to go into life, to see and to believe.

Father Collins and I want to thank the Parish Staff, the church cleaners, the church decorators, the musicians, the liturgists and all of the ministers of word and sacrament, who have spent much time and effort to make this Easter celebration beautiful, uplifting, and inspiring. A very Happy Easter to all of you.

SECOND SUNDAY OF EASTER[*]
Confirmation Day

ACTS 12:   "Many signs and wonders were done
              among the people."

PSALM 118:   "Give thanks to the Lord for he is good…"

REVEL 1:   "I was caught up in the spirit of the Lord's
              day…"

JOHN 20:   "Jesus said to his disciples, 'Peace be
              with you; as the Father has sent me, so I
              send you.'"

This weekend here in Rochester, about 200 young Catholics, sophomores in High School, will be confirmed in their Catholic Tradition of Faith, here at St. Pius X, at Resurrection, and at Pax Christi. Fifty-two are of our parish. Confirmation is a public expression and prayer and celebration which is about committed maturity. Confirmation is the willing acceptance for the Community, of a care, of a commitment, of a promise to grow up, to grow in to responsible be-

---

[*] Editor's note: This homily was originally presented on 4/18/04.

havior and thought which will contribute to and redeem the people with whom the confirmed lives, works and plays.

As we pray for our young people being confirmed, we can recall our own confirmation commitment, a few and many years ago, and we can recommit to the Gospel principles which Confirmation calls us to. Each Christian is necessary to further the cause of Christ, according to each person's talents, personality, and history.

Our world needs the presence and spirit of each person who has been given life. Confirmation calls us to give again our spirit, our thoughts, our convictions, our dialogue.
We are called to think clearly, to listen humbly, to study willingly, so that we can help direct the course of good creative, redemptive and saving energy, for the earth, for humanity, for all of creation.

On the front of the Worship Aid for the Confirmation Mass today is the listing of the seven gifts of the Holy Spirit, which we believe we all have, and we believe that these gifts are especially enlivened through our sharing the Sacrament of Confirmation. They have power to do good, and they are in all of us. They are WISDOM, UNDERSTANDING, COUNSEL, FORTITUDE, KNOWLEDGE, PIETY and FEAR OF THE LORD.

A second point of focus for us today is the celebration of and observance of Earth Day, which is celebrated around the entire world on Thursday, April 22, 2004. People all around the world observe this day. It is an opportunity to stop and consider the condition of our home, the earth. It is a day of Gospel responsibility, which asks us to examine our conscience as to how we use the earth, abuse the earth, nurture the earth, and live on the earth.

This year we are being asked to think about the water of the world. We have significantly polluted this basic resource of and for all of life during the last industrial century. We must pull together in study, courage and deliberate choice to protect our water.

We are being asked to study again what we are doing by depleting the rain forests of the world. We know now beyond doubt that the world's weather and regeneration are closely tied to the conditions of our forests, and we know that our oxygen supply is essentially tied to the health or lack thereof in this regard.

We are challenged to review how we generate, use, waste or abuse the energy of our day. Many problems exist in this area of life, and the solution to abuse must come from all of us. No one is excused from entering this difficult and controversial area of life.

Biodiversity is another focus point this year as we observe Earth Day. Biodiversity is all the Earth's plants, animals, ecosystems and genes. It includes the tallest tree, the smallest insect, the most delicate choral reef ecosystem. Biodiversity is what allows the Earth and all of its creatures to adapt and survive.

As humans, we are completely dependent on biodiversity for survival. Yet, we continue to pollute large portions of the earth and its living forms, causing the extinction of entire species.

Our Scriptures and our faith practice demand that we be good stewards of the earth, that we be responsible for the entirety of creation, that we participate in earth functions, never abusing the earth, always studying the earth, always standing in awe of her giftedness and gifting us every day of life.

THIRD SUNDAY OF EASTER*

ACTS 2:   "Jesus…was a man commended to you by God with mighty deeds, wonders and signs, which God worked through him in your midst."

PSALM 16:   "Lord, you will show us the path of life."

1 PETER 1: "Conduct yourselves with reverence during the time of your sojourning."

LUKE 24:   "Jesus took bread, said the blessing, broke it, and gave it to them. With that, their eyes were opened, and they recognized him."

In recent weeks we have heard, on National News, that our current space program is going to be retired in 2010. The space ships will be relegated to museums, thousands of people will lose their jobs, and space travel will be suspended as an American function for a few years, until the new space system is built, perfected, and professionally in place.

This current space effort has transformed the way we see life. This program has radically increased our knowledge of, our

---

* Editor's note: This homily was originally presented on 4/6/08.

180

respect for, and our wonder at, God's universe, our home. We, as Americans, have traveled to the moon, have cooperated with other nations in building and occupying the space platform, have conducted thousands of experiments, done countless hours of research, and have re-defined how we see our earth, our constellation, the Milky Way, and our universe, of which we now know, we are part of as a tiny speck of dust, as it were. The immensity, the simplicity, the mystery of God's creation, and the profound beauty of our life have been deepened beyond our dreams, since President John F. Kennedy, in the early 60's, stated that an American goal was to have people go to the moon and safely return to earth within ten years. As we all know, it happened within five years.

Our scriptures today speak of the same phenomenon two thousand years ago. The people were mystified by the life, the teaching, the entire experience of Jesus. Acts, our first reading states, "Jesus..was a man commended to you by God with mighty deeds, wonders, and signs, which God worked through him in your midst." Acts exhorts us to pay attention to the signs and wonders and mighty deeds which continuously transform our world, increase our knowledge of, and appreciation for, life, as God continuously gives it.

Psalm 16, our response today, reminds us that through our nature, our faculties, our intelligence, our emotions and passions, God will show us the path of life. The Psalm says, "Lord, you will show us the path of life." Life is constantly changing, for us as individuals, and for our world. We find

God only if we use all the gifts that God gives us. We must keep up with the knowledge, the new understandings, the new challenges that continue to unfold before us. The First Letter of Peter exhorts us, "Conduct yourselves with reverence during the time of your sojourning."

We no longer believe that the world is flat. Measuring generations in the conventional manner, that is, twenty years per generation, we have, in the last twenty-six generations, since Christopher Columbus in 1492, transformed our knowledge and appreciation of the nature and the function of our earth, of our galaxy, of our universe several times. The old and limited categories of knowledge do not apply any more, they do not work any more. They are inadequate, limited and limiting. St. Peter tells us to walk with reverence, humility and courage during our lifetime, when and where God has placed us. It is here that we find our salvation. Again, Peter says, "Conduct yourselves with reverence during the time of your sojourning."

And finally, we have the story of the disciples on the road to Emmaus, when Jesus joins them, but they could not see who He was. It was only when Jesus took bread, the commonest of foods of that day, blessed it, broke it, and distributed it to them, that they began to see who Jesus was. The Eucharist, celebrated as the road map and foundation of life today, still opens our eyes to the presence of God in all that life brings. In Eucharist, we see again and again the presence and power of God in our lives.

THIRD SUNDAY OF EASTER (2)[*]

ACTS 3: "I know, Brothers, that you acted out of ignorance, just as your leaders did."

PSALM 4: "Lord, let your face shine on us."

1 JOHN 2: "The way we may be sure that we know him is to keep his Commandments."

LUKE 24: "Then he opened their minds to understand the scriptures."

In a book published last year, entitled *Management Lessons From Mayo Clinic*[†], a delightful story is presented. The story actually happened some time ago. A huge semi truck pulled in to St. Mary's Hospital Emergency Room area, and the driver, a female, went into the emergency room for treatment. The medical team in the ER determined that the driver needed to be hospitalized. She protested, because her big

---

[*] Editor's note: This homily was originally presented on 4/26/09.

[†] Berry, Leonard L and Seltman, Kent D. *Management Lessons From Mayo Clinic.* New York: McGraw-Hill Books, 2008, pp. 33-34.

truck was illegally parked outside the hospital, and her little dog was locked in the cab of the truck.

One of the ER nurses volunteered to take her dog home and to care for it, until she, the patient, was well. Another nurse was a retired over-the-road semi truck driver, and still had his license. He assured the patient that he would contact the police and the mall in town to get permission to park the truck there until she had recovered. And he did just that.

The story is about the lessons contained in today's scriptures. In addition to the medical services, which the patient would pay for, the Hospital Staff went way beyond what they would have had to do. They did not act out of ignorance, when they were apprised of her difficult situation, as did the apostles and the believers did, when it came to Jesus. The Hospital Staff went the extra mile to bring comfort, reassurance, and peace of mind to the ill truck driver.

Psalm 4 states, "Lord, let your face shine on us." In 2009, we are challenged to remember that the face of Jesus that shines on each of us is the face in front of us in the moment. Jesus' face today is your face and mine, as we meet people, as we comfort people, as we serve people. We, as members of the Body of Christ, are the hands, the feet, the face of Jesus. What a great vocation, what a great meditation, what a great empowerment it is to remember this fact: Your face is the face of Christ, as you meet people.

First John reminds us today that the way we know that we know Jesus, is to keep his commandments. To work to have integrity of spirit and behavior, is the greatest possible path to happiness. To be at one with the Lord is peace, and happiness, and brings peace and happiness to those around us, to our communities, and to our world.

The 24th Chapter of Luke's Gospel, which we hear today, tells the story of Jesus opening the minds of his followers to understand the scriptures. Every Sunday the Scriptures are read for us. As we try to pay attention over the years, eventually more and more sense comes, more and more appreciation of these ancient sacred writings comes, empowering us to deepen our lives, to find more peace, to have more insight with which to help each other. This is one of the gifts of faithful, week by week, practice of our faith. We learn of God the same way that we experience everything else-slowly, with patience, with practice, with attention. Our hearts and souls are deepened as we spend the days that God gives to each of us, and our lives continue to be richer.

The nurses at the St. Mary's Hospital ER went the extra mile to help the patient who was alone, frightened and in need. Every day, someone crosses our paths in similar circumstances. If we are paying attention, we can respond according to the command of Jesus.

FOURTH SUNDAY OF EASTER

ACTS 4:   "Peter, filled with the Holy Spirit, said, 'Jesus Christ is the stone rejected by you, the builders, which has become the corner stone.'"

1 JOHN 3: "See what love the Father has bestowed on us."

JOHN 10: "Jesus said: 'I am the good shepherd. A good shepherd lays down his life for his sheep.'"

We continue with the Easter message of love, encouragement, life, growth, and depth. A story I heard recently perhaps can give us a new Easter insight into our lives. A young mother took her small son to a piano concert. A few minutes before the concert was to begin, the mother left the child in his seat and went out to the bathroom. As she was returning, the lights began slowly to dim for the beginning of the concert. She panicked as she approached her seat to learn that her son was gone, and at that very moment, the stage curtain parted, exposing a huge and magnificent Steinway Piano on the stage, and sitting at that piano was her little son, innocently picking out with one finger, "Twinkle, Twinkle, Little Star."

At that very moment, the internationally acclaimed pianist, Paderewski, made his entrance, quickly moved to the piano, and, whispering in the boy's ear, said, "Don't quit. Keep playing." Then, leaning over the little boy, Paderewski reached down with his left hand and began filling in a bass part. And with his right hand, he reached around the boy on the right and began a running obbligato.

Together the old master and the young novice transformed what could have been a frightening situation into a wonderfully creative experience. The story concludes with the audience having been so touched by this accidental and spontaneous moment, that they could not remember any of the great music Paderewski played that evening, only the beautiful duet by master and child, "Twinkle, Twinkle, Little Star."

The Easter message to us is, "Don't quit. Keep playing." The Spirit of the risen Christ, and the loving arms of God enfolding us, is the truth of Easter. The love that God bestows on us, as we were reminded in the second reading today, is absolutely adequate for a rich life. The Good Shepherd is always here for us. Learning this again and again is what dissipates our fears and anxieties, and enables us to live fully, to live in an Easterly manner.

Jonathan Swift had a favorite saying, "May you live all the days of your life." Easter tells us again that life is precious, life is present, life is for living. Thomas Edison is quoted as saying, "If we did all the things we are capable of doing, we would literally astound ourselves." Easter is about being astounded by the power in life that God has given to each of us.

Easter, then, is about new attitudes, rising spirits, confident minds. Easter is the reinvigoration of tired hearts, broken wills, discouraged souls.

Easter spirit is a living, moving awareness that calls us to deepen our life and appreciation of life each day. Easter is about paying attention. Easter is about focus. Easter is the annual invitation to new life, rich life, joyous life.

Easter teaches us again each year that, although we walk with some darkness, despair, discouragement and bitterness, we do have the strength within to rise again and to renew our spirit. It is a choice we make again and again. We balance our being as we use all of the powers which God has given to us. We learn strength and rejuvenation by the Easter discipline of getting up and walking with the Holy Spirit of God which resides in each one of us.

Easter is the story of homecoming every year. We come back to the basic truth of our dignity, of our worth, of our strength. Thomas Edison knew this Easter secret when he said, "If we did all the things we are capable of doing, we would literally astound ourselves."

FOURTH SUNDAY OF EASTER (2)

ACTS 13: "I have made you a light to the Gentiles, that you may be an instrument of salvation to the ends of the earth."

PSALM 100: "We are his people, the sheep of his flock."

REV 7: "I, John, had a vision of a great multitude, which no one could count, from every nation, race, people and tongue."

JOHN 10: "My sheep hear my voice....No one can take them out of my hand."

Maya Angelou, the well-known African-American Poet, wrote a poem in 2005 entitled, "Amazing Peace – A Christmas Poem."* The poem is short, and reads in part, "We clap our hands and welcome the Peace of Christmas. We beckon this good season to wait awhile with us. We, Baptist and

---

* Angelou, Maya. *Amazing Peace A Celebration.* New York: Random House, 2005.

Buddhist, Methodist and Muslim, say come. Peace. Come and fill us and our world with your majesty. We, the Jew and the Jainist, the Catholic and the Confucian, implore you to stay awhile with us so we can learn by your shimmering light how to look beyond complexion and see community. It is Christmas time, a halting of hate time. On this platform of peace, we can create a language to translate ourselves to ourselves and to each other."

This beautiful idea expressed by Maya Angelou is based on the fundamental truth that all people are one, and that we are commissioned to make and sustain peace. No individual or group of individuals is better than anyone else. We are the family of humanity. We are brothers and sisters. We are one.

The scriptures today remind us of this truth. Acts of the Apostles, our first reading, teaches not Jew and Gentile, but one people. Psalm 100, our response, refrains, "We are His people, the sheep of His flock." In Revelation, our second reading, John has a vision of a great multitude, from every nation, race, people and tongue. And our Gospel reminds us that we all hear God, not just the few, the privileged.

Pope Pius XII, in the late 1940's, wrote an Encyclical entitled, *Mystici Corporis*,† the mystical body of Christ, the Church. In that encyclical, the pope stated that, in some way, all human beings belong to the Church, all belong to God, all

---

† Editor's note: This encyclical may be found online at www.vatican. va/holy father/pius xii/encyclicals.

are one. Our life's work is to eradicate hate, prejudice and division, and to work tirelessly for peace, unity and respect for all.

We are reminded also today to take care of those among us who are vulnerable, weak, poor, lost, unimportant in the eyes of the world. We have, as the Lord reminded us, the poor and the marginalized with us always. It is easy to forget that. Perhaps a good practice for each of us would be to do some small kindness for someone in need each week. Each of us has a neighbor, an acquaintance, a family member, who is broken at the moment, who is lonely at the moment, who is in need of reassurance at the moment. A cup of water, a smile, a brief visit, can lighten the load.

Another aspect of the Easter message is that Christ has gone to the Father, and He has sent us, each and every one of us, to be his mind, his word, his hands, his heart. Easter reminds us that Christ can only be present through you and me. We call ourselves the Body of Christ, and that, indeed, is who we are. We teach that each of us is imbued with the Holy Spirit of God, and that too, is our great privilege and gift. We find our greatest peace and happiness in using these gifts of God with and for each other.

FIFTH SUNDAY OF EASTER*

ACTS 14: "They strengthened the spirits of the disciples and exhorted them to persevere in faith."

REV 21: "I heard a loud voice from the throne saying, 'Behold, God's dwelling is with the human race.'"

JOHN 13: "I give you a new commandment: love one another. As I have loved you so you should love one another."

The development of the English language was and is an interesting process. Many of our words came through the old classical languages, Latin and Greek. Some of the most interesting and graphic words for me are "courage," "encourage," "discourage." "Courage" comes from the Latin word *cor*, which is translated "heart." "Encourage" is from two Latin words, *en* and *cor*, which translates "to put the heart in." And finally, "discourage" comes from two Latin words *di* and *cor*, which means "to tear the heart out." The graphic imagery of these words says it all for me.

---

* Editor's note: This homily was originally presented on 5/9/04.

192

If you and I have heart, we are strong, we have courage. If some one else's word praises us, our heart is put in and we are ready to move. And, if someone else's word tears at us, the heart comes out, and we are weakened, perhaps defeated.

Our scriptures today revolve around courage, encouragement and discouragement. Acts says that Barnabas and Paul strengthened the spirits of the disciples, strengthening them to stay the course in the face of opposition. Revelation reminds us that God lives with us every day, and that truth is immediately encouraging. John's Gospel tells us how to encourage each other: simply love one another. How simple the truth, how difficult the practice sometimes.

Sociology tells us that most of the people behind bars, in our jails and prisons, experienced, among other things in their developing years, significant discouragement and very little positive reinforcement. We know that children who grow up in constant negativity are definitely affected in a negative manner. Conversely, we know that praise and support builds strong personalities in the young.

Each of us has probably experienced a few times in life, the pleasure of encouragement or the pain of having our heart cut out by sharp words. And, most probably, each of us has been the author, the source of words of encouragement and of moments of hurtful dialogue, wounding others through a lack of charity.

Life's quality is, to a great extent, determined by our willingness to be sensitive to the feelings of others, and to the condition of our own soul. To be encouraging and to avoid being a discouraging person, we need to establish continually a balance and health in our emotions and a discipline and calm direction in our spirit. This is the work of the growing human Christian being. The message of Jesus is fundamentally one of giving and receiving and sharing dignity. The Gospel lives and moves in our lives according to the courage we develop, the encouragement we are willing to give, and the discouraging attitudes and behaviors we are willing to curtail and avoid.

This approach to life demands a continuing maturity and a constant generosity. This way of life can only happen with deliberation. In other words, we are courageous and encouraging only by deliberate and thoughtful and mature choice. This gift does not come easy and is certainly not automatic. It is Gospel choice. It is virtue. It is difficult.

Fifty years ago, on May 6, 1954, with great courage and with constant encouragement, a young British medical student by the name of Roger Bannister became the first person in the history of the world to break the four minute mile record. He ran the mile in 3 minutes, 59.4 seconds, breaking a record people had been chasing for 20 years. (*Chronicle*, May 1954). The power of courage and encouragement is profound, is Gospel, is essential to happy life.

FIFTH SUNDAY OF EASTER (2)[*]

ACTS 14:   "(Paul and Barnabas) strengthened the spirits
            of the disciples and exhorted them to
            persevere in the faith."

PSALM 145: "I will praise your name forever, my King and
            my God."

REV 21:   "Behold, God's dwelling is with the human
            race."

JOHN 13:   "I give you a new commandment: love one
            another."

As we come to the month of May, we think again of all the
young people who will be graduating from high school and
college in the next few weeks. The students themselves, their
families and friends, really all of us, ponder the possibilities
for them as individuals, and as members of our society. The
students consider their gifts, their limitations, the possibilities
that lie before them. They know that life is going to change
significantly as they step in to more independence, and assume more responsibility.

---

[*] Editor's note: This homily was originally presented on 5/6/07.

The scriptures today give all of us, but especially these young graduates, some very good advice. In our first reading from Acts, we are told that Paul and Barnabas, "strengthened the spirits of the disciples and exhorted them to persevere in the faith." "Disciple" is a word from the Latin language, which literally is translated "student." What great advice for these young students and for all of us. Persevere in the faith!

The exhortation of the Psalm response, Psalm 145, is equally as important as persevering in the faith, or rather, it is part of the process of perseverance in the faith. "I will praise your name forever, my King and my God." The second reading from Revelation, helps the students and all of us remember the most important truth any of us will ever learn, and that is the fact that, "God's dwelling is with the human race." This truth is the foundation for happiness, for peace of mind, for success in any venture of life. God lives among us, within us, and in every moment and experience that life will ever present to us individually, and as citizens of the earth. Without this framework, life cannot be anything but empty, disappointing, bleak, and boring.

The Gospel of John sums up what the first three readings present as success, namely, to persevere in faith, to remember that God is always with us, and to pray and praise God. The Gospel simply says, "I give you a new commandment: love one another." This is the foolproof way to happiness: "Love one another."

In the current issue of *America* magazine, there is an article entitled, "Advice for College Grads."† One of the people offering advice in the article is Tim Russert, who is managing editor and moderator of NBC's "Meet the Press," and a political analyst for "NBC's Nightly News," and "The Today Show." He named his comments, "Now it is your turn." He begins his article thus: "I remember so vividly when, as a young boy, I heard John Fitzgerald Kennedy conclude his inaugural address this way: 'With History the final judge of our deeds, let us go forth to lead the land we love, asking God's blessing and God's help, but knowing that here on earth God's work must truly be our own.'" Then he gave some examples. In Albania, a young girl loses her father at age 8, and leaves home as a teenager, in her own words, "To care for the unwanted, the lepers, the people with aids, believing the works of love are the works of peace." This of course is Mother Teresa. In Poland, it was a young electrician named Lech Walesa, the son of a carpenter, who transformed a nation from communism to democracy. In South Africa, Nelson Mandela, President Nelson Mandela, a brave black man who worked his way through law school as a police officer, spent 28 years in prison to make one central point: we are all created equal. On September 11, it was the police officers, fire fighters, and rescue workers who redefined modern-day heroism.

---

† McDermott, Jim. "Advice for College Grads," *America*, May 7, 2007, p. 20.

And he concludes his article by saying to the graduates, "It is now your turn. You can help save lives, provide prosperity, record history, prevent disease and train young minds." The scriptures today remind all of us that we are extremely privileged, and it is now our turn to live the Gospel to the best of our ability.

Most of you are aware that yesterday and today is First Communion here at St. Pius. 34 second grade young people from our parish are receiving First Communion. Their names appear on the front of the parish bulletin. If you know one or another of these children, perhaps you could send them a note, give a small gift, or give them a call.

I recently learned that "bread," in most languages, is the same word as "food." So when Jesus wanted to say, I am your food, he didn't call himself meat or apples. "I am your bread," means "Stay alive by consuming me." These little people are joining us in the mysterious journey of staying alive by consuming Jesus in Eucharist.

SIXTH SUNDAY OF EASTER

ACTS 15: "It is the decision of the Holy Spirit and of us not to place on you any burden beyond these necessities..."

REV 21: "For the glory of God gave it light, and its lamp was the Lamb."

JOHN 14: "The Advocate, the Holy Spirit, whom the Father will send in my name, will teach you everything and remind you of all that I told you....I have told you this before it happens, so that when it happens you may believe."

Today's Scriptures lead us to see that our Roman Catholic tradition is indeed *a tradition of change*. Our identity, religiously, began in Bethlehem, when and where Jesus was born. One of the first changes in the plan came by way of a dream for Joseph, when he was told to leave immediately and unexpectedly, to save the life of the infant Jesus from the hand of hatred in the person of King Herod. This change gave birth to courage and to trust.

Twelve years later a big change happened when the parents found the child Jesus in the temple speaking with the teachers. When they questioned him, he told them it was his Father's will that led him to disobey them, his parents. Mary pondered these things in her heart, and learned the change of trust and openness to the providence of God, as life unfolds it for each and for all of us.

The lived tradition of the followers of Jesus lasted, we think, about 30 to 50 years, and then a huge change came to be. The stories began to be written down, by various and sundry people. We call this change our Holy Bible, our Scriptures. All through the first three centuries of Christianity, people were killed for their beliefs, because the Roman Empire leaders were afraid of this new movement. This painful chapter of our history inspired courage and perseverance. In the third century we began another change in worship of our Christian God. We began, for the first time to build churches. This change developed broader communities. A significant change came with the development of the Nicene Creed at the Council of Nicea in 325 CE. This change still is part of our worship mode today.

Throughout the centuries, corruption, renewal and expanding of the world to new nations brought changes through cultural filters, historical emphasis, and national personalities. The worshipping Church survived all of history and the ups and downs. We went through the big change from married clergy to celibacy in the eleventh century, through the foul corruption of the dark ages, leading to the protestant reformation, beginning in 1517, and the Council of Trent, which defined the behavior of the church from 1545 until modern times.

From the seventeenth century until fifty years ago, we experienced the Jansenist heresy which translated into almost no Catholic going to Holy Communion before going to confession. We experienced an overwhelming preoccupation with sin. Today, it appears that we perhaps have lost all sense of sin, and our culture is going through deep trials of no boundaries, limits and lost responsibilities.

Changes in the ability to travel have radically changed our church; from the Holy Land to Europe; from Europe to Africa and the New World called America. Changes such as the development of the university, agriculture, the city; literacy, the printing press in the 16th century; telephones, television, the computer and air travel in the 19th and 20th centuries.

We are coming to know through the Hubble Telescope that changes are constant in our universe, through medical science that changes enable us to live much longer and richer lives, through lived experience, that we must develop medical ethics, beginning and end of life issue ethics, and we know that the growing population of the world, the experience of our poisoning the earth, especially throughout the last century, and other issues demand the change of new ethical standards which will protect life at all levels.

We have been brought, through our practicing of faith and reading of scripture and worship of God, to the realization that all of God's creation is one, that all of life is one, that we humans are participants in the life of God, the life of the universe, the life of the earth, and that we may no longer abuse any portion of it without self-destruction and annihilation. We are asked today by the scriptures to continue to change and grow and become better people of God and more responsible participants in life. We are not asked to control life, but to be part of the wisdom of God in directing the life given us each day.

SIXTH SUNDAY OF EASTER (2)

ACTS 10: "The person of any nation who fears the Lord and acts uprightly is acceptable to God. The Holy Spirit descended on all who were listening."

PSALM 98: "The Lord has revealed to the nations his saving power."

1 JOHN 4: "Let us love one another because love is of God; everyone who loves is begotten of God."

JOHN 15: "Jesus said to his disciples: 'As the Father has loved me, so I have loved you. Live on in my love.'"

A very close friend of mine is an ELCA Lutheran Pastor. He and his wife have been close friends for years. He fondly tells the story about when He was attending Luther Seminary, years ago, in Decorah, Iowa, during which time he belonged to their world renowned choir. The choir took a trip to Germany to sing and perform in several towns. The students would be farmed out to families for their overnight accommodations at the various stops. At one stop, his name was drawn last, and he was assigned to an older couple, both of whom were in their eighties, and neither of whom spoke any English.

Don knew no German, so they had a German-English dictionary as the tool of communication between them. He felt he was destined to the worst three days of his life, but these three days turned out to be the highlight of the trip for him, and have been three of the best days of his entire life. Here is why.

He went home with the old couple. When they arrived, the wife served coffee and cake at the kitchen table. They took out the dictionary, and proceeded to talk into the late hours of the night. It turned out that the old man told my friend Don that the couple had had three sons. Two of the boys were killed during combat in World War II, while fighting against the American Army. The third son was captured by the American Armies, placed in an American prison camp for two years, until the war was over. Shortly after he was released from prison camp, he died of a disease which he contracted while in prison. Thus, his hosts had lost three sons, all of their children, to war, at American hands.

Don said that he was almost paralyzed with fear, not knowing how to try to dialogue with these people. They must have sensed his apprehension, and the husband, in very halting English, said something like, "We have forgiven the hatred which brings war between peoples and nations. We Germans were doing what you Americans were doing during that war, fighting for our side. Hopefully, our two nations have learned that war serves humanity very badly. Our boys lived and died for what they believed. They are with God. Our job is to live, and to promote peace through love and forgiveness of one another."

Don said that the next three days were a total joy, and that these people continued to be his friends until they died many years ago.

Our scriptures today lead us, as it were, to that humble kitchen table in Northern Germany. Acts 10, our first reading, reminds us that any person of any nation who fears the Lord and acts uprightly is pleasing to God. The old German Father who had lost three sons at war taught the young seminarian who came from the nation responsible for the death of his sons that we are all to seek the Lord, not revenge.

Psalm 98, our response, tells us again that every nation, if we are opened as a nation, can receive God's saving power.

The First Letter of John, our second reading, simply states a challenging truth, "Let us love one another, because love is of God."

And John's Gospel is a simple and fitting summary statement for today's teaching, "Jesus said to his disciples: 'As the Father has loved me, so I have loved you. Live on in my love.'"

The message of the Word is always universal, that is, given to and for all nations and peoples. And the message is love, forgiveness, and peace. This is every person's life's work.

THE ASCENSION[*]

ACTS 1:   "It is not for you to know the times or seasons that the Father has established by his own authority. But you will receive power when the Holy Spirit comes upon you, and you will be my witnesses...to the ends of the earth."

EPHES 1:   "May God give you a spirit of wisdom and revelation resulting in knowledge of him. May the eyes of your hearts be enlightened, that you may know what is the hope that belongs to his call."

LUKE 24:   "Repentance for the forgiveness of sin would be preached in his name...You are witnesses of this."

We observe today the Feast of the Ascension of Jesus. It is a day of study of the beyond, the indescribable, the transcendent. We continue to learn today, how to stand in awe, how to believe in something bigger than any one of us, bigger than all of us put together.

---

[*] Editor's note: This homily was originally presented on 5/23/04.

Today's observance is a continued call to humility, openness before the mystery of God present in our world, and of God being totally beyond our comprehension. The Ascension teaches us limits, and the wisdom found in believing, in our inability to figure out every truth.

Today teaches us that human mental analytical power is limited. Today shows us again that mental comprehension, intellectual analysis and human understanding only take us to the brink of mystery, of knowledge of the beyond. Indeed, as Scripture teaches, "God's ways are not our ways."

This past week brought me a special treat. Last Monday the United States Government announced that the great American National Bird, the Bald Eagle, had been taken off the endangered species list for the first time in over forty years. And on last Sunday, one day before this announcement, my brother and I watched for some time, a family of Bald Eagles in their nest high above the Root River, about fifteen miles southeast of Rochester. The parents and the baby eagles could be seen in the giant nest, which is perched near the top of a huge evergreen tree.

In the 40's and 50's, a herbicide and pesticide called DDT was used in agriculture in this country. It poisoned so many things, including the eagle, and took the species almost to extinction. I can remember not seeing a single eagle in the 60's, 70's and early 80's. It took 25 years to regain stability for the eagle. This was a story of rushing to judgment, of ignorance, of assuming that we had adequate knowledge to further creation. In our arrogance and near-sightedness, we destroyed many aspects of creation, perhaps some species of beings in creation.

The Ascension, on the other hand, is a story of standing in wait, a story of humility, a story of our admission that we are not God, but that we are creatures who participate in the grand mystery of creation, redemption, life. Ascension is about what the Scriptures speak to today. As Jesus says in Acts, "It is not for us to know the times and seasons the Father has established." Perhaps this is the manner in which we would be saved from our own arrogance. We participate in life, in mystery. We do not comprehend all. We understand and comprehend some truths. We always stand in awe before the large truth, called mystery.

Ephesians prays for us, "May God give you a spirit of wisdom and revelation resulting in knowledge of Him. May the eyes of your hearts be enlightened, that you may know the hope that belongs to his call." Knowledge, in other words, goes well beyond comprehension and analytical exactness and precision, to wonder, awe, appreciation, intuition, pondering, consideration. How deep is the power that God gives to us, as we share in this universe of life and destiny. We humbly and courageously address this reality today and each day of life. What a beautiful way to worship our God and to spend our time and energy!

And, finally, Luke's Gospel asserts that "We are witnesses of this." A witness is not the author, is not the creator, is not the provider and owner. A witness is a mindful, fully alive human, who appreciates living truth, who shares and bears it to others, who ponders its reality to further life, love and peace. Our vocation, it would seem, from the exhortation of Scripture today, is to be creature, fully alive, appreciative and alert, willing to further our participation and appreciation of the entire experience called life.

PENTECOST SUNDAY

ACTS 2:   "Now there were devout Jews from every nation
            under heaven…Galileans, Parthians, Medes,
            Elamites, Mesopotamians, Judeans,
            Cappadocians, people from Pontus and Asia,
            Phrygia and Pamphylia, Egypt and Libya,
            Romans, Cretans and Arabs."

1 COR 12: "For in one Spirit we were all baptized into one
            body, whether Jews or Greeks, slaves or free
            persons…"

JOHN 20:   "On the evening of that first day of the week,
            when the doors were locked where the disciples
            were, for fear of the Jews, Jesus came and
            stood in their midst, and said to them,
            'Peace be with you.'"

A volunteer mother, while working for an organization that
delivers lunches to elderly shut-ins, sometimes took her six
year old daughter on her afternoon rounds. The daughter was
unfailingly intrigued by the various appliances of old age,
particularly the canes, walkers and wheelchairs. One day the
mother saw the child staring a pair of false teeth soaking in a

glass. The mother was bracing for the inevitable barrage of questions, when her daughter simply turned to her and said, "Mommy, the tooth fairy will never believe this."

Today is Pentecost for the entire Christian world, for more than one billion people, more than one-seventh of the world's population. In the first reading, sixteen nations were listed dramatically to demonstrate the power of the movement in the ancient world. This feast is a teacher of universalism, a picture of the globe and its people. Pentecost is a reminder and a demonstrator of openness, inclusivity, Holy Communion of all of humanity. This feast speaks loudly of our need to be our brothers' and sisters' keepers.

Pentecost is about bringing peace in the midst of fear, sharing common humanity in the face of racism and nationalism. Pentecost is about focusing on God, our Creator, and then defining all people as brother and sister. This feast sheds the scales of prejudice from our eyes, and strips our hearts clean of the dross that condemns anyone as inferior or undeserving of our respect and protection.

Jesus' statement to the disciples locked in the room through fear was, "Peace be with you." Our world is anything but peaceful these days, and the call of today is to regroup, stay the course of peace, work for harmony and unity between peoples. Fifty years ago next month, when this parish was formed, our city and our parish were almost totally Caucasian. Today we are made up of dozens of races, nationalities and cultural backgrounds. Fifty years ago, Rochester was 99% Christian. Today several other world religions are represented in our midst. Pentecost calls us to this change, to this new horizon, to this uncomfortable stretch.

On an individual level, Pentecost is a reminder of the gifts and fruits of the Holy Spirit. The scriptures describe quite specifically what the powers are that we have as the gift of God. Each of us is endowed with a person power plan called personality, and each of us has been blessed with emotions, convictions, knowledge, prudence and wisdom; we have been given passion and vision and insight. We have the ability to analyze, manage, perform tasks, plan agendas and the ability to make life rich and gratifying. In short, the very spirit of God is to some degree operative in each of us.

Some of us, from our school days, remember Francis Thompson's "The Hound of Heaven."* This poem is perhaps one of the most well-known spiritual autobiographies. Thompson had suffered from a lifelong addiction to alcohol and drugs and dissipation. In desperation, he began to write to find his soul, his gifts of Pentecost, as it were. In his poem, "The Hound of Heaven," Francis Thompson begins,

> "I fled Him, down the nights and down the days;
> I fled Him, down the arches of the years;
> I fled Him, down the labyrinthine ways
> Of my own mind; and in the midst of tears

---

* Editor's note: This poem may be found, among other places, at http://poetry.elcore.net.

I hid from Him, and under running laughter."

Perhaps this poem is so well-known and so often read because it describes part of many of our journeys. From the depths of our own darkness from time to time, Pentecost is a new call to hope, to determination, to courage – to realize again that the power of God is in us, and that, if we can stop running away, we have the strength to overcome.

Life is a series of rebounds, an experience in getting back to our feet again and again, a call to believe in our strength rather that wallow in our victimhood of weakness and compromise, which is part of all human life. Pentecost is about radical and faithful life choice. As the Old Testament reminded the Jews and continues to remind us, "Choose life then." Pentecost is life and love and the essence of the journey from God, through time, space, energy and experience, back to God. The Psalms say, "The Lord is my light and my salvation." Pentecost says, "Let the Lord be your light and your salvation."

PENTECOST SUNDAY (2)

ACTS 2:   "When the time of Pentecost was fulfilled, they
            were all in one place together…there were
            devout Jews from every nation under heaven."

PSALM 104: "Lord, send out your spirit, and renew the face
            of the earth."

I COR 12:   "There are different kinds of spiritual gifts, but
            the same spirit."

JOHN 20:   "Jesus said to them again, 'Peace be with you.
            As the Father has sent me, so I send you.'"

On May 17, 1954, at the Supreme Court in Washington, DC,
Chief Justice Earl Warren announced the opinion of the Court
in "Brown vs. Board of Education." This historical ruling
stated that "separate but equal" schools were unconstitu-
tional. One year later, fifty years ago this year, the Supreme
Court ruled that this decision be enforced, "With all deliberate speed."

This ruling set off a period in American History which would
rival the power of Pentecost for the ancient Jews and follow-

215

ers of Christ, as the fire came upon them in that room in Jerusalem. Racism in America, until fifty years ago, was the reality that kept hatred, injustice, fear and deliberate human malice alive between races and classes of people, the haves and the have-nots. While racism is not totally defeated in America, the social fabric of this country has improved much; so it is with the Holy Spirit of Pentecost. Christians are not sin-free, perfect and totally God-like today, but the issues of divisiveness have been diminished significantly.

Pentecost and the end to racism in America are about unity: unity with God, with all people, with nature, with the earth, with the universe. Unity of mind, body, spirit; unity with all of reality, unity within society – these movements point to the truth that all of creation, all of life, is *one*. Humans have put up the arbitrary and incorrect boundaries and divisions which have led us into the lie, into death, into hatred and violence. Pentecost and racial respect are movements which bring healing, advancement, correction of life course and union with God, which is heaven. In each instance, the spirit of Pentecost, and racial respect, a continuing human choice is needed. We choose unity or we fall into divisiveness.

Fifty years ago, black people were not welcome in our schools, churches, hospitals, restaurants. Today they mostly are. At the time of Christ, gentiles were not welcome by the Jews. Today, they mostly are. The current call for all of us is to continue to work the Holy Spirit within for constant conversion and regeneration toward goodness, peace, respect and unity. It does not come easy, as history teaches clearly, at both the individual and social levels.

Today, a new dimension has appeared, and that is that the world has become smaller through transportation, communication and frequent social interaction between the hundreds of cultures, nations, philosophies and religions. The challenge of Pentecost and the challenge of being free from prejudice for each of us has moved to new and more demanding heights. God is calling us to live in peace on this planet, to respect all decency and to fight for the rights of all people. In other words, justice and honor and searching for truth are not optional. They are of the essence of the Christian life.

The scriptures offered for our reflection today point us toward unity. A concrete step toward unity within and among us is to identify, name and acknowledge our own biases. Am I biased against the old, the young, blacks or browns or yellows or white trash; do I scoff at long hair on males or poor taste in dress on females; are Republicans or Democrats in my crosshairs; and on and on they go.

There is a famous and effective Christian principle which states, "Identify, don't compare." To identify my biases will empower me to accept and address the biases which have become part of my consciousness, part of my journey, part of my identity. I do no good by comparing me to you or to Susan or to George. Pentecost invites me to come to a deeper knowledge, love and acceptance of me, so that, in health, I can reach out more effectively and generously. Identification of moral blindness in prejudice and bias is a huge step toward spiritual and a fuller human growth. That is, at least, part of the story of Pentecost.

PENTECOST SUNDAY (3)[*]

ACTS 2: "And they were all filled with the Holy Spirit."

PSALM 104: "Lord, send out your Spirit, and renew the face of the earth."

1 COR 12: "There are different kinds of spiritual gifts but the same spirit."

JOHN 20: "Jesus came and stood in their midst, and said to them, 'Peace be with you.'"

George Bernard Shaw wrote, "This is the true joy of life: the being used up for a purpose recognized by yourself as a mighty one; being a force of nature instead of a feverish, selfish little clot of ailments and grievances, complaining that the world will not devote itself to making you happy."[†]

This quote is perhaps a modern day statement about what Pentecost is to be about, the unselfish and deliberate giving

---

[*] Editor's note: This homily was originally presented on 5/27/07.

[†] Warren, Rick: *The Purpose Driven Life.* Grand Rapids: Zondervan, 2002, p. 33.

219

of our lives to each other. The scriptures today all speak of the Spirit of the Lord, given for and to us, for the development of, and salvation of, the world and all its people.

Acts states, "And they were all filled with the Holy Spirit." Our Psalm response, Psalm 104, has us speak the invitation, "Lord, send out your Spirit, and renew the face of the earth." In the second reading, Paul says to the Corinthians, and to us, "There are different kinds of spiritual gifts, but the same spirit." And John's Gospel states, "Jesus came and stood in their midst, and said to them, 'Peace be with you.'"

Pentecost is a day when we recommit to live our spirit, to share our spirit, to contribute our spirit, for the welfare of all. Pentecost is a celebration of the fact that we all share in the Holy Spirit of God, and Pentecost is an annual review as to how we tend and share that spirit. We have the Sprit of God in communion with each other and with all of creation.

Richard Rohr‡, the noted Franciscan speaker and author, contends that we find out who we are through this Pentecost spirit. He says that if we want to know who we are, we should study and prayerfully reflect on our relationships: our relationship to ourselves, our relationship to each other, our relationship with all creatures, the animals and the plants and the earth, our relationship to the universe, and our relationship with God. This study, he contends, will show us clearly

---

‡ Editor's note: More information on Fr. Rohr may be found at http://www.cacradicalgrace.org/richard-rohr.

who and what we are at any given point in life. This is truly the message of Pentecost. We are, and participate in, a holy communion with each other, with all of creation, with all of time, and with the eternal God. A Pentecost review of this truth redefines our focus, and redirects our spirit with, for and to our eternal God.

Pentecost is a wonderful celebration of our power, of our dignity, of our human nature, as we develop our lives in the time that God gives us. Pentecost is an invitation to true happiness, found by reaching out to others, to creation and to God. Pentecost is the annual reminder that to find happiness, we must lose ourselves. The ego must go! Jesus taught, "If you want to find your life, you must lose it, for the sake of others and of all."

George Bernard Shaw knew this truth as he wrote, "This is the true joy of life: the being used up for a purpose recognized by yourself as a mighty one; being a force of nature instead of a feverish, selfish little clot of ailments and grievances, complaining that the world will not devote itself to making you happy." This is the teaching of Pentecost.

On a personal note, 46 years ago today (tomorrow), I laid facedown on the Winona Cathedral Sanctuary floor and listened to the choir chant the Communion of Saints, as my five classmates and I prepared to be ordained to the priesthood. I was scared to death, and can remember thinking, "What on earth am I getting myself into?" Forty-six years later, I know that I have had a wonderful life as a priest, sharing the mystery of the Lord with others through word, sacrament and community.

I invite any man, young or old, if you are searching for a meaningful life, to consider priesthood. It is a very happy way to live. I will perhaps get in trouble for saying this, but I hope one day good women, as well as men will be welcomed to our priesthood in the Catholic Church. In conclusion, I thank you for your great kindness to me for the past four years here at St. Pius X. You have made this a most welcoming parish family, and I thank you.

Ordinary Time (2)

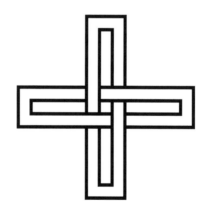

TRINITY SUNDAY

EXODUS 34: "O Lord, do come along in our company. Pardon our wickedness and sins, and receive us as your own."

2 COR 13: "Brothers and sisters, rejoice. Mend your ways, encourage one another, live in peace."

JOHN 3: "God so loved the world that He gave his only son."

An ancient poem states:
"When the lens you look through
    Reflects your personal bias,
    Your view of reality is clouded.
    Truth simply is.
    The clouded mind cannot know it."[*]

We Catholic Christians observe today the feast of the Trinity, the pre-eminent symbol with which we attempt to describe the Mystery of God. The Trinity is a good symbol, since it has lasted throughout the many centuries of Christianity. It is

---

[*] Soeng, Mu: *Trust in Mind The Rebellion of Chinese Zen.* Somerville: Wisdom Publications, 2004, p. 137.

part of the formula which we use most of the time to open and close our corporate prayer and worship, "In the name of the Father, and of the Son, and of the Holy Spirit."

The very observance of the Feast of the Trinity, however, reminds us that no formula, no grouping of words, is adequate to the Mystery of God. Our mind and its functioning are beyond words and concepts as we attempt prayer, communion with God. To seek God takes us beyond words, concepts and ideas, beyond human control and limits. The beautiful poem reminds us to let go and to stand in awe before the truth of God. "Truth simply is," states the poem, and it proves to be a wise admonition as we address the ultimate mystery of existence in God Almighty. God simply is as God is. And our life journey and agenda is to study and appreciate that ultimate truth.

This feast gives us an opportunity to stop and to consider what the habitual patterns are with which we attempt to access God. Am I stuck in a boring, mechanical and habitual mindset that comes alive when I consider prayer, or going to church, or addressing birth or death or suffering or fear? As each day of life comes and goes and is translated into history, our being changes, and our perceptions, and thoughts, and considerations are called upon to grow and change and become something more. This is how we journey effectively with the Lord.

Our appreciation of the Mystical, the Divine, the Transcendent – in short, our appreciation of God, must be a continuous and living modification of mind and soul and spirit. As we travel through infancy and childhood, through adolescence and into adulthood, with the many changes that we experience, our spirit is called to be alive and changing and growing as well. To relate to our old neighbor and good friend, God, demands that we truly be alert and alive, paying attention to the journey. Trinity Sunday renews the call for this attitude, this stance, this behavior in our being, so that we can remain plugged in to the life and interest of God. Carl Jung, the noted psychiatrist of a hundred years ago, observed that the most shallow of all human awareness is a purely intellectual experience. He knew that emotion, sensation, intuition, social involvement and awareness, and much more had to be part of a rich and fulfilling experience of any truth. And so it is as we address the ultimate truth of God.

Praying, reflecting, meditating, contemplating, remembering, wondering, questioning, doubting, considering, these are but some of the movements we engage as we address God. Our scriptures today give us plans for engaging God. Exodus asks us to invite God to come along with us, as it states, "O Lord, do come along in our company." Paul's letter to the Corinthians suggests, "Brothers and sisters, rejoice. Mend your ways, encourage one another, live in peace." And John's Gospel helps us to remember that, "God so loved the world that He gave His only son."

Trinity Sunday helps us review the truth which simply is, that we find God through total human engagement, through social involvement, through mystical experience, through personal search. Forty-four years ago this week, I was ordained a priest. One month before that experience, on April 12, 1961, Russia placed the first human being in space. Yuri Gagarin, the Soviet cosmonaut, was the pilot. On May 5 of that same year, Alan Shepherd became the first American to fly in space. During that same month, race riots were breaking out in the Southern part of the U.S. People were giving their lives to bring equality to black and white persons. Certainly, our images and appreciations of God were different before those world- and human-changing events. We commit ourselves to stay alive and alert in our search for our Trinitarian God.

TRINITY SUNDAY (2)*

PROVERBS 8: "Thus says the wisdom of God: The Lord possessed me, the beginning of his ways."

PSALM 8: "O Lord, our God, how wonderful your name in all the earth."

ROMANS 5: "The love of God has been poured out into our hearts through the Holy Spirit that has been given to us."

JOHN 16: "The Spirit of truth will guide you to all truth."

In Oslo, Norway, there exists one of the most beautiful statuary gardens in the world. It was sculpted by Norway's premier sculptor, Gustav Vigeland. It includes 121 larger-than-life pieces which depict the full range of human life and family, from infancy to old age.

Called "The Cycle of Life," the work traces the coming together of a young couple, the coming of their children, and then the changing relationship of parent and child. Finally,

---

* Editor's note: This homily was originally presented on 6/3/07.

the artist shows us the connection between the generations.[†] This sculpture garden is the story of relationships and is powerful.

Today we reflect on the life of God as Trinity, and the Trinity of Persons in God is all about relationship: God the Father, God the Son, God the Holy Spirit, or as the three are some-times described, God the Creator (Father), God the Redeemer (Son), and God the life-giver and teacher (Holy Spirit). The Trinity of Persons displays ultimate relationship.

Richard Rohr, the noted Franciscan speaker and author, says that if we want to learn who we really are, we should study and prayerfully reflect on our relationships: our relationship with ourself, our relationship with each other, our relation-ship with all creatures, the animals, the plants, the earth, our relationship with the universe, our relationship with God.

Relationship is the essence of communion, holy communion, the inter-connectedness of all of creation with our Trinitarian God. Right relationship empowers us to grow, to become more completely human and God-like. The Trinity calls us into relationship in all of life, and in all of God life within and among us.

In our Liturgical observance of the Christian calendar, we have feasts highlighting the three persons. As an example, on

---

† See Chittister, Joan. *The Ten Commandments Laws of the Heart.* Maryknoll: Orbis Books, 2006.

March 25th, God sends the angel Gabriel to Mary to announce His son to be born of her. Christmas highlights the birth of the Son of God. Pentecost holds up for our consideration the Holy Spirit. We begin and conclude most times of prayer, privately and publicly, with the Sign of the Cross, "In the name of the Father, and of the Son, and of the Holy Spirit. Amen."

The Trinity of Persons in one God is the basic foundation upon which our Christian and Catholic Theology is founded. Our appreciation of the mystery of God, of God's life, and of our involvement in that life, flows from the Trinity. The Christian story found in scripture and tradition flows out of Trinitarian language.

The hymns we sing and the prayers we utter, listen to, and participate in, flow from appreciation of Trinity. This Sunday observance, the Feast of the Trinity, gives us pause to stand before the mystery of our God, in respect, in awe, in appreciation of being involved in God's very life.

In another vein, as we worship today, we bless with our prayer and love and respect all the young people who are graduating this week, from the various levels of educational accomplishment. St. Pius kindergarteners, eighth grade students, and Lourdes Seniors graduated this past week. In the coming week all three Public High Schools, J.M., Century and Mayo, will graduate. We offer all of these good young people to our Trinitarian God and bless them on their way.

CORPUS CHRISTI

GENISIS 14: "Melchizedek, king of Salem, brought out bread and wine…"

1 COR 11: "The Lord Jesus, on the night he was handed over, took bread, and after he gave thanks, broke it and said, 'This is my body that is for you…'"

LUKE 9: "Then taking the five loaves and the two fish, and looking up to heaven, he said the blessing over them, broke them, and gave them to the disciples to set before the crowd. They ate until they were satisfied."

A seventeen year old daughter, about this time of the year, writes to her parents as follows:

"Dear Mom and Dad, As you know, I recently became seventeen years old. That being the case, I have decided to leave home and move in with my boyfriend. Now don't worry, because we have set up a plan to sell pot out of our house so as to pay rent and buy food.

"I also need to tell you that I am pregnant, and my boyfriend knows about this. He does not care that another boy is the father to the child. He says we can work this out. My boyfriend asked me if we could borrow $1,000 from you for a while since he thinks he may have AIDS, and we need to go to a doctor to find out. That costs money, you know, and neither of us has health insurance.

"Now, Mom and Dad, none of the above is true. But I wrote this to give you a framework for judging me tomorrow when you get my report card in the mail and find a D- in Biology. That doesn't sound too bad to me, compared with what you could have had to deal with."

Did you ever get a letter like this in the last 50/40 years?

In the history of the world, which has been in written form, we think, for about 11,000 years, many myths, customs, rituals, practices and social conventions have been recorded and described for our study and enrichment. These have been civic, national, racial, religious, cultural and more. One of the most beautiful and most frequently practiced is the prayer, the practice, the experience of Eucharist. Based on ancient Jewish ritual and practice of reading the scriptures together for spiritual nourishment, and of eating together, in order to nurture the body and the community, the Eucharist has become the cornerstone of Christian worship for the majority of Christian people around the world. We Catholics, especially, have placed Eucharist at the center of life observance and celebration.

Eucharist is celebrated in churches, in homes, on battlefields, in jails and prisons; Masses are offered at meetings and gatherings of so many descriptions. The Eucharist focuses our attention on the power and gift of History. Eucharist is the chariot we ride in to worship. Eucharist sets our gaze on mystery, the ultimate and profound truths of existence. Eucharist is the source for processing grief at times of death and loss, and it gives us comfort when we celebrate the great joys, accomplishments and successes of life.

Eucharist is the stage for weddings, funerals, commencements, family observances that mark precious moments in the journey. Eucharist is perhaps the main source of silence, reflection, meditation in life, which is riddled by noise, disturbances and constant movement. Eucharist has the power to calm our fears, to regenerate our courage and to refocus our energies. Eucharist enables us to reset priorities, when we get lost in the confusion of living, in the frantic need to accomplish, in the accelerating pace of modern life.

Eucharist calls us together, reminds us frequently that we are to be one with the Lord, with all of creation, with each other. Eucharist takes the simplest of God's gifts to make the magnificence of the moment. In Eucharist, we sinful human beings come as we are, and we offer the staples of life: forgiveness, bread, wine, generosity, sharing and blessing, and we are renewed. We come in all the circumstances of life, and of each moment of life, in order to grow as persons, as appreciative persons, as peaceful persons.

Eucharist is the grand teacher of generosity in sharing the life each of us has been given. Eucharist always begins with the call to reconciliation, which is essential to the continuance of life. Eucharist brings us together in a setting of self control, discipline, and with a call to attentive focus. Participation in this ritual empowers us to think of others, to share with others simply, to contribute to others by our presence, by our person, by our care and attention. Eucharist is the teacher of simplicity, of substance, of foundational truth as the basic needs of life. Eucharistic practice enables us to go where we normally do not go, because of discomfort, of inconvenience. This great gift strengthens our ability to pay attention to the truth within, to the movements within, to the condition of our soul. This is hard work, and Eucharist holds our feet to the fire in order to see the bigger and truer, and more complete picture of what our life is about or could be about.

As we observe this feast of *Corpus Christi*, we thank God for this vehicle of worship, the Mass.

CORPUS CHRISTI (2)

GENESIS 14:   "In those days, Melchizedek, king of Salem, brought bread and wine, being a priest of God."

PSALM 110:   "You are a priest forever, in the line of Melchizedek."

1 COR 11:   "Brothers and Sisters: I received from the Lord what I handed on to you, that the Lord Jesus, on the night he was handed over, took bread, and, after he had given thanks, broke it and said, 'This is me body that is for you. Do this in memory of me.'"

LUKE 9:   "Jesus spoke to the crowds about the kingdom of God, and he healed those who needed to be cured."

On this Feast of the Holy Eucharist, we are invited to make Eucharist out of our lives. The scriptures offered for our reflection take us all the way back to centuries before Christ, as Genesis speaks of the king of Salem, Melchizedek, who was also a priest, as he offered bread and wine, the staples of life for those agrarian and nomadic peoples, as an appropriate offering to the Lord.

Psalm 110, our response, also references the priesthood of the ancients, in the line of Melchizedek, stating, "You are a priest forever, in the line of Melchizedek." Luke's Gospel begins today's offering, speaking of the natural outflow of a Eucharistic people, namely, "Jesus spoke to the crowds about the kingdom of God, and he healed those who needed to be cured."

But the reading today that I would like to review with you is the second reading, Paul's first letter to the Corinthians, Chapter 11. The reading, as you remember, begins, "Brothers and Sisters: I received from the Lord what I handed on to you, that the Lord Jesus, on the night he was handed over, took bread, and, after He had given thanks, broke it and said, 'This is my body that is for you. Do this in remembrance of me.'"

This excerpt from 1 Corinthians states that the Eucharistic Memorial that Jesus gave us flowed out of betrayal, trial, difficulty: "the Lord Jesus, on the night he was handed over, took bread, and, after he had given thanks, broke it and said, 'This is my body that is for you. Do this in remembrance of me.'"

I mentioned earlier in these comments that we are invited on this feast of *Corpus Christi*, to make Eucharist out of our lives. A significant piece of Eucharist is trials, how we see them, what we feel about them, and how we handle the trials of life. Jesus, on his way to terrible betrayal, suffering, demeaning death, reached out and gave us the perpetual and wonderful gift of Eucharist, which defines for us all the sacred and important celebrations of living and dying.

You and I are invited, on this Feast of Corpus Christi, to among other things, look at how we deal with the trials of our lives. We don't know all the tests God will give us, but we can predict some of them, based on the scriptures. We will be tested by MAJOR CHANGES, DELAYED PROMISES, IMPOSSIBLE PROBLEMS, UNANSWERED PRAYERS, UNDESERVED CRITICISM, & SENSELESS TRAGEDIES, to name a few.

A very important test and trial is how we act and react when we cannot feel God's presence in our lives. Sometimes, it seems, God intentionally draws back, and we do not sense God's closeness or presence.

A king named Hezekiah, in the Old Testament, experienced this test that you and I experience from time to time. Chronicles 32 says, "God withdrew from Hezekiah in order to test him and to see what was really in his heart." Hezekiah had enjoyed a close fellowship with God, but at a crucial point in his life, God left him alone to test his character, to reveal a weakness, and to prepare him for more responsibility. Eucharistic spirituality asks us to remember that life involves trials, and that the trials are important in life, as much, or more so than comforts.

Part of today's teaching is to practice discipline as Eucharistic people, so that we do not fall apart when the dark days, the sad days, the problematic days come. And we all know that those days have come, perhaps are here currently, and will be part of future life. Eucharistic strength gives us what we need to utilize these days, as well as the comfortable, successful, and exciting days.

A final thought. Eucharist always is experienced in community. That, in itself, teaches us that we are to help each other to experience, outlast, and get through the trials of life. Eucharist is a magnificent gift and power in life. How lucky we are to be part of the Eucharistic Christ frequently!

ELEVENTH SUNDAY IN ORDINARY TIME[*]

EXODUS 19:   "You shall be to me a kingdom of priests, a holy nation."

PSALM 100:   "We are God's people; the sheep of His flock."

ROMANS 5:   "While we were still sinners, Christ died for us."

MATTHEW 9:   "Without cost, you have received; without cost, you are to give."

There is a widely acknowledged principle in psychology and spirituality that one must say "Goodbye" before one can say "Hello." As an example, a person must say goodbye to infancy before that individual can have a healthy and normal childhood. And one must say goodbye to childhood before one can mature in adolescence. The adolescent must bid farewell to adolescence before a mature adulthood can be entered and developed, and so it goes through the various and succeeding phases of adulthood. Goodbyes precede hellos.

---

[*] Editor's note: This homily was originally presented on 6/12/05.

Our scriptures today speak of various phases and experiences of life. Exodus calls us to a maturity called *holiness*: "You shall be to me a kingdom of priests, a holy nation." Psalm 100 calls us to a maturity called *humility*: "We are God's people, the sheep of his flock." Romans calls us to the maturity of *thankfulness*: "While we were still sinners, Christ died for us." And Matthew's Gospel quotes Jesus as calling us to the maturity of *generosity*: "Without cost, you have received; without cost, you are to give." Life demands attention, movement and ownership. To find meaning at all of the various phases of life, we say many goodbyes and express many hellos.

In a challenging book, entitled *Modern Man in Search of a Soul*†, Carl Jung, the noted psychiatrist, speaks of leaving the phases of life to find health and meaning. He states that we must find in the afternoon of life, a meaning which nurtures us and fulfills us, or we become lost. He challenges us to the fact that while the early stages of life are for development of person, family and strength, the afternoon of life, our later years, are for the development of *culture*. Culture development needs the combined wisdom and experience of each of us. We enable and empower society to grow, to mature, to stabilize, as we give of our energies, experiences, and of the wisdom garnered through having lived many years.

---

† Jung, Carl: *Modern Man in Search of a Soul.* Orlando: Harcourt, Inc., 1933, pp. 109-10.

Carl Jung and our scriptures call us to a maturing stance, and by being willing to grow, to change, to leave the preceding phase of life, we find richness in the new portion of our journey.

To be human beings, as God intends us to be, we are a work in progress. Never for a moment does our condition remain static. We are constantly changing. Whether or not that change is meaningful and has significance depends on our attitudes, dispositions, intentions. As we develop the willingness and maturity, the generosity and attentiveness to change, we are fulfilling the will of God. We are finding meaning in life, we are not just putting in our time. We are engaging life, contributing to life, helping to form culture, contributing our spirit to truth, to peace, to world unity and communion. God's call is simple but demanding. God intends that we not waste our gifts, that we continue to develop those gifts throughout every day of life.

And so we listen to the call of the Lord today to be human, to be a maturing human being, to be willing and ready for the inevitable change that is taking place. We recommit our life energy to growth and development. We fulfill what our scriptures today ask of us, namely that we be holy and humble and thankful and generous. That is the richness of living all along the way. Boredom, fatigue, disillusionment go when we live in this fashion. The engagement of our nature, as God gives it, is the only way to happiness and fulfillment. Our faith journey teaches us then to say goodbye to yesterday, to say hello to today and to say yes to the future God has in store for us.

Today we pause to honor and acknowledge our fathers. It is Fathers' Day. We thank you men who are fathers for all the good you have done and continue to do and offer for the stability of our culture, for the healing of our world, for the development of our young people. Our country needs the power of fathers and mothers who are holy, humble, thankful and generous perhaps more now than ever before. God bless our fathers.

ELEVENTH SUNDAY IN ORDINARY TIME (2)

2 SAMUEL 12:	"Nathan said to David: 'Thus says the Lord God of Israel:…you have cut down Uriah the Hittite with the sword; you took his wife as your own, and him you killed with the sword of the Ammonites.'"
PSALM 32:5:	"Lord, forgive the wrong I have done."
GALATIANS 2:16:	"I live, no longer I, but Christ lives in me."
LUKE 7:	"So I tell you, her many sins have been forgiven, because she has shown great love."

The focus of today's scriptures is mercy and forgiveness. In our first reading, we have perhaps the greatest account of very serious betrayal and sin, of equally serious repentance, and of God's total forgiveness.

King David, one of the best known people in the pages and history of the Old Testament, was the king of Israel. His nation was at war with their neighbors. His general's name was Uriah, and Uriah was leading the charge of war against the enemy. Uriah and his beautiful wife lived next door to King David's palace. Now remember David had many wives, as was the custom at that moment in history. But one day, he looked from his rooftop garden over at Uriah and Bath-sheba's house, and saw Bathsheba bathing on the roof. David lusted after her, sent for her, and when she came to him, he had sexual relations with her.

She became pregnant, and when she told David, he called her husband home from battle, hoping to get him drunk, and send him home to his wife. Uriah came to his king, as com-manded, but after meeting with David, refused to go home to the comfort of his wife, because his soldiers were still in bat-tle, and Uriah, being a general of integrity, would not accept comfort while his men were dying on the front line of battle, so Uriah slept outside of David's palace on the ground that night, before returning to battle.

So, David, his first plan to cover his sin having failed, called in the third in command in the army and told him to position Uriah in the hottest part of the battle, where he would surely be killed. That soldier obeyed David, and, sure enough, Uriah was killed by the enemy Ammonites.

The book of Samuel tells us that when David realized what he had done, he went to bed, turned his face to the wall, and prayed for death. David had, after all, sinned first by lusting after another man's wife, then seduced her and committed adultery with her. He had to lie by silence and by circumstance, to get Uriah home from battle, and when Uriah would not go to his wife, David arranged through another person, thus involving him in murder, to place Uriah in battle where he certainly would be killed. David further sinned by not having the courage to kill Uriah himself, but used other people, friends and foes to do the dirty work of murder. This is certainly one of the most tragic stories in the scriptures. A man of privilege, a king, who lived sumptuously, stooped to the lowest level of attitude, decision, and behavior, and then, despaired of God's mercy.

Psalm 32, our response today, says, "Lord, forgive the wrong I have done." This is a simple request of God to forgive deep betrayal. David actually wrote a psalm, number 51, begging God to forgive him. As you know the story of David's sin, a reading of Psalm 51 is a powerful expression of accepting forgiveness for serious sin.

In our second reading today, another serious sinner, St. Paul, who has repented of his serious sins of harassment of others, torture, and murder of those who believed differently than he did, sums up his current status by saying, "I live, no longer I, but Christ lives in me." If we work at letting Christ live in us, we will be saved from our sinfulness.

And finally today, in Luke's Gospel, we hear of the sinful woman who is forgiven much because she loved much. The message of Christ is simple and demanding. We must be fully alive and healthy in mind and spirit to live in Christ, to avoid sin, to be forgiven the sin we experience, and to love much. This is the formula of Jesus.

TWELFTH SUNDAY IN ORDINARY TIME*

ZECHARIAH 12: "Thus says the Lord, 'I will pour out on the house of David and on the inhabitants of Jerusalem, a spirit of grace & petition.'"

PSALM 63: "My soul is thirsting for you, O Lord, my God."

GALATIANS 3: "There is neither Jew nor Greek, there is neither slave or free person, there is not male and female; for you are all one in Jesus Christ."

LUKE 9: "If anyone wishes to come after me, he must deny himself and take up his cross daily and follow me."

Today in the Northern Hemisphere, we observe the Summer Solstice, the longest day of the year for daylight. In America today we celebrate Fathers' Day, a day of observance and honor for our Fathers. A police officer who also was a father tells the following stories: While taking a routine vandalism

---

* Editor's note: This homily was originally presented on 6/20/04.

report at an elementary school, the officer was interrupted by a small six year old girl. Looking at his uniform, she asked, "Are you a policeman?" "Yes," I answered, and continued to write my report. After a moment, she said, "My mother told me if I ever needed help, I should ask a policeman. Is that right?" "Yes, that is right," I told her. "Well then," she said, extending her foot toward me, "would you please tie my shoe?"

On another occasion, the officer pulled his van with his police dog in the back, up to the curb and stopped near where a little boy was playing. The boy came over toward the van, looked at the officer and then at the dog for a long time. Then, the child said to the officer, "Is that a dog you have back there?" "It sure is," I replied. Puzzled, the boy looked at me and then again at the dog, and after a pause, the boy asked, "What did he do?"

Our scriptures today, Zechariah and Psalm 63 from the Old Testament, and Galatians and Luke from the New, ask us to consider, to study, to review, the spirit of grace and petition, of thirsting for God, of unity between all peoples, and of the presence of the cross in life. Little children, police officers, fathers and mothers, and all of us need to address these pieces of life from time to time.

Zechariah teaches the need to develop the spirit of grace, which empowers us to be kind, civil, decent, mature in our dealings with each other. This old and wise book of wisdom also teaches us how to ask for help graciously and humbly, as did the little girl. We are interdependent beings, and giving and receiving on a daily basis is what produces peace, harmony, mutual respect, social health and comfort. Daily human decency to family, to co-workers, to "John and Suzie Q. Public," are needed from each of us and from all of us. As we celebrate the 150th birthday of Rochester, and the 50th birthday of St. Pius these summer days, no greater gift or contribution can be offered by each of us than to humbly recommit to decency, kindness, civility and gentle peace.

Psalm 63 leads us into the transcendent realm of life, as we pray, "My soul is thirsting for you, O Lord, my God." It would seem that we cannot be gentle and civil, if we are not daily, trying to connect anew to our God. This should be a deliberate and disciplined practice in life. None of us should be surprised that prayer is difficult, as is charity and control of emotions. Human life and the development of healthy human life is a science, an art, needing constant vigilance, discipline and direction. These are deliberate and life-giving behaviors, vigilance, discipline and direction. Society needs each of us to do these things, and each individual needs to give and to receive them, in order to be at peace.

St. Paul reminds the Galatian people and us, that we are one. No more Greeks, Jews, slaves, free persons, men or women. We are to be one. The air we breath, the water we drink, the food we consume, the airplanes we fly, the computers we operate, all these things, movements and experiences teach us the basic unity of all of creation. We humans must develop the art, exercise the practice, put into place the discipline it takes to be one every day. There is the tendency within each of us to be selfish at a very basic level. Never a day comes and goes that we do not need to struggle to be one, to be bearers of unity and peace. This is probably why Jesus is quoted often in the Gospel, reminding us that we have to take up our cross every day and follow Him. To follow Jesus, we must practice being a person of inner discipline, outer good behavior. We must daily make it our agenda to be people of peace and unity.

TWELFTH SUNDAY IN ORDINARY TIME (2)

JEREMIAH 20: "The Lord is with me, like a mighty
champion."

PSALM 69: "Lord, in your great love, answer me."

ROMANS 5: "The grace of God overflows for many."

MATTHEW 10: "Everyone who acknowledges me before
others I will acknowledge before my
heavenly father."

The presence of God is a deep, heavily and frequently proc-
essed truth. Millions of books have been written, speeches
delivered, prayers offered in this vein. How is the human
mind, limited as it is and must be by nature, ever able to deal
with the infinite, with the transcendent, with the limitless reality that we believe God to be? How does growth in faith
and hope take place? What is the appropriate approach to the
mystery of God? How does one teach this reality? How does
one find security in knowledge, in awareness, in the sense
that God must be?

We deal with this issue of God differently, it seems, than we do with our approach to all other reality. We go to the Lord in intuition as much as in intellection. We ponder possibility rather than measure quantity, in our effort to be with our God. We reverence God rather than analyzing structure. We worship, using the fullness of human spirit, rather than going to mathematical analysis.

The human soul and mind is capable of conscious awareness, intellectual analysis, intuition, emotional coloration. The mind can and does hunger for truth bigger than current condition and deeper than current quality. The human spirit is conditioned by nature, by God's creative intention, it would seem, to seek beyond our grasp, to ponder depth, to appreciate potential, to be in awe before mystery. The human person is capable of what we call trust, that is the stance of accepting life in all of its mysterious and potential dimension. It is there that God lives.

As humans, we deal with truth. Small truths we call facts, and we have some control over their place in life. Small truths are learning to drive an automobile, cook a meal, wash clothing, play ball. We also deal with big truths, and we call these mysteries. These truths include gestation, birthing, living, dying, love, God. We simply stand before BIG TRUTH in awe and wonder. We can never comprehend the big truth. We only participate in its being. We do not comprehend God. We simply share in God's gift of life and love.

Thus, our scriptures today invite us to trust God, as we hear in Jeremiah, chapter 20: "The Lord is with me like a mighty champion." And Psalm 69 states, "Lord, in your great love, answer me." Paul's letter to the Romans reminds us to thank God, "the grace of God overflows for many." And, finally, Matthew's Gospel teaches that we must continue the search for God, stating, "Anyone who acknowledges me before others I will acknowledge before my heavenly Father."

Our lives, our meaning, our destinies are all woven into the mystery of God. Ultimate questions and issues are the backbone of happiness for us. As we pray and ponder and wonder and question, we deepen our awareness, we enrich our appreciation, we strengthen our involvement in creation, and we open our being to the Creator. This is the spiritual journey. It is a life-long journey.

We pray together frequently to be encouraged, and to get the strength to persevere in this effort. It is never too late in life to start the search for God, and the more and longer we stay at it, the richer we become. The development of the spiritual life is truly the most significant thing any one of us can do. The possibility of happiness, the quality of life, the ability to see and perceive and open ourselves to new life possibilities, are tied intimately to the spiritual life being developed.

Prayer, practice, perseverance, patience are all needed to accomplish this life-giving, life-enriching dimension of life which we call the spiritual life. God, our neighbor, ourselves, creation, all come into focus as we work at our spiritual life. It is there that we find happiness and life.

TWELFTH SUNDAY IN ORDINARY TIME (3)*

JOB 38:   "The Lord addressed Job out of the storm, and said: 'Who shut within the doors the sea,when it burst forth from the womb?'"

PSALM 107: "Give thanks to the Lord, his love is everlasting."

1 COR 5:   "The old things have passed away, behold new things have come."

MARK 4:   "'Do you not yet have faith?' They were filled with great awe."

President Harry Truman, in his biography, is said to have responded to a question, after he had served as President for one year. The question was, "What is it like to be President of the United States?" Harry Truman answered, "It is like riding a tiger. You either keep riding, or the tiger will eat you." The scriptures today have something of that spirit in them, for our consideration and reflection. From the Book of Job, God reminded Job that God is in charge always, even in the storm.

---

* Editor's note: This homily was originally presented on 6/25/06.

We are to learn through the storms of life, and we all experience storms of many kinds and descriptions in life.

Psalm 107 reminds us to be thankful and to have the biggest possible realization of truth: "Give thanks to the Lord, his love is everlasting." There is an old saying that the more experience a person gets, the more education one receives, the more one realizes how little one knows! Arrogance is blindness to the truth. Humility in life is the road to wisdom.

On Thursday, December 14, 2005, the San Francisco Chronicle ran a front page story about a female humpback whale who had become entangled in a spider web of crab traps and lines. She was weighed down by hundreds of pounds that caused her to struggle just to stay afloat. She also had hundreds of yards of line rope wrapped around her body, her tail, her torso, and had a line tugging in her mouth.

A fisherman spotted her just east of the Farallon Islands (outside the Golden Gate Bridge), and radioed an environmental group for help. Within a few hours, the rescue team arrived and determined that she was so bad off that the only way to save her was to dive in and untangle her – a very dangerous proposition. One slap of the tail could kill a rescuer. They worked for hours with curved knives, and eventually freed her.

When she was free, the divers said that she swam in what seemed like joyous circles. She then came back to each and every diver, one at a time, and nudged them, pushed them gently around – she thanked them. Some of the divers said that it was one of the most incredibly beautiful experiences of their lives. The man who cut the rope out of her mouth said her eye was following him the entire time, and he said he will never be the same again. Psalm 107 tells us today what that whale instinctively knew, namely, "Give thanks to the Lord, His love is everlasting."

Paul's letter to the Corinthian People in Greece reiterates the profound truth that is really quite simple; "the old things have passed away, behold new things have come." The past is history, unchangeable, and not a good place to live. Regret, disappointment, bitterness can easily become the conditions of being. The future is not yet, unpredictable, and also not a good place to live. New things come to and make life rich in potential, in the present moment. Paul is telling us to "pay attention," and we will find new life every moment.

In a recent book, entitled *Let In the Light* by Patricia Livingston[†], the author speaks of prayer as the power of sharing and focus. She says, and I quote, "Energy is real. Physicists assure us that nothing that exists is static; everything is energy. Prayer is energy. It goes out from us and impacts reality. How this happens, how our prayer somehow interacts with the energy of the Divine, we cannot explain. But prayer makes a difference, as medical studies have shown."

---

† Livingston, Patricia. *Let In the Light Facing the Hard Stuff With Hope.* Notre Dame: Ave Maria Press, 2006, p. 93.

And, finally today, Mark's Gospel describes the disciples in the boat on the stormy sea as being frightened to death, having little faith, and being in awe of the power of Jesus, as he calmed the storm. "'Do you not yet have faith?' They were filled with great awe." To keep our balance in life is a challenging reality. We need to practice faith, hope, justice, kindness and forgiving love constantly, or we lose our way. A thankful heart will enable us to help each other out of our entanglements in life, and make us worthy ministers of Jesus Christ.

TWELFTH SUNDAY IN ORDINARY TIME (4)[*]

JOB 38: "The Lord addressed Job out of the storm and said, 'Who shut within doors the sea, when it burst forth from the womb...'"

PSALM 107: "Give thanks to the Lord; His love is everlasting."

2 COR 5: "Whoever is in Christ is a new creation; the old things have passed away; behold new things have come."

MARK 4: "Then Jesus asked them, 'Why are you terrified? Do you not yet have faith?' They were filled with great awe."

Many of us have not heard of a man by the name of Thomas Berry. He was a Passionist Priest, who died on June 1, 2009, in Greensboro, N.C. He was 94 years old, and had spent the vast majority of his life studying, writing and lecturing about the human relationship with the natural world, and its implications for religion. Father Berry was described by *Newsweek* Magazine in 1989 as "the most provocative figure

---

[*] Editor's note: This homily was originally presented on 6/21/09.

260

among the new breed of ecotheologians." He was the first to say that the earth crisis is fundamentally a spiritual crisis. Father Berry has been a profound gift to us. We do well to study his thinking and spirituality.

Father Berry believed that the only way to effectively function as individuals and as a species is to understand the history and functioning of our planet, and of the wide universe itself, like sailors learning about their ship and the vast ocean on which it sails. His teaching was a reminder that we, the Church, must keep up with other fields of learning, such as Cosmology, Anthropology, Quantum Physics, International Relations, and other developing areas of life, or risk the loss of the young people who have been born into our world in the last half of the last century. And, he was right, because that is what is happening. Our Gospel values never change, but life is changing all of the time, and our perceptions of life are changing all the time, and Jesus taught his followers to live in the real world, as God creates it, gives it to us, and asks us to be stewards of this creation, as it exists today, not the world as it was in the time of Jesus, as he walked this earth. We are to take his truth and apply it to today, as He applied the truth then.

Our spiritual values are addressed in the scriptures given to us today. In the Book of Job, given today, the Lord addressed Job out of the storm, and said, "Who shut within doors the sea, when it burst forth from the womb?" Basically, God is telling Job, in the midst of a frightening storm, that God is in charge, and that our job is to learn how God works, in storms, in quiet times, in all the circumstances, conditions and challenges of each new day. God's basic truth is that life is dynamic, ever-changing, alive, and moving. That is the life God gave to Job, and the life God gives to us. We accept life as it is offered, or like Job, we despair.

Psalm 107 reassures us, "Give thanks to the Lord; His love is everlasting." In other words, the Lord is much more faithful to us than we are to the Lord. God is with us always, in all of life.

Paul, in the second reading, reminds the Corinthians, and all the people throughout all of the centuries, including us today, that, "Whoever is in Christ is a new creation; the old things have passed away, behold new things have come." Again, the message is that life is change, and moving. The ancient scriptures, and great minds like Father Thomas Berry, in our day, remind us to keep up, to stay the course, to seek the truth always, as it is being offered at every moment. We are to remember that truth is always of God, and therefore, truth is safe. Our job is to figure the truth out all along the way of life.

Mark's Gospel offering today is a life-giving reminder: "Then Jesus asked them, 'Why are you terrified? Do you not yet have faith?' They were filled with great awe." Our job is to look, to listen, to learn today, and we, too, will be filled with great awe.

THE NATIVITY OF JOHN THE BAPTIST

ISAIAH 49: "The Lord called me from birth...He says...I will make you a light to the nations, that my salvation may reach to the ends of the earth."

PSALM 139: "I praise you for I am wonderfully made."

ACTS 13: "Brothers and Sisters, children of the family of Abraham, and those others among you who are God-fearing, to us this word of salvation has been sent."

LUKE 1: "All who heard these things took them to heart, saying, 'What, then, will this child be?' for surely the hand of the Lord was with him."

Today's feast of the birth of John the Baptist is a call to all of us to be people of the community, people of the government, people of the church, people of courage, people of the poor and marginalized, people of peace, and people of social justice. John the Baptist was murdered because he was all of the above, and more. The most challenging dimension of life is not and never has been, "God and Me," but it always has been and continues to be "God and You and Me and Us," the entire concept of social justice, and of care for and respect of all of God's creation.

A modern day true story gives us a challenging example. This true story is entitled, "Mothers of the Disappeared – Argentina 1977-1983."*

In 1976, the Military of Argentina accomplished a coup, and took over the government. The people, at first, were very happy, because the previous administration had been so corrupt. But soon, the military officers of Argentina began a horrible and savage oppression, whereby they silently and secretly murdered anyone who dissented from their oppressive policies. In the following six years, an estimated 20,000+ people disappeared from their homes, and were never heard from again. They were murdered in secret and their bodies were disposed of in secret. These people became known as the "desaparecidos," the ranks of the disappeared. The aim of this repression was to silence all protest, and it very nearly succeeded. Political oppression evaporated. The press was silent. Church leaders remained willfully blind. It fell to a group of women to find the courage to break this silence. These became known as the Mothers of the Disappeared.

These women had seen sons, daughters, husbands disappear from their homes in the night, never to be seen again. These

---

* Ellsberg, Robert. *Blessed Among All Women*. London: Darton Longman & Tod, 2006.

women went to jails, hospitals, and military installations to try to find their loved ones. In vain they pleaded with judges, government officials, and bishops for assistance. Always they were dismissed, sometimes with cruelty and cynicism. But the Mothers did not give up. In their grief, anger and frustration, they found each other.

It was against the law to hold any public protest during the state of siege. And so the women came together to support each other, and then they began a silent vigil each Thursday, in the Plaza de Mayo, a public square in Buenos Aires that faces the Ministry of the Interior. Each Thursday, scores of middle-aged women, known as the Madres de Plaza de Mayo, stood silently, identified only by their white kerchiefs, and sometimes by the pictures they held of their missing loved ones.

The Generals did not know how to respond to this mute outcry. They resorted to ridicule, and they called them the crazy women. Then they went to bullying and terror. Some of the mothers were kidnapped and disappeared. But these behaviors only strengthened their resolve. The women persevered, and despite a news blackout in Argentina, the Mothers' protest was reported throughout the world. The Mothers' silent vigil became the visible conscience of the Nation. In 1983, the military, by this time thoroughly discredited, yielded power to a civilian government. The Mothers' courage saved the people of Argentina.

John the Baptist calls you and me to courage, to contribution to the common good, to a renewed realization that we have social as well as personal responsibility. We are, each of us, our brothers' and sisters' keeper, in every phase of life.

THIRTEENTH SUNDAY IN ORDINARY TIME*

1 KINGS 9: "The Lord said to Elijah, 'You shall anoint Elisha, as prophet to succeed you.'"

PSALM 16: "You are my inheritance, O Lord."

GAL 5: "For the whole law is fulfilled in one statement, namely, 'You shall love your neighbor as yourself.'"

LUKE 9: "Jesus said, 'No one who sets his hand to the plow and looks to what was left behind is fit for the kingdom of God.'"

In 1905, 99 years ago, Albert Einstein published his famous and life enhancing statement of the modern theory of relativity.† This theory transformed the way the people of the world saw themselves and all of creation and energy in and of life. This theory continues to direct us in our realization that all things, movements, energies are one and that all is

---

*Editor's note: This homily was originally presented on 6/27/04.

† Einstein, Albert (Lawson, Robert W. trans.). *Relativity The Special and General Theory.* New York: Henry Holt, 1920.

changing. Movement, harmony, symmetry, predictability are conditions of our search, our appreciation, our learning and development.

Just a little more than 100 years ago, Emily Dickinson wrote a beautiful poem about the human brain, addressing the mystery and power of this human organ. She says, "The Brain-is wider than the sky, For-put them side by side- The one the other will contain with ease- and You-beside- The Brain is deeper than the sea-For-hold them-Blue to Blue-The one the other will absorb- As Sponges-Buckets-do-The Brain is just the weight of God-For-Heft them-Pound for Pound-And they will differ-if they do-As syllable from Sound."‡

These two great and insightful people, from different angles and motivations, address the tremendous potential that lives within each of us. We are creators, redeemers, life-bearers with God. The Scriptures today give us direction as to planning for the future, appreciating the past, behaving in the current scene.

In First Kings, our first reading today, the Lord directs the currently reigning prophet to provide for the future, and the continuance of providing access to God's Word, by appointing a new and younger prophet. We are to be aware, in our life efforts, that we contribute to the development and quality of life. We are called to be co-creators with the Lord. God's

---

‡ Editor's note: This poem may be read online at http://poemhunter.com/poem/the-brain-is-wider-than-the-sky/.

spirit is our spirit. We share in the very life of God and of God's creation. We are to participate and contribute according to our means, and thus insure a peaceful and quality future, for those who will come after us. Elijah, Elisha, Albert Einstein, Emily Dickinson made their respective contributions. We are to make ours.

Psalm 16 focuses our energy: "You are my inheritance, O Lord." Our eyes, our senses, our energies, our very life force – are to be focused on the source and substance of our lives, Almighty God. This will maintain our humility and gratitude, and keep us on the true path, or bring us back to the true path.

Galatians reminds us, "For the whole law is fulfilled in one statement, namely, 'You shall love your neighbor as yourself.'" We are to contribute to life generously, we are to keep a humble focus on God, and we are to remember that we are one with and for each other. We are to honor the other as we do ourselves. We are to be peacemakers at all times.

And, finally, Luke's Gospel quotes Jesus as reminding us to have courage and perseverance, "Anyone who puts his hand to the plow and looks back is not fit for the kingdom of God." Life demands courage, strength, perseverance, and these come with the exercise of discipline. Albert Einstein and Emily Dickinson had to discipline their lives significantly to give their gifts. We are called to no less focus, effort and generosity.

As we approach the birthday of our Nation on the 4th of July, we realize anew the fact that we live, at the providence of God, in the freest, richest, most opportune land on the face of the earth. The poorest of us financially is richer than the majority of the world's people currently. We have a heavy responsibility to contribute generously to life.

THIRTEENTH SUNDAY IN ORDINARY TIME (2)*

2 KINGS 4: "Later Elisha asked, 'Can something be done for her?'"

PSALM 89: "Forever I will sing of the goodness of the Lord."

ROMANS 6: "Just as Christ was raised from the dead by the glory of the Father, we too might live in newness of life."

MATT 10: "Whoever loses his life for my sake will find it."

Fifty years ago this past week, Disneyland opened in Anaheim, California. A man by the name of Walt Disney gave the world the first super playground comprised of 160 acres of rides, games, shows and wonderfully entertaining people, and the forever famous Mickey and Minnie Mouse, Goofy and companions. Disneyland is a word that everyone knows and many hundreds of millions of people have experienced in life.

---

* Editor's note: This homily was originally presented on 6/26/05.

Disneyland is about being good to people and making people happy, and entertaining people, and lifting up the spirits of people. Our scriptures today are about that same theme of kindness, service, caring for others and finding newness of life.

The prophet Elisha receives great kindness from a couple, and returns great kindness, the couple giving him a home and he promising them a child in their childless marriage. Psalm 89, our response, reminds us to be thankful before God for all the joy of life, "Forever I will sing the goodness of the Lord." Paul's letter to the Romans speaks of the newness of life, which comes through kindness, grace, care and concern for others. And Jesus tells us again that if we lose our life for others, it is there that we truly find life richly.

This past Tuesday, fifty years after Disneyland opened, we experience in the entire Northern Hemisphere, the summer solstice, which marks the day in the year here in the North that has more minutes of sunshine than any other day in the year. Tuesday marked the beginning of summer, which gives us all that is needed in nature, warmth, moisture, clean air, nurturance, which comes through new life in the plant, animal and mineral kingdoms. These gifts keep the world's people alive, safe, and well.

What great gifts nature and the talent of all people give to us. Each of us can recommit today to care for the earth, and all of nature around us, and also to develop our gifts to the best extent of our abilities. This is the way we show gratitude to God and to others, and this is the way that life continues to be rich, enriched and enriching for all. This is the foundation of our life. This is our vocation. This is the responsibility of each of us.

To bring peace of mind and human dignity to one another is the ultimate in kindness. We are to love as God loves, and that is in giving life, respecting life, sustaining life, enhancing life. To bring kindness is the richest gift one can give. We are all called to that disposition, conviction and behavior for those whose lives we touch.

Today, we here at St. Pius X, say goodbye to a wonderful man, a persevering priest, a spiritual leader, a steadying Pastor, in the person of Fr. Paul Surprenant. He has served St. Pius for twelve years. He has led well and has certainly tried to be kind and caring of people. His contribution here has helped many and has brought goodness and joy and comfort to many. We wish him well and send him with our prayer and respect, as he moves to Byron and Kasson to serve people there in the worship of God and in the development of Christian charity.

Next week, we will welcome Father Charles Collins as our pastor with the good spirit of this parish and congregation.

THIRTEENTH SUNDAY IN ORDINARY TIME (3)*

WISDOM 1:   "For God fashioned all things, that they might have being; and the creatures of the world are wholesome, and there is not a destructive drug among them."

PSALM 30:   "I will praise you Lord, for you have rescued me."

2 COR 8:   "You know the gracious act of Jesus Christ, that though he was rich, for your sake he became poor, so that by his poverty, you might become rich."

MARK 5:   "Jesus raised the daughter of the foreigner and cured the woman from a life-long illness."

The U. S. Government announced this past week that the American population will pass the 300,000,000 mark in October of this year. The U.S. Census Bureau estimates that world population has passed 6.5 billion people. Those figures say that the U.S. Population is 4.6% of the world's popula-

---

* Editor's note: This homily was originally presented on 7/2/06.

tion. We know that currently, we are the wealthiest people on the planet, the freest people on the planet, the most opportune people on the planet. We know that per capita, we consume more than any other people on the planet, and we produce more waste than any other people on the planet.

We know that, in our industrial approach to life, we are polluting the air, the earth and the water very irresponsibly. The United States Government continues to refuse to sign world treaties that would aggressively address pollution and earth warming. We have made a God of money, and everything has to worship at that altar, blindly ignoring life-threatening conditions.

The scriptures today teach us what the ancients knew in a rich and confident way, namely, that God's creation is sacred, wholesome, and for life. It is never to be abused. *Time* Magazine, in the current issue, has an editorial by Richard Stengel, Managing Editor, entitled "Why History Matters."† In the article, he quotes Thomas Jefferson as saying, "A Nation can never be ignorant and free." It seems that most Americans are choosing to be ignorant on the issue that is a universal moral imperative, namely, the care of planet earth. Aldous Huxley,

---

† Editor's note: This article was originally published in the Monday, June 26, 2006 issue of *Time* Magazine. It may be read online on the Time archives at search.time.com.

in his classic work entitled *Perennial Philosophy*‡, states, "If we don't know, it is because we find it more convenient not to know. Original ignorance is the same thing as original sin."

We study and discuss moral issues in the areas of human sexuality, human life, justice, international relations, but rarely do we ponder deeply the foundational moral issue of them all, and that is what our policies, intentions, and behaviors are doing or neglecting to do to our home, to our life source, to the children of the future, as we continue to significantly abuse the planet earth.

The *National Catholic Reporter* of June 30, 2006, has a story by Joseph Cunneen in it, on the issue of caring for the earth.§ The article states that virtually all of the world's scientists agree that we are on a wrong, and potentially disastrous course, by allowing our business and oil misbehaviors to warm the air and water of the earth. This is the most important moral issue before humanity today, and each of us is responsible to study, learn, and act in healing and protecting ways regarding Mother Earth.

---

‡ Huxley, Aldous. *The Perennial Philosophy An Interpretation of the Great Mystics, East and West.* New York: HarperCollins Publishers Inc, 2004.

§ Cunneen, Joseph. "The Last Days of the West." *National Catholic Reporter*, June 30, 2006. [Editor's note: This article may be read online at natcath.org/NCR_Online/archives2/2006b/]

This week, as we celebrate the birth of this nation, in addition to celebrating with our families and friends with picnics, parades, fireworks and parties, we can read, study, and research the entire issue of global warming, form a more educated opinion, and determine to do what we can to contact our legislators at local, state and national levels, to speak our mind on what arguably is the most fundamental moral issue of our time and for the rest of time. We must follow the wisdom of the Old Testament Book of Wisdom, which tells us today that it is the responsibility of everyone to keep the earth and its creatures and conditions sacred and safe for generations to come.

FOURTEENTH SUNDAY IN ORDINARY TIME

ISAIAH 66:   "When you see this, your heart shall rejoice
             and your bodies flourish like the grass;
             the Lord's power shall be known to his
             servants."

PSALM 66:   "Let all the earth cry out to God with joy."

GALATIANS 6: "For neither does circumcision mean
             anything, nor does uncircumcision, but
             only a new creation."

LUKE 10:   "The harvest is abundant but the laborers
             are few; so ask the master of the harvest
             to send out laborers for his harvest."

Bing Crosby and Count Baise and his band have recorded a
wonderful rendition of the song entitled, "Everything is
Beautiful." It is bouncy. living, inviting, and makes one want
to dance and be happy. One of the lines in the song, however,
hits the listener hard, if one really listens. The line states, "No
one is as blind as the one who refuses to see."

The context for that statement is the fact that we judge each other by outward appearance and that we do not look at what we do not want to see.

The scriptures today speak about the blindness that lives in us when we refuse to see. The scriptures today infer and explicitly tell us that we need to use our entire nature, including our ability to know, to think, to analyze, to create, as we address the unfolding of life within and among us. We have probably all experienced a little child, who in shyness covers their eyes and tries to hide behind Mom or Dad, when a stranger speaks to him or her. In children, this behavior is understandable and, at least in the beginning, it is acceptable. But, in adult life we are responsible for seeing as much of the truth as we are able to, and we are responsible for addressing as much of the unfolding mystery as we can.

As we live and become more aware of reality, it becomes increasingly obvious that change is the only constant in experience. Our bodies change from their beginning, times change, technology advances, systems of thought, of government, of practice come and go. We change our minds, our outlook, our direction. Change is all around us and within us. And so, our appreciation of who we are, where we are going, and what our existence means, change. Thus, our religious practices, our theological perceptions, our spiritual exercises must change. And this takes courage, discipline, thought, humble willingness to become more as God gives us more – more time, more experience, more history, more awareness.

This is the point that blindness, chosen out of fear and insecurity, enters and can become a problem. We cannot be an adult walking around in a child's appreciation of the mystery of God and of existence. We must continue to grow up, and to deal with life, joy, sorrow, suffering, death. In short, we are to engage all dimensions of our life and journey here. Our faith and the scriptures tell us that we need not be afraid of this process.

Isaiah today tells us as much. "When you see this, your heart shall rejoice and your bodies flourish like the grass; the Lord's power shall be known to his servants." As life comes, and as we open ourselves to that life, we change and grow safely. We are freed from the enslavement to naivety, habituation, a closed mind. Life unfolds in the present and the present is different in every way from any past point in history. Psalm 66 exhorts us today, "Let all the earth cry out to God with joy."

Paul's letter to the Galatians tells us that the religious practice of circumcision had lost its meaning when the church changed from being all Jewish, to include Gentiles. Paul says, "For neither does circumcision mean anything, nor does uncircumcision, but only a new creation." As life changes, intelligent humanity must make the change or become lost in the lie of rigidity, past custom and dead faith. Living faith is the fruit of human nature, fully alive before God, walking with the Lord, interpreting the Lord's creation with new, richer and more mature awareness and engagement.

In Luke's Gospel today, Jesus tells his followers, including you and me, "The harvest is abundant but the laborers are few; so ask the master of the harvest to send out laborers for his harvest." The same kernel of wheat is not harvested every year. Wheat is harvested each year, but new kernels are the enrichment and nourishment of new life. And so it is with the spirit.

Our faith practice needs to brush its teeth, comb its hair, bath its skin and exercise its being every day, or it shrivels up and becomes a paralysis. Living faith takes courage, study, prayer, openness to change, willingness to grow. This is the message of scripture today. Trust the Lord, Trust the Lord's grace in you, Trust God's call for us to grow and change with all of creation, with all of time, with all of experience. We walk with faith, not by incomplete and surface understandings born of chosen blindness. We courageously trust God and continue to participate in God's unfolding plan. Then we truly avoid what Bing Crosby sings about in the song, "Everything is Beautiful," when he croons, "No one is as blind as the one who refuses to see."

FOURTEENTH SUNDAY IN ORDINARY TIME (2)

EZEKIEL 2: "As the Lord spoke to me, the spirit entered into me and set me on my feet, and I heard the one who was speaking say to me: Son of man, I am sending you to the Israelites, rebels who have rebelled against me."

PSALM 123: "Our eyes are fixed on the Lord, pleading for his mercy."

2 COR 12: "Brothers and sisters: That I, Paul, might not become too elated, because of the abundance of the revelations, a thorn in the flesh was given to me, an angel of Satan, to beat me, to keep me from being too elated."

MARK 6: "A prophet is not without honor except in his native place and among his own kin and in his own house."

The scriptures today speak to us in several stories about qualities, conditions of soul, virtues of COURAGE, HUMILITY, and STRENGTH. Most of us could name persons who have exemplified courage, humility, and strength: for exam-

ple Helen Keller, Mother Teresa, Abraham Lincoln, Albert
Einstein, Peter and Paul, St. Catherine of Sienna, St. Teresa
of Avila, St. John of the Cross, and the list is endless.

A Canadian Theologian by the name of Bernard Lonergan
(born in 1904 in Canada and he died in 1984), spent much of
his life studying and writing about achieving personal development. David Tracy, another great theologian, says of Bernard Lonergan that Lonergan was the greatest theologian
North America has ever produced.

Father Lonergan, a Jesuit, invites us to take seriously our
own experience, to explore the way we function as knowers
and lovers, and to discern the patterns involved in human
growth. It is in this way that we can develop the virtues the
scriptures of today speak about, namely, courage, humility
and strength.

Bernard Lonergan suggests five general principles to guide
our development:
1. BE ATTENTIVE by probing the full range of our
   experience.
2. BE INTELLIGENT by cultivating an inquiring mind and
   spirit.
3. BE REASONABLE by gathering evidence & judging the
   validity of your insights.
4. BE RESPONSIBLE by giving back & acting on our
   valid insights.

5. BE LOVING by making charity the highest aspiration of
   our life.

This, he says, guarantees the highest development of our being, and insures happiness and peace of mind for those who
practice this discipline. Ezekiel tells us today that God has
given us of God's spirit and sends each of us out to share that
spirit, according to our personality, history and experience.

Psalm 123, our Psalm Response, reminds us to keep our eyes
fixed on God. Jesus taught that we must pray always. That
means, among other things, that we focus our energy, our
mind, our heart, our whole being on the mystery of God. The
first Commandment Jesus taught is, "To love the Lord your
God, with all your heart, with all your mind, with all your
soul, with all your strength." This is fulfilling what Psalm
123 exhorts us to do and be today.

St. Paul today tells the proud and self-serving Corinthians to
learn and to practice humility. He says that he was given ex-
traordinary revelations, and he was given a thorn in the flesh
to keep him humble. Paul is simply telling us what we all
know, namely, that we are made in God's image, that we are
good, but that we are also sinners, limited and needy creatures. The truth is that we need God and each other. A good
rule to follow in keeping ourselves humble is, "Identify, don't
compare." If I identify who I am, and not compare myself to
others, I will remain humble, thankful, and respectful of others and of all creation.

Jesus today in Mark's Gospel tells us not to be bossing each other around in our homes and workplaces. We are to be brothers and sisters, not bosses and slaves. The Gospels are wonderful collections of stories and examples, by which we can form, inform and reform all of life.

FIFTEENTH SUNDAY IN ORDINARY TIME

DEUTERONOMY 30: "For this command that I enjoin on you today is not too mysterious and remote for you...No, it is something very near to you, already in your mouths and hearts; you have only to carry it out."

PSALM 69: "Turn to the Lord in your need, and you will live."

COLOSSIANS 1: "For in him were created all things in heaven and on earth, the visible and the invisible."

LUKE 10: "You shall love the Lord, your God, with all your heart, with all your being, with all your strength, and with all your mind, and your neighbor as yourself."

Living faith is an experiment that becomes an experience.
Living faith is an experiment until it becomes an experience.
Living faith remains an experiment unless it becomes an ex-

perience. We humans are equipped to enter the arena of belief, faith, trust. This proves to be hard work at several junctures of life for most of us. To believe is to be vulnerable. To believe is to lack perfect control. To believe is to stand before truth much beyond our comprehension. In fact, to believe is to appreciate, not to comprehend. To believe places us before mystery, in awe. And this is always a powerful experience.

Our scriptures today, beginning with the Old Testament Book of Deuteronomy, assures us that we have tremendous power, the power to believe. Belief always takes us beyond ourselves. Belief always stretches us and introduces us to the bigger. Belief reminds us that we are participants, not the boss, not the one in charge, not in perfect control. Psalm 63 instructs us as to how to believe: "Turn to the Lord in your need, and you will live."

In our search for meaning in life, in our learning about existence, in our efforts to grow, we always go beyond current comprehension, knowledge, awareness. We are, in other words, curious, and curiosity leads us beyond the visible, the obvious. Paul's letter to the Colossians states it this way: "For in him were created all things in heaven and on earth, the visible and the invisible..." The invisible is as real as the visible. The vast majority of reality and creation is beyond our senses and much of creation is beyond our mental capacity. Thus, God empowers us to believe truth, based on human experience and prudence, but going beyond logic, perfect analysis and human comprehension. To believe places us again at the feet of the Lord, trusting life and humbly learning better to share with all of creation. Luke's Gospel today tells us how to exercise and experience the great power of belief, when he quotes Jesus. To believe and to love takes all of our heart, all of our being, all of our strength, all of our mind. Belief engages the entire human being, the total human capacity. Belief demands that we keep learning, that we keep open to further possibility, that goes beyond life, beyond death, beyond words and concepts.

The story of humanity, of our ancestors, perhaps can help us continue the experience of believing. In ancient times people dreamed that they could travel faster than walking, and so they domesticated animals, horses and camels and elephants, and satisfied with this new dimension of life, they went further and invented the wheel, which brought further possibilities. They learned to float on the water, building boats and ships and they then learned to go beneath the water in the submarine. We built cars, and then airplanes, and then space craft, ever expanding the horizon, opening up new mysteries, setting the stage for more believing, imagining, experimenting, experiencing. Belief empowers more belief.

A child comes from the womb and first learns to roll over, to sit, to crawl and at each level of development the child realizes a bigger part of self, more potential and possibility, and so the child believes in walking and does so. Faith enables us to believe more, to appreciate more, to enter more completely into awe and wonder and gratitude and peace.

And so it is with our growing appreciation of the universe. In pre-Biblical and Biblical times, the earth was understood very incompletely. A hundred miles was beyond the experience of most people. As the great civilizations began to unfold, knowledge and appreciation also increased. Hundreds of years later, with Galileo, Christopher Columbus and others, we realized that the earth was a round unit, but certainly not the previously accepted center of all of reality. Instead we grew in knowledge and appreciation of the Milky Way, which is the earth's home. And now, thanks to scientists like Hubble, space travel and scientific advances, we know the universe is still being created and is infinite. Our metaphors for God, for Creation, for Heaven and Hell must continue to unfold in a faithful and faith-filled way, so that we continue on our path to life with the Lord. Our faith makes it safe to love the Lord with all of our heart, soul, strength and mind.

FIFTEENTH SUNDAY IN ORDINARY TIME (2)

AMOS 7: "Amos answered Amaziah, 'I was no prophet...; I was a shepherd. The Lord took me from following the flock, and said to me, go, prophesy to my people Israel.'"

PSALM 85: "Lord, let us see your kindness, and grant us your salvation."

EPHESIANS 1: "In him we were chosen, destined in accord with the purpose of the one who accomplishes all things according to the intention of his will."

MARK 6: "Jesus summoned the twelve and began to send them out two by two, and gave them authority over unclean spirits."

Our scriptures today give us traveling light and confidence in the call of God for each of us. Amos tells the man who wanted to run him out of Dodge, as it were, "I didn't choose this prophesying business. God called me from being a shepherd and told me to do this work." Amos knew at a deep level that God was with him in all circumstances. Psalm 85, our response, reminds us to see the goodness of God all around us and within us: "Lord, let us see your kindness, and grant us your salvation."

Paul tells the people of Ephesus that we are chosen in Christ and are empowered and destined to do good with and for each other. And Mark's Gospel tells of Jesus sending the Apostles out and giving them what they needed to accomplish God's will in all of life.

Aaron Copland is universally recognized as one of the great American composers of the twentieth century. He was a Jew. He reminds us, in a book of his writings entitled, *Aaron Copland: A Reader,*[*] that we of the Americas have learned our music rhythm lessons largely from the Negro.

Copland writes that "it is impossible to imagine what American music would have been like if the slave trade had never been instituted in North and South America. The slave ships brought a precious cargo of wonderfully gifted musicians, with an instinctive feeling for the most complex rhythmic pulsations. The strength of that musical impulse is attested to by the fact that it is just as alive today in the back streets of Rio de Janeiro or Havana or New Orleans as it was two hundred years ago."

---

[*] Kostelanetz, Richard (ed). *Aaron Copland: A Reader: Selected Writings,* 1923-1972. New York: Routledge, 2004.

The Negro slave was the Christ to music in America, and you and I are the recipients of the glorious music of their culture. In spite of their suffering and enslavement, they produced for us some of the most inspiring music in the world. Dixieland Jazz, Negro Spirituals, and the magnificent rhythms of their culture fill our radio airways every day. The scriptures today remind us that we, like the Negro slaves of two hundred years ago, have power, talent, and the mission from God to develop those gifts for the good of all.

We spend a lifetime coming to know facts and the information of life. We spend a lifetime meeting new people, and keeping names and faces properly together. We spend a lifetime learning how to maintain intimacy with our family and closest friends, hungry to know more of relationships, their meaning, their richness for ourselves, their attractiveness in our desires. Hopefully, it is also in this way that we spend a lifetime coming to know God.

Patience, perseverance, openness of mind and spirit, creativity, courage to know truth, willingness and readiness to change, as did Amos, and Paul, and the Apostles – this is our agenda. We continue, throughout life, to change in habit, in mind, in perception, in conviction, and these are among the conditions of spirit which enable us to know self as maturing, others as growing, and our God as infinitely perfect.

And where do we find God's name described? Like Amos and Paul and the Apostles, we find God in obedience and in confidence and in courage to move on to each new circumstance, condition, and offering of life. We find God in each moment given to us, in every experience in life as we reflect on it, and in the silent wisdom of listening prayer. We find God in worship where two or three are gathered in God's name, in suffering and in pleasant times, in short, in all things, all circumstances and places. It is impossible, if we are paying attention and listening, to miss the evidence of God's presence in our lives.

FIFTEENTH SUNDAY IN ORDINARY TIME (3)

DEUTERONOMY 30: "Moses said to the people… 'this command that I enjoin on you today is not too mysterious and remote for you….It is something very near to you..already in your mouths and in your hearts; you have only to carry it out.'"

PSALM 69: "Turn to the Lord in your need and you will live."

COLOSSIANS 1: "Christ Jesus.. is before all things, and in him all things hold together. For in him all fullness was pleased to dwell."

LUKE 10: "'Which of these three, in your opinion, was neighbor to the robbers' victim?' He answered, 'The one who treated him with mercy.' Jesus said to him,'Go, and do likewise.'"

Christian and Catholic morality, we believe, is based on the Law of God. Moral standards developed, according to the plan of God, in ancient times, were codified in the Old Testament, modified and ratified by Jesus in the New Testament, and today act as guide, protector, and saving principle for all of us. Biblical moral standards and the ethical principles which flow from them, serve as strength, protection, safety and happiness in human life. There is no such thing as a happy life, a peaceful life, a meaningful life, if we do not learn and follow the law of God. This is called the "Discipline of Growth." If a person does not discipline and regulate his/her body with proper food, drink, respiration, exercise, and rest, the body breaks down and malfunctions. And likewise, if a person does not discipline and regulate his/her spirit with moral integrity, that spirit, soul, mind, personality, gets twisted, broken, confused and sick. In the case of the body, the breakdown is called ill health. In the case of the soul, the breakdown is called sin, selfishness, deterioration of humanity, in our being.

I want to share with you a true story, which graphically demonstrates the predictability and essential need for God's Law, whether the law be physical, chemical, biological, mathematical, spiritual or moral. The law of God is for life, to protect life, to enhance life.

On May 25, 1961, over 46 years ago, and two days before I would be ordained a priest, President Kennedy called the country to action and committed the United States to sending a man to the moon and safely returning him to earth within the decade. On July 20, 1969, 38 years ago this coming Friday, Apollo II astronauts Neil Armstrong and Buzz Aldrin planted an American flag on the moon's surface, leaving a plaque that read, "Here men from the planet earth first set foot upon the moon July 1969 A.D. We come in peace for all mankind." This was the moment when Neil Armstrong uttered the unforgettable words, as he stepped on the moon for the first time, "That's one small step for man, one giant leap for mankind."

This story points out in great detail, that the law of God, if used as God intended, is safe, powerful, life giving and life enhancing. Thousands of men and women worked tirelessly for over 8 years to accomplish this project of going to the moon, and "How did they do it?" They did it by paying the strictest attention to the mathematical, physical, chemical, astronomical and moral law of God. The law of God demands study, practice, discipline, thought and reflection, and cooperation with, and respect for, all other forces in nature. The law of God calls us to the fullness of our human nature.

As our scriptures are given today, Moses tells us and comforts us with, "this command I enjoin on you today is not too mysterious and remote for you…It is something very near to you…already in your mouths and in your hearts; you have only to carry it out. Psalm 69 tells us of God's law, by saying, "Turn to the Lord in your need and you shall live." In our second reading, Paul to the Colossians, we are reassured, "In

Christ Jesus, all fullness is pleased to dwell." The Gospel account concludes with Jesus saying to the people who heard the story about the victim of the robbers and of those who helped him, "Go, and do likewise."

God's Law is our life. God's Law is our salvation. God's Law is our discipline. We have only to carry it out.

SIXTEENTH SUNDAY IN ORDINARY TIME*

GENESIS 18:   "The Lord appeared to Abraham…"

PSALM 15:   "He who does justice will live in the presence of the Lord."

COLOSS 1:   "…the word of God, the mystery hidden from ages and from generations past…the glory of this mystery…teaching everyone with all wisdom."

LUKE 10:   "Martha, Martha, you are anxious and worried about many things. There is need of only one thing."

A little first grade girl had just finished her first week of school, when she came home and announced to her mother, "I am just wasting my time in school. I can't read. I can't write, and they won't let me talk." That dear little girl had, after one week, a very narrow understanding of what school was about and how things unfold there. And so it is sometimes for us.

---

* Editor's note: This homily was originally presented on 7/18/04.

The scriptures today speak about the appearances of God, the presence of God, the Mystery of God, the need to grow in the Lord. And sometimes, we get stuck in habituation, arrested thought patterns, emotional needs, a lack of courage or of vision. It appears that all of these conditions are treated in the scriptures today. In Genesis, we hear that Abraham was visited by God, who came in a vision. But Abraham could not recognize the Lord in the commonness of the situation. In Colossians, Paul speaks about the Mystery hidden from ages and generations. In Luke, Jesus tells Martha that she has to learn to see the bigger and more complete picture. Her view is too limited and too limiting.

In the newspaper, *USA Today* on this last Tuesday, there were two brief articles about search, vision, possibility. One was about the Hubble Telescope in space which, if not repaired, will probably fail in 2007. This instrument has taught the world more about space than anything ever known. And the hope is that it can continue to teach us, open our eyes to more of creation and to more of reality, which is found in the infinite power and gifts from God. The article states that NASA will make the decision before the end of September on this matter. The public is most interested in the fact that we should fix the Hubble because it is unfolding so much new understanding and appreciation of the Universe for us.

The second article is about white pelicans in North Dakota. For at least 100 years, white pelicans have called Chase Lake National Wildlife Refuge in central North Dakota home. But the nesting ground, usually noisy this time of year with the grunts and squawks of thousands of birds and their chicks, is strangely quiet. Most of the pelicans are gone and no one knows why. Nearly 28,000 birds showed up to nest in early April, but then took off in late May and early June, leaving their chicks and eggs behind. Normally the pelicans stay at the refuge through September, raising their young and feasting on crawfish and salamanders. Investigators have considered diseases, food supply, water quality, weather, predators and other factors, but have found no satisfactory explanation for the exodus.

These two stories demonstrate for us the fact that we humans want to advance, to learn about the universe of which we are a part, to have our minds and souls opened and nurtured, so that we can participate in the ongoing creation and redemption of our planet, of our lives in union with all of creation. Our Christian Catholic Faith calls on us to open our minds and hearts to the continued unfolding of God's creation, of the mystery of existence.

The story of Martha and Mary, offered again today for our reflection, is an enriching reminder that Martha lives in each of us. The tendency to be self-centered, self-focused, self-seeking is alive in each of us. Selfish thinking leads to smallness of thought, unimaginative spirit and to a lack of creative energy. Complaining never changes reality. Engagement does.

We open ourselves again then today as we gather in worship. We re-establish a mind-set that welcomes the Lord, that welcomes life now, that welcomes opportunities each of us has to become more, more of whom God intended each of us to be.

SIXTEENTH SUNDAY IN ORDINARY TIME (2)*

GENESIS 18: "The Lord appeared to Abraham… as he sat at the entrance of his tent. Abraham saw three men standing nearby and ran to greet them."

PSALM 15: "He who does justice will live in the presence of the Lord."

COLOSSIANS 1: "I rejoice in my sufferings for your sake, and in my flesh I am filling up what is lacking in the afflictions of Christ."

LUKE 10: "Martha, Martha, you are anxious and worried about many things. There is need of only one thing."

The last two weeks have been difficult ones for the Catholic Church in the world, and in the United States. Pope Benedict two weeks ago, announced in the headlines of the media that the Roman Catholic Church is the one true Church in the world, the only means to certain salvation. At the same time, Cardinal Mahoney, the archbishop of Los Angeles, is flying

---

* Editor's note: This homily was originally presented on 7/22/07.

to Rome twice within two weeks, to hammer out a deal to settle the biggest and most scandalous chapter in the sexual abuse of children, primarily by Catholic priests, but also by religious men and women and a few lay people. The headlines of all the papers of this country and the leading news programs of the electronic media announced that 660 million dollars is the settlement agreed upon by all parties involved. This does not preclude the possibility of civil law suites being brought forth.

Pope John Paul II, shortly before his death, in a message delivered publicly, said that one of the mistakes of Christianity is that we have traded the Gospel for a set of rules. Our church today is defined more by lawyers, legal systems, both civil and ecclesiastical, and by trying to present the best image of who we are, than the church is defined by the spirit of Jesus Christ and his teachings.

The sexual abuse of a minority of the clergy and church leaders, and the cover-up on the part of the Catholic hierarchy have been and continue to be a sad, horrible chapter in our history as a Church. We must humbly embrace the total dimension of this painful, destructive, and shameful phenomenon, or we will never heal and become again a church who has moral standing and moral integrity in our world, which is in such need of integral and faithful moral and spiritual leadership.

Our scriptures today tell us that we should be hospitable. In the Book of Genesis, we hear that the Lord appeared to Abraham, who was sitting at the entrance of his tent, his home. Strangers came by and Abraham invited them in, fed them, and welcomed them. Psalm 15, our response, speaks of living in the presence of the Lord by doing justice. Paul's letter to the Colossians tells of the sufferings we must endure along with Christ, as we help each other live the Gospel. And Jesus is said, in Luke's Gospel, to have told Martha that she was to be in union with God and not worrying about all the other issues.

The scriptures introduce us today to various concepts involved in everyday living. In Genesis, our first reading, we have strangers coming to Abraham. We all deal with strangers every day. We are all called to be hospitable, kind, welcoming, never excluding, demeaning, distancing. Our Psalm response asks for justice. We are to live with integrity every day, with concern for all people in our lives. Paul reminds us in the second reading that to live the Gospel sometimes involves some inconvenience, pain, and suffering. We are asked to do this in the spirit of Christ. And, in the Gospel, Jesus reminds the Martha in each of us that we are to get our priorities straight.

In view of the current condition of our church family, being riddled with scandal, negative press, and the deep need for moral renewal, at the local level, it would seem more in line with Christ to respect the religious convictions of all people who differ from us Catholics in their approach to the mystery of God, without having to remind them that we think we are right. Each of us has had many opportunities to meet people of other faith traditions, both Christian and non-Christian. I have met many people in my lifetime who believed differently than we Catholics do, and I don't think that I have ever met one of these good people who did not think that their faith practice was the right one for them. In other words, the religious convictions of each tradition and the moral integrity of each individual conscience is not in the purview of our business to judge as right or wrong. Jesus taught us not to judge but to love one another.

As followers of Christ, we believe that it is far more important to love than to be right. And at this point in the American Catholic Church, as one of many current religions being practiced in this country, it would seem better to be humble, reflective, and willing to reform our lives than to explain "the why" of our clerical sexual misconduct, and the attempts to minimize the significance of this behavior, explain away our sin, or to infer that the financial fallout of this issue does not fall on the shoulders of the Catholic Laity.

The scriptures today do indeed ask us to be hospitable, just, silent in suffering, and willing to re-establish our Gospel priorities. We seek God's continued blessing in all of this.

SIXTEENTH SUNDAY IN ORDINARY TIME (3)[*]

WISDOM 12:   "And you taught your people, that those who are just must be kind."

PSALM 86:   "Lord, you are good and forgiving."

ROMANS 8:   "The Spirit comes to the aid of our weakness"

MATT 13:   "The kingdom of heaven is like a mustard seed."

Forty years ago this summer, two famous Americans died, and left a powerful heritage. Helen Keller died on June 1, 1968, and Robert Kennedy was killed on June 6, 1968. Helen Keller was deaf and blind from 18 months of age. She was a feisty young girl. From age six, she was signing with her fingers, and reading a little Braille. Her well known teacher was Ann Sullivan, herself blind. Helen Keller graduated from Radcliffe College, Cum Laude. She learned to speak, ride horses, waltz, she loved German and Greek, and was an inspiration to all who knew of her.

---

[*] Editor's note: This homily was originally presented on 7/20/08.

Robert Kennedy was shot twice in the head at the Ambassador Hotel in Los Angeles. At his funeral, his brother, Senator Edward Kennedy, said among other things, "My Brother need not be idealized or enlarged in death beyond what he was in life. He should be remembered simply, as a good and decent man, who saw wrong and tried to right it, saw suffering and tried to heal it, saw war and tried to stop it." Senator Kennedy said that his brother Robert said many times, all across this country, "Some men see things as they are and say why? I dream things that never were, and say why not?"

Our scriptures today invite us and exhort us to do with our time on this earth, and with the gifts we have, to grow, to help make new horizons, to develop new opportunities for all of humanity.

Wisdom says, "And, Lord, you taught your people, that those who are just must also be kind." A constant need in this country, and all over the world, is that all people work for justice, fairness, and kindness. Society, to be safe, and to be a comfortable place to live, must be based on justness, fairness, patience, courage and kindness. This is the responsibility of each of us. Great strides among humanity have happened because of people like Helen Keller and Robert Kennedy, and of people like you and me.

Psalm 86 brightens our days with the promise, "Lord, you are good and forgiving." We believe that we are made in God's image, and that God's work is truly our own. Paul's letter to the Romans reminds us that the Spirit of God is alive in each one of us, as Paul says, "The Spirit comes to the aid of our weakness."

In Matthew's Gospel, Jesus is quoted as saying, "The kingdom of heaven is like a mustard seed." The mustard seed is among the smallest of seeds, but grows into a huge plant. Each of us begins our journey as a single cell, formed from two tiny seeds, one from Mother and one from Father. As the mustard seed has tremendous potential, so does each of us. Wisdom reminds us to be just, fair and kind. Psalm 86 reminds us to be like God, good and forgiving. Romans reminds us to have confidence in the Spirit of God, which we all share. And Jesus' words remind us to develop our potential.

The message is simple. The message is doable. The message is our blueprint.

SEVENTEENTH SUNDAY IN ORDINARY TIME

The readings offered for our consideration and appreciation today from Genesis, Psalm 138 and Luke all take us to a description or example of prayer. And prayer is central to our relationship with God and with the development of our spirit and soul. Prayer, communication, reflection, contemplation, meditation; singing, thinking, imagining, reflecting, remembering, pondering, wondering, questioning, doubting, speaking, listening, dialoging, studying, writing, reading, creating, dancing, changing. These and many other postures, exercises, and experiences are part and parcel of the prayer life of most of us.

Genesis gives us the story of selfish begging and bartering with the Lord. It is a good example, it would seem, as how *not* to pray. We can get into a mentality which tries to control God, barter with God, negotiate the situation. That is not prayer. Prayer is opening of self to the awe and mystery and possibility of existence. Prayer is journeying with trust, gratitude, love and respect. Prayer is the willingness to listen deeply and calmly to what is, to what is happening, to what is changing.

Psalm 138, today's response, states, "Lord, on the day I called for help, you answered me." This statement places the one praying in the presence of God, in the conscious focus of one's own being, and in a stance of belief, trust, obedience, reverence and awe. And Luke's Gospel presents the humble and universally accepted Christian prayer of liturgy and of private piety, The Lord's Prayer. Luke's Gospel for today ends with the statement that our God and Father in heaven will give the Holy Spirit to those who ask. What a comforting and reassuring statement that is.

Prayer comes through each person differently at each new moment of life. One day, we may pray out of fear, insecurity, vulnerability, restlessness and a lack of peace of mind. Another day may find us joyful and confident. Still other conditions of soul are deep wonder, radical doubt, deep and abiding questioning. Sadness, loss and grief bring a different experience of prayer, one that takes us to an entirely different place in our soul. Depression, darkness, hopelessness force us into a spiritual stance of learning the path by walking it.

Holiday spirit envelopes us with one approach to peaceful prayer. Funeral liturgy moves us along the painful prayer of Goodbye to life as it was before the death of a loved one. The birth of a child or of an animal, the beauty of a snowfall, the blossoming of a flower, the experience of a thunderstorm, all deepen our respect for, and appreciation of, the power of nature, and our prayer is pretty much speechlessness, wonder, awe.

We pray with our ears as we listen to a friend who is sad, or to a child with many questions about the journey. We pray with our lips as we offer a sincere kiss or a kind word. We pray with our nose as we appreciate the odors of life, those that are sweet and appreciated and those that warn us of danger to life and safety. We pray with our eyes as we see and study new pieces and dimensions of life each day. We pray with our touch as we do our work, as we play together. We pray with our body as we sit in peace, genuflect with reverence, kneel in respect. We pray with our soul as we bring our mind home, as we focus our attention, as we ponder and consider the passing of life.

We pray this morning as we listen to and sing the music, as we offer our donation, as we hear the ancient word, as we experience the sacrament, as we smile at our neighbor and look through the church window.

We pray differently as we say goodbye to our childhood and begin the stormy time of adolescence. We shift our prayer as the responsibilities of young adulthood come to play in our lives. Prayer flows differently in the power days of middle age and changes again as we learn the diminishment of our older years.

The prayer of creativity is different from the prayer born of guilt, and the humble prayer of defeat moves differently than the good prayer of success. Illness brings one kind of prayer while vigor shifts our soul differently.

Basically, prayer for us Christians is as essential as breathing, eating and walking. Prayer is the expression of our soul's deepest needs and movements. Prayer is the poetry that comes from each of us as we reach out for the transcendent, as we place our life in the hand of God, as we support each other in any good. Prayer is our highest human expression, our deepest glance, our fullest experience. Prayer is our walking stick into eternity. It works all along the way.

SEVENTEENTH SUNDAY IN ORDINARY TIME (2)

1 KINGS 3: "The Lord appeared to Solomon in a dream at night….. Solomon asked the Lord, 'Give your servant an understanding heart to judge your people and to distinguish right from wrong.'"

PSALM 119: "Lord, I love your commands."

ROMANS 8: "Brothers and Sisters: We know that all things work for good for those who love God, who are called according to God's purpose."

MATT 13: "Every scribe who has been instructed in the Kingdom of Heaven is like the head of a household who brings from his storeroom both the new and the old."

Today, we hear from Paul's letter to the Romans, "Brothers and Sisters, we know that all things work for good for those who love God, who are called according to God's purpose." We believe this to be the central core of our faith life and practice, the love of God and the development of goodness with and for each other. A Wisconsin poet, Father Gordon Gilsdorf, speaks about God's lexicon, and says, "I searched

God's lexicon to fathom 'Bethlehem' and 'Calvary.' It simply said: See 'Love.'"* In birth and in death and in everything in between, we find life through love, charity, the offering of goodness.

To accomplish this in life, we must develop the gift of Wisdom. Today's first reading from the Book of Kings, beautifully presents Solomon as asking for this life-giving gift of wisdom. "The Lord appeared to Solomon in a dream at night...Solomon asked the Lord, 'Give your servant an understanding heart to judge your people and to distinguish right from wrong.'" Solomon is one of history's heroes because he sought the gift of wisdom, knowing that it was foundational to the success of life for others and for himself.

Wisdom can be described as that condition of soul, mind, spirit that sees reality as it is, as sacred before God and Humanity. To develop wisdom demands that we pay attention to life as it comes, that we hunger for truth, and that we respect all of creation. To be wise means that we study life sincerely and constantly. To be wise is to have a humble heart, and to be open to new appreciations and perceptions of things, movements, relationships. To be wise is to stand in awe before all of life, and before all manifestations of life. To be wise is the ultimate goal of all human longing and all human possibilities.

---

* See Morneau, Robert F. In *Millennium Monthly,* May 1999, at http://www.americancatholic.org.

Think of the wise people in your life. Think of their qualities. Think of their responses to the circumstances of living. This is the way we learn. As we develop our own rendition of wisdom, we contribute to the spirit of the earth, the spirit of truth, the spirit of humanity. Great joy comes from a competent and generous willingness to share our gifts with others in as complete a way as possible.

Wisdom is insightfulness. Wisdom is a quality which brings hope and enables us to believe in truth bigger than our ability to comprehend. Wisdom enables us and empowers us to appreciate mystery. Wisdom is what enables us to know and to honor limits – limits in relationships, limits in power, limits in all of life.

Wisdom is the force which brings each person to his or her potential. Wisdom is the condition of soul which brings balance, respect for all truth, and a sense of awe. Wisdom brings richness to all of life.

Solomon was a wonderful example of wisdom for the ancient and biblical worlds. Another big name person who died fifty years ago is an example of deep wisdom and humble and grateful faith. This man is Albert Einstein. He was born in Ulm, Germany on March 14, 1879, and died on April 18, 1955. His humble wisdom has transformed our world so much that his contribution cannot be measured. We, like Solomon and Albert Einstein, are asked to contribute our share to the world knowledge pool in a humble and confident fashion. It is in that spirit that we truly find God, peace, happiness and goodness.

SEVENTEENTH SUNDAY IN ORDINARY TIME (3)

2 KINGS 4: "For thus says the Lord, 'They shall eat and there shall be some left over.'"

PSALM 145: "The hand of the Lord feeds us; God answers all our needs."

EPHES 4: "I, a prisoner for the Lord, urge you to live in a manner worthy of the call you have received, with all humility and gentleness, with patience, bearing with one another with love."

JOHN 6: "When they had had their fill, Jesus said to his disciples, 'Gather the fragments left over, so that nothing will be wasted.'"

In ancient times, our ancestors lived in small communities, and pretty much spent their lives in their respective community, because they moved from place to place by walking. And then came the domestication of animals, and people could move further because they rode on the animals. Then, perhaps the greatest invention of all time came into play, the wheel, and chariots and carts were developed so that many could be transported at one time, and the ancient world was significantly transformed.

Then people began to build boats and the world shrunk again, so that people could and did go to other nations, countries and places, on the water. Then roads were built to increase speed and safety in travel. A couple hundred years ago, the engine was invented, and this further transformed our existence. Within the last two hundred years, trains, automobiles, and planes came to be, and the speed with which our society changes was dramatic.

The last hundred years or so saw the telephone, the telegraph, the radio, and the television come along, and the modern world was born. Increasing our ability to move and to learn and to become, was our ability to experience space travel, the moon landing, the computer. In a few thousand years we have come from living in a small village with a few other human beings to now living in space. And currently, we can be in touch with almost anyone in the world by e-mail in a few seconds of time.

As we reflect on this history, we can see clearly that life is an ongoing experience of change, movement, development and growth. Our scriptures today teach us to be reverent and thankful for the simple presence of our human nature, of our intelligence, of our creativity, as we continue to enjoy all that has come to be, and as we struggle to contribute our portion to the goods of nature and to the welfare of humanity, as we continue to live.

In the first reading from the Second Book of Kings, a man told Elisha the prophet to use the food he had at hand with his community and it would be enough, and as Elisha obeyed, he learned that what was present was sufficient. Psalm 145, our response today, teaches us the lesson we must never forget, and that is, "The hand of the Lord feeds us." Humility, reality, awareness are essential to our moving along. Paul's letter to the Ephesians states again the simple and essential truth for life on this earth between individuals, within families and communities and among nations. Paul says, "I urge you to live in a manner worthy of the call you have received, with all humility and gentleness, with patience, bearing with one another through love, striving to preserve the unity of the spirit through the bond of peace: one body and one spirit, as you were also called to the one hope of your call: one Lord, one faith, one baptism; one God and Father of all, who is over all and through all and in all."

Basically, the scriptures teach us to use the gifts of God, to share the gifts of God, to protect the gifts of God. God's gifts include our ability to know truth, to share generously and unselfishly the goods of the earth, and to utilize always the spirit that is within each of us to preserve unity and the bond of peace.

We humans are very wealthy in our natural endowments of body, mind, and spirit. We humans are called to appreciate all that others have given to us throughout all of human history. We are exhorted to make our respective contribution to the ongoing development of God's plan through God's Holy Spirit which is within each of us. We pray for humility, gratitude, courage and generosity.

SEVENTEENTH SUNDAY IN ORDINARY TIME (4)

GENESIS 18: "In those days, the Lord said, 'The outcry against Sodom and Gomorrah is so great, and their sin so grave, that I must go down and see whether or not their actions fully correspond to the cry against them that comes to me. I mean to find out.'"

PSALM 138: "Lord, on the day I cried for help, you answered me."

COLOSSIANS 2: "Jesus Christ brought you to life along with him, having forgiven us all our transgressions."

LUKE 11: "Jesus said to them, 'When you pray, say: Father, hallowed be your name, your kingdom come. Give us each day our daily bread, and forgive us our sins, for we forgive everyone in debt to us, and do not subject us to the final test.'"

In everyday life, we humans need food, drink, oxygen, exercise, sleep, rest, love, and truth. Without any one of these, our lives become, to some degree, deformed, paralyzed, and broken. Each of us has experienced this paralysis, deformation, brokenness, when we cannot get our breath, when we need desperately, a drink, when we are exhausted or starved, and when we know that we do not have, tell, be, or receive the truth.

Our first reading today is an account of life involving truth, lies, exaggeration, calumny, slander, reality. Whenever we share in truth, we flourish; whenever we are part of an untruth, we and our environment go down. The individual and the society he/she is part of diminish when the lack of reality, or a lie is offered. God speaks in Genesis, "I mean to find the truth." Jesus, centuries later said, "Seek the truth, and the truth will set you free." Truth is reality, and truth is salvation. Truth is the only foundation of happiness.

On several occasions in my experience, I have visited a dying person, at home, in a nursing home, or in a hospital. Many times, early in our conversation, when the family is not present, the patient will say something like, "Father, I am dying, aren't I?" I try to respond attentively and gently, but honestly, by saying, "Yes, it appears that your body is shutting down," or "Yes, the medical people think you are failing physically." Almost always, the patient will say, "Thank you for talking about this business of my death. It is difficult for my family and me to talk about my dying, but I know I am dying, and it feels good to just talk about it." The truth sets the patient free. Fear is dissipated through acknowledgment of truth, in this case, the truth of accepting death.

Psalm 38, our response today, assures us that it is OK to cry for help. "Lord, on the day I cried for help, you answered me." The answer will not usually look like what I have in mind, but it is what we need to take the next step in this journey called life. In our second reading, Paul assures the Colossians and you and me that the Lord of life, the spirit of the Lord of life, walks with us unceasingly. We cannot get away from the truth of God. We can become delusional, filled with untruth of our own making, and untruth is always of our making, and we can live a lie in our mind, but we cannot avoid God Almighty. This is why a healthy conscience hurts, when we know that there is untruth within us or among us. Happiness is the absolute opposite of the lie.

Our Gospel account today gives us the greatest power, promise and assurance of happiness. It is through the medium of prayer. The disciples ask Jesus to teach them to pray. Prayer is the effort on our part to reach beyond human truth, to be open to the mystery of God-truth. Prayer is the ultimate in seeking the truth. Prayer quiets our soul, slows down human chatter within, and sets another stage for expansion of our appreciation of life, its meaning, its destiny. Prayer is a comprehensive engagement of our mind, our will, our awareness of the presence of our God. Jesus says that if our prayer praises God (Hallowed be your name), accepts God's will (Your kingdom come), if we are satisfied with what we need,

need, not want (Give us each day our daily bread); if we are humble, which means knowing our place and taking it, living the truth, if we ask forgiveness for our sins and forgive others, if we are open to the truth of life and the truth of death, then we are safe, we are saved, we are at one with the Lord and with each other, and with all of creation. This is the truth that sets us free.

EIGHTEENTH SUNDAY IN ORDINARY TIME

ISAIAH 55:   "Thus says the Lord: All you who are thirsty, come to the water. You who have no money, come, receive grain and eat."

PSALM 145: "The hand of the Lord feeds us; He answers all our needs."

ROMANS 8: "What will separate us from the love of Christ? Will anguish, or distress, or persecution, or famine, or nakedness, or peril, or the sword? No…"

MATT. 14:   The multiplication of the loaves and fishes.

The stories of plenty abound in America and in Rochester. The stories of freedom and opportunity abound in America and in Rochester. The stories of God's continued blessings abound in America and in Rochester. And the stories of worry and anguish and anxiety abound in America and in Rochester. Most of these stories have been or continue to be part of the experience of each of us. Many of us worry and fret and fear the hours and the days and the years of life away, by giving in to our self-focus, insecurity and vulnerability, rather than practicing the disciplines of trust in God, living in the present, and being very thankful for all that is available to us, in abundance.

The scriptures today beautifully and simply and briefly describe the bounty of God present to us here and now. Psalm 145, our response today, states well the richness of our experience of the gifts of God. Paul's letter to the Romans hits us hard by telling the truth that we worry and fret and fear, thus losing life. No, Paul says: NO. Much of the time we do not believe him. And Matthew's account of the multiplication of the loaves and the fishes reminds us again of the power that we humans have from God, having been given intelligence, courage, creativity and determination.

Our scriptures are telling us again the truths we learned as children and have chosen to forget as we live out adolescence, maturing adulthood, and our declining years. We are wealthy beyond what the vast majority of people on the earth can ever hope for. We are better educated than the people of the world generally. We enjoy freedom to travel, to create, to contribute, to share more than almost any other group who has ever lived. This setting is a blessing and, at once, a danger to us, because it allows us to become inordinately self-focused, anxious, and vulnerable.

The scriptures remind us that we must practice courage, living in the present, and trusting God. None of these experiences come easily, without practice, automatically, without decision, on our part. We seem to think that the spiritual life should be easy. We forget that the spiritual life, like human intimacy of any kind, is demanding, taxing and challenging. We must work calmly at being present to life, at trusting God, at being thankful, or worry, fear, anxiety take over and tend to increase as we allow this lazy and sloppy spirit to continue. For us Catholic Christians, the spiritual life involves the warmth and plenty of Christmas and the difficulty and challenge of Calvary and the Cross. Jesus taught that unless we take up the cross every day and follow him, we cannot be his disciples. And to be his disciple means that we live in the Kingdom of God, not in our own little worry and fret shop. To follow Jesus means we develop faith and hope and charity and unselfishness and calmness and confidence on an ongoing basis as the foundation of life. As we practice this, there is no room for fear and fretting, and anxiety and worry. We practice the way of Jesus or we practice and are enslaved to the way of self-centered worry. That is a radical Christian choice and decision. To follow Jesus means life and the kingdom. To follow the path of worry and fear means more worry and fear. Our job is to choose Christ, and His way, and His life, and His kingdom.

A recent book, entitled, *The Power of Now*, by Eckhard Tolle,[*] describes what our scriptures present today. It is a beautiful read and it has helped me very much to remember what my faith is about, and how my faith is to be practiced for life,

---

[*] Tolle, Eckhart. *The Power of Now*. Vancouver: Namaste Publishing, 1999.

and that is that we are to live in the present, as God gives life. The two greatest thieves, described in the Scriptures and in poetry, and experienced by all of us, are the *past* and the *future*. These two experiences rob us of the only chance at life, which is the *present*. We recommit ourselves as we pray today to live in the Kingdom of God, the present.

EIGHTEENTH SUNDAY IN ORDINARY TIME (2)

ECCLESIASTES 1: "Here is one who labored with wisdom and knowledge and skill, and yet to another who has not labored over it, he must leave property."

PSALM 90: "If today you hear his voice, harden not your hearts."

COLOSSIANS 3: "Brothers and Sisters, seek what is above. Put to death immorality."

LUKE 12: "You fool, this night your life will be demanded of you."

One of the most painful and beneficial experiences in life for a sixteen year old is to be beginning to take the driving road test in order to qualify to possess a driver's license, during which he or she breaks a law. Immediately the test is stopped, and the errant driver returns to the testing station to go home defeated and instructed to practice, study, and then return to try again at a later date. This is painful because it is a blow to one's ego, but it is also beneficial to the driver and to society, because one learns the heavy responsibility, as a driver of a road vehicle, to protect the safety for ones' self and society at large. The message, implicit or explicitly spoken is, "*get it right.*"

Get it right is the message found in our scriptures today as it pertains to life. *Get life right.* Learn the laws of life. Learn how to direct life. Learn to protect life. Learn the dimensions of life. Learn the limits of life. Learn the essence and nature of life. Learn the source and destinies of life and *get it right.*

Ecclesiastes instructs us not to confuse life with property, possessions, with greed for anything created. Psalm 90 teaches about spirit. Do not allow the burdens, disappointments, unfairness, injustice, any part of the dark side of life make one bitter and hardened in heart. Paul's letter to the Colossians exhorts us to see clearly, and beyond the obvious, and deeper than human conventions, into the transcendent mystery of God, eternal life, truth and love beyond imagining. Further, this reading names several possible pitfalls which can confuse and disappoint us in selfishness, body and soul indulgences which are immoral. Discipline is the lesson to be learned in this scripture.

And Luke's Gospel offers very important and very heavy wisdom. To learn that life is not all in the mind of God, is not all in the womb of our mother, is not all in the body on this earth, is not all in human control, is not finished at the limit of our comprehension, is so important. To ponder the meaning, direction, possibilities, and eternal dimensions of our existence is essential for a happy and peaceful life. Until and unless we learn to live in FAITH, seeking bigger truth, HOPE, opening us to more life than meets the eye or is able to be comprehended by the human brain, and CHARITY, which is the very life of God within and between us, we are paralyzed and we miss the richness intended by our God. Letting go of life is a portion of Luke's story today. Possessions, power, seeking total control of our environment, are all illusions. We live at the will and pleasure of God for as long as God intends and permits. And this is utterly a safe plan for all of us in life. It is essential that we learn the exhortation of Jesus to the effect that, "Unless we are willing to lose our life, we will not find it."

EIGHTEENTH SUNDAY IN ORDINARY TIME (3)

ECCLESIASTES 1: "What profit comes to man from all the toil and anxiety of heart with which he has labored under the sun?"

PSALM 90: "If today you hear God's voice, harden not your hearts."

COLOSSIANS 3: "If you were raised with Christ, seek what is above where Christ is seated."

LUKE 12: "Take care to guard against all greed, for though one may be rich, one's life does not consist of possessions."

In a book published in 2006 entitled, *THIRST, Poems by Mary Oliver**, the author writes in her epilogue the following meditation: "Another morning and I awake with thirst for the goodness I do not have. I walk out to the pond and all the way God has given us such beautiful lessons. Oh Lord, I was never a quick scholar but sulked and hunched over my books past the hour and the bell; grant me, in your mercy, a little

---

* Oliver, Mary. *Thirst, Poems by Mary Oliver.* Boston: Beacon Press, 2006.

more time. Love for the earth and love for you are having such a long conversation in my heart. Who knows what will finally happen or where I will be sent, yet already I have given a great many things away, expecting to be told to pack nothing, except the prayers, which, with this thirst, I am slowly learning." (P. 69)

Greed is a universal experience in all of humanity. In addition to owning our own body, our soul and our life, we hunger for security, which we frequently and mostly translate as the need for possessions. And it seems, the more possessions we get, the more we want and need. When is enough, *enough*? This is one of the constant life challenges for us.

The wisdom of the ancient peoples, as recorded so many times in the Old Testament, and as given to us today in our first reading, Ecclesiastes, Chapter 1, speaks to this reality, as it asks, "What profit comes to a man from all the toil and anxiety of heart with which he has labored under the sun?" Our response Psalm, Psalm 90, exhorts us, "If today you hear God's voice, harden not your hearts." We are to work every day to focus on the God of life, so that we do not become preoccupied with the possessions of life, and greed leads us, inevitably, down that road toward possessions, and we never find peace. We are further taught, in our second reading, Paul to the Colossians, "If you were raised with Christ, seek what is above...."

And our Gospel today is direct in telling us that Jesus said clearly, "Take care to guard against all greed." The vast majority of our Native American brothers and sisters, in their tribes and communities, had, before Christianity came, holidays dedicated to giving things of value away, as a way to counter greed. The Indian People believed that they belonged to the earth, and that they did not own the earth. They were guests on the earth, which was their home, and in life, and should treat all possessions as though they did not own them; thus, the annual give-away. This was a practice and a discipline which prepared them for the ultimate give-away of all things in death.

Jesus taught on several occasions that we should seek first the kingdom of God within, and then all other things and experiences would make sense. Mary Oliver, in her book of poems, asks, "How many mysteries have you seen in your lifetime?" It seems that one of the mysteries we deal with almost constantly is greed. We need to be aware of this tendency toward greed within ourselves, this fruit of original sin, if we hope to place God first always, if we hope to find peace always, if we want a rich life always. Wealth is never about possessions, it is always about spirit.

In another poem, Mary Oliver states about life, "This is our school." There is perhaps no more important lesson for us to learn in life, than to identify greed within ourselves, name greed within ourselves, and control greed within ourselves. Greed, while most of us do not get as excited about it as we do about sexual lust, is just as lethal, as controlling, as demanding as lust, and not dealing with greed can destroy portions of our lives just as devastatingly as can lust.

We pray God for wisdom in dealing with our greed.

THE TRANSFIGURATION OF THE LORD

DANIEL 7: "All peoples, nations and languages serve the Lord. His dominion is an everlasting dominion."

PSALM 97: "The Lord is king, the most high over all the earth."

2 PETER 1: "We possess the prophetic message that is altogether reliable. You will do well to be attentive to it, as to a lamp shining in a dark place."

MARK 9: "Peter said to Jesus, 'Lord, it is good that we are here.'"

The Feast of the Transfiguration draws our full attention to the greatest mystery of existence, the truth and mystery of the presence of God. To grow in holiness is to journey into mystery, into the very life of God. Often the result and experience is not clarity, but a different vision of life with different questions. Light does not necessarily dispel all the darkness, but the light can be a guide to us as we continue the search for meaning.

The essence of mystery is incomprehensibility. God is our inspiration. We stand in awe!

God calls us from our depths to be inclusive and appreciative of all of creation, of all of humanity, of all of existence. We address our God through experience of faith and hope and charity and wonder and awe. We are tempted to seek God through intellect and cognition primarily, because we tend to want to be in control. When we approach the Lord, we do so in vulnerability as creatures not in control. The Feast of the Transfiguration Scriptures show us how to address the mystery of God.

The Book of Daniel reminds us, "All peoples, nations and languages serve the Lord; God's dominion is an everlasting dominion." Seeking God is the gift given to every single human being, and the search for God is a fundamental defining experience throughout all of each life. We seek the Lord by loving God above all things, and by loving our neighbors and ourselves. What a wonderful insight and continued learning!

We have a common experience in the search for the Lord, and we have a unique experience in that search. In this part of life, we do well to heed the spiritual principle, "Identify, don't compare!" No one else can do our search for us, and we can do little except encourage one another in this effort.

St. Peter expresses the truth in this way: "We possess the prophetic message that is altogether reliable. You will do well to be attentive to it, as to a lamp shining in a dark place." The journey to God for most of us is more in the dark than in the light. This is perhaps a helpful truth to review from time to time, because the spiritual life can get frustrating, just as any other dimension of life can tax our nerves and determination and perseverance.

Perhaps Mark's Gospel today gives us the deepest hints about pursuing the Mystery of God. Mark tells the story of Jesus taking the three disciples up into the isolation of the mountains, away from noise, away from the crowd and away from the business of everyday living. Jesus takes them into the cloud, where they cannot see, and experience being lost. They experience hearing a strange voice coming from the cloud, and their senses and intellectual hunger are frustrated. The message seems to be that we open our hearts, we correct our expectations concerning the Lord, and that we do what the prophet Micah very clearly and succinctly tells us of the search for God, "You have been told, O Man, what is good, and what the Lord requires of you: Only to do the right and to love goodness, and to walk humbly with your God." (Micah 6:8)

Henri J. M. Nouwen, the famous author who writes about the search for God has a book entitled, *The Return of the Prodigal Son.*[*] The book is inspired by Rembrandt's painting of the same title. Nouwen says of his own journey to the heart

---

[*] Nouwen, Henri J. M. *The Return of the Prodigal Son.* New York: Doubleday, 1992.

of God, "At the heart of this adventure is a seventeenth –century painting and its artist, a first-century parable and its author and a twentieth-century person in search of life's meaning." The work of every man and woman and child is that pursuit of deepening appreciation of the mystery of God, in all of the circumstances, conditions and opportunities of life. Let us continue to give ourselves to this enriching and deepening movement toward the Lord of life.

NINETEENTH SUNDAY IN ORDINARY TIME

1 KINGS 19: "The Lord said to Elijah, 'Go outside and stand on the mountain before the Lord; the Lord will be passing by.'"

PSALM 85: "Lord, let us see your kindness, and grant us your salvation."

ROMANS 9: "Brothers and Sisters: I speak the truth in Christ."

MATT 14: "Jesus went up on the mountain to pray."

Perhaps you have heard the story about the man who desperately wanted to win a lot of money by winning the Powerball lottery. He prayed and prayed and nothing happened. Then, one day the man was desperately praying, and he begged God, "Please tell me how to win the Powerball." And a rather impatient answer came from the clouds, "Buy a ticket."

Mystics, scholars, philosophers, theologians, people of every description, have throughout the history of humanity, searched for the Mystery of God, with accompanying emotions, doubts, questions, fears. Deep in our hearts resides the need to approach God, to know the truth, to experience beyond our reach, beyond our comprehension, beyond our nature.

Our scriptures today revisit that condition with us. The first reading from the Book of Kings tells of Elijah who is seeking God in a cave, which is in the dark, on the side of the mountain, which allows him to see a long distance. Elijah also looks for God in a heavy wind, in an earthquake, in fire, and in a tiny whispering sound. And on that particular day at least, Elijah found God in the tiny whispering sound. And what did Elijah do when he found the Lord? The account tells us that he hid his face in his cloak. Elijah was afraid of this overwhelming truth of God.

Psalm 85, our response, says, "Lord, let us see your kindness, and grant us your salvation." The author believes that he can find God in kindness. St. Paul writes to the proud and powerful Romans and says, "I speak the truth in Christ." Paul's conviction is that he finds God in Christ. And in the Gospel account by Matthew, we are told that Jesus went up on the mountain alone, and prayed. Jesus was finding God in solitude, quiet, and the movement and experience of prayer.

Dear friends, we have freely come together at this time, in this place, to participate in, to contribute to, to derive from – the Mass. This ancient prayer has been the medium through which we have searched for God for most of our lives. This experience of word and sacrament, of forgiveness and peace sharing, this hour of silence and song, this pausing for reflection, is our search currently for God.

All of life is a search for the mystery of God. Our entire base for happiness is the search for, and experience of, God. Our hearts are deepened, our souls are expanded, our minds are developed, our emotions are enriched, as we pray and ponder, and search and wonder.

Prayer and communion with God is a deepening of our being and of our experience and of our awareness. Emily Dickinson, in one of her poems, writes, "Exhilaration is the breeze that lifts us from the ground and leaves us in another place whose statement is not found."* Prayer and search is the breeze that lifts us from the ground. And prayer always leaves us in another place, and prayer never exhausts the possibilities of reality, of life, of experience.

As we pay attention to our journey and as we reflect on our thoughts, feelings, experience, and current condition, through our prayer, we do find a bit more of God. And we do find a bit more of ourselves and of our relationships and of our accomplishments. Through prayer we are able to deal with our selfishness and sin without despair. In this search for God we are renewed in humility, so that we can know our place and take it calmly and richly. Life makes more sense when we punctuate it with prayer and reflection and with the search for

---

* Editor's note: This poem, "Exhilaration is the Breeze," may be viewed on the Internet at www.americanpoems.com.

God. What a rich gift our curiosity and sense of wonder is, as we apply that power to the search for our God.

NINETEENTH SUNDAY IN ORDINARY TIME (2)

WISDOM 18:   "...with sure knowledge of the oaths in which they put their faith."

HEBREWS 11: "Faith is the realization of what is hoped for and evidence of things not seen..."

LUKE 12:   "For where your treasure is, there also will your heart be."

In a wonderful book entitled *Waiting for God**, its author, Simone Weil, states that faith is a "marvelous invitation into the wholeness of life." In his article, "Deeper Into Love†," Henri Nouwen suggests that faith empowers us to realize that God does not shout, scream or push. The voice of God is soft and gentle, like a small voice. And there is an old saying that goes:

> "All bondage is in the mind.
> All freedom is in the mind.
> The truth of selfhood brings clear faith."

---

* Weil, Simone. *Waiting for God.* New York: HarperCollins, 1973.

† Nouwen, Henri. "Deeper Into Love," *Weavings,* September/ October 1995, p. 25.

Faith is an essential part of life and living and is a map for negotiating this gift of life. Faith is a quality and experience and movement that has been described and studied in so many veins and ways and manners. Faith involves speculation, risk, mature letting go of selfish and narrow perceptions, and faith is learning how to negotiate through growth, development, change in heart, mind, soul. Faith is about dreaming, curiosity, conviction. Faith is a full and joyful and confident interpretation of life. Faith addresses the big truths called mystery, the transcendent. Faith takes us beyond logic and limited comprehension. Faith, we say, is the search for God. Faith is a disposition of soul and mind and spirit.

Faith is God's gift, a religious experience. Faith includes moral conviction, growth, willingness to reconcile. Faith is openness to life, suffering through dialogue. Faith is about simplicity. Faith is spiritual integration. Faith means that we must be committed to an intellectual life, a life of thought, openness, probing, curiosity, readiness to change. Faith helps us remember that intellectual activity, however, is only a small portion of the big truth of humanity.

Mortimer Adler, in a book entitled *The Great Ideas*[‡], states, "Man first turns from himself and his immediate surroundings to the larger universe of which he is a part, and this provides the person with a visible boundary to his universe and

---

[‡] Adler, Mortimer. *The Great Ideas, A Syntopicon of Great Books of the Western World* (2 vols). Chicago: Encyclopaedia Britannica, Inc., 1952, p. 37, seq.

becomes an inescapable object of contemplation.." Faith involves contemplation, meditation, pondering and consideration. Faith is found in the humility of prayer, in the admission of our humanity, of our limits, of our true condition as creatures.

Emmanuel Kant, the Enlightenment philosopher, stated, "Two things fill the mind with ever new and increasing admiration and awe, the starry heavens above me and the moral law within me."§ Faith is about appreciating the reality without and the spirit of integrity within. Tolstoy, the great Russian author, says, "the impulse to seek causes is innate to the soul of man."** Curiosity and the God-given human desire to know truth are big parts of our healthy faith life. Faith is about progress and healthy aging and maturing. Faith is the soul exercising toward eternity. Faith is the experience of checking regularly our world-view, our self-view, our God-view. Faith is about asking the same old questions with new appreciation, with new insight, with new energy. Faith is the exercise which keeps our soul and spirit healthy and positive, alive and changing.

Jesus told his followers that they had to become like little children if they hoped to experience the power of faith and

---

§ Kant, Immanuel. *Critique of Practical Reason.* New York: Macmillan Publishing Company, 1985, p. 166.

** Tolstoy, Leo, Garnett, Constance (trans). *War and Peace.* New York: The Modern Library, ND, p. 918.

hope and pure charity. Children are generally curious, open, appreciative and enthusiastic. "Enthusiastic" means literally to have God in us. Faith is then the grid of full truth and potential. Faith then is the way of growth into bigger truth and life.

WISDOM 18: "The night of the Passover was known beforehand to our Fathers, that, with sure knowledge of the oaths in which they put their faith, they might have courage."

PSALM 33: "Blessed the people the Lord has chosen to be his own."

HEBREWS 11: "Brothers and Sisters: Faith is the realization of what is hoped for and evidence of things not seen. Because of it the ancients were well attested."

LUKE 12: "Jesus said to his disciples, 'Do not be afraid any longer, for your Father is pleased to give you the kingdom.'"

When parents have come to see me, over the past several years, and want to talk about some problem with one of their children, if I know the person well, as they leave my office after our talk, and if they are feeling some better about the problem as they leave, I say jokingly something like, "I know that I am smarter than you, because I never had any kids."

There is usually a moment a laughter at that point, and then, I tell the truth, and that is, "I am basically a coward, not having had children." I thought, at age 26, when I was ordained a priest, that I was a hero, giving up a wife and children. God taught me better, by assigning me to be a high school teacher and principal for over twenty years. Adolescents are wonderful human beings, and one of their missions is to teach, humble and ignore us adults.

Courage is the topic of our scriptures today. Courage is about the long view in life. Courage is about wisdom, prudence, clarity of thinking. Courage flows from a spiritual life, a life of prayer, contemplation, reflection. Courage is the state of soul that empowers us and enables us to stay the course in the face of difficulty, discouragement, and sometimes, defeat.

Courage is really the foundational quality of person that gives us the strength of ethics, values, morals. Courage is the power of recovery, after we have failed in some dimension of life or another. We are able through this virtue to get up, dust ourselves off, and start all over again, as the popular song proclaims.

Our first reading tells us that courage is the fruit of fore-knowledge, prudence, fore-sight and focus. The Book of Wisdom states, "The night of the Passover was known beforehand to our fathers, that with sure knowledge of the oaths in which they put their faith, they might have courage." Courage results in deep strength, perseverance, and determination. Courage gives us backbone. Paul, in the letter to the Hebrews, takes a slightly different approach to courage, as he says, "Faith is the realization of what is hoped for and evidence of things not seen." Courage directs our efforts as we address the unknown, the future, the threatening. Courage teaches us to act out of vulnerability with a calm confidence, with a steady gait, with a firm resolve. Courage is one of the most important foundation blocks of every person's life.

Luke's Gospel has Jesus telling his followers, "Do not be afraid any longer, for your Father is pleased to give you the kingdom." As we embrace our faith, as we grow in that faith, we come more and more to realize that all things unfold somehow, in the hand of God, and being part of God's kingdom gives us what we need to dissipate the fears that can paralyze us, if we allow them to take over.

And so, parents of children, children of parents, siblings and friends and neighbors dealing with each other, this day reminds us to practice courage, to review its condition within us, to continue to develop its power and energy within, so that life can continue to unfold in peace, in richness, in meaning for all of us together and for each of us individually. Courage exercised in each of us is what brings, renews, and assures a quality and peaceful society. Courage is the responsibility of each of us, and a wonderful gift to offer to all.

TWENTIETH SUNDAY IN ORDINARY TIME[*]

ISAIAH 56:   "For my house shall be called a house of prayer for all peoples."

PSALM 67:   "O God, let all the nations praise you."

ROMANS 11:   "Brothers and Sisters: I am speaking to you gentiles...For the gifts and the call of God are irrevocable."

MATTHEW 15: "Then Jesus said to her in reply, 'O woman, great is your faith. Let it be done to you as you wish.'"

An ancient Oriental poem reads, "But small minds get lost. Hurrying, they fall behind. Clinging, they go too far, sure to make a wrong turn."[†]. Small minds are operative in our world. And the "Small Mind Temptation" is a reality that we all face from time to time in life. Sometimes, it seems, the world is too big or too dangerous or too out of control for us

---

[*] Editor's note: This homily was originally presented on 8/14/05.

[†] Soeng, Mu. *Trust in Mind The Rebellion of Chinese Zen.* Somerville: Wisdom Publications, 2004, p. 148.

to handle, and we retreat into the smallness of our little and personal view. We refuse to become part of the human family and of its efforts to deal with the realities of which life is made.

Our scriptures today challenge us to avoid the small mind and to get in to the world view, to see as closely as possible, as God sees, that is, the entire picture. This is a challenge demanding a healthy and courageous spirit. Isaiah speaks of all people, "My house shall be called a house of prayer for all people." How tempting it is to be Catholic before being human. How easy it is to think that we have all the truth, when, in reality, we share in the truth. A small mind excludes others, but for as long ago as when Isaiah wrote, God is saying to have an open mind, open to all people.

Our response today, Psalm 67, exhorts us, "O God, let all the nations praise you." The Psalm does not say, "let all praise you as I do," but rather, it opens our minds, which tend to be closed, to embrace all peoples and their approach to God. What a great impact our new Holy Father made, when, in his first public statement, he said that it was of greatest importance that we Catholics open ourselves to the other world religions. We are not God's people in isolation from all of creation, in isolation from the entirety of humanity. We are one with the Lord, and we are one with all of God's creation, and we must have big minds, open minds, in order to access the rest of humanity. We are to reach out of openness, and we are to reach out of sincerity and of respect for all other people and for their approach to the mystery of God. Psalm 67 is a mind opener: "O God, let all the nations praise you."

Paul writes as a Jew to the Gentiles in Rome and says that we must all have big minds, open minds, and we all have to learn to hear the call of God and accept the gifts of God. A small mind does not hear the call of God. Prayer, if it is authentic, does not close our minds or make our minds smaller. Prayer opens and expands and unfolds and welcomes others, and other ideas, and other opinions, and other approaches to the mystery of life, the mystery of God. Paul learned the hard way that his small mind got lost. He was dramatically knocked off his horse and was physically blinded and was humbled, and in that way he was healed, and he grew, and he opened his mind, and he found his way to fuller truth.

Matthew's Gospel today tells of a foreign woman coming to the Jews and to their leader of the moment, Jesus. She begged for help and Jesus tested her and learned that she had a big mind, and that she had big trust, and that she believed outside the dogma of her small approach. She was willing to trust Jesus and his approach to the truth. He allowed her in and praised her for having an open mind. He said, "O woman, great is your faith."

Our scriptures and our traditions and our history are full of challenges and stories of openness. This is God's call – to be inclusive, never exclusive, to have big minds, courageous minds, open spirits, willing hearts. It is in this way that we can contribute to the world and its growth and its salvation.

Sixty years ago last week, America dropped two atomic bombs on Japan. We killed thousands of innocent people. Now North Korea and Iran and some other people we Americans do not like and do not trust are threatening to do what we did, what we started, and we are demanding that they stand down. They apparently see us as hypocrites and as double-dealers. This is but one example of how small minds can get us in trouble as individuals, as Church, as a nation.

Our faith practice and our scriptures today ask us to open ourselves to the hard things of life. We are challenged to be authentic, not dogmatic. We are asked to dialogue with all the people of the world, not to try to dictate our narrow way. We Catholics, and we Americans, have plenty to think about in terms of having an open and a big mind.

Our Oriental poem is a gift for today:
> But small minds get lost.
> Hurrying, they fall behind.
> Clinging, they go too far,
> Sure to make a wrong turn.

TWENTIETH SUNDAY IN ORDINARY TIME (2)

JEREMIAH 38: "A court official said to the King, 'These men have been at fault in all they have done to the prophet Jeremiah, casting him into the cistern.'"

PSALM 40: "Lord, come to my aid."

HEBREWS 12: "Let us persevere in running the race that lies before us."

LUKE 12: "From now on a household will be divided, three against two and two against three."

Every human life comes to that point, sooner or later, when one must learn to stand on one's own two feet. If we want to be humanly, personally, socially mature and functional, we have to decide who we are, what we stand for, what is worth living and dying for, or we will never find happiness.

We are social beings, it is true, but to be an effective social being, one must become who God has made us to be, personally, individually. Personality is a wonderful gift, as it defines each of us as individuals, as unique human beings. It takes each of us to contribute our image of God to the entire community, or the community is lacking to some degree, because our contribution is missing.

Jesus said, "I am the vine, you are the branches. Unless you abide in me, you cannot have life, any more than the branch can have life apart from the vine." The branch, you and I, must know who and what we are, or our union with the vine is dead, ineffective, a waste. We place, at the command of God, heavy responsibility upon ourselves, in loving, forgiving, serving and caring for each other. This is because we believe that each individual is important, a child of God, a person to be respected, and a person to be taken seriously. To be taken seriously, we must develop our gifts, as individuals, or the body hurts, the community suffers, and the individual withers and dies.

Our scriptures today speak to us about standing on our own two feet, standing alone sometimes, getting through the hard and frightening moments of life, deciding what we stand for, and who we are before each other.

From the first reading, in the Book of Jeremiah, we hear the account of Jeremiah being thrown into a deep cistern by his enemies, to sink in the mud at the bottom, and to die. Lucky for him, some friends came along, learned of this crime, and went to the authorities, to plead for Jeremiah. Jeremiah was saved. Jeremiah got into the cistern because he spoke up, he told the people some things they did not want to hear. Jeremiah was like a responsible parent, a good political or spiritual leader, who speaks to what is best for the family, the entire community, the citizenry. This takes courage, clarity of thinking, determination to stand up and be counted.

Psalm 40, our response, teaches us again, that the source of our strength when we are alone, lonely, isolated, defeated, wounded, afraid, is God Almighty. St. Paul, in our second reading, speaks of the fruit of knowing who we are, where we are going, what we intend to do, as he exhorts, "Let us persevere in running the race that lies before us." Paul takes for granted that if we know who we are, then we know where we are going. Part of following Christ is to keep a focus, to know the conditions and the direction of the path ahead, and to calmly muster courage, as we go, to make the journey.

To practice the discipline of knowing who we are gives us a continued ability to know what we need to do and to understand how to accomplish the task at hand.

Luke's Gospel depicts the reality that all of life, in families, in communities, in churches, in any gathering of human beings, does not go smoothly, nor does life develop easily sometimes. We do divide, we are divided, we experience division. But this division serves as the fertile ground out of which we make stability, through which we promote forgiveness and peace, by which we accomplish our salvation. The cross is present in each life and in all of life. If we continue to develop and clarify our strength, we can make the grade, and we can contribute to the community in a meaningful fashion. This is the Christ-life in the healthy and strong individual.

TWENTIETH SUNDAY IN ORDINARY TIME (3)*

PROVERBS 9: "Forsake foolishness that you may live; advance in the way of understanding."

PSALM 34: "Taste and see the goodness of the Lord."

EPHESIANS 5: "Watch carefully how you live, not as foolish persons, but as wise."

JOHN 6: "Jesus said to the crowds, 'I am the living bread that came down from heaven; whoever eats this bread will live forever.'"

Forty years ago this summer, on July 20, 1969, Americans landed on the moon, marking the first time that a human being ever visited the moon. Neil Armstrong was the first to step onto the moon. He was joined 19 minutes later by Edwin Aldren. These two men explored the moon, set up an American flag, and took a telephone call from President Nixon, who said that this phone call, "certainly has to be the most historic telephone call ever made." While these two men explored the surface of the moon, the third member of the team

---

* Editor's note: This homily was originally presented on 8/16/09.

of Apollo 11, Michael Collins, orbited the moon in the command ship.

This experience represented the wisdom of thousands of people whose work, careful thought, and prudent wisdom, enabled this profound feat to happen. Our scriptures speak of this wisdom and careful knowledge today.

The Bible, especially in the Wisdom Literature of the Old Testament, exhorts the reader to be wise and prudent. Avoid foolishness, we are told today. Only the correct use of the healthy mind that God gave us leads to life, success, growth, peace of mind, and fulfillment as a person. The moon landing could never have happened without great prudence, careful planning, exact calculations, and persevering study of all the elements by all the people involved.

Proverbs today tells us that we will live only if we exercise prudence, avoid foolishness, and utilize all the wisdom that life experience gives.

Psalm 34 reminds us to, "Taste and see the goodness of the Lord." Our lives are to be anchored on the source of all truth, wisdom, and knowledge. God is the origin and the sustenance of human wisdom. Truth will set us free, empower us to do great things, and enable us to save our souls. Happiness comes from the living knowledge of God in all of life.

Ephesians reminds us a second time in today's readings to live wisely, prudently, and carefully. Paul says, "Watch carefully how you live, not as foolish persons, but as wise." We have a moral obligation before God and each other, to develop intelligence to the best of our ability. In other words, it is a sin to waste our intelligence, to neglect our potential, to be careless with our talents.

And, finally today, our Gospel tells us to look to Jesus Christ for the source and substance of knowledge. If we live in and through Jesus, we will enjoy eternal life. How blessed we are to be invited to Eucharist frequently. This gift is food, and wisdom, and the way to life and truth.

TWENTY-FIRST SUNDAY IN ORDINARY TIME

JOSHUA 24:   "If it does not please you to serve the Lord, decide today whom you will serve."

EPHESIANS 5: "Defer to one another out of reverence for Christ."

JOHN 6:   "Simon Peter answered him, 'Lord, to whom shall we go? You have the words of everlasting life. We have come to believe...'"

St. John Chrysostom once said that our poverty is measured not so much by how little we have as by how much we want. Our worst poverty is experienced when we lack God, when we do not seek God. Joshua today exhorts his contemporaries and us to decide today if we are seeking God, and if not, whom or what we seek. And, hopefully, we, like the ancients, say that we will seek the Lord. We experience a mysterious moment when we step out of inordinate self-concern into listening to the silent truth of life, of soul, of hunger within. That is where we seek the Lord.

We find God as we listen. We avoid God as we strain not to listen, as we choose to be distracted constantly, by TV, by worry, by too much work or business. We have the richness of power within to listen deeply to all things, including God. At the core of our lives, there is the power to practice listening. We can focus attention if we want to and if we practice. We can sift through the many voices which crowd the human heart. We can go on the journey of *intentional listening.* Joshua says to listen and to choose.

Mary Rose O'Reilley* says, "Try to learn tranquility, to live in the present a part of the time every day. Sometimes, say to yourself, 'Now, what is happening now.'" This is where we find the still point of life. This is where we find God.

Ephesians today directs us to defer to one another out of reverence for Christ. What a beautiful thought, and what a powerful motive to charity. He sets his remarks right where it would seem to be the most difficult to practice – the home, the family, the marriage, the place of intimacy. Only if we continue to grow, and to seek a solid center, can we do this difficult work called kindness, charity.

And, John's Gospel today calls the bluff of Peter and the others. And, when challenged, Peter usually came through. Lord, you have the words of eternal life. In 1973, Doctor Karl Menninger wrote a wonderful book, entitled, *Whatever Be-*

---

* O'Reilley, Mary Rose. "Deep Listening: An Experimental Friendship." *Weavings*, May/June, 1994, p. 24.

came of Sin?[†] And as a psychiatrist, not as a preacher, he challenged his readers to seek truth about sin in our own lives, because sin is what separates us from God. I would recommend this book to your attention.

[†] Menninger, Karl. *Whatever Became of Sin?* New York: Hawthorn Books, 1973.

TWENTY-FIRST SUNDAY IN ORDINARY TIME (2)

ISAIAH 22:   "I will place the key of the house of David on Eliakim's shoulder; when he opens, no one shall shut. When he shuts, no one will open."

PSALM 138:   "Lord, your love is eternal; do not forsake the work of your hands."

ROMANS 11:   "Oh, the depth of the riches and wisdom and knowledge of God."

MATT 16:   "You are Peter, and upon this rock I will build my church...I will give you the keys to the kingdom of heaven...."

The first reading today and the Gospel account both speak of keys. And the Psalm response and the second reading from Romans speak of the eternal love of God, of God's depth, wisdom, riches and knowledge. These are profound stories and accounts of power, responsibility, invitation and opportunity.

Keys, in our culture, signify many things. When a teenage young person is responsible enough, he or she gets keys to the car. But first, they must know the terribly heavy burden that accompanies those keys, and they must appreciate the power they possess in driving an automobile. When we buy a home the realtor or old owner hands over the keys. Ownership, possession, responsibility, and taxes come with the keys. When a dignitary comes to town, he or she is given the keys to the city. They are most welcome here.

Keys to offices, machinery, vaults, jewelry boxes, drug stores, liquor cabinets, gun cabinets and cedar chests all have significance, meaning and responsibility attached to them. Symbolically, keys ask us to grow up, to be responsible, to contribute to the common good, to protect the rights and safety of all people.

Our faith and faith practice are central keys to life. Life on this planet is given to us as individuals and as a community, and the journey of maturing, growing, changing, and becoming is a call to balance the meaning, the emphasis, and the priorities which we give to self as individual and to the people around us as community. Neither undue selfishness nor being consumed by the wishes of others is healthy or holy or human. Responsible living asks us to continue to learn the path of life by walking it unselfishly and in a balanced fashion.

Peace comes to families, to communities, to nations and to the world, as we human beings continue to serve, seek appropriate return, and involve our energies in a corporate and calm way. Our society today seems to be preoccupied with power, control of others, and self-seeking as individuals and as a nation. The key to all of this is to see as God sees, in other words, to seek and to participate in the depths of the wisdom and the knowledge and the power of God, as St. Paul pointed out to the Romans in today's second reading.

We as Church members are called to and expected to continue that deepening throughout life. Peace does not exist because of human wisdom, human power, human knowledge. Peace comes as we are humble enough to seek together the wisdom and the knowledge of God. This involves continuous conversion of heart and mind and of soul in us as individuals and in society. We are called by the scriptures of our Church to be responsible ourselves, and to call others, especially our leaders, to be responsible in decision making matters.

Part of happiness is to deepen our wisdom, as each day of life comes. We contribute to world, family and personal peace each day or we choose to destroy that reality by a bit. No life is static, but is in the process of contributing to or taking from the pool of human experience, knowledge, wisdom, and development.

As one looks at human growth, we have only to look at the past century. Had we lived one hundred years earlier than we have, most of us would not have owned and driven automobiles. Most of us would never have experienced an airline flight. Most of us would have died much earlier than we are going to die. In other words, the scriptures are telling us that each person and each generation is to contribute to the common good as well as to enhance our personal goals. God's call for each of us is to contribute to each other.

JEREM 20: "I say to myself, I will not mention God, I will speak in his name no more. But then it becomes like a fire burning in my heart, imprisoned in my bones; I grow weary holding it in, I cannot endure it."

PSALM 63: "My soul is thirsting for you, O Lord my God."

ROMANS 12: "Do not conform yourselves to this age but be transformed by the renewal of your mind, that you may discern what is the will of God, what is good and pleasing and perfect."

MATT 16: "Jesus said to his disciples, 'Whoever wishes to come after me must deny himself, take up his cross, and follow me.'"

The goal of life is to be conformed to the will of God, to the truth of nature, to the standard of charity and reconciliation. This is not an easy agenda for anyone. This call is rooted deeply within us, and demands the best that our human nature can imagine and produce. This call has to be heard all along the road of life, as perspectives change and as the circumstances of life are altered. We truly are to be students in the classroom of the Lord all the days of our lives. This is the only road to salvation and life.

The vast majority of the astronauts and cosmonauts who have visited space in the last 40+ years have described on their return to earth, how their views were changed, how their hearts were struck with deep awe as they saw their home, the earth, from space. They indicated that their attention was focused, that their appreciation of reality and life was deepened, that their respect for all of creation and all of energy, and all of life was opened up considerably. They were inspired.

In our first reading today, we hear the story of a man named Jeremiah. He is, at the point of this story, tired, bored, fed up with the search for God, ready to quit. He says, "I say to myself, I will not mention God, I will speak in His name no more." We get to that point from time to time. Our souls become listless, afraid, tired. We experience doubt and confusion and a devil-may-care attitude. But almost immediately, Jeremiah felt something else in his soul. He says, "But then it becomes like a fire burning in my heart, imprisoned in my bones. I grow weary holding it in, I cannot endure it." If we are willing to return to the classroom of the Lord, we will be given that same burning, that same hunger, that same curiosity. The nature of life is that it is to be enhanced always. This is God-given to all of us.

Our Psalm response today repeats that same energy and desire that we have. It says, "My soul is thirsting for you, O Lord my God." St. Augustine, the patron of the church I started in 45 years ago, and spent my last ten years as a pastor, tried throughout much of his life to avoid God, but finally, after running away in so many ways, Augustine found the energy to embrace life, and he cried out that famous quote, "O Lord God, you have made us for yourself, and our hearts are restless until they rest in you." Another well known person who ran away from the Lord much of his life was Francis Thompson, the famous poet who wrote the classic, "The Hound of Heaven."* In this biographical poem, Thompson says, "I fled Him (God) down the nights and down the days, and down the labyrinth of my mind..." And Francis Thompson came to know that God relentlessly loved him and pursued him as the Hound of Heaven.

St. Paul advises the Roman people and ourselves today, "Do not conform yourselves to this age but be transformed by the renewal of your mind, that you may discern what is the will of God, what is good and pleasing and perfect." Paul asks us to have the larger view, the view from space as did the astronauts, basically, to see as God sees. That is where life begins, functions and ends.

---

* Editor's note: This poem may be read on the Internet at http://poetry.elcore.net/HoundOfHeavenInRtT.html.

And, finally, Matthew's Gospel quotes the famous word of Jesus, which calls us to grow up and to be all that we can be, as Jesus says, "Whoever wishes to come after me must deny himself, take up his cross, and follow me."

The journey of life for us Christians is rich, promising, demanding. Life as given by God must be earned and developed. Each of our lives is a unique expression of a portion of the Spirit of God, and must be lived out in God's Spirit, and according to God's way.

TWENTY-SECOND SUNDAY IN ORDINARY TIME (2)

SIRACH 3: "My child, conduct your affairs with humility, what is too sublime for you, seek not, into things beyond your strength, search not."

PSALM 68: "O God, you have made a home for the poor."

HEBREWS 12: "Brothers and Sisters, you have not approached that which could be touched,… but the God and judge of all."

LUKE 14: "When you are invited to a wedding, go and take the lowest place."

I, like you, have had many, many teachers over all the years of schooling that we have experienced. All of my teachers were good human beings, most were very good teachers, and a few of them were excellent teachers. The excellent teachers were able to express themselves easily and simply and directly. They never put on aires or seemed artificial. They were able to inspire us students to want to learn, to work, to deepen our understanding and appreciation of the topic or issue at hand.

One of these excellent teachers was Father Joe McGinnis. He taught us Latin, Marriage and Philosophy at St. Mary's College in the 1950's. One of his pet phrases, which he used often, was, "Humility is knowing your place and taking it." He said this at various times, when, I suppose, one or another of us, his students, appeared to become a bit arrogant, puffed up or superior. He wanted his students to not only be informed and competent in the subject matter. He wanted us to be balanced, secure, and real people. He wanted us to be who God made us to be.

Humility is knowing your place and taking it. Humility is the fruit of being in touch with who I truly am. Humility is the security of person that enables me to live comfortably and confidently in my own skin. Humility is finding happiness in being who I am, not needing to aspire to be like someone else. Humility is the power and ability to identify who I am without the need to compare myself to someone else.

Humility is the wisdom to be aware of the fact that there will always be people present to me who are superior to me in one category or another of the human condition, and humility is also the knowledge that I will always be better at some aspect or another of life than other people. In the first instance, if I focus on those who are stronger than me, I can tend to get petty and jealous, depressed and discouraged. If I look at my greater ability in one thing or another as compared to other people, I can become puffed up with pride and a false sense of self importance. The stances of jealousy, pettiness, discouragement, and arrogance, are destructive and defeating to happiness, because all are figments of my imagination. Humility truly is, "Knowing my place and taking it. Amen." We pray today for this wisdom to grow within us.

An author by the name of John Powell, who studies us humans, writes, "I am afraid to tell you who I am, because, if I tell you who I am, you may not like who I am, and it is all that I have."* If I practice humility, my mind is at peace, I know deep truth about myself, I am satisfied with who I am, and with what I have, and I know more deeply that I am the person God intended me to be. It is from that stance that we find peace, hope, strength, and satisfaction with life.

Our scriptures today speak to this profound truth. Sirach advises wisely, "My child, conduct your affairs with humility, what is too sublime for you, seek not, into things beyond your strength, search not." Psalm 68, our response, tells us that God has made a home for each of us, as we are, where we are, while we live. St. Paul writes to the Hebrew People, and reminds them that they cannot touch God, they need not touch God, but in all of life, they and we approach God, our life, our judge who made us, our protector. And Luke's Gospel simply tells us to always know who we are, and where we

---

* Powell, John. *Why Am I Afraid To Tell You Who I Am?* Resources for Christian Living, 1990.

intend to go, and to seek peace in that humble and stable knowledge.

TWENTY-THIRD SUNDAY IN ORDINARY TIME[*]

WISDOM 9:   "Who can know God's counsel, or who can conceive what the Lord intends?"

PSALM 90:   "In every age O Lord, you have been our refuge."

PHILEMON 9: "I, Paul, an old man, and now also a prisoner for Christ Jesus..."

LUKE 14:   "Anyone of you who does not renounce all his possessions cannot be my disciple."

There is an old saying, "Life is what happens while we are making our plans." Our scriptures today, in a rather round-about way, remind us of this reality. We learn each day that we are human, incomplete, fallible; we learn that we have dignity and responsibility. In short, we learn that we are creatures, and that we live at the pleasure of, and within the providence of, God Almighty.

We learn that we live with God and each other, and that we live in the context of earth, body, soul, community, creation.

---

[*] Editor's note: This homily was originally presented on 9/5/04.

377

As we experience life, as we make wise and unwise choices, as we grow, fail, recover, and heal, we become more aware of mystery, of providence, of truth beyond words, concepts, and definitions. We come more and more to stand in awe of being, of living, of possibility, of dying. Experience empowers us to go deeper into this journey, if we choose. To deepen our being, we must be as open as possible each day. We must be as aware as possible each day. We must be as willing as possible to deal with all that the day brings each day.

The Book of Wisdom asks today, "Who can know God's counsel, or who can conceive what the Lord intends?" This reading teaches us to be humble, to know our place and to take it, to trust- to trust providence, to trust success, to trust failure, to trust life, to trust death. This is a difficult learning. To learn to trust is a life-time journey. It is a bumpy ride for most of us, because we betray and are betrayed. We expect things to go our way, when, in fact, they do not sometimes. Especially when we experience hurt, we tend to become very self-centered, self-focused, self-protective. Psalm 90, our response today, directs us in this regard when it says, "In every age, O Lord, you have been our refuge." To trust God is, then, our vocation. It is a practice that is as needed as the ability to breath air, to digest food, to exercise body and mind. Our spirit must practice trust, or we become paralyzed in life.

The 9/11 Commission Report[†], the final report of the National Commission on terrorist attacks upon the United States, contains so much information about trust, betrayal, the need to be wise and trust wisely. The report tells the reader that on the morning of 9-11-01, three years ago next week, the Federal Aviation Agency ordered all domestic flights to be grounded immediately at the airport nearest to where they happened to be at that moment in flight. Within two hours, 4,500 commercial aircraft landed safely at the closest airport. What an example of trust between airline pilots, air traffic controllers and airport managers! Tens of thousands of passengers were downed safely through trust, confidence, and wise attention.

St. Paul, in his letter to Philemon, teaches us something about trusting in hard times. He says, "I Paul, an old man, and now also a prisoner for Christ Jesus...." He writes and tells the people to be good to the former slave who is coming in Paul's name and in his place, since Paul is in jail. Paul is calm, even in the face of danger, fear, personal concern. This is a difficult thing to learn for most of us, but our faith tradition, our scriptures, our traditions assure us that all is safe, even death.

Finally today, Luke's Gospel quotes Jesus as saying, "anyone of you who does not renounce all his possessions, cannot be my disciple." Jesus is telling us that possessions, relation-

---

[†] Editor's note: The 9/11 Commission Report may be obtained online at www.911commission.gov/report/911Report.pdf.

ships, plans, life itself, all these dimensions of being, are transitory, ever changing, unfolding, but, *but*, all is happening in the providence of God. We trust that providence of God. We ask God to teach us to trust, to practice calmness in times of disturbance, to live each moment as fully and as momentarily as possible. We all live and move and have our being in the loving providence of God. We trust that, and we live.

TWENTY-THIRD SUNDAY IN ORDINARY TIME (2)*

EZEKIEL 33: "Thus says the Lord: 'You, son of man, I have appointed watchman for the house of Israel.'"

PSALM 95: "If today you hear his voice, harden not your hearts."

ROMANS 13: "Owe nothing to anyone, except to love one another; for the one who loves another has fulfilled the law."

MATTHEW 18: "Jesus said to his disciples: 'If your brother sins against you, go and tell him his fault between you and him alone.'"

At graduation from medical school, doctors take the Hippocratic Oath, swearing to "do no harm" in using the power that modern medicine has entrusted to them. Today's scriptures remind us of the weighty responsibility Christians have been given, through our baptismal commitment, to love one another. The Hippocratic Oath is needed for safe and good

---

* Editor's note: This homily was originally presented on 9/4/05.

381

medicine, and brotherly and sisterly love is needed to keep society together and at peace.

The prophet Ezekiel reminded his contemporaries of their responsibility to look out for each other, to protect each other from the enemy without, and from the enemy within themselves. He said, "You, son of man, I have appointed watchman for the house of Israel." They were to protect individuals and be responsible for society, keeping both healthy, directed, and functioning well for the benefit of all.

About the same time in history, roughly twenty-five hundred to three thousand years ago, the Psalms were being composed and written down, as the ballads and songs of the people, and each Psalm highlighted some important truth. Psalm 95, our response today, states, "If today you hear his voice, harden not your hearts." The people were exhorted to pay attention to God, to listen attentively, and to behave responsibly. The author somehow knew that, if the heart becomes hard and bitter, life is partly lost. God's way is the truth. God's way is safe. God's way brings health and harmony and healing for the renewal of society.

A modern novel was written about a nursing home, life there and intrigue there. If my memory is correct, I believe that the novel was entitled, *A Bed By the Window*.† The story line was about love and care, about betrayal and murder. It runs the

---

† Peck, M. Scott, M.D. *A Bed By the Window.* New York: Bantam Books, 1990.

gamut of human history, human potential for good and for evil. I read the book about fifteen years ago, and at that time, I was visiting a woman in a rest home in Owatonna. She was totally paralyzed from the neck down, and she had lived in the same bed by a window of the rest home for fourteen years. Every time I came to visit and give her Communion, she had a big smile and a happy heart. She was the inspiration of all the people there, the workers and the patients. She embodied what our scriptures today describe. She had a very difficult life and an equally happy life, and it formed that entire community. She inspires me yet, years after her death.

Paul gives us, in the second reading today, a high standard to work toward: "Owe nothing to anyone, except to love one another; for the one who loves another fulfills the law." And, in the Gospel today, Jesus speaks of the best forgiving love there is: "If your brother sins against you, go and tell him his fault between you and him alone."

This weekend, here in America, we observe a holiday which gives each of us pause to reflect on what we do for a living. We are to consecrate our efforts as a gift to society, as our offering to the welfare of self and others. All labor and work is of value. This day offers an opportunity for us to thank God for the health of mind and body and emotions we enjoy, in order to do good work. Wendell Berry, an American Poet, says of this time of the year, "The summer ends, and it is time to face another way."‡ Labor Day directs our thoughts and efforts in another way, as we go back to the structures of society.

We seek the blessing of God on our work, on our lives, for this new season.

---

‡ Editor's note: This poem by Wendell Berry, "The Summer Ends," may be found online at <u>writersalmanac.publicradio.org/</u>.

TWENTY-FOURTH SUNDAY IN ORDINARY TIME*

Exodus 32:   "They have soon turned aside from the way I pointed out to them, making for themselves a molten calf, and worshipping it."

LUKE 15:   "I will rise and go to my father."

1 TIMOTHY 1:   "Beloved: I am grateful to him who has strengthened me, Christ Jesus."

LUKE 15:   "My son, you are here with me always; everything I have is yours. But now we must celebrate and rejoice, because your brother was dead and has come to life again; he was lost and has been found."

Perhaps the greatest temptations in life are not to greed, lust, gluttony, pride, envy, hatred, and resentment. The toughest temptations are to the molten calves of our lives: the false gods which we create, and cling to, and refuse to discard. These false gods look real, because we want them to look real. They feel real because we want them to feel real. They become real, because we want them to do so. False gods

---

* Editor's note: This homily was originally presented on 9/12/04.

make us to lose our souls, because they are not real. Lost souls are the victims of false gods.

False gods are made up stories, made up in our own heads. These gods paint an entirely unreal picture, and they lead to nowhere: not to depth, not to growth, not to change, not to abandonment, not to letting go. And salvation is found in depth, growth, change, abandonment, and letting go.

The ancients, under the direction of Moses, who was leading them in the difficulty, the danger, the reality of the desert, chose to leave the real God, trust their own shallowness, collect their gold, and burn it into a large chunk of gold, into a golden calf. They presumed that the calf would feed them, would comfort them, would reassure them, because they could see it, could control it, could force it to stay in their midst. But false gods are an illusion. They lead to hell and death and meaninglessness. False Gods are the ultimate danger.

The ancient Jews, like ourselves sometimes, did not want to move on through the dangers and fears of life. They got tired and self-focused, and then felt that they knew better who God is and ought to be. Fear and self-focus are the raw materials of the false gods of life.

The real God challenges us to find God every new day, changing as we experience the gift of life more, calling us always onward, in to maturity, in to awe, in to abandonment of our mental images which falsely attempt to define God. The real God, the Mystery, the Awe-invoking source of life is traveling along with us all the way, and the real God invites us to keep up: to keep up with life, to keep up with growth, to keep up with emotional and spiritual maturity. The real God invites us and commands us to grow as individuals and as communities. We are swept along by time, by the passing of the years of our lives. We must choose to have our spirit move in the same God-given pattern, or we become the victims of false and comfortable gods. The real God is the source and essence of real life, and that is where our faith practice calls us to be.

Luke 15, our response today to the first reading, is a beautiful prayer of daily recommitment, "I will rise and go to my father." Daily renewal of imagination, openness to mystery, readiness to change – these are the avenues which guarantee that we find the real God and travel in the presence of the real God. Fears, compulsions, old habits won't make the real God present. Only true, growing, willing humanity empowers us.

Paul's first letter to Timothy, from which we learn today, says among other things, "I am grateful to him who strengthens me, Christ Jesus." Jesus does show us the way to God, and that is why we study Jesus, and that is why we constantly read His teaching, and that is why we daily open our lives to His spirit. Jesus shows us the way to God.

And, finally, the story of the prodigal son, the silly son and the pacifying father, is such a good one. Both boys had the wrong idea of God. The younger son looked for God in pleasure, selfishness and irresponsibility. The older son stopped his search for God in bitterness, resentment, and in a stubborn unwillingness to change. The father called both boys to life as it is now. That is the way, the truth, the life. It is there that they and we will find the true God.

Today (yesterday) marks the tragic third anniversary of the terrorist attack on this country. As we mark this moment, we offer the lives of all who died, we support the lives of their loved ones, and we recommit our lives to peace, forgiveness, and the promotion of respect for all people of every religion. The power of God's love will conquer the violence of hatred in the human heart. Each of us offers his/her part.

THE EXULTATION OF THE HOLY CROSS

NUMBERS 21: "With their patience worn out by the journey, the people complained against God and Moses."

PSALM 78: "Do not forget the works of the Lord."

PHILIPPIANS 2: "Christ Jesus...emptied himself, taking the form of a slave, coming in human likeness."

JOHN 3: "God did not send His Son into the world to condemn the world, but that the world might be saved through Him."

The cross, the reality, the sign, the prayer, the symbolic jewelry, the wooden crucifix, the Liturgical expression, the human experience in every life, is our focus today.

Jesus, almost 2,000 years ago, was hung on the cross, by his enemies. Crucifixion was the normal manner of killing people who had broken the law in those days. That commonplace experience of 2,000 years ago has led to, perhaps, the most well-known symbol and sign on the face of the earth, the Cross. Every Saturday evening and Sunday morning, approximately twenty-five million Catholic people begin and end their Mass signing themselves with the cross. Tens of thousands of Catholic Churches in the United States, and throughout the Catholic World, have, as the most visible, central, and obvious, symbol, the crucifix hanging over the altar. The cross is, indeed, everywhere.

Our culture, as formed by our Christian traditions, has been informed by the cross in so many ways. And, perhaps that is a very good thing, because, in addition to all the behavioral crosses we make in prayer and worship, and beyond the artistic expressions of the cross, in metal, in wood, in ceramic, in stone, in fabric, and in the many other artistic forms, each person is involved with his or her personal cross of suffering, of limitations, of pain physically, socially, relationally, psychologically, spiritually, mentally and emotionally.

The cross is a teacher. The cross is a test. The cross forms us in perseverance. The cross invites us into the sufferings of Christ, in and with our fellow human beings.

The scriptures given for our reflection today tell stories of the cross. The Book of Numbers tells us of the grumbling of the people toward Moses and God in the desert. This behavior brought on the cross of the snakes, who bit the people, killing some of them.

Psalm 78, our response, reminds us, "Do not forget the works of the Lord." Remembering God's Law, God's works, God's Commandments, enables us to avoid some suffering, and empowers us to deal with the crosses we can't avoid.

Paul's letter to the Philippian people reminds them and us that Jesus Christ came among us, and became one of us, willingly embracing the human crosses that we all experience and share. This union with Christ empowers us to bear our share of the cross.

And John's Gospel recalls for us again that Jesus saved our world partly through the cross. The cross is part of every life. How we choose to embrace that part of our existence determines to some great degree our continuing happiness and peace of mind. We pray that we can and will bear our cross in union with each other and with the Lord. Therein lies our salvation.

TWENTY-FIFTH SUNDAY IN ORDINARY TIME

ISAIAH 55:   "Seek the Lord while he may be found, call him while he is near."

PSALM 145:   "The Lord is near to all who call upon him."

PHILIPPIANS 1: "Christ will be magnified in my body... For to me, life is Christ."

MATTHEW 20:   "Jesus told his disciples this parable: 'The kingdom of heaven is like a land owner who went out at dawn to hire workers for his vineyard.'"

Approximately twenty-five years ago, a small publishing company in Dubuque, Iowa named Brown-Roa Publishing, came out with a textbook on human sexuality, anatomy, decision-making and behavior, and the teaching of these facets of sexuality to young people, sixth grade and older. It was a wonderful text and was widely used. The main reason that it was such a success, in my opinion, was that it contained a list of approximately 150 words and brief phrases about human sexuality, divided into 16 lists, one for each chapter, to be used, one chapter per week, for 16 weeks, the length of the course. Thus 10 words and/or phrases, and their definitions, would be read each week, at the beginning of class.

Instructions to the teachers were that the word or phrase should be stated to the class, and the definition of that particular word or phrase should be immediately stated to the class, without any other comment. The intention was to give clear information, and to give proper vocabulary to our culture, because we do not know how to speak of sexuality. I have heard several times from young adults, who were my students back then, as to how fortunate they had been to have had that teaching and learning experience. They feel more at ease now, teaching their own children about sexuality. Clear thought and simple definition had power in this instance.

Our scriptures today ask us to have clear thought and simple definition about another very important life truth, which is our knowledge of, and appreciation of, God Almighty. As sexuality gives life if properly understood and appreciated and protected, so does our knowledge of God give life to us.

Isaiah, our first reading, says quite simply, "Seek the Lord while he may be found, call him while he is near." To be healthy before God, we seek God with every waking moment and with constant openness and energy. We live in God's presence. God is here, there, and everywhere. Be aware of this life-giving truth, says Isaiah. Psalm 145, our response today, emphasizes the same truth when it says, "The Lord is near to all who call upon him." God wants to be the core of our life and is present always, if we are willing and welcoming.

St Paul takes a slightly different approach to the mystery of God present, as he states, "Christ will be magnified in my body...For me, life is Christ." Paul equates life with the willing openness to God present in Jesus and His church and sacraments and brothers and sisters. And the parable offered by Jesus today reassures us that God has a call and destiny and plan for everyone, and that God very constantly and generously makes available the sources of life for us.

There is, as I have referenced before, a principle in current day counseling which states, "Identify, do not compare." And it means that I find the truth about me, not by comparing myself to you or to anyone else. I simply identify who I am and what I look like at this moment. That is as close to the truth about me that I can get. Again, our scriptures today are asking us to identify who God is for us today, and to know that that concept and appreciation keeps changing with each living moment. We deepen our union with, and appreciation of, and commitment to, our God as we pay attention, as we stay in God's presence, as we seek the Lord while he can be found.

TWENTY-FIFTH SUNDAY IN ORDINARY TIME (2)[*]

WISDOM 2: "The wicked say, 'With revilement and torture let us put the just one to the test that we may have proof of his gentleness and try his patience.'"

PSALM 54: "The Lord upholds my life."

JAMES 3: "Beloved: Where jealousy and selfish ambition exist, there is disorder and every foul practice."

MARK 9: "Jesus was teaching his disciples..., 'The Son of Man is to be handed over to men and they will kill him, and three days after his death the Son of Man will rise.' But they did not understand... and they were afraid."

In just over six weeks, Americans have the privilege and responsibility of going to the polls to vote for governmental leaders, and perhaps for some issues which may be on the ballot. The scriptures today offer some insight into a spirit which, in recent years, has become quite wide-spread in the

---

[*] Editor's note: This homily was originally presented on 9/24/06.

American political scene, in campaigns, in public debate and in discussions between individuals and small groups of people.

Wisdom, our first reading today, speaks of hatred, plotting, revenge. The Book of James, our second reading, reminds us that jealousy, selfish ambition, and foul practice all contribute to disorder in society. And Mark's Gospel has Jesus telling His followers that He will be betrayed, and killed, by people who do not like his message. Perhaps this is a good time for all of us to examine our political attitudes, convictions, involvements, as well as the comments we make concerning political candidates with whom we disagree.

In the September 25, 2006 issue of *America* Magazine, the Jesuit periodical, there appears an edited rendition of a speech which was given by Cardinal Theodore McCarrick, the retired archbishop of Washington, D.C., to the Catholic members of Congress on June 20, 2006. The title of the article is "Restoring Civility to Political Discourse." The article highlights some very challenging principles which can help all of us be civil and respectful and kind to those candidates and political parties with whom we disagree.

The article reminds the reader that God's love is demanding. We are to love God, neighbor and self, and thus in our political life, we are to work at building bridges to common sense in pursuit of the common good, even across partisan lines. The just ordering of society and the state is the essential responsibility of politics, and thus of each citizen. We must work at restoring civility to public discourse, so that we attack problems and not each other.

To allow ourselves to become bitter in politics serves no purpose for the good of society, and is a divisive stance between people. To exercise restraint in our emotional and judgmental life in politics is a gift to society, and strengthens the fabric of our culture.

Civic responsibility, manners and respect for different ideas is essential to the stability of society. Psalm 54, our response today states, "The Lord upholds my life." It is good to remember this truth as we come to the civic responsibility to involve ourselves in the respectful debate which is how we clarify issues, and arrive at the best solution to the needs of society. In a current book, entitled *American Gospel*[†] by Jon Meacham, the author states, "The great good news about America-the American Gospel, if you will-is that religion shapes the life of the nation without strangling it." Our roll as citizens and as candidates is to bring our convictions to the table respectfully, and trust that our contribution will help the entire body of the country.

Recriminations, blaming, insulting the other, do nothing positive, and instead bring a cynicism to the arena of politics, which is counter-productive. We owe it to our youth to speak

---

[†] Meacham, Jon. *American Gospel*. New York: Random House, 2006, p. 5.

respectfully, responsibly, accurately in our public discourse and dialogue about the issues that affect all the citizenry.

We ask the Lord for prudence, reverence for contrasting views, and courage as we exercise our civic duty to educate ourselves and prepare to go to the polls in early November.

TWENTY-SIXTH SUNDAY IN ORDINARY TIME *

AMOS 6:   "Thus says the Lord the God of hosts:
            Woe to the complacent in Zion."

PSALM 146: "Praise the Lord, my soul."

1 TIM 6:   "But you, man of God, pursue righteousness,
            devotion, faith, love, patience and
            gentleness."

LUKE 16:   "Then Abraham said, 'If they will not listen to
            Moses and the prophets, neither will they be
            persuaded if someone should rise from the
            dead.'"

Perhaps the greatest and most dramatic example of complacency, naivety, and lack of attentiveness was the experience we all encountered and shared in, leading up to the attack on the United States on 9-11-01. The devastation which we experienced that day has had and continues to have, deep financial, spiritual, psychological, and international relationship consequences. The world and this Nation were significantly changed that day. We were put on immediate and continuing

---

* Editor's note: This homily was originally presented on 9/26/04.

notice that day that we as Americans are not safe in spite of our financial wealth, military prowess, and perceived international standing as the most powerful nation in the world, perhaps in all of human history.

The scriptures today, beginning with the Prophet Amos, our first reading, tell us as much. The humanity of 2,500 years ago, in the Middle East, where much of our attack on 9-11-01 was inspired, planned, and ultimately initiated, were warned through Amos, "Thus says the Lord, the God of Hosts: Woe to the complacent in Zion." When people of any timeframe, age, or condition of life become too selfish, too self-focused and self-absorbed, our spirit bloats and becomes blind to those around us, and selfish complacency sets in, only to deepen until calamity visits. This has been recorded throughout human history. Our humanity, our faith, human decency, all call us to a balance which is inclusive of others, which is concerned for others, which values others, as the self, or we, as individuals or as societies, become ill with complacency.

1 Timothy, our second reading, relates some of the tools needed to avoid complacency, some of the attitudes which empower us to be balanced between self-interest and interest in other people and in all of creation. "But you, man of God, pursue righteousness, devotion, faith, love, patience and gentleness." Disciplined development in these areas costs us attention, devotion, application of sincere and costly effort. These are character building pieces of human effort which insure the fact that self cannot become too out of control.

Luke's Gospel gives us the story of being complacent, self-absorbed and increasingly more selfish as time and self indulgence go on. The rich man becomes so self-consumed, that common sense, human logic and obvious responsibility are no longer real to and for him. He is blind because he has chosen to be blind for so long. When it becomes obvious to him that it is all too late for him he is astounded, when he asks for the unusual experience of someone coming back from the dead to warn his brothers, when he is told the obvious, that if they cannot see, hear, appreciate the normal delivery system of life and truth, even the unusual will not do the trick. Deep wisdom here for all of us. Pay attention. Pay attention to the inner movements of our spirit. Pay attention to strength and weakness and patterns of thinking, feeling, perceiving, concluding within our hearts on a day-to-day basis. Life management, life balance, life integrity – these are the lessons to be studied today in the Holy Word.

Life patterns, strengths, deformities, form slowly and over time, being reinforced by attitudes, behaviors, dispositions, and atmospheres of mind and spirit. Good habits and bad habits are children of repetition. It takes deliberate neglect to allow bad habits to develop, and it takes concerted effort to build good habits, which nurture and protect life within us, among us and all around us.

A wonderful example in life of persons being vigilant, attentive, and protective is good parents. Loving parents pay attention to the welfare and safety of their children. Complacency is not allowed in this setting. Virtues, good teachings, and healthy modeling are the rule of the day. This seems to be what nature intends. Part of holiness and health in life is to pay attention calmly and surely as each moment of life unfolds. Let each of us recommit to this spirit today.

TWENTY-SIXTH SUNDAY IN ORDINARY TIME (2)*

EZEKIEL 18: "But if the sinner turns away from the wickedness he has committed and does what is right and just, he shall preserve his life."

PSALM 25: "Remember your mercies, O Lord."

PHILIPPIANS: "Have in you the same attitude that is in Christ Jesus"

MATTHEW 21: The story of two brothers making decisions and carrying them out.

The cover story of *Newsweek* Magazine for 09-05-05 is entitled, "Spirituality in America." The issue discusses what we believe, how we pray, and where we find God. It speaks of Islam, Judaism, many strains of Christianity, and of other religions. One article in the magazine is written by Professor Martin E. Marty, an eminent and highly respected American Protestant Theologian and Historian. The article is entitled, "The Long and Winding Road." It spells out three general ways that Americans seek the Mystery of God. The American

---

* Editor's note: This homily was originally presented on 9/25/05.

spiritual journey can best be appreciated, according to this approach, by studying these three ways.

First, most people in America still pursue their spirituality in traditional churches, as most of us do, but with the difference, in the last forty years since Vatican II, that most of us are much more open and ecumenical. We are becoming more aware that we are human beings together before we are Catholic, Protestant, Jew, Islamic or Buddhist. We are appreciating better that all people, all races, all religions, all cultures, are of God. We are together, God's People, none better than the other.

A second experience of Americans in seeking their spirituality is through activism. People are taking political stands, pro and con, on many issues of concern. People find their God in hands-on helping others in the person of the poor, the elderly, the lonely, the vulnerable. As an example, many of you spend time in rest homes, the hospitals, our schools, our food shelves, in working for the missions.

And, finally, the third path is that of "being spiritual but not religious." Many of America's young belong, at least temporarily, to this group. They are deeply concerned about their spiritual health, but do not find inspiration in organized religion. This phenomenon causes many parents and spiritual leaders grave concern. These people do not usually "go to church," but they do sincerely seek the Lord, according to polling data.

Each of these three paths is real and the way for many people. Our scriptures today remind us, as does this issue of *Newsweek*, that the journey to God is, as the article is entitled, "a Long and Winding Road." Ezekiel speaks of sinners turning from wickedness, without saying that he or she must belong to a church. This is a wonderful reminder to us church-goers that we must be very careful not to become judgmental, self-righteous, and exclusive, thinking that ours is the only, or even the best approach. It is good for us, or we probably would not be here, but it does not touch all other good people as it does us. We are not to manipulate each other. We are to support one another in the search for God.

And our Psalm response teaches us again, "Remember your mercies, O Lord." We are all in need of the mercy of God. No one is without sin. We walk humbly with God and with each other, not necessarily on the same path.

Paul tells the Philippian people to, "Have in you the same attitude that is in Christ." Jesus always welcomed those who were not Jews, those who were different, those whom some judged to be unbelievers. That is to be our stance: open minded, ecumenical, welcoming. None of us has been appointed judge over another adult.

And Matthew's Gospel today presents the story of all of us from time to time. Like the brothers described in our Gospel today, we sometimes commit ourselves and we take it back. We say "No," and regret our decision. We experience the entire gamut of being human, inconsistent, generous, changing and growing.

America is changing more today than ever before in our history. New religions, new cultures, new races, new ways are all around us and these people and movements touch us and give us an opportunity to keep growing, to keep changing, to keep welcoming other people. Jesus was always inclusive, never exclusive. We are called to be no less, to be one with Jesus.

TWENTY-SIXTH SUNDAY IN ORDINARY TIME (3)

NUMBERS 11: "Taking some of the spirit that was on Moses, the Lord bestowed it on the seventy elders; and as the spirit came to rest on them, they prophesied."

PSALM 19: "The precepts of the Lord give joy to the heart."

JAMES 5: "Behold the wages you withheld from the workers who harvested your fields are crying aloud; and the cries of the harvesters have reached the ears of the Lord."

MARK 9: "Anyone who gives you a cup of water to drink because you belong to Christ, will not lose his reward."

Several years ago, I took a graduate course. One of the assignments in the course was to choose three photographs, which I thought were three of the best pictures I had ever seen, and then I had to show the pictures and talk about them to the class. I chose a picture taken in the 1940's by the

United Nations Children's Division, which depicted two infants sitting on a blanket totally naked. They were reaching out to each other. They looked to be about ten months to a year old. One of the babies was black and the other child was white. The picture was intended to break down racism which was bad at the time all over the world.

The second picture was entitled, "The Whole Earth," and was taken from space as the astronauts were going to the moon in 1969. The picture shows the absolute unity of the entire planet, and makes the observer know, at a very deep level, that all of God's creation is one on this earth, that all people are one.

And my third choice of a picture was the picture of Pope John Paul II, sitting in a jail cell with Ali Ağca, the man who had tried to kill the Pope by stabbing him. The Pope was there to forgive his assailant. These three pictures, I still say today, are among the best and most provocative pictures I have ever seen.

Each week in our experience of Mass we are given three or four pictures from the scriptures. These pictures are intended to make us think, ponder, wonder and grow. These biblical and historical pictures have the power to deepen our soul, and to inspire our lives, if we pay attention to them. This is why the liturgy takes place in a setting of reverence, silence, and attentiveness. This is why the lector announces at the conclusion of each reading, "The Word of the Lord," and the rest of us respond, "Thanks be to God." And this is why the priest, at the conclusion of the Gospel reading proclaims, "The Gospel of the Lord," and the people respond, "Praise to you, Lord Jesus Christ."

Today, the Old Testament reading from Numbers gives us a picture of the Lord giving the spirit which Moses had to the seventy elders, and shows us some jealousy that others were getting the spirit also. This is a story about inclusion, not exclusion; this is a story about equality, not about classism. This is a story about humility and gratitude.

The Psalm today gives us the picture of God's law bringing joy to our hearts. This is a picture of challenge, a picture of integrity, a picture of an invitation to be authentic.

The Book of James shows us a picture of injustice, of the wealthy withholding the wages from the poor and vulnerable workers who did their harvest. This is also a picture of God's vengeance on anyone who takes advantage of another, especially of the vulnerable.

And finally today, the Gospel gives us a simple picture of giving a cup of water to someone in the name of the Lord. This is a profound picture of the simplicity of the Gospel, a picture of every person being able to live the way of the Lord, if we choose to do so.

We are invited to carry these pictures with us throughout the week, and then next week we will be given new pictures to consider, ponder and reflect upon. The faith we share is indeed a rich gift, and it is available for all of us. Thanks be to God!

TWENTY-SEVENTH SUNDAY IN ORDINARY TIME*

ISAIAH 5: "Now I will let you know what I mean to do with my vineyard: Take away its hedge, give it to grazing, break through its wall, let it be trampled."

PHILIPPIANS 4: "Have no anxiety at all, but in everything, by prayer and petition, with thanksgiving, make your requests known to God."

MATTHEW 21: "The kingdom of God will be taken away from you and given to a people that will produce its fruit."

This past week, the vast majority of the priests of the Winona Diocese, about 95 of us, spent Monday through Wednesday at a conference center at Okoboji, Iowa. We spent our time praying together, studying together, and even playing together for one afternoon and evening. All work and no play makes Jack a dull boy, you know.

---

* Editor's note: This homily was originally presented on 10/2/05.

The theme of the conference was spirituality and unity between and among priests and bishop for the sake of the
Kingdom of God. The conference director, Father Ronald
Knott, challenged all of us to be authentic, healthy and holy,
as men and as priests. And, in the process of listening to him
and discussing with each other, it became clearer than ever
before, that to be authentic, healthy and holy is a demanding
agenda. Human growth does not come automatically, easily
or readily. Spiritual and human growth is a process, involving
time, attention, spirit and determination, openness and generosity.

The scriptures today from Isaiah and Matthew paint sad and
frightening pictures of what happens when people are not
authentic, healthy and holy. Both accounts describe scenes
where the workers in the vineyard are dishonest, corrupt and
self-serving. They shirk their duty, refuse to be dependable
and responsible, and experience the consequences that are
painful, embarrassing and defeating. These stories remind all
of us that there is a consequence to every decision we make.
If the decision is positive, life-giving and respectful, the consequence will be positive. If the decision is hurtful to others,
disruptive and destructive, the appropriate consequence will
follow. Responsibility is a necessary part of a happy and
healthy and holy life.

Paul's letter to the Philippians presents a positive and productive approach to life and a strong relationship with the Lord:
"Have no anxiety at all, but in everything, by prayer and peti-

tion, with thanksgiving, make your requests known to God." To practice this approach to spirituality, we must learn about directing our lives in a wise and fully human fashion. And to do that requires attention, reflection, meditation. In short, if we want to be responsible workers in the vineyard of life, we must learn to be silent and centered.

Throughout the history of Christianity, spiritual leaders and teachers have spoken of at least three levels of silence which are necessary to find peace of mind and soul, and a sense of communion with God and with others and with all of reality and creation.

The first level of silence which is essential to spiritual growth is SILENCE FROM WORDS. We must learn to close our mouth and stop the idle chatter so that we can better focus attention on life and spirit, communion and rest. This is a first step toward no more anxiety and toward thankfulness and prayer.

A second level of silence is SILENCE OF IDEAS. In addition to not speaking, we exercise the discipline needed to slow and hopefully, stop, the ceaseless flow of ideas, notions and perceptions which occupy our consciousness during all waking hours of life. Those who study our minds and the processes of living tell us that ideas are ever present in the mind, and a discipline needs to be developed to slow this process down, to focus energy on being, rather than on thinking. This second level of silence moves us more deeply in to a place where we can access the mystery of God and communion with all of creation.

And finally, the third level of silence is SILENCE OF EMOTION AND FEELING. We learn to befriend our feelings, emotions, and passions in such a way that we can get through them, beyond them, into a silence which is truly life-giving. This is called meditation, contemplation, union with God. Probably, none of us can do this totally, but we can practice these silences toward the end of union and communion with God and with self and with all of creation.

A healthy, balanced mind and soul need silence, focus, and opportunities for growth as a human being and as a Christian. We renew our willingness to be workers in the vineyard of the Lord, and we ask for the grace to be healthy, balanced and reflective workers for the Lord and with each other.

TWENTY-EIGHTH SUNDAY IN ORDINARY TIME[*]

2 KINGS 5: "Naaman went down and plunged into the Jordan seven times at the word of Elisha, the man of God. His flesh became again like the flesh of a little child, and he was clean of his leprosy."

PSALM 98: "The Lord has revealed to the nations his saving power."

2 TIMOTHY 2: "But the word of God is not chained."

LUKE 17: "Ten were cleansed, were they not? Where are the other nine?"

The healing of bodies and souls is the topic being offered for our consideration through the scriptures today. Naaman was healed bodily at the word of Elisha. Ten lepers were healed bodily at the word of Christ, but only one leper was healed in soul by the word of Christ, and Christ rhetorically asks his disciples what went wrong in that scene. Only one soul was healed enough to say, "Thank you."

---

[*] Editor's note: This homily was originally presented on 10/10/04.

In the last year, I have learned a lot about healing. For the first 42 years of my priesthood, I do not think I lost over five days total to ill health. In the last year I have experienced three surgeries, and treatment for a herniated disk in my back. I have indeed learned that the machinery does not run as it used to. And I have learned that there is tremendous healing at the hands and the word and the talent of others. I thank you for your kindness most recently as I underwent surgery for acute appendicitis. Two weeks ago last Friday at around noon, I became immediately and extremely ill. I went to St. Mary's emergency room, and several hours later, was diagnosed and had the appendectomy at three o'clock on Saturday morning. I currently feel very strong physically, and very peaceful spiritually, emotionally, mentally, largely due to your kind calls, cards, messages and prayer. Thank you very much.

I just returned from the east coast yesterday. I had gone to Maryland to witness the marriage of two of my high school classmates. One was a widow and the other had never before married. It was a joyful experience. While in the East, I went to New York City for a few days of rest and recreation. The hotel at which I stayed was just across the street from a twenty-five foot terra cotta statue of Venus Demilo. Up close it looked like a pile of steel, but from across the street, 150 feet away, Venus came to life beautifully. People would rush by the statue, and then, across the street, would turn to look at it and comment to their friends on its presence and beauty.

From a distance, we become aware of the healings of life available to us. The scripture stories do as much today. Our life journey is about healing. We get wounded, and we become ill, and our hearts are disappointed, and our paths fall into darkness. We experience bitterness. We come to know pain, physically, spiritually, emotionally, mentally. Our moods become dark and our histories are not perfect. Our families are broken and relationships become strained. Violence unfairly visits us or loved ones, and so-called bad luck comes around occasionally. These and many other experiences and conditions of our journey are part of life. We need constant healing, and thus, we need constantly to learn how to heal, how to open ourselves again to healing, how to reach out in exhaustion to heal others, when we really do not feel much like doing that.

Healing involves *nature*, that is, what we are given, and *intention*, that is, what we bring to each new moment of life. We are learning, as the scriptures teach us, that the manner in which we proceed each day is the empowerment for growth, or becomes the paralysis that leads to bitterness and death. We are the masters of our own destiny, and no one can take our responsibility for that nor can we assume that responsibility for others totally. We learn to heal, to stand on our own two feet, to engage life in a positive fashion or we don't do so. That is our radical choice.

And so the scriptures today teach us not to complain, to be responsible, to be thankful, to listen to others, to generously contribute to life on this planet. We are empowered to be healers and to be healed. It will happen if we choose it.

TWENTY-EIGHTH SUNDAY IN ORDINARY TIME (2)

THE EUCHARIST

Today in the Diocese of Winona, all 115 parishes are reflecting on the historic development, the prayer, the mystery, the experience, the reality of Eucharist. This afternoon people will gather at St. John's Church here in Rochester for a prayer and then will process with the Eucharist through the city of Rochester, stopping three times at various sites for a prayerful experience with Vietnamese Catholics, Hispanic Catholics, and African Catholics, reflecting on some of their customs which surround the Eucharist.

This day gives all of us a chance to reflect on this central truth of our religious faith, and to consider again its impact on our lives personally, and as a society and culture. The reality of Eucharist accompanies and punctuates our lives as Catholics, from the cradle to the grave, and has been, throughout Christian history, the unifying and defining expression and experience of our faith practice.

The Eucharist developed, as the Scriptures describe it, as the celebration of the Word, as was the center of ancient Jewish religious practice, and as obedience to the command of Jesus to his followers to, "Do this in memory of me." Throughout history, Word and Sacrament have been the two foundational portions of Eucharist. Accidental practices have changed from culture to culture, from language to language, from age to age, but the core of Eucharist has always involved essentially, the Word of God and the Body and Blood of Christ, experienced, perpetuated, remembered, enlivened.

The Eucharist is our prayer and experience in moments of joy and in times of loss and sadness. The Eucharist empowers us in times of tragedy and on the road of celebration. The Eucharist is the setting for the celebrations of most of our Sacramental experiences throughout life. The Eucharist is the Catholic gift to all of culture, all around the world. The Eucharist is the most celebrated religious ritual in all of religious history. The Eucharist defines life and frames life for more people than any other experience or observance. The Eucharist is a world-wide experience and expression of the human spirit, as we seek the mystery of God.

The ritual of Eucharist begins with greeting, and flows immediately to the confession of sin, our need to be forgiven, and our need to forgive. Society cannot exist in peace and the individual cannot experience peace without this constantly renewed posture of humble presence with and for each other. This movement is foundational to life, to spiritual life, to prayer life, and is repeated every time the community gathers for Eucharist.

We move from the gathering prayer to the lessons from the Holy Word of God. Here we are instructed, inspired, challenged and comforted. We are asked through the scriptures to be students again, students of life, of love, of community relations. And rounding out this first of two portions of Eucharistic feeding, those being Word and Sacrament, the community prays for the needs of the people of the world, and for the needs of those gathered in the respective celebration.

Moving into the second phase of Eucharistic prayer, we make an offering from our resources of material possessions and spirit. Having given, which is a need we all have, we move to remembering, the human experience which brings wisdom, and is the recitation by the priest for the community of the Eucharist prayer. This moment is called *Anamnesis* or remembering. Jesus said, "Do this in memory of me."

We conclude this rich and ancient ritual by receiving the life of God, the body and the blood of Jesus Christ, and we go forth from the respective gathering with a blessing and as a blessing.

Song and silence, speaking and listening, kneeling and standing and sitting, are the behaviors and postures of this sacred prayer. And so, as we reflect on this great expression of our Catholic worship, we realize that each time we share this gift, we are led through the life-giving experience of humility and forgiveness, we are instructed by the ancient word, we are invited to give of possession and person, we remember our ancestry, our history, our spiritual foundation, we share in being one through Holy Communion, and we are sent back to the rigors of life with all these gifts to let them be lived out in all of our moments, experiences and awarenesses.

The Eucharist is indeed, a fully human and profound experience. That is why we say *Eucharistia*, translated, "Thank you."

2 KINGS 5: "Naaman went down and plunged into the Jordan seven times at the word of Elisha, the man of God. His flesh became again like the flesh of a little child, and he was clean of his leprosy."

PSALM 98: "The Lord has revealed to the nations his saving power."

2 TIM 2: "But the word of God is not chained."

LUKE 17: "Ten were cleansed, were they not? Where are the other nine?"

The healing of persons, bodies and souls is one of the topics given for our consideration in the scriptures today. In 2 Kings, we are told that Naaman was healed in body at the word of Elisha. Ten lepers were healed bodily at the word of Christ, but only one leper was healed in soul by the word of Christ, and Jesus rhetorically asks his disciples what went wrong in that scene. Only one leper was healed enough to say, "Thank you."

A significant portion of our life journey is about healing. We make mistakes, we make poor choices and decisions, we become wounded, we become ill, our hearts get disappointed, and our paths fall into darkness. We experience physical breakdown, mental bitterness, and emotional pain. Our histories are not perfect, our moods become distorted and dark, and we lose faith and hope.

Our families are broken and relationships become strained. Violence unfairly visits us or our loved ones, and so-called bad luck comes around occasionally. These and many other experiences and conditions of our journey are part of life. We need constant healing, and thus, we need constantly to learn how to heal, how to open ourselves again to healing, how to reach out, even when we are exhausted, to attempt to heal others. Jesus said that we must take up our cross daily, if we choose to be His disciples, and it would seem that to heal, and to be healed, significantly involves that cross.

This is probably why we Catholics have been taught to practice the three theological virtues, Faith, Hope, and Charity. These attitudes, decisions, and behaviors – Faith, Hope and Charity – are healing postures of person and soul. Healing involves *nature*, that is, what we have been given, and healing involves *intention*, that is what we choose and bring to each new moment of life.

Our scriptures today are teaching us that the manner in which we proceed each day is the empowerment for healing and growth, or becomes the paralysis that leads to bitterness and death. We are, to a degree, the masters of our own destiny in life, and no one can take that responsibility from us in life, nor can we assume that totally for others in life. We have the choice. We are to learn to heal, to stand on our own two feet, to engage life in a positive fashion, or we won't do so. That is a radical healing choice, and it belongs to each of us.

And so the scriptures today teach us not to complain, to be responsible, to be thankful, to listen to each other, to generously contribute to life on this planet. We are empowered to be healers and to be healed. It happens, as we choose it.

A concluding story: A man, roughly my age, who has been a life-long friend, but one whom I haven't seen in ten years because he moved to a far distant part of the world, called me last week to thank me. I have been writing to his son, who is in a state prison in a distant state. The man is in prison for a crime he committed several years ago. The man in prison has made a life out of serving the other prisoners through his talent to plan and lay out plans for buildings which make life a bit easier in prison for all involved there. This prisoner chooses to be productive rather than to choose to continue down through life on a path of crime, hatred and violence.

Life offers us choices, every day, in every circumstance, in every moment given to us. The teachings of Jesus Christ empower us to make the right choices.

TWENTY-NINTH SUNDAY IN ORDINARY TIME

2 TIMOTHY 3: "Remain faithful to what you have learned and believed...The sacred scriptures are capable of giving wisdom."

LUKE 18: "Jesus told his disciples a parable about the necessity for them to pray always without becoming weary."

In the 1960's, when astronauts were traveling to the moon, American astronaut John-David Bartoe said while looking back at the earth from outer space, "As I looked down, I saw a large river meandering along for miles, passing from one country to another without stopping. I also saw huge forests, extending across several borders. And I watched the extent of one ocean touch the shores of separate continents. Two words leapt to mind as I looked down on all of this: commonality and interdependence. We are one world."*

Our scriptures read aloud today speak about that same awareness, asking us to continue to pray, to seek wisdom, to

---

* Keck, L. Robert. *Sacred Quest: The Evolution and Future of the Human Soul.* West Chester: Swendenborg Foundation Publishers, 2000, p. 150.

unfold new dimensions of truth. New understandings and new awareness and new appreciations are what learning is all about. This is how humanity participates in the creative and redemptive work of God. We are exhorted never to be afraid of new truth, new insights.

In 1605, Miguel de Cervantes published *Don Quixote*, in which he expressed the belief that there are "no limits but the sky." The modern phrase that owes its heritage to Cervantes is, "the sky is the limit." The word "sky" comes from an ancient word meaning covering, so it is understandable that Cervantes thought then that the sky was the ultimate limit. The sky was thought to be a cover for the earth, a rather low cover at that.

Recently however, our minds and spirits have been liberated from small special limitations. Astronomy and cosmology have removed the cover and have expanded our awareness of a sky of seemingly limitless grandeur. The sky, as we now know it, is not a cover or restriction of our imagination. It is a mind-boggling and spirit-stretching window into an awe-inspiring, miraculous and wonder-filled universe. We need today to have flexible souls that can stretch to lengths, depths, heights and periods of time which were previously unheard of.

A healthy soul is one that is unafraid of new possibility, one which is excited about God's universe continually being unfolded for all of humanity. Our appreciation today is so much greater than it was for folks in biblical times. This is why we do consider the word of God as living, life-giving. We do exercise our minds to wonder, awe, wisdom and insight. And we exercise our souls through prayer, contemplation, meditation, reflection. Our prayer will, as Jesus promised, keep us from becoming weary.

From the political realm we hear Vaclav Havel, President of the Czech Republic, say: "The main task in the coming era is a radical renewal of our sense of responsibility. Our conscience must catch up to our reason, otherwise we are lost... We must divest ourselves of our habit of seeing ourselves as masters of the universe who can do whatever occurs to us. We must discover a new respect for what transcends us: for the universe, for the earth, for nature, for life and for reality. A better alternative for the future of humanity, therefore, clearly lies in imbuing our civilization with a spiritual dimension."[†]

To realize a new and life-giving spiritual dimension, each of us must continue to grow, to courageously learn the new and constantly changing understanding and appreciation of all of reality. We are asked to keep eyes, senses, mind and soul open to the unfolding of God's creation. We are reminded that we are to bless all of God's gifts, never abuse or misuse them.

---

† Ibid, p. 104.

We are profoundly blessed to live at a time when the speed of becoming aware of new information is always increasing. We are challenged to use our mind and soul individually and collectively in participating in this grand plan of God almighty, as it unfolds right before our eyes. We are to be healthy in mind and soul and body so as to contribute our share. God is working through each and every one of us. We pray for readiness, courage and generosity to be equal to the task at hand.

TWENTY-NINTH SUNDAY IN ORDINARY TIME (2)*

ISAIAH 53: "Because of his affliction, he shall see the light in fullness of days."

PSALM 33: "Lord, let your mercy be on us, as we place our trust in you."

HEBREWS 4: "Let us approach the throne of grace to receive mercy and to find grace for timely help."

MARK 10: "Can you drink the cup that I drink or be baptized with the baptism with which I am baptized?"

The scriptures today lead us where we probably never want to go. We are asked to face suffering, defeat, rejection, difficulty, pain and sorrow in life, in each of our lives. Jesus asked the two brothers if they could drink the cup and be baptized in pain. At another time, he reminded his followers that if they wanted to follow him, they had to take up the cross. In other words, there is suffering in life, and part of our growing up and maturing is to learn how to face, experience,

* Editor's note: This homily was originally presented on 10/22/06.

tolerate, and survive suffering. This is a demanding class-room. This is a challenging piece of the truth of life.

Last month, when the Amish families in Pennsylvania were horribly attacked in the death of their small daughters, they became an international example of facing suffering and overwhelming sadness, as they prepared their children for burial, and with great simplicity and dignity took their small bodies to their respective grave sites and buried them. They also said quietly, and with great humility, that they forgave the man who committed this horrible crime. This attitude and decision is a heroic and profoundly challenging example for all of us to emulate and struggle to practice.

The passengers of flight 93 on 9-11who rebelled against their attackers, and brought down the fourth plane in Pennsylvania, before it could crash into the White House or the capital building rejected victimhood. They chose instead to make their lives a sacrificial offering for the common good. This is an extreme example of courage, but it reminds us that the Lord does offer us empowerment through our human powers, if we choose to practice mental, spiritual, emotional and physical courage.

Some of you can remember, as can I, the Civil Rights Movement of the 1960's. I can graphically remember the Sunday in 1963 when four little African American girls, Addie Mae Collins, Carole Robertson, Cynthia Wesley, and Denise McNair, were killed while attending Sunday School at their Baptist Church in Birmingham, Alabama, by a bomb placed in their classroom by a white supremacist. This suffering is still seared into the minds of people today, as other ethnic, racial, and religious hatreds continue to persist all around the world.[†]

Suffering, and dealing with tragedy in our lives as individuals, as families, as a society, is never done perfectly, but given a spirit, a state of mind, a determined effort, union with Christ, we can experience the agony in the garden, the carrying of the cross, the crowning with thorns, and the crucifixion, as this portion of life comes to each of us.

The poet William Stafford, in a poem entitled "You and Art," offers this reassurance: "You live on a world where stumbling, always leads home."[‡] We don't suffer willingly, but with strength, determination and the practice of the virtues of courage, trust in God, perseverance, long-suffering, and Gospel support for each other in community, we can get through the suffering that inevitably is a part of our journey.

Our spirit and attitude, if it is that of Christ, empower us to undergo the sufferings of life according to the manner and experience of Jesus. As children, many of us heard from our parents that we should offer suffering up. Good advice! Je-

---

[†] See *Time* Magazine, October 23, 2006, p. 60.

[‡] Stafford, William. "You and Art," *Weavings,* September/October, 2006, p. 14.

sus, during the passion, said, "My God, My God, why have you forsaken me?" and he also said in his suffering, "Father, into your hands, I commend my spirit." Both of these utterances are human expressions, and both are understandable, and both are of Christ. We pray today that both can be part of our approach to the suffering that visits our lives.

TWENTY-NINTH SUNDAY IN ORDINARY TIME (3)

ISAIAH 45: "I have called you by your name,
giving you a title, though you knew me not.
I am the Lord and there is no other."

PSALM 96: "Give the Lord glory and honor."

1 THESS 1: "Know..Brothers and Sisters, you are loved by
God, you were chosen."

MATT 22: "Then repay to Caesar what belongs to Caesar
and to God what belongs to God."

Robert Frost, the great American poet (1874-1963), wrote a wonderful poem which has been quoted thousands of times, over the past fifty years. The Title of the poem is, "The Road Not Taken." I want to share this classic with you.

Two roads diverged in a yellow wood,
And sorry I could not travel both
And be one traveler, long I stood
And looked down one as far as I could
To where it bent in the undergrowth;

Then took the other, as just as fair,
And having perhaps the better claim,
Because it was grassy and wanted wear;
Though as for that the passing there
Had worn them really about the same,

And both that morning equally lay
In leaves no step had trodden black.
Oh, I kept the first for another day!
Yet knowing how way leads on to way,
I doubted if I should ever come back.

I shall be telling this with a sigh
Somewhere ages and ages hence:
Two roads diverged in a wood, and I-
I took the one less traveled by,
And that has made all the difference.[*]

Our Scriptures today speak to the issue that Robert Frost considered, namely, "The Road Less Traveled." In Isaiah, God says, "I have called you by name, giving you a title, though you knew me not. I am the Lord, and there is no other." To live the life of God in a Godly way is a choice, a difficult choice, and many times in life it becomes the road less traveled, because it is difficult, demands discipline, focus, perseverance. But that is precisely what Frost said made all the difference, a chosen direction, a deliberate choice. Our lives

---

[*] Lathem, Edward Connery (Ed). *The Poetry of Robert Frost.* New York: Holt, Rinehart and Winston, 1972, p. 105.

unfold as magnificent gifts from God, and our lives develop beauty, depth, meaning and satisfaction through choice of the roads we choose to follow. Our choices make all the difference.

Our Psalm today, 96, reminds us to give God glory and honor in response to this wondrous gift of life in which we participate with each other and all other beings, energies, and expressions of life. We live in a setting of mystery and potential. Many roads are offered for our consideration, all along the way. As we find wisdom, hopefully our choice of the road we take develops richly.

Paul tells the Thessalonians, "Know, Brothers and Sisters, you are loved by God. You were chosen." We have great potential to choose good roads, to make mature decisions, to be confident in our journey, because we have the love of God deep within us. We have been chosen, each and every person ever to have been born. And finally, Matthew's Gospel reminds us to give to God what is God's, and to each other what will make us grow. This choice demands wisdom, insight, self discipline, prudence, generosity.

As our lives continue to unfold, hopefully we are able to say with Robert Frost, "I took the road less traveled by, and that has made all the difference."

THIRTIETH SUNDAY IN ORDINARY TIME

JEREMIAH 31: "Thus says the Lord, Shout with joy for Jacob…The Lord has delivered His people."

PSALM 126: "The Lord has done great things for us; we are filled with joy."

HEBREWS 5: "…it was not Christ who glorified himself in becoming high priest, but rather the one who said to him, 'You are my Son: This day I have begotten you.'"

MARK 10: "The blind man said to Jesus, 'Master, I want to see.'"

"During World War I, when blood was in short supply, wounded soldiers were sometimes transfused with sea water – and it worked. We are all made up of the same stuff. We are all children of the universe."* We believe that we are children of God and that we are one with all of God's creation. It can be no other way.

---

* Taylor, Barbara Brown. *The Luminous Web*. Lanham: Cowley Publications, 2000, p. 29.

Our scriptures today reiterate this truth of unity among all people with and for the Lord. We are one in our desire to see and in our desire to be joyful. John Keats, the English Poet (1795-1821), reminds us of this truth, "A thing of beauty is a joy forever."†

To be able to see and to find joy, we must be one with the God of creation, and be one with creation and all of its laws and truths. We must look beyond what the eye can see as did Helen Keller. We must continue to think beyond what has been, as did President Kennedy, when he said to the world of science, "Send people to the moon." We must have the generosity of Jesus, described in today's Gospel, when he said to the blind man who asked to see, "Go your way; your faith has saved you."

To see and to be happy, we Catholics believe that we must be filled with, that we must practice all days, the ability to see and to be happy and joyful through FAITH seeking TRUTH, HOPE seeking LIFE, and CHARITY seeking UNITY with God, creation and each other. These movements, these gifts of God, are the powers we have, and the powers that we can choose to engage, to find sight, insight, foresight, wisdom and salvation.

---

† Editor's note: This poem by Keats, "A Thing of Beauty (Endymion)," may be found at http://www.poemhunter.com.

Father Avery Dulles, in his book, *Reshaping of Catholicism*,[‡] quotes a theologian named Friederick Von Hugel, saying that Christianity, through our faith and hope and love, has the power to hold in balance three elements of religion: Institutional integrity and unity, Intellectual integrity and clarity, and Mystical openness to new insight and appreciation of God and of God's presence in all of creation, including all of us.

Institutional integrity and unity is the responsibility of each of us. Intellectual integrity and clarity must be sought by each of us. And Mystical openness to new insight and appreciation of God and of Creation and of Humanity is our life call every day. In the last years when astronauts flew through space, they recorded their appreciations. Aleksei Leonov, an astronaut from what used to be the USSR, Soviet Russia, spoke feelingly of the earth as "small, light blue, and so touchingly alone, our home which must be defended like a holy relic," and James Irwin, our US astronaut wrote, "The earth reminded us of a Christmas tree ornament hanging in the blackness of space. As we got further and further away it diminished in size. Finally it shrank to the size of a marble, the most beautiful marble you can imagine. That beautiful, warm, living object looked so fragile, so delicate, that if you touched it with a finger it would crumble and fall apart. See-

---

[‡] Dulles, Avery Robert. *The Reshaping of Catholicism: Current Challenges in the Theology of Church.* New York: Harpercollins, 1988.

ing this has to change a person, has to make a person appreciate the creation of God and the love of God."[§]

We pray God today for a renewal in each of us of the unity and truth and joy of which our scriptures speak.

[§] Editor's note: This quote, along with more links to James Irwin, may be found online at www.brainyquote.com/quotes/quotes/.

THIRTIETH SUNDAY IN ORDINARY TIME (2)*

EXODUS 22: "Thus says the Lord: You shall not molest or oppress an alien for you were once aliens yourselves in Egypt."

1 THESS 1: "Brothers and sisters: You know what sort of people we were among you for your sake."

MATT 22: "Teacher, which commandment in the law is the greatest? Jesus said to Him, 'You shall love the Lord your God with all your heart, with all your soul, with all your mind. This is the greatest and first Commandment. The second is like it: You shall love your neighbor as yourself.'"

I spent a few days in Boston this last week. While there, I saw a very moving memorial just outside City Hall in downtown Boston. The memorial is a park of about one-half a city block. Seven glass towers are set there in a straight row. The glass towers are each about six feet square and rise to a height of approximately 30 feet. On the pains of glass on all four sides of each of the towers, are printed the numbers, not

---

* Editor's note: This homily was originally presented on 10/23/05.

the names, but the numbers identifying all Holocaust Victims – millions of numbers, each representing one person whose life was taken in hatred.

On the cement slab that serves as a walkway through the seven towers of glass, there are printed sayings, quotations, reminders. One of the blocks of print in this walkway said something like the following: "They came for the Communists, but I was not a Communist, so I did not speak up. They came for the Jews, but I was not a Jew, so I did not speak up. They came for the Unionists, but I did not belong to a Union, so I did not speak up. They came for the Catholics, but I was not a Catholic, so I did not speak up. They came for the Black people, but I am not black, so I did not speak up. Then one day, the came for me, and no one spoke up."[†]

The message is clear, and it is the message in our Scriptures today. Exodus states, "Thus says the Lord: You shall not molest or oppress an alien for you were once aliens yourselves in the land of Egypt." First Thessalonians remembers, "Brothers and sisters: You know what sort of people we were among you for your sake." And Matthew's Gospel demands, "You shall love your neighbor as yourself."

Our faith demands of us that we continue to grow, as life changes. Our faith demands that we must continue to think

---

[†] Editor's note: This is a quote from Martin Niemöller. More on this may be found online at www.history.ucsb.edu/faculty/marcuse/niem.htm.

and judge with fairness, as life changes. Our faith demands that we be socially responsible and address the problems and issues that present themselves, as life changes.

Robert Wuthnow is the director of Princeton University's Center for the study of American Religion, and he has written a new book on religious change in America. The book is entitled, *America and the Challenges of Religious Diversity.* ‡ The author says that, although 80% of Americans still call themselves Christians, and like to think of America as a Christian nation, the fact is that we in America are becoming much more religiously diverse. Until recent times, we said America was Catholic, Protestant, Jewish. This no longer describes America religiously. Best estimates now say that 1.3 million Hindus live here, about 2 million Muslims live here, and anywhere from 2.5 to 4 million Buddhists live here. Add to that list Native American Religions, New Age groups, and many other spiritual movements. We are, according to our own scriptures and theology, told to welcome these people, learn about them, never exclude them. To do that we must study their cultures, examine our prejudices, and search our fears.

Our souls must be open and healthy and willing to change. This is religious conviction coming from our Church. How easy it is to think that the new, the different from us, is a danger to our welfare or even to our country. Our ancestors came

---

‡ Wuthnow, Robert. *America and the Challenges of Religious Diversity.* Princeton: Princeton University Press, 2005.

here, and most of them were not welcomed by those already here. We Catholics were hated and feared. A Catholic could not be a school Superintendent or a public official for the first three hundred years of our history. Not until approximately 40 years ago could a Catholic participate politically and publicly.

America allowed slavery for two hundred plus years, and prejudice against women which, even in our Church, continues today. Race, and religion, and culture, and class, and status, and profession, can do strange and immoral things to us if we do not continue to grow and change as the realities of life around us are altered and become something new.

Our scriptures today demand that we have new hearts, changing hearts, open hearts, toward all of our brothers and sisters. This is no small challenge. We pray to be equal to the call.

THIRTIETH SUNDAY IN ORDINARY TIME (3)*

SIRACH 35: "Though not unduly partial toward the weak, yet God hears the cry of the oppressed."

PSALM 34: "The Lord hears the cry of the poor."

2 TIM 4: "The Lord stood by me and gave me strength."

LUKE 18: "The tax collector stood off at a distance and would not even raise his eyes to heaven, but beat his breast and prayed, 'O God, be merciful to me a sinner.'"

We are finishing the annual observance of October as "Respect for Life Month." We will initiate, on this coming Thursday, the month of November, a month dedicated, in our liturgical and faith tradition to remembering the dead people of our lives. These two months, coming in the fall, as they do, invite us to reflect, to remember, to appreciate, the current mystery of life that all of us are experiencing here on earth today. These months also invite us into the mystery of eternal life, which our ancestors who have died eternally ex-

---

* Editor's note: This homily was originally presented on 10/28/07.

445

perience. This is sacred time, and this is sacred reality – life, death, living, dying, meaning for life on earth, meaning of life in eternity. These are days of growth each year, as we choose to engage them and listen to them.

Ancient peoples have given us many gifts. One of the most important gifts they have offered us is remembering. They had no text books, no radios, no public records, no TV, no internet, for constant and immediate recall. They had to learn to remember, and they taught their children to remember, the important truths of life. Most of our holidays and most of our rituals in society are radically born in, and come from, the remembering of ancient people, They learned to observe annually issues, experiences, relationships, that were important to them, so that they would remember the most foundational and basic truths of life.

A very important piece of our Mass ritual, every time we come together to worship at Mass, is remembering. The Canon of the Mass, or, as we more frequently call it, the Eucharistic Prayer, is about remembering, and about rooting ourselves in the history and lived experience of our ancestors over all the centuries.

We begin the Eucharist by recalling where the gifts we offer in this prayer come from, and we pray about, "the work of human hands, and the fruit of the earth," as we prepare the bread and the wine. This prayer also includes a reminder that the money collected is to continue the work of the centuries, in spreading the Gospel of love and forgiveness, and in rendering the services needed currently by all the members of the Body of Christ.

We continue our prayer in the Mass by remembering that, "Christ has died, Christ has risen, Christ will come again." We remember that Christ is present in history and in the current time, and directs our destiny into the future. In this prayer, we remember that Christ is our constant focus, leading us through the Spirit to God the Father, to the fullness of eternal life.

We continue in the Eucharist Prayer to remember the Saints, publicly acknowledged as our mentors, and we name our own patron, Pius X. In addition, we remember the deceased people who have more immediately touched our lives, our family members, our friends, our neighbors, our benefactors. And finally, we remember to pray for ourselves, that we can enter these memories to be enriched, to be inspired, to be reassured that we are one with each other, with our ancestors, with the Body of Jesus Christ, with the fruits of the earth, with the energy of human hands. We remember, too, that we are the Christ today, and, as we leave each other, when we finish praying, we receive a blessing to go forth to continue this living, this remembering, this involvement in all of God's call and life.

The Mass, our coming together, is so foundational to the health of our culture, to the stability of our society, to the richness of our life experience, that it comes and happens and moves us, because we remember. We remember who we are. We remember why we are here. We remember what is our mission. We remember what is our destiny. Remembering is a beautiful prayer. Remembering is a wonderful experience and behavior. Remembering is our life blood for time, leading to eternity.

THIRTY-FIRST SUNDAY IN ORDINARY TIME[*]

WISDOM 11: "Before the Lord the whole universe is as a grain from a balance or a drop of morning dew come down upon earth. Lord, you love all things that are and loath nothing that you have made."

Psalm 145: "I will praise your name forever, my king and my God."

2 THESSAL: "We always pray for you...that our God may bring to fulfillment every good purpose in you, and that the name of Jesus may be glorified in you."

LUKE 19: "Jesus said, 'Zacchaeus, come down quickly, for today I must stay at your house.'"

I recently read an account of what happened to five seventeen year old teenagers in a small Texas town. A boy was driving his car and his girl friend was with him. They were being followed by three friends in another car, all of whom were girls. Somehow, as the two cars approached a bridge, the second

[*] Editor's note: This homily was originally presented on 10/31/04.

car rear-ended the first car, which somehow flew over a small bridge railing, landed on its top and immediately sank with the two teens in it. The three young people in the second car were terrorized and screaming, when out of nowhere came a man who took off his shirt and dove into the river twenty feet below. After a few seconds he reappeared with the first teen, took a breath and disappeared beneath the surface of the river a second time, reappearing in thirty seconds with the second teen, who was unconscious. He gave CPR until the boy regained consciousness. By this time the police and emergency medics were present at the scene. After a minute or two of examining the participants, the police asked to speak with the person who had rescued the two people in the water. Nobody was around and the young people could not describe him. He had done the good deed and disappeared.

The people of that small town and many more of us have been touched by the kindness of this unknown man, who gave what he could at the moment of need and then moved on without fanfare or recognition. Somehow that man must have known what Wisdom states today. He understands and appreciates all the good of creation, and that each of us is to participate and contribute calmly, generously, and as needed in the present moment to the ongoing reality of and need for unity. His courageous behavior is a wonderful example for all of us to do what is needed calmly, quietly and with kindness.

The Gospel today has another story of a man who quietly climbed a tree because he was small in physical stature, and also because he was a hated tax collector, and not welcome with the masses of people. Jesus welcomed this hated man and stayed with him, and said, "this man too is a child of Abraham." We are to work tirelessly to bring peace, to work for unity, to forgive sin, to be people who unite rather than categorize and divide.

We celebrate a great Christian and American holy day and holiday this weekend, Halloween, the holy eve, by sharing gifts, treats, kindness and time together. We do this in honor of all who have gone before us. Our ancestors are the conduit of life for every single one of us. God gives us life through other human beings, tying all of us together as one. This is why we hold the gift of human life in such high regard. And this is also why we work for unity, harmony, and respect for all. The celebration continues for us Catholics as we observe All Saints Day tomorrow. We renew our appreciation that we are one with the living and with the dead, that we pray some-how together with and for each other, that we are safe in life and in death. Our minds are stretched and our imaginations are enlivened, our memories are stirred through the obser-vance of All Saints. This feast stirs our intuitive side and en-ables us to be open to life way beyond comprehension, un-derstanding and analysis. We come to deeper appreciation of the grand mystery that all of life is, and we grow in awe and wonder. These are dimensions of soul that enrich our journey, and strengthen our resolve to change and become all that God intends.

And All Souls Day on Tuesday asks us to look at sinfulness and the need of forgiveness in life and in death. The mystery of God present to us from our vantage point asks for different appreciations and awarenesses as we live and die. We grow in trust of life and death as we experience these days. We are thankful.

THIRTY-FIRST SUNDAY IN ORDINARY TIME (2)*

MALACHI 1: "Have we not all one father? Has not the one God created us?"

1 THESAL 2: ".. in receiving the word of God from hearing us, you received not a human word but, as it truly is, the word of God, which is now at work in you who believe."

MATT 23: "The scribes and the Pharisees preach but do not practice. All their works are performed to be seen. They love places of honor at banquets."

This week on October 31 and on November 1, we celebrate the many dimensions of what we call life, in the practice of our faith, as we honor the dead on Halloween, the eve of All Souls Day, and as we salute the living and the dead, God's Saints, on All Saints Day. We take a comprehensive look at the various stages of our journey, and of our existence, on these two days.

---

* Editor's note: This homily was originally presented on 10/30/05.

Life is a mystery which engages us in time and in eternity, in partial comprehension and in appreciation of its nature, being much bigger than our minds can comprehend. Our faith teaches that each of us has been created by God, as our first reading today indicates, "Has not the one God created us." We somehow lived in the mind and spirit of God for all eternity, or we would not be here. We lived safely and developmentally, in the womb of our mother for approximately nine months, during which time our mother ate for us, drank for us, breathed for us. That was a different life than our independence now, as we individually walk this earth, eating and drinking and breathing for ourselves. And as we live and age on earth, the manifestation in and of life continues to change for all of us, physically, emotionally, spiritually, and in various other ways. And death introduces us to another dimension and manifestation of life, which we call eternity.

Halloween and All Souls and All Saints Days invite us into prayer, pondering, considering the possibilities involved in this new life. As we cannot and do not know what tomorrow is to bring, so we find ourselves blind as to eternal life, its meaning, its quality, its substance, its experience. And we trust that just as life in the mind of God was safe, life in the womb of our mother was safe, life on this earth is safe, so will the doors we call death safely deliver us to yet another mode of existence and experience. All of this happens in the providence and under the direction of the great conductor of life, whom we call God. These two feasts, All Souls and All Saints, take us annually into the arena of communion with the living and the dead. The Communion of Saints does cover time and eternity, the living and the dead, comprehension of portions of life, and appreciation of all of life.

November continues to be the month in our faith experience that invites us into deeper appreciation of all of life, through faith, seeking deeper and clearer knowledge; through hope, which empowers us to enjoy new possibilities of life; and through charity, which is that movement in life which brings color, and fabric, and complexion to human life.

November is a month which is intended, through our faith practice, to expand our horizons, to deepen our appreciations, and to give us courage to deal with life on earth now, and to prepare for our death, as that day approaches. November invites us to be creative in our search for life, for the richness of life, for the unpredictability of life. Thus the month begins with it the feasts that enable us to pray with and for the dead, for our intentions and for theirs, so that our respective lives in time and in eternity may unfold richly in the presence of God, according to the will of God.

We are invited to face our fears about living and about dying. We are given the opportunity each year through this month to reflect on how we appreciate life, and how we stand before death. These are maturing exercises, and these attitudes enable us to know our vulnerability, and to know our tentativeness in the face of living and dying. These are prayerful opportunities to grow as persons of faith, and to discuss important issues of life and of death with our family and friends. Society is served through each of us, as we deal with these universally important issues of life and death.

A final thought: Our second reading today from Paul to the Thessalonians reminds us that the truth of life and death is truly the word of God. Paul says, "in receiving the word of God from us, you received, not a human word, but, as it truly is, the word of God, which is now at work in you who believe." We know that we are truly safe as we live in and through the word of God.

ALL SAINTS & ALL SOULS

In the acclaimed book, *Parting of the Waters*, by Taylor Branch[*], the first sentence of the Preface reads, "Almost as color defines vision itself, race shapes the cultural eye – what we do and do not notice...." This is a book about America and racism and it brought to the attention of the reader the reality and the consequences of racism in this country.

As color defines vision, and as faith defines life itself, All Saints and All Souls shape our approach to seeing life and death, and everything in between and prior to and beyond. These two days ask us to be attentive students of Mystery, truth that is bigger and deeper than our ability to comprehend. These two days call us to appreciation more than to comprehension.

The feast of All Saints is celebrated every year on November 1st and the feast of All Souls is observed annually on November 2nd. These two religious holidays are most mysterious and beautiful. These two days ask us, as believing Christians, to look to our history, our ancestry, our origins, our destiny, our identity.

---

[*] Branch, Taylor. *Parting the Waters: America in the King Years 1954-63.* New York: Simon & Schuster, 1988, p. xi.

These two days also ask us to look into our own grave, our final meaning, our eternal life and salvation. With fear and with full human attention and emotion, we are invited to do this together. We think of and we thank all those who have lived, died, and remain for us, important parts of our existence – our ancestors, our heroes, our saints. We enter in to a new look at God and at life, from the perspective of the people who have given us life and example for living, the saints and relatives of times past.

We look at history from the viewpoint of God and eternal being, the eternal call. We challenge our thinking again each year to know that our meaning is not confined to temporal history, limited geography and mortal human blood. We ask difficult questions; we experience pure faith, and we feel the insecurity of full life in the unknown realities of time and eternity.

All Saints Day is an observance in our faith practice which calls us to Holy Day status, because important truths for all of us are being experienced. All Saints reminds us, that, in some way, we are united to every human being, to all beings, to Being, with a capital "B." We are people of all that history holds. We reflect again that we are our brothers' and sisters' keeper. We are taught by this day that everyone who has been given life in the womb has the right to live it in God's plan.

On All Saints Day we study again the lesson which says that skin color, gender, age, financial or educational condition, status, nationality, religion or other secondary conditions all bow to the truth of the sacredness of each person. Persons are saints. We are persons. We believe that God is person. All Saints expresses the truth of the human soul that we are eternal in some way. We share in the life of dead people and they share in ours.

Our memories are enlivened, our imaginations awakened, our hearts are touched by this day so that we can see better and know more completely the mystery of love, sainthood, personhood, communion with each other and with all things. This day asks us to snap to attention and to look at God, and at ourselves, and at each other, and at our dead relatives, and at our life today, and at our death tomorrow. Truly, All Saints Day is a mysterious gift for us. Let us accept it thoughtfully and reverently and prayerfully.

All Souls Day is a call to be at one with the dead in gratitude and prayer. We are pulled beyond logic and comprehension to the fullness of life's possibilities. All Souls Day challenges us to remember, to appreciate, and to pray with and for the deceased. This day demands that we let go of our limited understanding, and that we trust life beyond our control. This day reminds us that it is natural to die, that it is safe to die, that part of our very meaning and reality is the experience of death and of those whom we have known, loved, and let go. All Souls Day teaches us again to treat life and death with utmost respect. All Souls is an experience in humility, in reality, in truth bigger than any one of us and of all of us.

These two days invite us to look more directly into each other's eyes, in to deep truth, in to new images, in to richer philosophy and theology. These two days shake our old ways of thinking and invite us to a new and happier walk on this earth, into eternity, with and for each other. These two days invite us again to ponder the fact that we are the Body of Christ, the Communion of Saints, citizens of eternal life. These two days stretch and bless us into maturity, humility, into the deep and blessed total life offered to us by God.

WISDOM 6: "Resplendent and unfading is wisdom, and she is readily perceived by those who love her, and found by those who seek her."

PSALM 63: "My soul is thirsting for you, O Lord, my God."

1 THES 4: "…we shall always be with the Lord. Therefore console one another with these words."

MATT 25: "…stay awake, for you know neither the day nor the hour."

There is a wonderful old saying that goes something like this: "Knowledge is what we gain by doing things correctly. Wisdom is what we reap, when we do things incorrectly and wrong, and then recover from the error or mistake." The Old Testament Book of Wisdom, an excerpt of which is today's first reading, is one of the most beautiful books in the Bible, in that it takes the reader to the heart of humanity, to the soul of Christianity, to the depths of truth. Wisdom is the condition of the human soul at its best and richest moment.

The portion we heard today begins, "Resplendent and unfading is wisdom, and she is readily perceived by those who love her, and found by those who seek her." Wisdom is the fruit of the deepest hunger and need in our nature. Wisdom is the result of life lived reflectively, thoughtfully, attentively, perceptively. Wisdom is the seat of power and the fountain of the strength of our nature. We are never better than when we think, consider, choose and act with wisdom. Wisdom is the glue that keeps society healthy and together in peace.

Wisdom in our soul enables us to contribute well and productively to others. The wisdom of a good parent, as an example, saves the life of the child when he or she is young, by total protection, and as the child develops, by slowly allowing the child to explore life and possibility under the guidance and surveillance and protection of the parent. The wisdom of the airline pilot safely enables millions of people every day to fly all over the world. The wisdom of doctors and nurses and medical people restores and promotes health for us when we are ill and hurt. The wisdom of the teacher forms and informs the lives of her/his students. The wisdom of the farmer keeps good and healthy food coming for our livelihood and enjoyment. It is a tremendous gift that we give to others and to self and to culture, as we each develop our portion of wisdom, and as we are willing to share that goodness with others. The hope of the world, and the possibility of peace in our world, is dependent on the wisdom that we develop and share and receive and engage.

Psalm 63, our response today, speaks to us about the source of wisdom: "My soul is thirsting for you, O Lord, my God." Deep within us is the hunger for God, for wisdom, for richness of spirit. Wisdom is the treasure that holds appreciation of God, the sense of the Almighty, the experience of the Holy Spirit. Wisdom is generated as we live with deliberation, focus and determination. Wisdom is the reflection and manifestation of goodness coming from the ways we choose to live our lives, and it is in wisdom that we find peace of heart, richness of spirit and the generation of enthusiasm, which keeps life rich, satisfying and encouraging.

Wisdom also includes what St. Paul says to the Thessalonian people: "We are always with the Lord. Therefore, console one another with these words."

And finally, Jesus is quoted in Matthew's Gospel, as urging us on to the development of wisdom. Jesus says to his followers, "Stay awake, for you know neither the day nor the hour." We know that every minute of life is given once, and having passed, it can never be retrieved. We, in wisdom, develop a deep regard for the time given to each of us. We stay awake in order to utilize this rich gift. Wisdom sets reality clearly before us, so that we see as accurately as possible the passing of time, the opportunities of life, the richness of every minute given to us.

THIRTY-SECOND SUNDAY IN ORDINARY TIME (2)*

2 MACC 7:   "It happened that seven brothers and their mother were arrested and tortured with whips and scourges by the king to force them to eat pork in violation of God's law."

PSALM 17:   "Lord, when your glory appears, my joy will be full."

2 THESS 2:   "May the Lord Jesus Christ encourage your hearts and strengthen them in word and deed."

LUKE 20:   "God is the God of the living, for to him all are alive."

In 1905, just over 100 years ago, Albert Einstein published his famous and life enhancing statement of the modern theory of relativity.† This theory transformed the way people of the world saw themselves and all of creation and energy in

---

* Editor's note: This homily was originally presented on 11/11/07.

† Campbell, Joseph. *The Inner Reaches of Outer Space: Metaphor as Myth and as Religion.* Novato: New World Library, 1986, p. 3.

and of life. This theory continues to direct us in our realization that all things, movements, energies are one and that all is changing. Movement, harmony, symmetry, predictability are conditions of our search, our appreciation, our learning and development.

At about the same time, the famous American poet, Emily Dickinson, wrote a beautiful poem about the human brain, addressing the mystery and power of this human organ. She says, "The brain is wider than the sky, for put them together side-by-side. The one the other will contain, with ease – and you beside."‡

About 50 years ago, Bing Crosby and Count Baise and his band recorded a wonderful rendition of the song entitled, "Everything is Beautiful." The song is bouncy, living, inviting, and makes one want to dance and be happy. One of the lines of the song, however, hits the listener hard, if we listen. The line states, "No one is as blind as the one who refuses to see."

Bing Crosby and Count Baise tell us, in the medium of music, that we must be aware of the world around us if we want to be happy. Emily Dickinson tells us in poetry to use the brain with its power and mystery to enrich life, and Albert Einstein invites us beneath the surface, to appreciate and understand, to some degree, the power that holds us all safely in

---

‡ Editor's note: This poem may be read online at http://poemhunter.com/poem/the-brain-is-wider-than-the-sky/.

life. These are relatively recent and current expressions of the unfolding of God's creation.

Our scriptures today tell of other stories, conditions, aware-nesses, of God's presence. In the Second Book of Maccabees, we hear the story of a mother and her sons, strengthened in suffering, and in facing death. None of us knows how to face death, and none of us wants to go there, but, eventually, it is part of the journey of each person. And we, like the mother and her sons, will approach death, as we approach life. Psalm 17, our response, reminds us again that we find our joy and peace in the Lord, in God's truth, whether in peaceful or ex-tremely trying times of living and dying.

Paul reminds the people of Thessalonica, and you and me, that we find our strength and courage in the Lord, and in God's word. And Luke's Gospel states again for all to hear, God is the God of the living, and all that we are, all that we have, all that we can and will experience, is in the Lord. Meditating, contemplating, reflecting on this truth, namely, that all things, all dimensions of life are from, involved with, and happen in, the Lord God- our faith is a constant call for us to go to this study hall, to ponder this part of life, to be open to an increasing appreciation of the fact that we live and we die in the Lord God.

In the current issue of WEAVINGS (Nov/Dec 2007, p12), a wonderful author by the name of Wendy M. Wright, speaks of the need to pay attention to the Spirit within. She says, "I am aware, however, that it is a significant part of the Christian life to be alert to the way the Spirit moves in the midst of the ordinary fabric of our everyday lives, to work at ferreting out, in the sometimes murky interior of the human heart, where and how God calls us into the fullness of being. Being alert to these movements is part of the life of discipleship."§

§ Wright, Wendy M. "To Be Alert: A Rumination." *Weavings* XXII: 6 (November/December 2007): 6-14, p. 12.

THIRTY-THIRD SUNDAY IN ORDINARY TIME

MALACHI 3: "But for you who fear my name, there will arise the sun of justice with its healing rays."

PSALM 98: "The Lord comes to rule the earth with justice."

2 THESAL 3: "We hear that some are conducting themselves among you in a disorderly way, by not keeping busy but minding the business of others. Such people we instruct and urge in the Lord Jesus Christ to work quietly and to eat their food."

LUKE 21: "By your perseverance you will secure your lives."

Responsibility, accountability, generosity, maturity, just and generous behavior, reverence before the mystery of God – these are the lessons presented in our scriptures today. This is a demanding agenda, and it belongs to each and every one of us.

I recently read a story about a man who was flying from Denver to Chicago. As he found his seat on the plane, he found himself sitting next to a young Air Force Academy cadet, a young woman with her companion. Her companion was a young peregrine falcon, tethered to, being cared for, and sitting majestically on the gloved hand of its trainer, the young female Air Force cadet. The cadet told the man that she and the falcon were on their way to Notre Dame University, where the next day, the Air Force Academy football team would be playing Notre Dame. She and the falcon were to perform and demonstrate on the field at half time of the game.

The demonstration would involve the falcon to be flying away from her hand to circle around and above the football stadium, soaring so high as to almost be out of sight to the spectators, and then diving at speeds of up to 220 miles per hour as it returned to her gloved hand, which held a morsel of food for the falcon.

The man said that he spent two wonderful hours looking at the bird and speaking with the cadet about the discipline, attention, training, trust and confidence needed to successfully control, work with and demonstrate the power of nature in the falcon for the spectators. The falcon, the mascot of the Air Force Academy, had been trained by the cadet in hours and hours of practice, respect for nature and for each other, with attention, discipline and care for each other.

Today, Malachi directs us to fear God's name through all of nature, in order that one may be healed through this process. The falcon and the trainer had to be very cognizant of nature and reverent before it to succeed. Psalm 98 teaches us again that the Lord rules all things, times, choices by justice. We are responsible to learn that profound truth, or stand ready to receive the consequences. Paul in Thessalonians reminds us that there must be order in our lives, unselfishness, responsibility for one another and a spirit of industriousness which empowers us to make our contribution and share responsibility for the community. And Jesus, in Luke's Gospel, tells us anew that, "By your perseverance you will secure your lives."

We know today, better than ever before in history, that nature is of God, from God and essentially demanding from us humans, study, respect, careful participation, and strict observance. We thank God for the freedom we are given, and for the education which has enabled us to learn well this life-giving and life-saving truth.

THIRTY-THIRD SUNDAY IN ORDINARY TIME (2)

The scriptures today speak of ordinary and common experiences, persons and conditions. The first reading from Proverbs describes a worthy wife, a good spouse. The response Psalm, 128, reminds us to revere the Lord, "Blessed are those who fear the Lord." Paul's letter to the Thessalonians speaks of times and seasons, darkness and light, and paying attention to life. And Matthew's Gospel presents one of the stories about the talents, and their use and of the consequences of neglecting the gifts we are given.

The ordinariness of life and the circumstances of life are the stage and raw material out of which we are to make a life. I recently was given a beautiful story which highlights this truth, and I wish to share it with you now.

A little girl named Tess went to her bedroom and pulled a glass jelly jar from its hiding place in the closet. She poured the change out on the floor and counted it carefully. Three times she counted it, because the total had to be perfect. No chance for mistakes here. Carefully placing the coins back in the jar and twisting on the cap, she slipped out the back door and made her way the six blocks to the Drug Store.

She went to the pharmacy and waited patiently for the pharmacist to give her some attention but he was too busy at this moment, so Tess twisted her feet to make a scuffing noise. Nothing happened. She cleared her throat with the most disgusting sound she could muster. No good. Finally she took a quarter from her glass jar and banged it on the counter. That did it!

"What do you want?" the pharmacist asked in an annoyed tone of voice. "I am talking to my brother from Chicago whom I haven't seen in years," he said without waiting for a reply to his question. "Well, I want to talk to you about my brother," Tess answered. "He is really, really sick... and I want to buy a miracle." "I beg your pardon?" said the pharmacist. Tess responded, "My brother's name is Andrew and he has something bad growing inside his head, and Daddy says that only a miracle can save him now. So, how much does a miracle cost?"

"We don't sell miracles here, little girl. I am sorry but I can't help you," the pharmacist said, softening a little. "Listen, I have the money to pay for it," said Tess. "If it isn't enough, I will get the rest. Just tell me how much a miracle costs."

The pharmacist's brother was a well-dressed man. He stooped down and asked the little girl, "What kind of a miracle does your brother need?" "I don't know," Tess replied, with her eyes welling up. "I just know that he is very sick and Mommy says that he needs an operation. But Daddy can't pay for it, so I want to use my money." "How much do you have?" asked the pharmacist's brother, who was from Chicago.

"One dollar and eleven cents," Tess answered, "And it is all the money I have, but I can get more if I need to." "Well, what a coincidence," smiled the man from Chicago. "A dollar and eleven cents is the exact cost for a miracle for little brothers." He took her money in one hand and with the other hand, he grasped her hand and said, "Take me to where you live. I want to see your little brother and your parents. Let's see if I have the miracle you need." That well-dressed man was Doctor Carlton Armstrong, a surgeon specializing in neurosurgery. He performed the needed operation free of charge, and it wasn't long until Andrew was home again and doing well.

The parents were overjoyed and talked about how much the surgery must have cost. Tess knew exactly how much it cost. One dollar and eleven cents and the faith of a little child.

Engaging life as it comes is what our faith asks us to do. We are sometimes asked to see beyond vision, to hear beyond words, to explore beyond normal boundaries. To be kind family members, to trust God, to get through darkness and light, to use the gifts which God has given to us – this is the way that leads to fuller truth and enriches and sustains life for all of us. Our scriptures today give a strong formula for the common-place things in our lives.

CHRIST THE KING SUNDAY

2 SAMUEL 5:   "All the tribes of Israel came to David...
                 and said, 'Here we are, your bone and
                 your flesh.'"

COLOSSIANS 1:   "Let us give thanks to the Father, who has
                 made you fit to share in the inheritance of
                 the holy ones in light."

LUKE 23:   "Jesus said to the thief, 'Amen, I say to
                 you, today you will be with me in
                 Paradise.'"

Christ the King Sunday: November 20/21, 2004. It is the last
celebration of our Catholic Liturgical observance for this
year. This feast brings us to the early dark afternoons and
long black evenings. It always appears on the calendar very
close to our feast of Thanksgiving. It reminds us through the
scriptures we hear that all of life is connected – to God, to all
of creation, time and space, as a part of one universe – life
functioning through the law of God, the mysterious power of
reality as it has been presented by the Creator.

The darkness of the evening itself, on this feast, speaks to us. God's plan makes light travel at the speed of 186,000 miles per second. That being the case, scientists tell us that it takes 8 minutes for the light of the sun to reach the earth. And we see the light of the nearest star in our galaxy, named Alpha Centauri, as it was four and a half years ago, the light taking that long to come that distance to our eyes. And the nearest galaxy, named Andromeda, can actually be seen with the un-aided eye, but is some two-million light years away.[*] The immensity, the simplicity, the mystery of all of reality brings us to our knees in worship, in awe, in thanksgiving and gratitude for the gift of life, and for our participation in it.

Our scriptures today remind us of beauty and truth, about who we are, where we are, and about the sentiments we can bring to each moment of this journey. In the account of 2 Samuel, we find the people coming to David and saying that they realize that they are bone of his bone and flesh of his flesh. In other words, they realize their communion, their union with the king and with each other and with all. Paul's letter to the Colossians renews the realization that we share in the inheritance of all people and of God and of creation. We are one. And Jesus tells the thief, as recorded in Luke's Gospel, that we will be together after this life in paradise. We are one.

---

[*] Keck, L. Robert. *Sacred Quest: The Evolution and Future of the Human Soul.* West Chester: Swendenborg Foundation Publishers, 2000, p. 245.

Christ is our king and is one with us. The Colossians are our
ancestors and are one with us. The thief is a sinner, redeemed, and is one with us. We live and move and have our
being with Jesus Christ, God and human, and are one with
Him.

Another dimension of life is given for our reflection today.
And it is that of finishing something, of saying "Good-bye."
This day is about closure, and about being willing to start
over again with a portion of life, in this case another liturgical year. We are people of portions, of limits, of being in need
of renewal. We finish a day by going to bed, to be renewed
through restful sleep. We finish a meal by cessation of eating,
allowing our body to digest food into new energy. We learn,
as we go through life how to begin and how to finish well.
Christ the King feast and observance gives us a pause in order to reset our worship focus, in order to re-establish authentic prayer, in order to rest with the challenge and difficulty of
intimacy with God. As we observe this finish of a year of
prayer, we offer all that has been to the Lord, and humbly ask
to be renewed in attitude, willingness, readiness, and openness to the mystery of the Godhead, to the richness of worship, to the possibility of charity and service for, with, and to
each other.

As Catholic Christians we thank God for the richness of our
tradition on this day. As Catholic Christians, we ask God's
forgiveness, as a Church and as individuals, on this day. As
Catholic Christians, we recommit our lives to each other and

to God on this day. As Catholic Christians, we promise to remember who we are and who we hope to become, in union with God, with God's creation, with God's people, on this day. As Catholic Christians we recommit to being ecumenically open to other Christians, to all people of differing and of no religious affiliation, on this day.

Our scriptures teach us well on this day: God created us as ONE with each other. God created us as people of great DIGNITY with each other. God created us, and Jesus reminds us, of our great DESTINY with each other, eternal life. Christ the King Feast is a great gift for all of us. We are thankful.

CHRIST THE KING SUNDAY (2)[*]

The Twenty-fifth Chapter of Matthew's Gospel is a magnificent summation of the Liturgical Year, which we finish today, because it draws us to the simplicity of the message of Christ our King. It says, "I was hungry and you gave me food, I was thirsty and you gave me drink, a stranger and you welcomed me, naked and you clothed me, ill and you cared for me, in prison and you visited me." The Gospel always calls us to the simple, basic needs of our humanity. The Gospel is not dramatic. It is thoroughly authentic, and it is terribly demanding, and insists that we Christians continue every day, to be more and more authentic.

When the righteous people asked the king, "When did we see you hungry, thirsty, naked, sick, imprisoned," and so on, the King said, "Whenever you did it to the least of my brothers and sisters, you did it to me." This past week, I was privileged to celebrate the School Mass here at St. Pius X. A child read a beautiful introduction to the Mass before we began our worship and prayer. She said something like, "How do we make the kingdom of God present? She answered herself with,"When we smile at someone, the Kingdom of God is made present. When we help someone, the Kingdom of God

---

[*] Editor's note: This homily was originally presented on 11/20/15.

is present. When we are kind, the Kingdom of God is present." This humble and clear statement set a wonderful tone for the Mass and could be felt throughout the entire liturgy.

America Magazine is a National Catholic Weekly Magazine, published by the Jesuits. It always has articles which challenge the reader to grow and to be authentic in spirit. Last week's issue featured a woman by the name of Dorothy Day, to honor her and renew her memory on the twenty-fifth anniversary of her death. She died on November 29, 1980. Boys and girls and young people, Dorothy Day was a woman who was a totally non-religious person, who joined the Catholic Church, and spent her entire life doing what our Gospel teaches us today. She served the poorest of the poor and the outcasts of society. She established programs which continue today. She opened houses for the poor. We have a Dorothy Day house for the poor here in Rochester, and these houses are found all over the country.

She opposed all wars of any kind all through her life. She was a Pacifist, which means that she did not agree with violence and war to settle human problems. Her entire life was rooted in solidarity with the poor and with those who suffered. She believed that all individuals are important. Each person is a child of God and deserves our respect. She believed in the Sacrament of the Present Moment. She believed that we should do what we can, in small ways and sincerely, to help others. She loved to quote the Russian author, Dostoevsky, "The world will be saved by beauty."[†]

Dorothy Day taught the Gospel simplicity with her entire life. We are called today, as we finish this church year, to be renewed in that Gospel simplicity, with and for each other.

This coming week, we Americans celebrate Thanksgiving. We, in America, are five percent of the world's people, and we have the vast majority of the world's wealth. We are asked to be humbly thankful for all we enjoy. This holiday is an excellent reminder to all of us that we must continue to grow in generosity, sharing, outreach, and caring. This feast reminds us how easy it is to be selfish and excessively self-focused.

Thanksgiving Day is a wonderful moment for individuals and families to pause and consider again how we are blessed, and to think of our heavy responsibility to be blessing for others.

Advent begins next weekend, and calls us to be renewed in our worship readiness, in our worship willingness, in our attitudes toward each other, as we continue to be a parish family, a compassionate community, a welcoming center for strangers and guests.

[†] Ellsberg, Robert. "Five Years With Dorothy Day." *America The National Catholic Weekly*, November 21, 2005, p. 8, seq.

Advent is a wonderful time for quieting our souls, for focusing our minds, for deepening our appreciations of the various facets of life. Advent calls us to be centered totally on the mystery of God, and on the rich life God continues to give us. Advent is a time of light, a rich opportunity for growth in spirit.

Christ the King Sunday, and the coming of Thanksgiving and Advent are great observances for us. We pray to enter all of these observances as completely as possible.

FINIS